LAW IN MANY SOCIETIES

LAW IN MANY SOCIETIES

A Reader

EDITED BY

LAWRENCE M. FRIEDMAN,

ROGELIO PÉREZ-PERDOMO,

AND MANUEL A. GÓMEZ

STANFORD LAW BOOKS

An Imprint of Stanford University Press
Stanford, California

Stanford University Press
Stanford, California

Printed in the United States of America on acid-free, archival-quality paper.

Library of Congress Cataloging-in-Publication Data

Law in many societies : a reader / edited by Lawrence M. Friedman, Rogelio Pérez-Perdomo, and Manuel A. Gómez.
    pages cm
 Includes bibliographical references and index.
 ISBN 978-0-8047-6373-8 (cloth : alk. paper)--ISBN 978-0-8047-6374-5 (pbk. : alk. paper)
 1. Sociological jurisprudence. I. Friedman, Lawrence M. (Lawrence Meir), 1930- editor of compilation.
II. Pérez-Perdomo, Rogelio, editor of compilation. III. Gómez, Manuel A. (Manuel Alejandro), 1971- editor of compilation.
 K376.L384 2011
 340'.115--dc22   2010048550

Typeset by Bruce Lundquist in 10/13.5 Minion

To Leah

To Andrea, Sofia, and Camila

To Maria, Marco, Max, and Miriam

CONTENTS

ACKNOWLEDGMENTS

We would like to thank those who helped us with the research for this project and who helped us transform the raw material into the final product offered here. The many students who have taken our courses both at Stanford University and Florida International University helped us deepen our understanding of the materials and raised our awareness about the important similarities and differences in the life of the law around the world. We thank Kate Wahl and Joa Suorez at Stanford University Press for their diligent assistance throughout the process. We also thank the anonymous reviewers for their insightful and encouraging comments and suggestions. We thank Florida International University College of Law Dean R. Alexander Acosta for his generous support. We are grateful to the Library Staff at Stanford Law School, Florida International University College of Law, and the International Institute for the Sociology of Law in Oñati, Spain. We would like to thank at Stanford, Sonia Moss, Alba Holgado, Erika Wayne, George Wilson, Kate Wilko, Sergio Stone, and Paul Lomio; at Florida International University, Marisol Floren-Romero, who, in addition to her wonderful assistance in locating materials, also dealt with the arduous copyright clearance process with her usual warmth and wonderful demeanor; and at the International Institute for the Sociology of Law in Oñati, Elvira Muñoz. We also thank our secretaries, Mary Tye, who provided assistance to Professors Friedman and Pérez-Perdomo, and Goritzia Rodriguez, who provided assistance to Professor Gómez. Florida International University student Leanna Loucks contributed with research assistance and helped with the proofreading process.

We obviously thank our families for their enduring support and encouragement.

Stanford, Mexico City, and Miami, April 2010

LAW IN MANY SOCIETIES

INTRODUCTION

This is a collection of readings about many societies, for scholars in many societies, and students in many societies—in short, for everyone who is interested in the basic questions of the relationship between law and society. There is a large literature on this relationship, most of it about law and society in specific countries. There is a much smaller literature that compares the legal systems or legal cultures of more than one country, from the standpoint of scholarship in law and society. But most collections of materials that exist are geared almost exclusively toward audiences in the United States; they are drawn largely or entirely from the experience of the United States and present research done chiefly within the United States. There are also some law and society readers in other languages, such as Spanish (Añón et al. 1998), but in this case all the articles dealt with Spain. Ferrari (1990) published a worldwide documentary enquiry with law and society bibliographies of thirty-five countries; this shows that most publications are national in scope. It is our aim to begin at least to fill the gap in the literature; to put together a reader that is truly global and international; a reader that samples the literature about law and society in many countries and from many different parts of the world.

When we talk about law and society, we have to remember that each country has its own legal system that interacts with the society that encircles it. When we talk about law and society, and speak in general terms, a reader might think that we are implying that there are essential similarities that bind all legal systems and even that different societies are also alike in some fundamental ways. We are implying that there are some generalizations that can be made about the relationship between law and society in all or perhaps most societies.

This book is meant to explore this general issue—that is, the question whether there are "laws" or at least generalizations that apply to whole groups of societies—and investigate its complexity. There is no doubt that many legal systems, especially those of contemporary societies have striking similarities. This is precisely why we can, for example, compare German with Mexican law, and indeed these two systems do have features in common. But, at the same time, it is obvious that they are not identical, and they may have some quite basic cultural and structural differences. The political systems of Germany and Mexico also have distinctive features that allow us to consider them as separate, and we cannot say that those differences are unimportant.

The many differences that exist demonstrate that each country not only has its own legal system, but that each legal system is unique. In addition, the reach of every legal system goes no further than its own national borders. This makes the serious study of legal systems peculiarly difficult. Physics is physics everywhere; so too of all of the natural sciences. It is even true, to an extent, of the social sciences; they too are transnational (though this is a bit more controversial and complex). What makes a science a science is the very fact that it is universal, that it rests on theory and research that is not limited to any particular country. For this reason, it is hard to imagine a "science" of law that is really parallel to the science of astrophysics or even parallel to economic or political science. However, there most certainly can be science about law: careful, rigorous study of particular legal phenomena. Therefore as we pile up more and more of these studies, we may be able to formulate some interesting, and valid, general statements about how legal systems behave—if not all legal systems, then at least legal systems in classes or groups of societies.

It is conventional to divide legal systems into "families" (common law, civil law, Islamic law). Membership in a family does tell us something about the particular legal traditions of a country and its legal history, but it tells us very little else. The legal systems of France, Haiti, Japan, and Argentina are all members of the civil law family and share some of the traits of that family. But the differences between them are arguably more important than the similarities. One only needs to look at the works of Toharia (2003), Rodriguez, Garcia-Villegas, and Uprimny (2003), and Cepeda Espinosa (2005) to realize this fact. We can take for example, Spain and Colombia, two countries with relatively new constitutional courts. This is a change related to the judicialization of politics, a recent development in the transformation of law and legal culture in modern times. Notwithstanding their similar origin and scope, the two courts have played their roles under different circumstances and the reactions of their respective political systems have also been very different. In other words, the divergence in national contexts may compel similar institutions to have different effects and operate differently in each country.

The same is true of common law countries—Australia, India, Barbados, and Ireland have some traditions in common; and perhaps the way lawyers in Australia think about legal problems is different in some characteristic way from the way a lawyer in Italy might think about similar problems. But in many ways the legal system of Australia might have more in common with the legal system of Argentina than with Jamaica or Nigeria.

Why should this be the case? The most general answer is that what molds a legal system decisively is not so much its tradition, formal juridical norms, habits of lawyers and jurists, or the rules and codes of the statute books, but more the culture, economics, and political structure of that country. This is the main focus of the law and society movement: what the legal system in operation is really like, and why; and it is the main focus of the readings in this book.

Studies of law and society have emerged and developed in great part because traditional legal scholarship—largely focused on the analysis of purely legal materials like legislation and court decisions, and in concepts developed in the academic or professional legal field—could not explain how legal systems function. But ever more serious is the fact that traditional scholarship never even tried to understand *law in action*. And it paid little or no attention to legal impact, that is, to the way in which legal rules, doctrines, and institutions impacted society, or failed to, and what were the conditions that determined whether an impact would be small, large, or nonexistent. Nor did traditional legal scholarship really explore what made legal systems grow and change; it was curiously static. There is no doubt that traditional legal scholarship can be very useful for the practice of law, but if we accept that the *law in the books* is different from the *law in action*, then the latter should more and more become the focus for research; scholarship on law in action may, indeed, also influence the practice of law.

We can make a distinction between external and internal scholarship about the legal system. "Internal" scholarship accepts the formal norms, the official texts, and the inherited doctrines and rules of the legal system, and it works within that tradition. It is a style of legal scholarship that is familiar to almost all lawyers and law students, and it dominates the teaching and scholarship of the law in every country, to the best of our knowledge. Traditional legal scholarship is also highly normative. It tends to ask what the right answer is to legal questions, and its criteria for deciding the right answer comes from the thoughts and writings and habits of legal scholars or judges.

"External" scholarship is study and scholarship about the legal system; it is scholarship that looks at the legal system from the outside and, specifically, from the standpoint of one or more of the social sciences—sociology, anthropology, psychology, political science, economics, and history. It tends never to ask what the right answer to a legal question might be. Rather, it asks questions about how and why and to what effect. Why did this rule arise or persist? Why was this statute passed, and what interest groups benefited from it? What were the forces that led to some particular reform of the law? Who followed the dictates of some regulation strictly; who disobeyed, and why; and who tried to find ways to get around it? What role do lawyers play in economy and society? Roughly, law and society studies have the same relationship to "internal" scholarship that the sociology of religion (for example) has to theology. Doctrines of the Catholic Church, or Islam, or any other religion, can be studied for their own sake and for religious enlightenment. One can ask, within the religion, questions of right or wrong. If Islam forbids *riba*—lending money at interest—then what strategies can banks follow to satisfy Islamic theology? The sociology of religion cannot and does not ask or answer such questions. Sociology of religion might ask: why do more women than men go to mass on Sunday in Spain; why did Buddhism spread through various countries of the Far East, and dozens of other questions, all from an external viewpoint. The same point, more or less, could be made about the relationship between the social study of law and the traditions of internal legal scholarship.

Law and society is obviously a label that encompasses a broad range of approaches and directions. It basically refers to the legal scholarship that employs social science tools and methodologies. There are studies that stress the relationship with culture, that is, the perceptions, attitudes, and opinions that people have about the law. Others give more importance to the relationship with legal structure and formal institutions. Some studies have a sociological focus. In others, more anthropological or ethnographic, the center of attention is on the structure of traditional societies and the exploration of the behavior of individuals according to their social roles in different historic periods. Another subfield pays attention to the relationship between law and the economic behavior of individuals and focuses on institutions like property or contracts, which are in turn essential for the comprehension of economics and the law. Law and society research may also focus on language. It can focus on the analysis of a given situation at present time, or use a historical perspective, with particular attention to changes over time.

We have already mentioned what we think is the basic axiom or proposition on which the law and society movement rests: the primacy of culture, social norms, and economic and political forces in the genesis and impact of law. Another way of putting the matter is this: the legal system is not autonomous. A system is autonomous if it operates under its own rules, if it grows, changes, and develops according to some sort of inner program. If the legal system were truly autonomous, then outside forces would have little or no impact. No serious law and society scholar believes this. Many of them do believe that legal systems are or can be at least partially autonomous. How much so, and in what regard, is (in theory at least) an empirical question—something we could investigate and measure. Of course this is easier said than done.

One of the major concerns of law and society scholars is impact. A law is passed: Does anyone behave differently? Does the law change people's minds and actions? Is the law obeyed or ignored, and to what extent? This is always an empirical question. There is no truly general answer—at least none at the present time. Hopefully, careful scholarship could at least turn up patterns and make statements that are valid for more than individual instances.

We cannot say anything very general about impact, but we can say this: whatever the impact is, it depends almost entirely on what is happening "outside" the law, that is, in the real world. Something in the social order determines impact, much more than the text of the law. If people in New Zealand tend to obey traffic laws and people in Italy do not, the texts of the laws themselves are very unlikely to give us a satisfying explanation. Nor does the fact that New Zealand is a common law country and Italy a civil law country explain the difference. The answer—if we can find it at all—will probably lie in the local legal culture. Of course, compliance with the law depends on all sorts of factors. The level of enforcement is one of these factors, but levels of enforcement are themselves influenced by elements of the local legal culture.

Another general point worth making is this: any major change in society is bound to be reflected somehow in the legal system. This can be an external event—a war, or a devastating epidemic. Or it can reflect changes in science and technology. Just consider how the invention of the telephone, the automobile, the jet airplane, antibiotics, or the computer has influenced the law. There is, to begin with, the obvious fact that the law will have to deal directly with the consequences of new technology—think of the development of a huge body of traffic law, which the rise of the automobile made necessary. But technological changes can, in turn, lead to major social changes, and major social changes—like the so-called sexual revolution or the rise of modern individualism—have an even greater impact on the law than the technology itself.

Law, after all, is never static; it is constantly in motion, constantly reworked and recon-figured. There is a common belief—or myth—that the law is extremely conservative, that it hates change, that it worships the past. Nothing could be further from the truth. The law sometimes cherishes archaic terms, but legal systems are not sentimental. Something old persists in the law only because it is useful or valuable to some concrete, contemporary in-terest group. Otherwise, it is ruthlessly discarded. The common law doctrine of precedent is another aspect of many legal systems that creates an impression of reluctance to change—an impression that the legal order loves the antique and the time-honored. However, this is a misunderstanding of what the doctrine of precedent means—and an even greater misun-derstanding of how it works in practice.

We should also dispose of the opposite misunderstanding: because law is plastic, because it is intensely practical, one might think that the legal system always "works," that it is always efficient, that it is always adaptive, and that it always fits its society like a glove fits a hand. Legal systems always reflect their society, but that society itself can be full of conflict and inconsistency. It can be a dictatorship, with a ruling clique that is more concerned with lin-ing its own pockets than anything else, and so on. Open, democratic societies tend to be less corrupt than closed, authoritarian societies. Additionally, their legal systems tend to reflect not just the interests of narrow elites, but also (to some extent) the interests of broad masses of the middle classes. The contents of this reader introduce the student to a wide range of societies, some of which have highly efficient and functional legal systems and some of which do not. Some readings will show the ways in which individuals and businesses learn to cope with incomplete or malfunctioning systems of formal law.

Another proposition, which is clearly linked to the others, is that particular types of society produce particular types of legal order, or configurations within the legal order. A capitalist society generates capitalist law—law that provides for markets, private prop-erty, enforcement of contracts, free enterprise (within limits), stock exchanges, and so on. A feudal society generates laws that promote and reflect the feudal system. A socialist system, or a fundamentalist Islamic system, similarly creates a legal system that will per-form in such a society. The modern welfare-regulatory state, in Western Europe and North America (among other places), produces certain kinds of law that fit the state—in fact, the state is in a way defined by the type of law it generates. A welfare state is a state that has a set of welfare laws. And a regulatory state is a state that has given up the idea of laissez-faire (if it ever had it), and elected to pass laws that call for the control and supervi-sion of business.

The novelty of this book is to call attention to both diversity and similarities among legal systems, in what we hope will be a systematic way. Our plan has been to include works on law and society that cover the different thematic areas of this field within the largest possible geographical area, but in a way that keeps this volume to a manageable size.

Since each country is unique, and each legal system is unique, the reader might well ask what can be learned from this book. We draw on studies from many different legal sys-tems, and even though quite a few countries are represented in this book, there are more than two hundred independent countries in the modern world, and most of them are absent from this collection. We think, nonetheless, that the student of law can learn quite a bit from looking at a range of topics, drawn from a range of countries. The very diversity of the settings is important; it teaches us something about the way the legal order relates to the society in which it is embedded.

The diversity extends not only to the settings but also to the methodologies the authors have used. Among the authors are sociologists, political scientists, historians, psychologists, economists, as well as legal scholars and jurists, who use the law and society approach in their work. Some of the readings are quantitative; some are qualitative. Some use elaborate statistics; some make use of interviews, or of ethnographic techniques. Some are strongly theoretical; others are light on theory and heavy on description and analysis. Works that are rigorous, that reflect careful research, or which embody theory about such research, make up the contents of this volume. We have avoided studies that view legal scholarship as a self-referential discipline, or which are solely about the formal analysis of legal doctrines, divorced from context.

The topics covered are listed in the table of contents. Hard choices had to be made about what readings to include and exclude and about what topics to cover. There is material on the legal profession, on criminal justice, on globalization, on litigation and other forms of dispute processing; material, too, on the importance of legal culture, and the influence of the structure of legal systems. Structure and culture are key concepts that reverberate throughout the book. Substantively, the topics range from divorce law to crime and punishment and to contract making among business people.

A word should be said here about language. The readings included in this book deal with countries whose citizens speak many different languages, European languages like Dutch and German, as well as Asian languages like Chinese and Japanese. But the original articles for the most part were written in English. Interestingly, during the last decades the salience of English as a lingua franca has successfully moved beyond the natural sciences and medicine into the social sciences. English has also become the language of finance, international trade, and development. International aid agencies, nongovernmental organizations, and other global institutions have embraced English as their language of choice, thus influencing the way in which people communicate with these institutions and how they in turn communicate with the rest of the world. Nowadays, English is not viewed necessarily as the language of a dominant culture or powerful nation, but rather as a pluricentric one, and this perception has facilitated its acceptance and success as a global language (Kaplan 2001). English is the language that more and more professionals and scholars must acquire. It is the second language for millions of people; and the second language, very notably, for international-minded legal scholars. Of the three editors of this collection, only one speaks English as his native language.

The dominance of English in sociolegal scholarship, as in other fields, is itself a consequence of globalization. In many contexts, there simply has to be an agreed-upon international language. The most obvious case is air-traffic control. A Brazilian airliner approaches the Istanbul airport. Nobody in the cockpit can communicate in Turkish with the air-traffic controllers, and none of the air-traffic controllers speak Portuguese. Nor do the air-traffic controllers speak Japanese, if the next plane due is from Tokyo, or French for the plane arriving out of Paris. There has to be, by common understanding, some way for the air-traffic controllers to communicate with the pilots—some language that they, and everybody else in this position, must share. That language, for various reasons, turns out to be English, and once established as such, its position as the international language only grows and grows.

English has also penetrated the legal jargon of many countries, in spite of the formalistic, conservative, and static nature of their traditional judicial language. English (as Latin or French were in the past) is now the dominant language of international and comparative law, the United Nations, the International Court of Justice, and the European Court of Human Rights. Academics have also felt compelled to use more English than in the past as it has become the default language for international conferences, and many of the leading scientific journals are also published in English. Our particular field is not an exception. After browsing through the International Institute for the Sociology of Law's database, we found out that of 1,497 works published in the field of law and society between 2000 and 2007, 942 were in English. These numbers continue to grow at a fast pace. The fact that the vast majority of the law and society literature is in English clearly facilitates our task in addition to assuring a broad audience for our book.

With respect to language, globalization also means that people have become more aware of cultural diversity and many learn other languages in addition to English. In the scholarly legal community people who speak two or more foreign languages are common. For this reason we have included in this volume some bibliographical references in Spanish, French, and Italian.

In broader terms, modernization and globalization are social facts. But it is not clear that all societies are bound to modernize or globalize, or in the same way. And both modernization and globalization have plusses and minuses. Paradoxically, one aspect of modernization is respect for tradition and culture, which leads to a certain revival of aspects of society that in theory modernization was meant to destroy. The growth of fundamentalism, or the movements for indigenous rights, shows how complex "modernization" is in practice.

Globalization, in turn, has not meant the end of national identities, or of nationalism itself. The modern world is the world of the European Union, Mercosur, the African Union, and the United Nations, but it is also the world in which Nauru and Vanuatu are independent countries, in which the Soviet Union is now sixteen different countries, and Yugoslavia at least six, in which the Czechs and the Slovaks decided they were separate entities, the Basques and the Welsh have more autonomy than they had before, and Belgium is in danger of splitting into two or more pieces. Moreover, there is a global culture of human rights, a World Trade Organization, an International Criminal Court, and a worldwide spread of judicial review. But there is, by contrast, the threat of terrorism, a kind of worldwide cancer, reflecting a vibrant and dangerous culture of extremism and intolerance. Terrorism is a threat, not only to the lives of innocent people but also to the rule of law itself, in that it leads to anti-terror campaigns in the developed countries that are widely popular, but that include important restrictions on liberty and human rights.

A final word: we think the law and society approach is important—indeed, fundamental. Law is too important to leave in the hands of orthodox legal scholars. One of the basic facts about modern societies is that they are societies with enormous and complex legal systems.

No modern society can function without an elaborate framework of law. It does not matter whether it is capitalist or socialist, whether it is committed to privatization or government ownership. In all cases, it needs a huge amount of law.

But that legal framework is not just the visible, obvious framework of constitutions, statutes, ordinances, rules and regulations, and decisions of courts. It is also a framework of behaviors and attitudes. A legal system is a moving, functioning machine. What makes it move is not texts and words so much as the social context, the legal culture, the society itself. What do we learn about a society from its written constitution? The constitution might be, for example, full of noble words about the rights of the citizens, but what does this mean, if the government violates those rights consistently and if a corrupt court system fails to enforce the rights? A country can enact a beautiful code of commercial law, but the living law of commerce, which might well be influenced by the code, will also include norms and values and customs of supreme importance that are not included in the code. And so it goes.

There is nowadays a vast production of nonacademic materials that are relevant to law and society studies. For example, Amnesty International publishes an annual report and other important documents on the human rights record of governments. Transparency International does the same with regard to corruption. These materials are important and useful, but we also need basic research, more studies, more understanding of how legal systems actually operate. Our hope is that the studies included in this book contribute to that end.

REFERENCES

Añón, M. J., R. Bergalli, M. Calvo, and P. Casanovas, eds. 1998. *Derecho y sociedad*. Valencia, Spain: Tirant lo Blanch.

Cepeda Espinosa, Manuel J. 2005. The judicialization of politics in Colombia: The old and the new. In *The judicialization of politics in Latin America*, ed. Rachel Sieder, Line Schjolden, and Alan Angell. London: Palgrave-McMillan.

Ferrari, Vincenzo. 1990. *Developing sociology of law: A worldwide documentary enquiry*. Milan: Giuffrè.

Kaplan, Robert B. 2001. English: The accidental language of science? In *The dominance of English as a language of science*, ed. Ulrich Ammon. New York: Mouton de Gruyter.

Rodriguez, Cesar, M. Garcia-Villegas, and R. Uprimny. 2003. Justice and society in Colombia: A sociolegal analysis of Colombian courts. In *Legal culture in the age of globalization: Latin America and Latin Europe*, ed. L. Friedman and R. Pérez-Perdomo. Stanford: Stanford University Press.

Toharia, José-Juan. 2003. Evaluating systems of justice through public opinion. In *Beyond common knowledge*, ed. Erik G. Jensen and Thomas C. Heller. Stanford: Stanford University Press.

I PROFESSIONAL ACTORS IN THE LEGAL SYSTEM

INTRODUCTION

Everyone who lives in a modern society is, in some way, an actor in the legal system, but there are those who have a more intense relation with the system. A *legal professional* is a person with specialized education in law and whose main activity is concerned with the functioning of the legal system. Lawyers and judges are the archetypical legal professionals, but there are other people with other functions who also can be given this label. Among these are notaries, law professors, and, in some countries, prosecutors and police officers. The legal profession is considered unified when the specialized education is common for the different occupations and when, for example, a lawyer can become a judge at some point during the lawyer's life. In some countries, however, the profession is divided into separate branches that are, in a real sense, separate professions; the educational process is different from one to another, and it is practically impossible to shift from one branch to another. This is the case of barristers and solicitors in England and of lawyers and judges in France. Of course, there are professionals who are not, strictly speaking, "legal" professionals, whose work matters greatly to the functioning of the legal system—detectives, for example, or experts in forensic medicine, or even gangsters in some countries (West 2007). In this book, however, we will confine our treatment to lawyers and judges, the two best-known and best-studied legal professions or branches within the legal profession.

Legal education is a topic essentially connected to the study of the legal profession because legal education is a constitutive element of the profession. From a law and society perspective, law schools or equivalent institutions are vital organizations with respect to socializing members of the profession, selecting who becomes a member of the profession, classifying the members, and communicating values and skills to professionals. Abe's article, which is Chapter 1 in this book, points to the important functions of official Japanese judicial institutions in selecting and socializing Japanese judges (Abe 1995). Other works deal with the values and skills communicated by law schools in the United States (Mertz 2007) and in Latin America (Pérez-Perdomo 2006) and the important role of law schools in forming the political elite in countries like Germany (Dahrendorf 1971), Japan (Miyazawa and Otsuka 2002), Mexico (Lomnitz and Salazar 2002; Fix-Fierro and López-Ayllón 2006), Europe as a whole

(Clark 1999), and Latin America (Pérez-Perdomo 2006). Legal education frequently disseminates politically liberal values, which perhaps has an important impact on the political role of lawyers (Halliday and Karpik 1997; Halliday, Karpik, and Feeley 2007; Falcão 1979; Winn and Yeh 1995; López-Ayllón and Fix-Fierro 2003; Gostynski and Garfield 1993).

Judges are not necessarily legal professionals in the technical sense in all societies. In many small, traditional societies, judges are elders, wise men, or leaders, without specific legal training (Gulliver 1963; Gluckman 1967; Nader and Todd 1978; Kouassi 2000). In European societies, in the past, commercial judges and justices of peace were not trained in law (Czap 1967), and in many countries they still are not. In Cuba, for example, lay judges continue to play an important role in the operation of the judiciary (Evenson 2003), and in France, administrative judges have only recently been recognized as professional judges (Boigeol 2003). With very few exceptions (Vermeule 2006), the judges who decide important criminal, civil, and administrative cases in most modern nations are required to undergo formal law training.

The judiciary constitutes one branch of government. There is a strong and deep-seated assumption that the judiciary should be independent; that is, none of the other branches should be able to influence or coerce the judges or dictate their decisions, or otherwise encroach on their jurisdiction. Only independent judges, it is thought, can make impartial decisions. Of course, the independence of judges is usually more an aspiration than a reality. Every political system has a way of influencing or controlling judges, even in societies that on the surface seem to have strong, independent judiciaries. The two selections on judges (Abe 1995, on Japan; Bogoch and Holzman-Gazit 2008, on Israel) deal with these *liaisons dangereuses* of judges. In the case of Japan, systemic control is so structured as to discourage any kind of judicial activism. In the Israeli case, the alliance of judges and the media puts important limits on political power, but the relationship between government and judiciary can be quite tense. In many countries—certainly in authoritarian countries—the judges may be directly subservient to political power either formally or informally. The Japanese experience is peculiar in that it reflects a very high level of bureaucratic control. In the United States and most Latin American countries there is direct political control over the appointment of judges. In Spain, the political marginality of judges protected their relative independence during the authoritarian Francoist regime (Toharia 1975), and a similar situation was present in Mexico under the long-ruling political party, the PRI (López-Ayllón and Fix-Fierro 2003). In other Latin American countries, the military dictatorships of 1970s and 1980s led to massive violations of human rights. Although, from time to time, judges corrected some of these abuses as a way of proclaiming their independence or in order to help create the perception that the military juntas were law abiding, the reality is that judges commonly supported or sanctioned these repugnant practices (Pereira 2005; Osiel 1995; Groisman 1987).

The Israeli case included as Chapter 2 in this book (Bogoch and Holzman-Gazit 2008) fits into a trend we can label as the judicialization of politics: active judges intervening in the political process and exercising a certain amount of control over the exercise of power by political figures. This trend is quite general in Europe and America (Guarnieri 1993, 2003; Garapon 1996; Sieder et al. 2005, for Argentina, Colombia, Chile, Mexico, Venezuela). Even East Asian countries, where Confucian thinking supposedly promoted a culture of respect for political power, courts have acted politically, though in rather moderate ways (Ginsburg 2002). The establishment of constitutional courts has strengthened the trend toward politically powerful courts in Europe (Germany, Italy, and Spain, for example) and Latin America (Colombia, Costa Rica, and Guatemala). In other countries, the political importance of the Supreme Court or constitutional court has been reinforced, and even lower courts have become more important political players (Epstein, Knight, and Shvestsova 2001; Tate and Vallinder 1995; Jacob et al. 1996). The importance of the constitutionalization of justice is striking, also in the case of Brazil (Arantes 2005; on the political background of constitutionalization and its economic and political effect, see Hirsch 2004).

The Italian experience, where prosecutors and judges pursued an anticorruption campaign (*mani pulite*), represents an extreme case of judicial influence on politics. Legal professionals (prosecutors and judges) started a moralization crusade that brought about a political crisis and a realignment of the Italian political system (Guarnieri 1993; Ferrari 1996).

Judges of international courts are a new phenomenon. These courts (such as the International Court of Justice, the European Court of Justice, the European Court of Human Rights, the Inter American Court of Human Rights, and the International Criminal Court) lack any police force or army to enforce their own judgments. But their decisions are generally respected and have had an influence on the affected countries (Koch 2003; Arold 2007; Santos et al. 2008).

The importance of judges can vary from one society to another, but in most countries, they seem to be more important now than in the past (Tate and Vallinder 1995). Corruption scandals involving politicians have only enhanced their power (Pujas 2000; Roussel 2000; Garapon and Salas 1996). Judges have often been able to place limits on the power of the political branches, and they also are playing an important role generally in society—in cases, for example, on product liability, large-scale accidents, financial fraud, medical malpractice, urban planning, and so on. A regime of "total justice" (Friedman 1985) has helped "judicialize" the entire society and not only the political system (Garcia de La Cruz Herrero 1999; Vianna et al. 1999; Moustafa 2003, 2007).

The power of judges has its definite limits. Judges are not like white knights, or Don Quixotes, going after wrongs to correct. They are generally reactive, since they can only decide cases brought to them by disputants and their lawyers, or by prosecutors. Moreover, a number of national legal systems traditionally regarded as predominantly inquisitorial have shifted to an adversarial, party-controlled model of judging. In some countries, slow or corrupt judiciaries, or very expensive procedures, legal fees and other costs, can contribute to create a sense of distrust in the justice system and a barrier to access the courts. Or a revival of religious beliefs can also make the people avoid courts (Engel 2005). The role of judges, then, cannot be understood separately from the legal culture of citizens and the role of lawyers in society.

In Europe and America until the early twentieth century, lawyers were not especially numerous; they were exclusively male and tended to come from the upper classes. They tended to staff the high state hierarchies and to form a kind of political elite (Karpik 1995; Pérez-Perdomo 2006; Abel 1989; Friedman 2005; Rueschemeyer 1973). In the late twentieth century the demographics of the profession began to change radically. The profession grew in size rapidly in country after country. Women entered the profession in great numbers. Lawyers were drawn from a wider range of social classes and ethnic groups. Lawyers perceived themselves (or were perceived) as primarily loyal to clients, rather than to the courts or the political system; their role was to advise and defend clients, particularly business clients, and to act as social brokers (Gómez 2009). Businesses have become the greatest source of demand for lawyers, and the work of an increasing number of lawyers is connected to business clients. This transformation, however, did not happen in socialist countries where the number of lawyers did not increase and where lawyers tended to be more subservient to the state (Clark 1999).

One modern development is the rise to prominence of the in-house counsel (Nelson and Nielsen 2000; Van Houtte 1999). The in-house counsel in a way contradicts the ideal of the lawyer as an independent professional. The in-house counsel is the lawyer for a single client; she works on the premises of the client and receives a more or less fixed salary, like any other employee. She is, nonetheless, supposed to provide an independent assessment of the issues submitted to her, based on her own knowledge of law. The number of lawyers working as in-house counsel is related to the size of the business, but clearly this type of arrangement is more frequent than in the past and is gaining acceptance in the profession. The in-house counsel is generally an important player within the organizational structure of any large business; she gives advice, hires outside counsel or law firms when necessary, controls the payments for legal services, and in general monitors the legal position of the company.

Another striking aspect of the modern profession is the rise of the large law firm. Some of these firms have become truly enormous. The first examples of megafirms were from the United States, but there are now large law firms in Europe, Asia, and Latin America, and most of them have a presence in several jurisdictions, thus giving rise to a truly globalized legal practice. In 1960, an American firm with one hundred lawyers was considered very large (Smigel 1964). Today, the largest firms have thousands of lawyers, and many branches spread all over the world. The growth of the large firm is related to the expansion of transnational or multinational enterprises, facing complex regulations in several countries (Flood 1996; Trubek et al. 1994). Law firms with offices in several countries, or networks of law firms operating across national boundaries, are increasingly common (Abel 1993–95; Sokol 2007). In other cases, for example, the lawyers of Silicon Valley, California, a capitalist culture has encouraged the rise of entrepreneurial lawyers who have adapted their activity and skills to the quite specific world of venture capital in the high-technology business (Friedman et al. 1989; Suchman and Cahill 1996). In some areas, notably mass tort litigation, consumer defense, and human rights litigation, lawyers have formed transnational networks that have enabled them to represent large groups of clients in different jurisdictions, mobilize economic and political resources, and exert influence on policymaking. An increased demand for specialized legal services coupled with skyrocketing legal fees have also prompted lawyers to rethink their practice and outsource some of their work to companies or individuals located thousands of miles away (Daly and Silver 2007). This trend has reached the public sector as courts of some jurisdictions have also begun to contract out nonessential tasks like the processing of minor traffic violations and transcription services (Borsand and Gupta 2009).

Today's law firm is a service enterprise that, typically, consists of a small number of managing partners and a cohort of subordinate personnel (junior partners, associates, paralegals, secretaries, and so on). The structure is hierarchical; associates can, after a certain number of years, become partners. Most, however, fall by the wayside in what Galanter and Palay (1991) have called the "tournament of lawyers." Big businesses require teams of lawyers to give them continuous, speedy, and high-quality legal service. For a long time, nothing seemed to impede the rapid growth of the big firms. At the time of writing (2010), however, the world financial crisis has called a halt—perhaps temporarily—to this period of growth; indeed, many young lawyers have lost their jobs.

The changes in recent years to the organization and function of the legal profession have not diminished the political importance of lawyers. Many lawyers maintain high state positions, in the government or in legislative bodies. Lawyers are found on both sides of most issues of policy and in the service of every regime. Lawyers have collaborated with dictatorships, contrary to the supposed ideals of the profession and the principles of the rule of law, in Nazi Germany, Fascist Italy, and in Latin American dictatorships (Halliday and Karpik 1997; Halliday, Karpik, and Feeley 2007; Correa Sutil 1997). Lawyers, notwithstanding, have also been at the forefront of the struggle for human rights and democracy by becoming engaged in political activism and employing their skills to promote political and social change (Gómez 2010). See, for example, the work of Win and Yeh (1995), included here in Chapter 4, on the important role of lawyers in the democratization of Taiwan, and the research of Sajo (1993) about Hungary.

REFERENCES AND SUGGESTIONS FOR FURTHER READING

Abe, Masaki. 1995. The internal control of a bureaucratic judiciary: The case of Japan. *International Journal of the Sociology of Law* 23: 303.

Abel, Richard L. 1993–95. Transnational law practice. *Case Western Reserve Law Review* 44: 737.

———. 1989. *American lawyers.* New York: Oxford University Press.

Arantes, Rogério B. 2005. Constitutionalism: The expansion of justice and the judicialization of politics in Brazil. In *The judicialization of politics in Latin America*, ed. Rachel Sieder, Line Schjolden, and Alan Angel, 232–62. London: Palgrave Macmillan.

Arold, Nina-Louisa. 2007. *The legal culture of the European Court of Human Rights.* Leiden, Netherlands: Martinus Nijhoff Publishers.

Bogoch, Bryna, and Yifat Holzman-Gazit. 2008. Mutual bonds: Media frames and the Israeli High Court of Justice. *Law and Social Inquiry* 33: 53.

Boigeol, Anne. 2003. The rise of jurists in France. In *Legal cultures in the age of globalization: Latin America and Latin Europe*, ed. L. Friedman and R. Pérez-Perdomo. Stanford: Stanford University Press.

Borsand, Shasha, and Amar Gupta. 2009. Public and private sector legal process outsourcing: Moving toward a global model of legal expertise deliverance. *Pace International Law Review Online Companion* 1: 1. Available at: http://digitalcommons.pace.edu/intlaw/301

Clark, David S. 1999. Comparing the work and organization of lawyers worldwide: The persistence of legal traditions. In *Lawyers practice and ideals: A comparative view*, ed. J. Barceló III and R. Cramton. The Hague: Kluwer.

————. 1987. The role of legal education in defining modern legal professions. *Brigham Young University Law Review* 2: 595–612. (Comparative Law Symposium). Also published in *Laws and rights: Proceedings of the International Congress of Sociology of Law for the Ninth Centenary of the University of Bologna*, ed. Vincenzo Ferrari, 103–22.

Correa Sutil, Jorge. 1997. No victorious army has ever been prosecuted. . . . The unsettled story of transitional justice in Chile. In *Transitional justice and the rule of law in new democracies*, ed. A. J. McAdams. Notre Dame, IL: University of Notre Dame Press.

Czap, Peter. 1967. Peasant-class courts and peasant customary justice in Russia, 1861–1912. *Journal of Social History* 1: 2.

Dahrendorf, Ralf. 1971. Las facultades de derecho y la clase alta alemana. In *Sociologia del derecho*, ed. V. Aubert. Caracas: Tiempo Nuevo.

Daly, Mary, and Carole Silver. 2007. Flattening the world of legal services: The ethical and liability minefields of offshoring legal and law-related services. *Georgia Journal of International Law* 38: 401.

Engel, David M. 2005. Globalization and the decline of legal consciousness: Torts, ghosts, and karma in Thailand. *Law and Social Inquiry* 30: 469–514.

Epstein, Lee, J. Knight, and O. Shvestsova. 2001. The role of constitutional courts in the establishing and maintenance of democratic systems of government. *Law and Society Review* 35: 117.

Evenson, Debra. 2003. *Law and society in contemporary Cuba*. The Hague: Kluwer Law International.

Falcão, Joaquim. 1984. *Os advogados: Ensino jurídico e mercado de trabalho*. Recife, Brazil: Fundação Joaquim Nabuco y Editora Massangana.

————. 1979. Lawyers in Brazil: Ideals and praxis. *International Journal of the Sociology of Law* 7: 7.

Ferrari, Vincenzo. 1996. Seguridad jurídica y crisis del estado de derecho en Italia. In *Seguridad jurídica y competitividad*, ed. M. E. Boza and R. Pérez-Perdomo. Caracas: Ediciones IESA.

Fix-Fierro, Héctor, and Sergio López-Ayllón. 2006. Muchos abogados pero poca profesión? Derecho y profesión jurídica en México contemporáneo. In *Del gobierno de los abogados al imperio de las leyes: Estudios sobre educación y profesión jurídicas en el México contemporáneo*, ed. H. Fix-Fierro. Mexico City: Universidad Nacional Autónoma de México.

Flood, John. 1996. Megalawyering in the global order: The cultural, social and economic transformation of global legal practice. *International Journal of the Legal Profession* 4: 1–2.

Friedman, Lawrence M. 2005. *A history of American law*. 3d ed. New York: Simon and Schuster.

————. 1985. *Total justice*. New York: Russell Sage Foundation.

Friedman, Lawrence M., Robert W. Gordon, Sophie Pirie, and Edwin Whatley. 1989. Law, lawyers, and legal practice in Silicon Valley: A preliminary report. *Indiana Law Journal* 64: 555.

Galanter, Marc, and T. Palay. 1991. *Tournament of lawyers: The transformation of the big law firm*. Chicago: University of Chicago Press.

Garapon, Antoine. 1996. *Le gardien des promesses: Justice et democratie*. Paris: Odile Jacob.

Garapon, Antoine, and D. Salas. 1996. *La République penalisé*. Baume-les-Dames: Hachette.

García de La Cruz Herrero, Juan José. 1999. La cultura de la reclamación como indicador de desarrollo democrático: Tres perspectivas de análisis. *Politeia* 22. Caracas: Universidad Central de Venezuela.

Ginsburg, Tom. 2002. Confucian constitutionalism? Globalization and judicial review in Korea and Japan. *Law and Social Inquiry* 27: 763.

Gluckman, Max. 1967. *The judicial process among the Barotse of Northern Rhodesia*. Manchester, England: Manchester University Press.

Gómez, Manuel A. 2010. Political activism and the practice of law in Venezuela. In *Cultures of legal-*

ity: Judicialization and political activism in Latin America (Cambridge Studies in Law and Society), ed. J. Couso, A. Hunneus, and R. Sieder. Cambridge: Cambridge University Press.

———. 2009. Knowledge and social networks in the construction of elite lawyers in Venezuela. *Sociologia del Diritto* 3: 113–35.

Gostynki, Zbigniew, and A. Garfield. 1993: Taking the other road: Polish legal education during the past thirty years. *Temple International and Comparative Law Journal* 7: 23.

Groisman, Enrique. 1987: *La Corte Suprema de Argentina durante la dictadura, 1976–1983*. Buenos Aires: Centro de Investigaciones Sociales sobre el Estado y la Administración.

Guarnieri, Carlo. 2003. Courts as instruments of horizontal accountability: The case of Latin Europe. In *Democracy and the rule of law*, ed. J. M. Maravall and A. Przeworski. Cambridge: Cambridge University Press.

———. 1993. *Magistratura e politica in Italia: Pesi senza contrapesi*. Bologna, Italy: Il Mulino.

Gulliver, P. H. 1963. *Social control in an African society*. Boston: Boston University Press.

Halliday, Terence C., and L. Karpik, eds. 1997. *Lawyers and the rise of western political liberalism: Europe and North America from the eighteenth to twentieth centuries*. Oxford: Clarendon Press.

Halliday, Terence C., L. Karpik, and M. Feeley, eds. 2007. *Fighting for political freedom*. Oxford: Hart.

Hirschl, Ran. 2004. The political origins of the New Constitutionalism. *Indiana Journal of Global Legal Studies* 11: 71–108.

Jacob, H., E. Blankenburg, H. Kritzer, D. M. Provine, and J. Sanders. 1996. *Courts, law and politics in comparative perspective*. New Haven, CT: Yale University Press.

Karpik, Lucien. 1995. *Les avocats: Entre l'État, le public et le marché*. Paris: Gallimard.

Koch, Charles H. 2003. Envisioning a global legal culture. *Michigan Journal of International Law* 25: 1.

Kouassi, Edmond Kwan. 2000. West Coast diplomacy among the Akan and their neighbors. In *Traditional cures for modern conflicts*, ed. I. William Zartman. Boulder, CO: Lynne Rienner Publishers.

Lomnitz, Larissa, and R. Salazar. 2002. Cultural elements in the practice of law in Mexico: Informal networks in formal systems. In *Global prescriptions: The production, exportation, and importation of a new legal orthodoxy*, ed. Y. Dezalay and B. Garth. Ann Arbor: University of Michigan Press.

López-Ayllón, Sergio, and Héctor Fix-Fierro. 2003. "Faraway, so close!" The rule of law and legal change in Mexico, 1970–2000. In *Legal culture in the age of globalization: Latin America and Latin Europe*, ed. L. Friedman and R. Pérez-Perdomo. Stanford: Stanford University Press.

Mertz, Elizabeth. 2007. *The language of the law school: Learning to "think like a lawyer."* Oxford: Oxford University Press.

Miyazawa, Setsuo, and H. Otsuka. 2002. Legal education and the reproduction of the elite in Japan. In *Global prescriptions: The production, exportation, and importation of a new legal orthodoxy*, ed. Y. Dezalay and B. Garth. Ann Arbor: University of Michigan Press.

Moustafa, Tamir. 2007. *The struggle for constitutional power: law, politics and economic development in Egypt*. Cambridge. Cambridge University Press.

———. 2003. The judicialization of politics in Egypt. *Law and Social Inquiry* 28: 883.

Nader, Laura, and H. Todd. 1978. *The disputing process-law in ten societies*. New York: Columbia University Press.

Nelson, Robert, and Laura B. Nielsen. 2000. Cops, counsel, and entrepreneurs: Constructing the role of inside counsel in large corporations. *Law and Society Review* 34.

Osiel, Mark J. 1995. Dialogue with dictators: Judicial resistance to authoritarianism in Brazil and Argentina. *Law and Social Inquiry* 20: 481.

Pereira, Anthony. 2005. *Political (in)justice, authoritarianism and rule of law in Brazil, Chile and Argentina.* Pittsburgh, PA: University of Pittsburgh Press.

Pérez-Perdomo, Rogelio. 2006. *Latin American lawyers: A historical introduction.* Stanford: Stanford University Press.

Pérez-Perdomo, Rogelio, and J. Rodríguez. 2006. *La formación jurídica en América Latina: Tensiones e innovación en tiempos de globalización.* Bogotá: Universidad Externado de Colombia.

Pujas, Véronique. 2000. Les pouvoirs judiciares dans la lutte contre la corruption politique en Espagne, en France et en Italia. *Droit et Societé* 44/45: 41.

Roussel, Violaine. 2000. Scandales politiques et transformation des rapports entre magistratura et politique. *Droit et Societé* 44/45: 13.

Rueschemeyer, Dietrich. 1973. *Lawyers and their society: A comparative study of the legal professions in Germany and in the United States.* Cambridge, MA: Harvard University Press.

Sajo, Andras. 1993. The role of lawyers in social change: Hungary. *Case Western Reserve Journal of International Law* 25: 137.

Santos, Cecilia M., A. C. Santos, M. Duarte, and T. M. Lima. 2008. *O Tribunal Europeo dos Direitos Humanos e Portugal: uma revisao bibliográfica.* Coimbra, Brazil: Oficina de CES.

Sieder, R., L. Schjolden, and A. Angell, eds. 2005. *The judicialization of politics in Latin America.* London: Palgrave Macmillan.

Smigel, Erwin O. 1964. *The Wall Street lawyer: Professional or organizational man?* New York: Free Press of Glencoe.

Sokol, Daniel. 2007. Globalization of law firms: a survey of the literature and a research agenda for further study. *Indiana Journal of Global Legal Studies* 14: 5–28.

Suchman, Mark, and M. Cahill. 1996. The hired gun as facilitator: Lawyers and the suppression of business disputes in Silicon Valley. *Law and Social Inquiry* 21: 679.

Tate, C. Neal, and T. Vallinder, eds. 1995. *The global expansion of the judicial power.* New York: New York University Press.

Toharia, José-Juan. 1975. Judicial independence in an authoritarian regime: The case of contemporary Spain. *Law and Society Review* 9: 3.

Trubek, David M., Yves Dezalay, Ruth Buchanan, and John R. Davies, eds. 1993. Global restructuring and the law: Studies of the internationalization of legal fields and the creation of transnational arenas. *Case Western Reserve Law Review* 44(2): 407–98.

Van Houtte, Jan. 1999. Law in the world of business: Lawyers in large industrial enterprises. *International Journal of the Legal Profession* 6: 7.

Vermeule, Adrian. 2006. Should we have lay justices? Harvard Public Law Working Paper No. 134. Available at SSRN: http://ssrn.com/abstract=943369

Vianna, L. W., M. A. R. de Carvalho, M. P. C. Melo, and M. B. Gurgos. 1999. *A judicialização da política e das relações sociais no Brasil.* Rio de Janeiro: Revam.

West, Mark D. 2007. Making lawyers (and gangsters) in Japan. *Vanderbilt Law Review* 60: 439.

Winn, Jane Kaufman, and Tang-chi Yeh. 1995. Advocating democracy: The role of lawyers in Taiwan's political transformation. *Law and Social Inquiry* 20: 561.

1

THE INTERNAL CONTROL
OF A BUREAUCRATIC JUDICIARY

THE CASE OF JAPAN

Masaki Abe

INTRODUCTION

Most Japanese judges, like those in the Continental European countries, are recruited to the judiciary just after completing legal education and training, and remain there for a long period of time. Those who become judges after some experience of private practice are rare. On the other hand, there is no court of special jurisdiction, such as administrative law courts and labor law courts, except for family courts, and the Supreme Court retains the final say in all legal matters in Japan as in the Anglo-American countries.

The aim of this article is to elucidate one purely Japanese characteristic, that is, the bureaucratic nature of the Japanese judiciary. The formal institutional framework of the Japanese judiciary provided by the Constitution and some statutes and the de facto delegation of powers concentrated enormous power of judicial administration on the central managerial staff of the judiciary, and the managerial staff has fully utilized this power in order to control the behaviors of lower-court judges. As a result of such centralized hierarchical control, the Japanese judiciary as a whole has come to be a bureaucratic organization, which is unique among developed democratic countries. A bureaucratic judiciary like that of Japan can be found neither among the Continental European countries nor among the Anglo-American countries.

. . .

In the following pages, the mechanism of strict hierarchical control over Japanese lower-court judges will be delineated. Following this, it is argued that this hierarchical control is exerted not in accordance with some capricious preference of those who happen to be at the top of judicial administration, but in conformity with consistent criteria which have developed as the products of organizational responses of the judiciary to its changing social and political environments. Finally, it is noted that this mechanism of internal control within

Reprinted from Masaki Abe, "The Internal Control of a Bureaucratic Judiciary: The Case of Japan," *International Journal of the Sociology of Law* 23: 303 (1995), with permission from Elsevier.

the Japanese bureaucratic judiciary is self-reproductive in its nature, and that shared tacit norms are likely to emerge within the judiciary because of the consistent internal control attributable to this self-reproductive control mechanism.

THE MECHANISM OF CENTRAL CONTROL

In Japan, the judiciary as a whole is a single bureaucratic organization to which all judges belong. A judge is appointed as a member of the judiciary, frequently transferred from one court to another, and gradually promoted to a higher position. In spite of the formal authority of the Conference of Supreme Court Justices over all aspects of judicial administration, real power to transfer and promote judges is held by the General Secretariat (Jimu-Sokyoku) of the Supreme Court. Using this power as sanctions, the General Secretariat exerts strict control over lower-court judges. Therefore, it is difficult for those lower-court judges who seek better positions within the judiciary to deviate from what the General Secretariat expects of them.

There are many points at which the General Secretariat can determine the fate of a judge. At these points, the General Secretariat can utilize its power to transfer and promote judges in such a way as rewarding the obedient and punishing the deviant.

In Japan, legal education occurs at the undergraduate level. One who wants to be a judge, a public prosecutor, or a private practitioner must study law at a law department of a university for four years and then pass the National Legal Examination (Shiho Shiken). The National Legal Examination is one of the most difficult examinations in Japan. Until recently, about twenty-five thousand people took the examination every year, and only about five hundred examinees passed. The percentage of passing was only 2 percent. While some scholars argue that this extremely low pass rate is a manifestation of a governmental policy of restricting citizens' access to courts by keeping the number of legal professionals low in order to maintain an apparently nonlitigious society (Haley 1978), the Ministry of Justice and the General Secretariat of the Supreme Court claim that the low pass rate is largely due to the limited capacity of the Legal Research and Training Institute (Shiho Kensyujo), where successful examinees get practical legal training. Three years ago, the capacity of the institute was enlarged, and now about seven hundred examinees pass the examination. But still the pass rate is only about 3 percent. It is rare to pass the examination on the first attempt. On average, the successful examinee passes on his sixth try at the age of twenty-nine years.

The National Legal Examination is administrated by the Administration Commission of the National Legal Examination (Shiho Shiken Kanri Tinkar), a quasi-independent administrative agency formally belonging to the Ministry of Justice. The examination tests only the legal knowledge and analytical skill of examinees. There is no clear ideological bias in questions asked in the examination. But if an examinee manifests a critical attitude toward the precedents of the Supreme Court in his answers to questions requiring essay-style answers, he may not be able to pass the examination. Even if this is not the case, many would-be examinees believe that the best way to pass the examination quickly is memorizing the precedents of the Supreme Court without paying attention to scholarly arguments criticizing those precedents, and they study in this way. Therefore, whether intentional or not, there is some possibility that the examination produces lawyers who are not critical of Supreme Court precedent and willing to accept the status quo.

Those who pass the National Legal Examination enter the Legal Research and Training Institute and get a two-year practical legal training. Formally, the institute is under the control of the Conference of Supreme Court Justices, and the instructors are to be selected by the conference from experienced lower-court judges, public prosecutors, and private practitioners. In fact, the General Secretariat selects instructors and the Conference of Supreme Court Justices only confirms them. The training at the institute includes training to be a judge, training to be a public prosecutor, and training to be a private practitioner. As well as learning the skills of writing legal documents from instructors within the institute, apprentices spend sixteen months of the two years at their assigned districts in order to get field training in district courts, public prosecutors' offices, and private law offices.

An apprentice who wants to be a judge makes an application to the Supreme Court in his second year at the institute. The Constitution prescribes that "lower court judges shall be appointed by the Cabinet based on the nomination list made by the Supreme Court" (Constitution Art. 80, §1). But, in fact, the General Secretariat makes the list, the Conference of Supreme Court Justices approves it without any modification, and the Cabinet appoints all of those put on the list. Therefore, the real decision to admit an apprentice to the judiciary rests not with the Cabinet but with the General Secretariat.

Every year, 60–100 apprentices apply, and almost all of them are admitted. Of 3,440 apprentices who applied for admission from 1947 to 1994, only 50 applicants (1–5 percent) were not put on the nomination lists made by the General Secretariat and hence not appointed by the Cabinet (data on file with the author). However, a significant amount of informal screening occurs during the apprenticeship. Instructors of the Legal Research and Training Institute who were selected from lower-court judges repeatedly persuade those would-be applicants whom the instructors think not suitable to the judiciary not to apply, and in most cases, those who are so persuaded give up applying. Only when an apprentice is tough enough to apply in spite of the persistent persuasion of judge-instructors, and the General Secretariat refuses to put his name on the nomination list, is an application formally rejected. As a matter of course, those apprentices who gave up or were rejected from becoming judges can enter into private practice, and hence, there is no fear of unemployment. But it is certain that an apprentice can never enter into the judiciary if he is regarded as not suitable to the judiciary by the General Secretariat or judge-instructors of the Legal Research and Training Institute appointed by the General Secretariat. In other words, the General Secretariat successfully refuses admittance to the judiciary to those who may be disobedient to it. This makes it easy for the General Secretariat to control those who enter the judiciary.

The new graduates of the Legal Research and Training Institutes admitted to the judiciary are first appointed as assistant judges. The difference between assistant judges and full judges is that the law imposes some limitation on the power of assistant judges. For instance, assistant judges may not preside over a three-judge panel, cannot become high-court judges, and may not participate in the decision-making of the conference of judges of the court where they are assigned within the first five years of their appointment (Judiciary Act Art. 27, Art. 28; Act Providing the Exception to the Limitation of the Power of Assistant Judges Art. I, Art. 1–2).

Assistant judges are transferred from one court to another about every three years. The law gives the Conference of Supreme Court Judges exclusive power to assign judges to particular courts (Judiciary Act Art. 47), and no one outside the judiciary can meddle in the decisions of the Conference. But, in fact, those decisions are made by the General Secretariat. The law also provides that a judge shall not be transferred against his will (Judiciary Act Art. 48). Therefore, on the face of the law, if a judge does not want to be transferred, he can remain in the same post. But if a judge ever refuses the decision of the General Secretariat to transfer him to a particular court, it is certain that he will never be transferred to a better place in the future. In addition, if he is an assistant judge, he may not be promoted to a full judge; and if he is a full judge, he may be judged unsuitable to the judiciary in an eligibility examination which judges must pass every ten years to retain their office. For these reasons, the decisions of the General Secretariat to transfer judges are rarely refused.

Both assistant judges and full judges think that there are good places and bad places to be assigned. Good places are district courts or high courts in urban areas where stimulating lawsuits frequently occur. In contrast, bad places are branch offices of district courts and family courts located in rural areas. The General Secretariat and the Legal Research and Training Institute are among the best places. In addition, temporary transfer to the Ministry of Justice as a solicitor to represent the government in civil and administrative lawsuits is regarded as an assignment to a good place. Generally speaking, judges assigned to good places have a greater chance of promotion to higher positions in the future than those assigned to bad places. Therefore, most judges want to be assigned to good places. Herein lies the possibility that the General Secretariat's de facto power to assign judges to particular places functions as a strong tool of controlling judges. The General Secretariat can, and often does, assign obedient judges to good places and disobedient ones to bad places. This power makes it difficult for judges to act in such a way that the General Secretariat deems disobedient.

With regard to assistant judges, however, the policy of the General Secretariat is that most assistant judges should experience both a large court in an urban area and a small court in a rural area in their first ten years, in order to learn various aspects of judicial work. Those decisions to transfer assistant judges are made in a relatively routine manner. Therefore, the possibility that the General Secretariat's power of assignment functions as a tool of controlling assistant judges is not very high. The only exception is assignment to the General Secretariat itself. Only a small number of assistant judges are assigned to the General Secretariat as research staff. These assignments imply that the General Secretariat expects those assistant judges to be in the judicial elite responsible for judicial administration in the future. In fact, most of those who have experienced the work at the General Secretariat during their assistant judge days are promoted to higher positions of judicial administration after they become full judges.

After ten years, assistant judges are promoted to full judges. Like the appointment of new assistant judges, these promotion decisions are formally to be made by the Cabinet based on the list made by the Supreme Court (Constitution Art. 80, §1), but the real decision rests with the General Secretariat. If an assistant judge is refused promotion to a full judge, he cannot remain in the judiciary, although he can still become a private practitioner. Therefore, this ten-year point is crucial for those who want to continue their judicial work. Actually, refusal is rare. From the end of World War II to this day, there has been only one assistant judge who has not been promoted. It was in 1971, in the midst of political attacks against the allegedly biased judiciary described below. In this case, the General Secretariat admitted that one reason for the refusal was that the assistant judge had been an active member of the Young Lawyers League (Seinen Haritsuka Kyajai), a liberal association of young legal professionals which took a critical stand on some governmental policies. This case might have been an abnormal one. But it seems that this one instance was enough for most assistant judges to fear possible denial of their promotion. At least, it became widely recognized within the judiciary that the General Secretariat was willing to block a promotion if it judges that refusal was really imperative. Because of this recognition, even the mere potential to refuse promotion is now a powerful threat that the General Secretariat can utilize in order to control assistant judges.

Even if assistant judges are promoted to full judges, their dependence on the General Secretariat is little changed. They are forced to be transferred by the determination of the General Secretariat from one court to another at about two-to-five year intervals. For full judges, however, transfers are more closely related to the possibility of promotion to higher positions than for assistant judges. While some full judges are repeatedly assigned to good places and gradually promoted to higher positions, such as chief judges and the heads of district courts, others are transferred from one bad place to another. Those whom the General Secretariat ranks highest are often assigned to the General Secretariat itself, then promoted to the heads of high courts, and finally selected as Supreme Court Justices.

Full judges are also examined every ten years and forced to resign if they are judged deficient (Constitution Art. 80, §1). Although this eligibility examination is formally to be administered by the Conference of Supreme Court Justices and confirmed by the Cabinet, in reality, the General Secretariat examines the eligibility of each full judge and neither the Conference of Supreme Court Justices nor the Cabinet has ever disapproved the result. After World War II, ten judges were denied their eligibility. The last instance was in 1969. In this case, as well as in former cases, the reasons for the denial were not officially announced. But it is widely recognized that it was because the judge had refused to be transferred that his eligibility as a judge was denied. This instance shows that a judge's refusal to be transferred may lead to the General Secretariat's denial of his eligibility as a judge and hence makes it difficult for judges to refuse their transfers.

THE CRITERIA OF INTERNAL CONTROL

What behavior does the General Secretariat require from lower-court judges? Does it demand more than just following its statutory interpretations presented at conferences of lower-court judges? If so, what is it?

As the managerial personnel of the General Secretariat are constantly being replaced by other lower-court judges, it is impossible that a particular person dominates the General Secretariat according to his will for a long period of time. Nevertheless, it seems that the General Secretariat has exerted its control over judges in a remarkably consistent way for at least the last two decades. This suggests that the General Secretariat has not forced judges to obey some arbitrary preferences of those who happened to be on its staff, but rather required judges to behave in accordance with certain invariable criteria and examined their actual behavior in light of those criteria. Such criteria have never been articulated by the General Secretariat itself. However, it seems that judges who are under the control of the General Secretariat are conscious of the existence and the contents of those criteria at least in general terms. Although thorough empirical research has yet to be done, comments of some judges and retired judges, as well as some anecdotal data, suggest the existence of at least two important criteria, that is: (1) the criterion of efficiency; and (2) the criterion of organizational autonomy.

The Criterion of Efficiency

The criterion of efficiency means that judges should process cases as expeditiously as possible. Those who are not sufficiently expeditious in their processing of cases should be regarded as deficient and hence should be treated disadvantageously in the judiciary. It seems widely recognized among lower-court judges that efficiency is one of the criteria the General Secretariat uses for evaluating their performance. One retired judge even tells that efficiency is the faculty which all judges are required to have more than anything else. According to this criterion, those judges who pay attention to all details of the uniqueness of each case and deliberately examine all of the various issues comprising a case are to be regarded as less talented and to be treated less favorably than their colleagues who simplify a case by limiting points of contention and quickly deliver judgment in accordance with Supreme Court precedents and General Secretariat's statutory interpretations presented at conferences of lower-court judges.

The Criterion of Organizational Autonomy

The criterion of organizational autonomy means that judges should avoid bringing about such a situation that invites the intervention of the political branches of the government into the judiciary and hence should refrain from behaving in such a way as to generate doubt that the judiciary might be biased against the will of the political majority. If the majority of the political branches of the government suspect that the judiciary is prejudiced against their policy preferences, they might intervene in judicial administration for the purpose of correcting the bias. Such political intervention would deprive the judiciary of the autonomy it now enjoys and destroy the principle of judicial independence. In order to avoid such an occurrence, the criterion of organizational autonomy requires judges to regulate their behavior.

In concrete terms, this criterion restrains judges from two sorts of seemingly antimajoritarian behavior. First, judges should not participate in any organization which takes a critical stance on some governmental policies. Secondly, judges should neither invalidate important policy decisions of the Diet, the Cabinet, or ministries, nor interfere with administrative bodies implementing those policies. The self-restraint of the Japanese judiciary from disturbing governmental policymaking and implementation is widely recognized. Such judicial passivity can be understood as a result of the effective restriction which the criterion of organizational autonomy imposes on the behavior of judges.

While the criterion of efficiency can be seen mainly as a response of the judiciary to a changing social environment which manifests itself in the increase of lawsuits, the criterion of organizational autonomy is a product of the historical experience of a judiciary once surrounded by an antagonistic political environment.

In short, the turn to judicial self-restraint in the early 1970s is to be understood not as an example of successful intervention of the political branches of the government into the judiciary, but as an anecdote of how the judiciary, with its scanty political resources, managed to maintain its organizational autonomy in an antagonistic political environment.

In addition, it should be emphasized that what judicial elites learned from those events was not that the judiciary should stay away from partisan politics. The criterion of organizational autonomy is exactly the product of this lesson. It is true that both obedience to politics and avoidance of politics result in abstention from invalidating policy decisions of the political branches of the government and administrative decisions implementing them. Therefore, for those who expect the judiciary to be a champion of subordinated people fighting against political majority, the difference between them must seem trivial. As far as the independence of the judiciary is concerned, however, the difference is important. While obedience to politics means dependence, avoidance of politics implies independence, even if this independence is nothing more than the indifference of political branches of the government to the self-restraining judiciary. What judicial elites have tried to do is to maintain the independence of the judiciary by keeping the whole judiciary away from the politics.

THE SELF-REPRODUCTION OF INTERNAL CONTROL
AND THE EMERGENCE OF INTERNAL NORMS

The internal control mechanism within the judiciary which, as has been discussed, is operated in accordance with the criteria of efficiency and organizational autonomy, continually reproduces itself. Under this control mechanism, those judges who perfectly internalize these criteria and behave in accordance with them are treated favorably by the General Secretariat. They are transferred to good places, promoted faster, and as a result are soon assigned to positions responsible for judicial administration. It is these judges who can join the high-ranking managerial staff of the General Secretariat. In turn, they require judges in younger generations to obey those criteria they have internalized, that is, the criteria of efficiency and organization autonomy. Among judges in the younger generations, those who also internalize those criteria and can perform well in accordance with them succeed to responsible positions in judicial administration. There is no factor within the judiciary which is likely to stop this process, and in this sense, this internal control mechanism is self-reproductive. For this reason, the criteria of internal control is consistently maintained in spite of the totally informal nature. As for the criterion of organizational autonomy, although some scholars suggest a continual intervention of politicians of the Liberal Democratic Party into judicial administration for the purpose of checking the reemergence of judicial activism (Ramseyer and Rosenbluth 1993, 152; Ramseyer 1994), the political branches of the government need not, and in fact do not, continuously intervene into the judiciary because the self-reproduction of the internal control mechanism within the judiciary makes such external control unnecessary.

It is only when changes in the social and political spheres surrounding the judiciary generate new demands on it that this self-reproduction comes to an end. There is little possibility of such an occurrence, however. As the number of lawsuits will continuously increase, efficiency will never become unimportant for the judiciary. Insofar as the judiciary maintains its posture of self-restraint, the political branches of the government will not impose some new demand on the judiciary as intensively as they did in the late 1960s and early 1970s. In particular, it is unthinkable that the political branches will demand that the judiciary aggressively intervene into policymaking and implementation processes. Bar associations, legal scholars, mass media, interest groups, or the general public may pressure the General Secretariat to change in the style of judicial administration. But it is unlikely that the General Secretariat will favorably respond to such external pressures because it has never been so responsive. While there have been frequent criticisms against judicial administration by the Japan Federation of Bar Associations (Nippon Bengoshi Renguken), some local bar associations, law professors, and retired judges, no criticism has been effective. Therefore, without some unforeseen exogenous change, the internal control mechanism will continue to reproduce itself.

This stable self-reproduction of the internal control mechanism may someday make the criteria of efficiency and organizational autonomy authoritative norms shared by everyone, not only controllers but also those who are controlled, within the judiciary. Sooner or later, those judges who still criticize the present judicial administration will leave the judiciary. Many newly recruited judges will take the existence of these criteria and their obedience to the criteria, and also the centralized judicial administration, for granted and sincerely obey these criteria. When this generational change has been completed, lower-court judges may not only expect but also come to require the General Secretariat to treat them in accordance with those criteria in a consistent manner without exception. If this happens, those criteria will no longer be just convenient guidelines of judicial administration at the disposal of the General Secretariat. They will solely be shared norms of the whole judiciary from which even the top of the judicial hierarchy, the General Secretariat, will not be able to deviate easily at their will.

REFERENCES

Haley, J. 1978. The myth of the reluctant litigant. *Japanese Legal Studies* 4: 359–90.

Ramseyer, M. 1994. The puzzling (in)dependence of courts: A comparative approach. *Journal of Legal Studies* 23: 721–47.

Ramseyer, M., and F. Rosenbluth. 1993. *Japan's political marketplace*. Cambridge, MA: Harvard University Press.

2 MUTUAL BONDS

MEDIA FRAMES AND THE
ISRAELI HIGH COURT OF JUSTICE

Bryna Bogoch and Yifat Holzman-Gazit

In Israel, as elsewhere, there has been an expansion of the role of the Supreme Court and a growing media concern with rights consciousness, alongside a shift to a more aggressive style of journalism. These trends are not unique to Israel. Studies of the coverage of the Supreme Courts of the United States and of Canada—countries that have witnessed similar developments—have found that these trends have resulted in increased, though still sporadic, coverage of specific cases, particularly those involving civil rights and those with immediate political significance that emphasize easily identifiable winners and losers. These studies have also shown that coverage of Supreme Court decisions and of the Court as an institution has remained largely favorable, despite occasionally sharp criticism. Some have claimed that instead of providing critical and skeptical coverage of the Supreme Court, the U.S. media has been co-opted into producing the public image that the Court seeks to foster, essentially serving as the Court's publicist. It is precisely the unique function of the Israeli H[igh] C[ourt of] J[ustice], whose sole purpose is to hear petitions against state entities and actors, that invites consideration of the wider political implications of the media coverage of supreme courts.

Because all petitions filed with the HCJ are complaints against state actors and institutions, the HCJ is inevitably situated in opposition to the government of the day, the Knesset (Israel's parliament), and other public institutions. Israeli governing coalitions have become increasingly fragile in the last two decades, and political bodies have been substantially weakened, while the Supreme Court has gained power. Thus, we argue, coverage of the HCJ by both elite and popular newspapers typically frames the Court as a powerful, rule-governed, effective protector of the citizen against corrupt, self-interested, or merely incompetent politicians and bureaucrats.

Reprinted from Bryna Bogoch and Yifat Holzman-Gazit, "Mutual Bonds: Media Frames and the Israeli High Court of Justice," *Law and Social Inquiry* 33: 53 (2008). Copyright © 2008 *Law and Social Inquiry*. Reproduced with the permission of Blackwell Publishing.

THE SUPREME COURT OF ISRAEL

The Supreme Court of Israel has two distinct functions. One is as the final Court of Appeals, in which it hears appeals in both civil and criminal cases. The other is as the High Court of Justice (HCJ), which has original jurisdiction over petitions seeking relief from administrative decisions of public agencies. Judgments of the HCJ are final and cannot be appealed.

A person who has reason to believe that an action of the state or a public agency has violated her legal rights may petition the HCJ and apply for an *order nisi*, which the Court will issue if it decides that the complaint has merit and is justiciable. An *order nisi* requires the public entity to explain why it will not accept the demands of the petitioner, and it is often accompanied by an interlocutory order preventing the public agency from further action for a specific period of time. The Court will then hear the explanation of the public agency, and it can either nullify the *order nisi* (i.e., dismiss the petition) or make it absolute (i.e., accept the petition). A total of 1,330 petitions were submitted to the HCJ in 1996, and 344 *orders nisi* were issued.

It is mainly for its actions as the HCJ that the Supreme Court of Israel has developed a reputation of being a powerful, influential, and activist court. Although Israel has no written constitution, from the beginning the Court developed, through its decisions against state agencies and administrative regulations, a jurisprudence of basic civil rights, such as freedom of speech and association, freedom of religion, freedom of occupation, and freedom of movement.

In the first three decades of its existence, within the prevailing ideology of legal formalism, Israel's Supreme Court drew a sharp distinction between politics and law. Petitions involving issues of foreign policy, military actions, and other questions concerning sensitive political matters were considered unsuitable for judicial determination and therefore nonjusticiable.

In the 1980s, the Supreme Court substantially reduced the requirements for proving standing and justiciability, allowing more petitioners to reach the Court. The Court also applied new standards of judicial review, based on the doctrines of reasonableness, rationality of the decision-making process, and proportionality, to decisions, which until that time had been traditionally immune from judicial oversight, such as decisions of the various state security organs. In 1992, in what has been hailed as a constitutional revolution, two Basic Laws on human rights were enacted by the Knesset. These Basic Laws have been applied by the Court in a number of controversial decisions, including on matters of collective identity, distributive justice, and administration legitimacy. The Basic Laws allowed these disputes to be phrased as rights entitlements and value issues, and thus subject to judicial review. In addition, the Court used these Laws to claim for itself the power of judicial review of legislation, an act that in effect confirms the supremacy of the Court over the Knesset. The Court's role in resolving fundamental societal dilemmas based on these laws, as well as on notions of collective values, not only enhanced the Court's power but also made it more difficult for the Knesset to contemplate overturning these decisions.

The increasingly central role of the HCJ in Israeli public life is thus commonly regarded as a consequence of the transfer of political power from the legislature to the Court. This shift of power occurred alongside a weakening of the country's political bodies and a growing public distrust in the good faith of politicians. Although the trust rating in the HCJ has fallen slightly in recent years, it is still higher than the trust rating accorded any other institution in Israel, with the exception of the military, and it is considerably higher than that reported in other countries.

The expansion of the Supreme Court's powers of review coincided with a growth in the number of media sources available to Israelis. In addition, in recent decades there has been a growth in the subjects and institutions that an increasingly competitive and investigative press scrutinizes. Since the 1980s, in light of severe criticism of the failings of the press prior to the Yom Kippur War, media professionals have approached their watchdog role more seriously. In fact, Peri (2004) claims that, except for coverage of matters of national security, the approach of Israeli journalists to politicians has gone beyond the critical adversary model in which politicians are aggressively criticized. They have now adopted a competitive model, in which the media "do politics" by undermining the legitimacy of public institutions and officials, and compete with political institutions for the leadership of public opinion and the mobilization of the public for political actions and social legitimation.

Another change that has marked the Israeli media scene is the increasing tabloidization of the popular press. However, contrary to the tabloid press in other countries, the Israeli popular press, like its quality counterpart, strongly emphasizes politics and current affairs.

METHOD AND SAMPLE

We selected for analysis every article mentioning the HCJ during the months of January, March, June, and November in 1972, 1981, 1994, and 2000 that appeared in two of the three national Hebrew-language dailies for the general population: *Haaretz*, the elite Israeli daily; and *Yedioth Aharonot* (commonly called *Yedioth*), the popular daily with the highest circulation in the country. We chose one year of each decade in which a different chief justice of the Supreme Court presided, avoiding years that were marked by war or concentrated terrorist activity, as well as months when the Court is typically in recess. Although increasing the number of years in our sample would have improved the general conclusions of some of our findings, we have attempted to limit the factors that would have skewed the coverage of Court activities in the years that were omitted. Altogether, our sample consists of 1,334 articles.

A distinction was made between those articles that dealt specifically with the HCJ and those that referred to the HCJ in passing in the context of a different story. Each article that dealt specifically with the HCJ was analyzed by a code that examined the prominence of the coverage and the media frames used in reporting about the HCJ. The prominence of the coverage was measured by a number of variables, including the size (area) of the report, the size of the headlines, the location of the article within the newspaper, and the use of visual elements such as photographs, illustrations, and other graphics. Two types of variables provided the basis for the frame analysis: (1) the type of report (i.e., a news report, opinion piece, or other type of article, and the identity and profession of the writer; and (2) the legal issues described in the article, the stage of the proceedings covered, the identities of the petitioners and the respondents, the results of the proceedings, and the evaluation of the Court's decision. In addition, other variables that were coded were the identities of the judges and lawyers, as well as the extent to which various descriptions of the Court's activities were included in the article. The coders were law or communications students, who were in constant contact with each other and with the principle investigators of the study to ensure consistency of the coding. A random sample of 5 percent of the total database of articles was double coded to examine reliability. Agreement between the coders was generally high, ranging from 78 percent to 100 percent, with an average of 94 percent.

RESULTS

Extent of Coverage

The main finding of virtually all previous studies of the coverage of the U.S. and Canadian Supreme Courts has been the paucity of the coverage and the fact that these Courts are covered mainly in the context of judicial decisions. The results from Israel are quite different.

Although Israel's Supreme Court carries out two distinct functions, the press is mostly interested in its role as the HCJ. Altogether, over the years covered by our research, there were only 200 articles dealing with civil appeals and 289 with criminal appeals, compared to 1,334 articles reporting on the Court's role as HCJ, despite the fact that there were somewhat more civil and criminal appeals combined than HCJ petitions. We suggest that the preference for HCJ stories ties in with our general thesis that these are particularly attractive to the media in that, unlike most civil or criminal appeals, HCJ petitions are directed against the activities of the government and public bodies.

Clearly the coverage of the HCJ has increased substantially over time in both newspapers, with a sharp distinction between the early years (1972 and 1981) and the later years (1994 and 2000). In fact, almost half of the total number of articles in both papers appeared in 2000 (48 percent *Haaretz*, 43 percent *Yedioth*).

However, not only are there more articles covering the HCJ over the years, but by 2000 the HCJ had become a routine, almost necessary, element in every edition of the newspaper. Whereas in the early years only one-third to one-half of the issues carried items about the HCJ, in the year 2000, 101 of the 105 issues of *Haaretz* contained a reference to the HCJ, with slightly fewer, 82, in *Yedioth*. In fact, in the last two years of our sample, there was an average of three to four articles on the HCJ in each issue of *Haaretz* and between one and two in *Yedioth*. Thus, unlike the U.S. Supreme Court that "disappears [from the media] for months at a time," the HCJ now maintains a constant presence in the press.

It can be argued that the growth of the HCJ coverage is due to the increase in the number of petitions filed with the HCJ and the expansion of the Court's activity. However, while three and a half times as many petitions were submitted to the HCJ in 2000 as compared to 1972 (from 491 to 1,686), the number of articles covering petitions to the HCJ has grown almost sixfold in *Haaretz* (from 45 to 255) and more than fourfold in *Yedioth* (from 26 to 115). Obviously the newspapers are devoting more coverage to petitions submitted to the HCJ *over and above the actual increase in the number of petitions filed with the Court*. The expansion of both direct and indirect coverage of the Court's activity in the elite and popular press alike keeps the HCJ on the public agenda and is an element in the constitution of the Supreme Court as a central institution in Israeli society.

Prominence of Coverage

There has been a steady increase in the number of HCJ articles appearing on the front page in *both* newspapers. The increase in the quality press was more gradual, while in *Yedioth* the main increase occurred in 2000. Despite the fact that in 2000 there were double the number of HCJ articles in *Haaretz* than in *Yedioth*, the two papers carried a similar number of articles on their front page (thirteen in *Yedioth*, fifteen in *Haaretz*). For *Yedioth*, these accounted for 20 percent of the articles in that year, whereas for *Haaretz* they amounted to only 10 percent. It seems that when *Yedioth* covers the HCJ, it tends to report the more dramatic stories that warrant front-page status, whereas *Haaretz* routinely reports on less dramatic HCJ cases as well.

What is interesting is that although there is almost no difference in the *number* of HCJ stories that appear on the front page of the two newspapers in 2000, only one story—a decision regarding procedures related to the dissolution of the Knesset—appeared on the front page of both newspapers. This story, which attests to the power of the HCJ over the Knesset even in matters of parliamentary procedure, was covered in a series of articles in both newspapers.

The other HCJ front-page stories in 2000 seem to reflect the nature and ideological bent of the paper. For example, six of the front-page stories in *Yedioth* dealt with petitions against prosecutorial decisions in cases involving infractions of norms of behavior by left-wing politicians, whereas in *Haaretz* the most frequent topic on the front page (appearing three times) was religion-state issues. By contrast, no religion-state decisions, which have been among the most controversial issues in Israel, appeared on the front page of *Yedioth*. Hence, while *Yedioth* gave prominence to the issues for which Court intervention is widely accepted, *Haaretz* highlighted the cases that were more controversial among the general public but that are consonant with the ideology of the secular, educated readership of the paper.

Identity of Petitioner

It could be claimed that the growth in the reports of petitions to the HCJ is due to the increase in the number of nongovernmental organizations (NGOs) that have emerged, especially in the last two decades in Israel with the explicit goal of promoting social and political change. Israeli NGOs view petitions to the HCJ not only as an important avenue for achieving reforms but also as a means of gaining publicity and public support. Some NGOs maintain large legal and public relations departments that are heavily involved in petitioning the HCJ and in publicizing their efforts at all stages of litigation.

There was indeed a steady rise in the reports of petitions by NGOs in both newspapers. By 2000, about 35 percent of the articles dealt with NGO petitions, compared to less than 10 percent in 1972. In fact, Dotan and Hofnung (2001) found that petitions by NGOs accounted for about 12 percent of the HCJ docket in 1993 and 1995, which suggests that these petitions may even be overreported in the media. However, while the activity of NGOs can no doubt contribute to an explanation of the increase in the media coverage of the HCJ, it cannot be the only reason. First, there was also an (albeit more modest) increase in the proportion of other petitioners reported in the media, such as business groups and public corporations. Moreover, the fact that NGOs invest tremendous energies in an effort to publicize their activities still does not explain why the media are particularly responsive to their petitions to the HCJ. Although the increase of NGO petitions may contribute to the heightened media coverage of the HCJ, we suggest that there is an additional element to petitions to the HCJ that is related to the antigovernment nature of these petitions, and this is what makes them so attractive to the media.

Stage of Proceedings

Since the 1980s, coverage of the HCJ has been extended to a wider array of Court activities. Just the intention to submit a petition to the HCJ (or the threat of submitting) is considered newsworthy, even before any legal proceedings have been initiated. In the earliest period most reporting centered on the decision, whereas by 2000 the decision and its aftermaths constituted only about 25 percent of the coverage in both papers. In fact, there was more coverage of the phase prior to the issuing of an *order nisi* (about 60 percent of the articles in 2000 in both papers) than after an *order nisi* was issued.

Unlike the media portrayal of Supreme Court decisions in the United States, in Israel it is not only who won or lost that is considered newsworthy but also the process of enlisting the Court against the government or other public entities. Rather than a game frame, it is a due process frame that characterizes media coverage of Israel's HCJ. Articles about the various stages of the proceedings, and even about the intention to petition the Court, keep the HCJ in the news and on the public agenda. More importantly, by reporting the process regardless of the final decision, the press emphasizes the unique rule-governed nature of the judicial process and identifies the Court as the institution that individuals and public interest groups can turn to in their fight against the government.

Outcome of Decisions

The reporting of the final result is not dependent on coverage of the decision regarding the *order nisi*. Nevertheless, it is clear that with the exception of the coverage by *Haaretz* in 1994, in both newspapers the granting of an *order nisi* or a final decision in favor of the petitioner was reported more frequently than its denial. In other words, the press reports many more instances when the citizen succeeds in enlisting the Court to overrule the government than when the Court aligns itself with the regime. Not only is this contrary to data from the C[entral] B[ureau of] S[tatistics], but it also contradicts a number of articles based on substantive analyses of decisions that claim that the HCJ, in fact, legitimates the dominant ideology and endorses government positions. Thus, the press frames the Court as a powerful, independent institution that frequently takes the government to task for violating the rights of citizens.

Topic of Decisions

The subject of judicial decisions has been considered among the most important factors predicting coverage of the U.S. Supreme Court. Human rights, discrimination, and First Amendment issues are more frequently covered than other, sometimes legally more significant topics. In Israel, complaints alleging violations of human rights by state authorities or the inappropriate behavior of public officials are lodged directly with the HCJ, and thus we expected that media coverage of the HCJ would focus on these issues. We also expected that intensified commercial pressures in more recent years would be associated with an increase of press coverage of highly divisive religion-state and security matters.

There has been a sharp decline in the coverage of one area for which HCJ intervention is most controversial. The proportion of religion-state issues reported has declined from a high in 1972 of 29 percent and 33 percent in *Haaretz* and *Yedioth* to 7 percent and 9 percent, respectively, in 2000. On the other hand, civil rights issues have increased fourfold in *Haaretz* and more than doubled in *Yedioth*, to about one-fifth of the articles in 2000. In that year, the most frequently reported issues were economics, public norms, and civil rights. All the other topics reported in 2000 comprised 10 percent or less of the press coverage, including only 5 percent and 8 percent of the articles in *Haaretz* and *Yedioth* that covered often controversial security issues, and only 2 percent and 4 percent, respectively, on freedom of expression cases.

While there are no data with which we can compare the actual Court docket with reports in the press, there is abundant evidence of the increased activism of the Court, especially on issues of civil rights and the regulation of norms of behavior by public officials. These are also the topics where Court intervention is accorded widespread public legitimacy, compared to more controversial decisions in security matters and in religion-state issues.

Our findings on the extensive reporting of areas of HCJ activity that are widely approved of by the Israeli public, such as civil rights issues and public norms, are consistent with our assumption that the framing of the HCJ in the press serves two functions: (1) it provides the press the opportunity and the ammunition for criticizing government actions on issues for which there is widespread popular support both for media criticism itself and for the role of the Court; and (2) it constructs the Court as an institution that deals with issues that are central to public life, that preserves order in the public sphere, and that promotes equality.

The large proportion of articles covering economic activities adds another dimension to the media's construction of the power of the Court. While the coverage of decisions concerning public norms and civil rights typically appear in the news section of the newspapers, more than two-thirds of the reports of judicial proceedings involving economic issues appeared in both papers in a separate economic section. These items were also generally considerably shorter than articles covering civil rights and public norms. Thus, the frequent coverage of economic petitions demonstrates that the Court is heavily involved in the economic life of the country. The framing of economic petitions as less prominent topics of specialized interest preserves the centrality of the Court's role in maintaining public order and furthering the protection of human rights.

Evaluation of the HCJ

Various commentators have noted the increase in investigative reporting in Israel over the years, and the fact that there are very few institutions in the country that have not been demythologized or at least challenged by critical reports. Peri (2004, 92) claims that, similar to the U.S. model, in all matters not related to security, the Israeli media have adopted a role of confrontation, challenge, criticism, and scrutiny of all government institutions. Not only does the coverage of the HCJ belie the critical stance of adversarial journalism, but it suggests a congruence of interests between the media and the Court in upholding the legitimacy of the Court and undermining the other political institutions.

Only some 10 percent of the articles in both the elite and popular press criticized the decisions of the HCJ, compared to between 23 percent and 33 percent that supported the Court's decisions, and about 60 percent that were neutral. This consensus of support in the coverage by both papers has fluctuated only slightly over time, and although it appears that there are more critical articles in 2000 in *Yedioth* than in the early years, the difference is not statistically significant. Compared to the treatment of other political institutions, there is very little of the skeptical or critical news coverage of the HCJ. Moreover, both the popular and elite press are more than twice as likely to support Court decisions that in effect challenge governmental policy and decisions. Praise of the Court's decisions is often explicitly contrasted to the government's inadequacies.

"The HCJ declared in a courageous decision worthy of the utmost praise that Arab citizens can no longer be adversely discriminated against in the distribution of state lands. . . . From now on, declared the HCJ, the State will no longer be able to maintain discriminatory policies against its Arab citizens" (*Haaretz*, March 10, 2000). *Yedioth* was even more blunt in its comparison of the Court and the government:

> For the first time in the history of the state a deep fissure was created in one of the biggest racist and embarrassing bluffs that the state bluffed itself and its citizens, the bluff that transformed Israel into the only democratic state in the world in which it is possible to maintain racially pure settlements. . . . The HCJ did not yet break down the wall and perhaps in its wisdom it did not yet do so. . . . Again we can feel real pride in the Supreme Court of the State of Israel. (*Yedioth*, March 10, 2000)

In effect, it seems that the Court provides the media with ammunition in their monitoring of and confrontation with political institutions, while the media provides the Court with the legitimacy and support it requires.

However, there is also evidence that the media in general reflects the prevalent power structure and reinforces hegemonic values and institutions. The extensive and favorable framing of the HCJ as an institution that regularly rules against government bodies and acts to curb government power detracts from the role of the Court in legitimating government policies. Most petitions, after all, are not accepted, and in most cases the Court upholds rather than rules against prevailing government practice. It is in the politicians' interests to foster a belief in the independence of the Court, although in fact, in most cases, they actually receive the Court's blessings to do what they want. It is similarly in the interest of the media to participate in cultivating the image of a powerful activist Court; this allows the press to present itself as the watchdog of democracy that exposes government abuse of power, backed by the authoritative and independent HCJ, without really challenging the status quo.

There is another sense in which the coverage of the HCJ serves a hegemonic function. It has been claimed that, following their loss of control over the Knesset, the old-time political elite colluded in the transfer of power to the Court, where demographically and ideologically they still prevail, thus ensuring the continued supremacy of their values and policy preferences. To the extent that this is indeed the case, the disparate interests of the Supreme

Court, the former political elites, and the media all coincide—and the extensive coverage of the HCJ petitions serves all these actors.

This is especially true of the elite press. Although on most indices there was no difference between the elite and popular press and both were supportive and largely uncritical of the HCJ, *Haaretz* provided far more extensive coverage of HCJ petitions, including the more routine cases, as might be expected of a serious elite newspaper. This greater exposure not only emphasizes the importance of the HCJ to the economic and social life of the country, but in the Israeli context it also accentuates the opposition and contrast of the Court to the political sphere. In addition, *Haaretz* gave greater prominence to those Court interventions that were consonant with its own liberal, secular stance and were often highly controversial decisions among the general public. By contrast, the popular press emphasized the more universally sanctioned role of the Court in curbing political corruption. The salience of the coverage of HCJ petitions and the nonconsensual topics that are highlighted in *Haaretz* seem to indicate that the elite newspaper endorses and promotes the transfer of power to the Court on a wider range of issues than does the popular press. Both views of the elite press thus seem to be supported by these data—the view of the elite press as providing deeper and more informative coverage of important societal issues, as well as the view that the elite press reinforces the legitimacy of certain professional and institutional elites—and serves as a powerful mechanism for these elites to preserve their hegemony.

In Israel, it is widely held that the Supreme Court, particularly in its role as the HCJ, serves as the bulwark against the deterioration of democratic values that the political sphere is too self-interested or corrupt to confront. This is the view that is promulgated and constantly reinforced by the press, which seems to regard the legitimacy of the Court as too fragile and precious to endanger by extensive criticism, or at least the type of skeptical coverage accorded other institutions. Our analysis of the HCJ has shown the benefits for the media and for the Court that this type of coverage affords. The question that remains is whether it also serves the best interests of the Israeli public.

REFERENCES

Dotan, Yoav, and Menachem Hofnung. 2001. Interest groups in the Israeli High Court of Justice: Measuring success in litigation and out-of-court settlements. *Law & Policy* 23: 1–27.

Peri, Yoram. 2004. *Telepopulism: Media and politics in Israel*. Stanford: Stanford University Press.

3

LAW, LAWYERS, AND LEGAL PRACTICE IN SILICON VALLEY

A PRELIMINARY REPORT

Lawrence M. Friedman, Robert W. Gordon, Sophie Pirie, and Edwin Whatley

What do lawyers contribute to technological change and economic development? Much popular opinion assumes that the contribution is mostly negative, that the vast amounts of legal time billed to corporate enterprise (US$38 billion worth annually, according to a 1984 estimate) are the pathological symptoms of an overregulated, excessively litigious culture that diverts resources from productivity and innovation into wasteful paper pushing. Other, more sanguine observers—usually lawyers—argue to the contrary that legal services are valuable, even indispensable parts of the infrastructure that support the efficiency of transactions, even if their value is not always appreciated by clients or the general public. The debate has been chiefly at the level of assertion because there has been so little serious research since James Willard Hurst's monumental study in 1964 of the ways in which lawmakers and lawyers designed and operated the legal-institutional frameworks for the growth and organization of the lumber industry in nineteenth-century Wisconsin.

Inspired by the example of Hurst's work, the authors have begun to study the lawyers who work in Palo Alto, California—the legal hub of the computer-products industries of the Silicon Valley. As a subject of study, the Silicon Valley is nearly ideal. It has a dense concentration of lawyers and a dense concentration of new industry. The lawyers claim that their role in the Valley's boom has been extremely influential. The industry and the legal practice that has grown up around it are both young; their entire histories are within the grasp of living memories. The explosive pace of growth gives us the chance to watch basic changes in form unfold even as the study progresses. This brief paper describes, in general terms, some of the observations and hypotheses arrived at after preliminary work on the project.

Even when Silicon Valley was still largely agricultural, more famous for prunes than for computers, the small city of Palo Alto was home to a fair number of lawyers. Minor league though it may have been, Palo Alto was a thriving legal center compared to its neighbors.

Reprinted from Lawrence M. Friedman, Robert W. Gordon, Sophie Pirie, and Edwin Whatley, "Law, Lawyers, and Legal Practice in Silicon Valley: A Preliminary Report," *Indiana Law Journal* 64: 555 (1989). Permission courtesy of the authors.

In the 1920s, when Sunnyvale, Menlo Park, and Mountain View each had one or two law-yers, and two county seats, San Jose and Redwood City had about twenty lawyers each. Tiny Palo Alto had fourteen. This number grew to fifty lawyers by the 1950s, then to two hundred fifty in the 1960s. Today (1988), Palo Alto, with a population under sixty thousand, has over one thousand lawyers practicing within the city limits—perhaps the highest ratio of lawyers to population anywhere in the United States outside Manhattan and perhaps Washington D.C.

In the 1950s, there were already some lawyers in the Palo Alto bar who had begun their careers on the East Coast, or in the industrial heartland, or in San Francisco. Quite likely, no explosion of lawyering in Palo Alto could have occurred without lawyers who had a strong professional background and useful skills. But it was not at all inevitable that local lawyers would be able to take hold and provide services for new industry. Local lawyers, after all, had chosen (for whatever reasons) to practice in the backwaters of Palo Alto, rather than in the great centers like San Francisco or New York. The experienced firms of San Francisco were not far away. Clients could ride the Southern Pacific to "the City" just as the lawyers did. Why use a small-town lawyer when you needed infusions of capital or big-scale advice on corporate structure?

LEGAL SERVICES REQUIRED BY NEW BUSINESS

Before we suggest some reasons why a flourishing local bar emerged to handle the legal business of high-tech industries, it might be useful to specify more generally the types of legal services that new industries ordinarily seem to need. Historical experience suggests the following loose sketch that describes the evolving demand for legal skills.

In the start-up phase, small businesses, especially those run by scientists and engineers without business experience, need access to elementary advice about such matters as re-cord-keeping for tax and accounting purposes, and such basic legal services as the drafting of partnership agreements and secured financing documents. Lawyers in this society have often also been used as repositories of general knowledge of business practices, for advice that the client can neither generate internally nor afford to buy from other outside sources. A business must also hire and pay lawyers for services only they can legally perform. Thus, the added cost of general business advice is low, especially when lawyers can draw upon experience with similar clients who have faced similar problems. Lawyers in this phase also function as all-purpose intermediaries, as links between entrepreneurs and financial sources, as well as between business and government agencies at all levels. When giant enterprises formed in the late nineteenth and early twentieth centuries, lawyers made key links between management of railroad and manufacturing corporations, on the one hand, and, on the other, the investment banking houses of Wall Street and Europe. Lawyers designed the risk-reward-and-security structures to attract different types of investment and often acted as salesmen of new issues of securities.

The maturing of an enterprise, in the regulatory environments that have been constructed in this country starting with the Progressive movements and New Deal, has called for a dif-ferent, and much more specialized, range of legal services. Companies usually identify the stage at which their consumption needs for lawyers sharply changes as the decision to "go public." The legal job of registering the company's stock issues under the federal and state securities laws calls for disclosure of company information and preparation of incredibly detailed forms, specialists in securities law, a staff of paralegals, and secretaries to do the routine state "Blue Sky" registrations, and, perhaps most important, enough experience with similar transactions to have produced files full of forms to copy. Mistakes in these transactions can be very costly, exposing companies to civil damage actions and heavy fines.

The decision to go public usually also entails changes in management and organization that call for other new legal tasks: design of executive compensation plans, employee pension plans, tax plans, and the like. City law firms with divisions of specialists and established reputations in corporate work have an obvious edge in their ability to attract such business. At this stage, it is not efficient for these companies to hire an internal legal staff that can handle going public. But neither can the companies continue to rely on solo practitioners and small partnerships for this complicated, specialized work. At this stage—which many industries in Silicon Valley have reached—midsized companies tend to use midsized firms, although the biggest downtown firms, who are afraid of losing business to in-house counsel, have tried to move in on the midsized market as well.

If the company continues to prosper and grow and avoids the need for the ghoulish services of bankruptcy specialists (another booming Silicon Valley legal field), its legal needs may change yet again. It may reach a third stage in which the company may want to take over or merge with other companies, or, conversely, defend itself against takeover attempts. It may wish to acquire foreign subsidiaries, or to engage in joint ventures or arrangements to cross-license its technology. It may need legal help with union recognition or collective-bargaining negotiations (although unions have not gotten a firm foothold in the Valley so far). It will probably need antitrust advice. It is likely to be dealing constantly with regulatory authorities on health, safety, and environmental matters. It is likely to be embroiled in litigation to protect its intellectual property rights and market share. And finally, it may, through its trade association or on its own account, see itself as having a major stake in or entitled to a major influence over the information of public policies regarding taxes, labor, intellectual property, tariffs, trade, and regulation.

For such needs as these, companies tend to adopt a two-tiered strategy. They are likely to bring an increasing amount of work in-house, not only the more routine legal work that they formerly contracted out to firms but also the general business advising function. The company's general counsel's office assumes the important function of deciding when to stay inside and when to contract outside, with whom, and on what terms; it also serves as the chief monitor of the outside work. House counsel will draw on outside legal and business counsel only for specialized and nonroutine matters and will spread such transactions—a new stock offering, a piece of litigation business, the job of designing an employee stock-option plan—around different outside firms rather than placing all their eggs in a single firm. The outside firms capable of such specialized work are usually either the very largest downtown metropolitan firms, who can muster large forces of specialized manpower at short notice to counter a takeover bid or an antitrust suit, or else smaller, super-specialized "boutique" firms.

LEGAL SERVICES AND HIGH TECH IN SILICON VALLEY

How does this very general model of the phases of the evolution of corporate needs for legal services map onto the Silicon Valley experience? Many of the high-tech companies began as tiny outfits—twentieth-century analogs to bakeries or dry-cleaning shops. When they found themselves, often to their surprise, with revenues in the millions, they needed lawyers who could provide the same services, especially in fields like securities regulation, that big-city lawyers were providing large, established clients elsewhere. So naturally, in the early years of the high-tech boom, companies entering the second phase thought of going to San Francisco for legal services, rather than to local lawyers who had chosen to practice in the provincial backwaters of Palo Alto. The resulting division of labor between San Francisco and the Peninsula bar was, in the main, acceptable to Palo Alto lawyers.[1] Most were solo practitioners, each with a mix of civil and criminal work. A few had banded together into loose associations, sharing common office space; a few had formed two-man partnerships, in which one partner concentrated on litigation and the other on corporate work. Local lawyers tended to believe that only big firms, staffed with experts, could handle public offerings of stock. The accounting firms, which figure in any major financing, hesitated to let their clients use Peninsula lawyers: they too preferred legal opinions from brand-name firms.

Ultimately, two Peninsula lawyers—John Wilson and Leo Ware—decided, independently of each other, to take the plunge. They saw no reason why *they* could not cope with public offerings. After all, securities work is not the only form of practice that takes skill and experience. Ware and Wilson were general practitioners. They were used to learning new legal skills on short notice. They had stood on the sidelines while their clients went public. They had observed and felt ready to participate; they did not think of themselves as country bumpkins. And, significantly, they found some indulgent clients, guinea pigs willing to resist the "Go North" tradition.

> Because [we] had been in big law firms . . . we did think that given an opportunity we could develop whatever expertise necessary. . . . [O]ur first client that wanted to go public, we didn't think about sending it out to somebody else. We took it public ourselves. When it became important to struggle with complicated tax matters, why we recruited people out of the NYU graduate tax program.

The crucial decision was far-reaching, but it was perhaps idiosyncratic. Other lawyers, who had equal stature in the legal community, and clients ready for large infusions of capital, chose not to join the bandwagon. Today, the firms of Wilson and Ware are the two biggest, most successful Silicon Valley firms. One contemporary of Wilson and Ware, who chose to stay put, is still a general practitioner, in a small, three-lawyer office, modern only in that the other two partners are women. This lawyer is not a failure; he has a thriving practice. After all, Silicon Valley is not just the location of a spectacular industrial boom. Real people live there, with real if mundane legal problems—people who marry and divorce, buy property and sell it, make out wills, and even die. But the lawyers who "stayed

---

1. The Peninsula refers here to the cities that are south of San Francisco.

behind" were nonetheless affected by the high-tech boom. It brought them work, simply by increasing the need for building permits, drafts of condominium agreements, and the incorporation of sushi bars and car washes. These lawyers were and are busy at their usual jobs—as pervasive facilitators in society. Their ranks have been swelled by a new generation of solos and small-firm lawyers, some of whom have deliberately turned their back on high-tech practice.

For present purposes, however, high-tech firms like Wilson, Sonsini or Ware & Friedenrich are the more interesting story. As the high-tech clients grew in number and size, hired more employees, and increased their revenues, the law firms grew as well; they acquired more clients, hired more associates, and raised their fees. In one sense, they were merely riding the waves. Or did the firms help *make* the waves? Did they make the boom possible by clearing away legal obstacles, by finding and brokering the union of brains and money, and by structuring arrangements?

There is no way, as yet, to answer these questions. But the two opposing perspectives on practice are each important. They influence the way the lawyers perceive themselves, and perhaps they influence the practice as well. To understand law and lawyers in Silicon Valley, it is probably best, paradoxically, to accept both perspectives as reasonably accurate: lawyers reacted to the high-tech boom, but they also helped to shape it. It is interesting to ask *how* they reacted, how they shaped events, and what effect their actions had on their rhetoric, their practice, and their social utility.

Some of the leading lawyers themselves, pressed to describe their contribution to the high-tech industries' growth, tend to stress those aspects of their practice roles and styles that in their view distinguish them from big downtown firms of corporate lawyers, especially in New York. They can offer their clients, they claim, service that business lawyers outside the high-tech regions cannot offer: general business advice based on local industry-specific knowledge, access to local sources of venture-capital financing, a facilitative, or "engineering" approach to the client' problems, and, very notably, a style of law practice—informal, practical-result-oriented, flexible and innovative, keyed to high-trust business relations—that matches the business culture of Silicon Valley. Each of these types of service needs a little elaboration.

General Advice

Silicon Valley lawyers typically service the full range of legal needs of high-tech clients. These lawyers are highly specialized with regard to the *type* of client they serve, but not with regard to the *kind of work* they do for these clients. They can give "full-service" advice because they know the industry and don't have to be educated constantly in every new client's problems at the client's expense. A lawyer famous in the Valley chiefly as a licensing specialist, for example, says:

> I would say, "I'm a high-tech company lawyer," and every word in that description is limiting. I represent the companies, not the investors, and I try to keep up in many areas of the law: securities, corporations law, tax law, copyright law, trade secret law, antitrust law, foreign trade, Export Administration Act. I try to read the legal periodicals, and stay current and give advice in all these areas as they affect local high-tech companies.

Access to Capital

In the start-up phase of the Silicon Valley companies, for example, local lawyers seem to have performed, as they still do, the classic functions of general business advising and financial intermediation. It may well be that one of their most important contributions has come from the fact that they knew all the venture capitalists personally and could set up lunches with them for their scientist and engineer clients.

> Our clients needed money, so we would try to come up with ideas for this, and of course the client also had ideas. . . . [T]here weren't very many, but what resources there were for venture capital, we knew about. For example, one of our early clients was funded by Du-Pont and then DuPont decided to cut back and sold out to Laurence Rockefeller, so we did a deal with Laurence Rockefeller, so we knew Laurence Rockefeller's office. . . . [W]e got to know Tommy Davis and Art Rock a little bit, and then as the venture-capital community grew, why we kind of grew with it.

Facilitative Law

The Silicon Valley lawyer not only works with engineers, he thinks of himself as a kind of engineer—a legal engineer. His job is not just counseling or advising on what the law is; his job is to solve problems: to take a principle, a task, and "engineer" it legally, showing how it can be done, or be done best. It is not his job to say something can't be done, but to show how it *can* be done. In his view, the New York or Boston lawyer lacks this facility, this attitude, or has it to a lesser degree:

> I think the most interesting legal problems are the ones where a client comes in with a new technology or a new problem and there is no form book to go and change the dates and names. You really have to stare at the ceiling and say, "Gee, if I were in this business, what would be the asset I would want to protect, and how would I commercialize it, and what would have to be the legal form of protection, and what would the documents have to look like, so that commerce wouldn't be impeded every time you wanted to make a sale?" . . .
>
> [The clients] operate at high speed, expect your lawyers to operate at high speed. They are mostly engineers, and they approach problems that way. The protector, the person who prevents somebody from violating the law or saying something can't be done—our clients continually complain about lawyers who say no. They say, "OK, here's what we want accomplished. Here's the legal problem. What's the work-around?" That's literally the vocabulary they use, and they assume there's a legal barrier somewhere. They don't mean, "How do I violate the law?" but "How do I structure the deal, so I don't have that problem?" And I think in many cases lawyers are satisfied when they say you can't do what you propose to do, because it would violate the law. . . . And here the clients expect you to take the next step and solve the problems.

Congruence of Legal and Business Styles

The claim that the legal style of Valley practitioners suits the clients' styles of doing business is one of the most intriguing, if also one of the hardest to pin down. We have been told by some local lawyers, for example, that the typical venture-financing document is shorter than its New York City counterparts (such as the trust indentures that secure large-scale corporate debt). Its language is more general. It does not try to spell out contingency plans for every conceivable event that could go wrong, but assumes that the parties will be able to cooperate sufficiently to work out flexible adjustments to changing circumstances. Such deals have the "high-trust" or "relational" character that sociologists of law and business attribute to communities of traders or firms engaged in long-term ongoing relations. If these claims that Silicon Valley law practice differs from New York City and San Francisco practice are at all valid—at this stage the claims are plausible but unproven—it remains unclear how best to go about explaining the differences. Many of the features of local law practice seem exactly what one would expect, given the ideal-typical model of the evolution of corporate legal needs sketched above. General business advice, as previously remarked, is what relatively small-scale clients, simple organizational structures, and no efficiency drives to internalize the lawyer's type of expertise. Financial intermediation is a classic lawyers' contribution to start-up entrepreneurs. An "engineering" or facilitative style of advice also seems to be the dominant mode of the early phases.

In a market where there are many small, starting firms, a shake-out period arrives, sooner or later. Many businesses fail; others merge into larger units. In the consolidation phase, competition between units in the industry becomes fiercer; companies struggle to gain and hold territory. The focus shifts somewhat away from wealth creation forward to wealth conservation. The "engineer" lawyer may decline in value, to be replaced by the warrior-litigator, or the defensive planner. The relative informality of the legal practice in the Valley may thus reflect the needs of start-up ventures and is therefore likely to fade over time, as enterprises mature. On the other hand, this style may affect the structure of the market for venture capital, which links capitalists and entrepreneurs in long-term relationships whose survival calls for a high degree of reciprocity, flexibility, and mutual trust. Or some of the differences in style may simply reflect differences in East and West Coast corporate cultures (this theory could be tested by comparing the Valley to high-tech law in the Route 128 industries around Boston).

There is nothing determined or inevitable about the ideal-typical model of the evolution of law practice. Distinctive modes of practice in Silicon Valley, if real, may well survive into the mature phases of those industries and firms which are the lawyers' major clients. At the time of writing (October 1988), however, there have been many signs that the big local firms are undergoing the kinds of strains of growth that are common elsewhere. As business clients expanded and became large enterprises, the law firms that had linked their futures with those clients expanded too; this brought with it severe shocks and tensions in the organization and cultures of the firms. Like firms in San Francisco and other cities, the major law firms of Palo Alto are bigger, more bureaucratic, and more specialized. The largest firm has grown from seven partners and fifteen associates in 1980 to forty-one partners and eighty-eight associates in 1988. The major firms have demanded longer and longer working hours of their associates and created severe dilemmas for associates—often, but not always, women—who also want time for family life. Some associates—again, by no means all of them women—have dropped out (or allowed themselves to be pushed) into other forms of practice such as small-firm or in-house work. "Boutique" firms are beginning to appear, looking for niches in the market, and contracting for fragments of legal business. Litigation practice is on the rise.

One useful way to track a number of these shifts is through study of the work of corporate general counsels' offices. These men and women have the major voice in deciding what legal services their companies will buy and from whom. Not surprisingly, house counsel staffs have grown in numbers and specialization with their companies: Hewlett-Packard had thirty-four lawyers in 1982 and has forty-seven now. The pattern of jobs these lawyers do varies widely: some (often, these days, JD-MBAs with a preference for mixing business with legal work) displace outside lawyers as repositories of general business advice and become important senior managers, playing a broad executive role in which legal affairs are only one among several responsibilities; others are hired simply for cost-cutting reasons, to perform routine legal tasks (drafting and reviewing contracts, handling employee complaints) more cheaply than outside lawyers can. Other in-house lawyers are specialists. A high-technology company is likely first to hire a general counsel. When a second lawyer is added, he or she is often a patent lawyer, whose work will consist chiefly of developing and filing patent applications, though later this lawyer may draft confidentiality agreements, review scientific papers before publication to ward off issues of intellectual-property law, and supervise litigation related to patents. Outside the patent area, few in-house specialties are consistent across companies: whether company lawyers primarily do contract, labor, tax, or securities work seems largely to depend on their prior experience in the outside firms from whom virtually all in-house lawyers are recruited. The larger companies, besides adding specialists in substantive legal areas, assign general lawyers to specific product lines and regions of the country.

The growth in size and responsibilities of these in-house staffs is clearly beginning—though only just beginning—to affect the structure of outside practice. It is still the custom that a company will lean primarily on a single law firm, with which it develops a long-standing relationship, and which does all or most of its legal business. These relationships sometimes grow out of personal and business connections between company founders and their first lawyers; the lawyer often cements the relationship by serving on the board of directors. Sometimes the general counsel of the company simply retains his ties to the firm where he used to work. But the old arrangements are beginning to erode. Most in-house lawyers we interviewed reported a gradual shift of work from primary outside counsel to a multifirm system, often using smaller boutique firms that specialize in tax, international, labor, immigration, benefits, or real estate law, either because the primary firm had become too costly, or did not give enough partner-level attention to the client, or because it could not service the specialty. Corporate cost-consciousness, in addition to pulling many legal jobs inside the company, has shifted authority to buy legal services from top management to functional departments less concerned with maintaining personal ties with outside lawyers and more with balancing cost and quality of service and keeping control over services performed.

In-house counsel have all developed techniques to monitor the quality and control the cost of outside work. Some of these are quite stringent: detailed and regular accounting of all bills, refusal to pay unacceptable items, negotiated fee discounts, detailed specification of the amount and type of the work to be done and of the particular partners and associates to perform it, and transferring of business, after unsatisfactory experiences, to a different firm, or to inside lawyers. Similarly, all of them keep close control over major litigation—reviewing all filings in draft form, holding strategy conferences with outside counsel, and managing costs through budget ceilings or by insistence on detailed itemization of bills. Inside lawyers also participate more and more in major lawsuits—conducting depositions, preparing witnesses, and reviewing documents during discovery—though the prevailing pattern is still to delegate this work to the outside firm.

The emerging trend in the Valley, then, seems quite similar to those that have already overtaken major businesses and their lawyers in big-city practice: a gradual shift away from the single outside provider to the spreading of specialized transactions among outside firms, and a gradual shift of some legal work, and especially of authority to control the terms and costs of legal work, away from outside firms into corporate staffs. The conventional wisdom, in the past, was that house counsel work was less independent, less "professional" than practice in law firms. But most of the in-house lawyers we talked to expressed a great deal of satisfaction with their work and spoke of it as *more* independent and professional than the outside-firm jobs they had left. This view had much to do with their relative freedom from the detailed monitoring, supervision, and time-and-cost accounting that outside lawyers must now endure, as associates dance to the tune of the partners, and partners dance to the tune of their clients.

CONCLUSION

All sorts of assertions are commonly made about the relation of lawyers to industrial change. Lawyers are often said to be either indispensable to entrepreneurship or a wasteful drag on it. These assertions are completely untested, and necessarily so. From a research standpoint, the underlying questions are tough and intractable. For one thing, there is not and cannot be anything even remotely resembling a control group. There is no way to examine what America would be like if, everything else remaining the same, lawyers disappeared off the face of the earth. This might make an interesting thought experiment, but not much more. Nor does salvation lie in "natural" or quasi-experiments. Underlawyered Japan is thrown up as just such a happy instance—a major industrial power without hordes of lawyers. But again there are so many obvious differences between the two societies that it would be presumptuous to claim much from the comparison of numbers of lawyers, or from differences in modes of lawyering, in the two countries. The Japanese experience is no doubt full of interesting lessons, but it has to be approached with extreme caution. But even if the global question is intractable, it might be possible to examine particular industries or states of the economy, at particular times. To find out what is happening to law practice in a single regional economy dominated by high-technology firms would be a modest start, at best, on such a project.

4   ADVOCATING DEMOCRACY

THE ROLE OF LAWYERS IN TAIWAN'S POLITICAL TRANSFORMATION

Jane Kaufman Winn and Tang-chi Yeh

LAWYERS UNDER AUTHORITARIAN RULE

From the 1940s through the 1980s, the autonomy of the R[epublic] O[f] C[hina] legal profession has been limited by a variety of techniques, such as severely restricting the number of lawyers passing the formal bar examination, the indirect political screening of lawyers by manipulating conditions for entry into the profession, the subordination of the civil justice system to the military justice system on politically sensitive issues, and the rigorous suppression of most forms of political dissent whether undertaken by lawyers or ordinary citizens. Many of these impediments to the development of an autonomous professional bar have been removed in whole or in part in recent years.

On November 1992 the ROC Lawyer Law was amended to restrict access to the profession through various alternatives to the formal bar examination and to make the professional bar more autonomous. But reform of the Lawyer Law is only one step toward a legal profession that would be willing and able to use the ROC legal system as a tool for achieving significant social reforms. In addition, reformist judges have been agitating for greater autonomy for the judicial system from the oversight of the executive branch of government.

Examination System

The number of practicing lawyers in Taiwan historically has been very restricted. In 1991, the ROC Ministry of Justice estimated that there were only 2,254 members of the private bar. Given Taiwan's 1990 population of 20.5 million, this represents a ratio of about 1 lawyer per 9,000 persons, which is equivalent to the Japanese ratio of 1 lawyer to 9,400 persons but much lower than the ratios of other civil code countries such as France, with 1 per 2,000 persons or the former West Germany with 1 per 500.

In his recent study of Japan's legal system, [John] Haley has pointed out that the relatively small number of lawyers admitted to the bar in Japan creates a problem of institutional incapacity for the legal system. Haley argues that Japanese citizens rely on mediation or other dispute-resolution mechanisms rather than on litigation because the Japanese government has purposefully limited the resources committed to the legal profession and the court system, thus increasing the relative costs to litigants in terms of expense and delay. The severe limitations on membership in the ROC legal profession may likewise evidence an official commitment to discourage reliance on dispute resolution by dispute litigation and encourage reliance on informal dispute resolution techniques that are more amenable to elite control.

One important factor keeping the number of lawyers in Taiwan low has been the high failure rate for the official bar examination. From 1950 to 1992, of a total of 40,604 candidates sitting the official bar exam, 2,072, or 5.10 percent, passed. This average disguises the fact that prior to 1989, of 2,000–3,000 candidates sitting for the official bar exam each year, as few as 6 might pass the exam (as was true as recently as 1982). For the years 1950–88, only 782 persons passed the official bar exam. In 1989, the pass rate shot up to 288 out of 2,698 candidates, or an unheard-of 14 percent, and it has remained above 10 percent ever since.

The dramatic increase in the number of candidates passing the bar exam coincided with the appointment of a new examination minister, Wang Zuorong, who has adopted a two-pronged policy of increasing the pass rate for the official exam and closing the various back doors to the bar. Precisely why the pass rate of the official bar exam suddenly more than doubled is a matter that has never been addressed publicly by Ministry of Examination officials, although it had long been advocated by many lawyers and legal academics. That such sudden policy changes with such a large potential long-term impact on the progress of democratization and liberalization can still be made in Taiwan without any public debate would seem to indicate that the KMT [Kuomintang] retains considerable power to implement its policies outside conventional political channels. While the manner in which the change in policy was achieved remains obscure, plausible justifications for the change in policy are not hard to find. The ROC authorities are pursuing liberalization in many economic and financial arenas, and a sophisticated practicing bar often plays a significant role in facilitating interaction between local economic interests and global markets.

Following the increase in candidates passing the official bar examination, demand for legal education in Taiwan rapidly increased, leading to the opening of several new law faculties at existing universities. One way to gauge the popularity of various fields of study is preferences expressed by students taking the joint university entrance examination, which is administered annually. The law faculty of National Taiwan University, the leading university in Taiwan, is now the first choice of students receiving the highest grades in the joint entrance examination, replacing business and international trade as the former majors of choice.

Back Doors to the Profession

Until the very recent dramatic increase in the number of candidates passing the official bar exam, the tiny number of successful candidates was never adequate to meet even the limited demand for lawyers recognized by the ROC authorities. The number of lawyers in Taiwan was therefore supplemented by admissions to the bar under other criteria. These back doors to admission were open to lawyers who either did not have to pass a formal qualifying examination, or who passed a less rigorous qualifying exam. In recent years, ROC officials have taken steps to close the back doors to the legal profession, creating the possibility of a more autonomous practicing bar in future years.

From 1950 to 1991, a total of 3,241 candidates were admitted to the bar without any qualifying exam (2,882 persons), or by passing a less rigorous exam than the official bar exam (358 persons) because of their status as magistrate, prosecutor, law professor, doctor of laws, senior judicial administrator, legislator, military judge, or military prosecutor. The 1992 reform of the Lawyer Law limits access to the practicing bar without a qualifying examination to experienced judges, prosecutors, or military judges. While access to positions such as magistrate or military judges may in turn be based on competitive examinations, the pass rates for those exams have historically been higher than the pass rates for the regular bar exam. For example, pass rates for the magistrate/prosecutor exam ranged from 5 to 10 percent from 1981 to 1991, while the military judge exam had pass rates from 40 to 78 percent during the same years.

The system of a very restrictive official bar examination, combined with a series of back doors to the profession, undermined the autonomy of the professional bar in Taiwan because of the possibility of covert political screening of candidates. One of the most popular back doors to the legal profession was to study law outside the ROC, obtain a PhD or JD in law, return to Taiwan, and find employment for five years as a lecturer in law, usually as a part-time adjunct, in one of Taiwan's law faculties. This maneuver worked only if one was able to secure employment as a lecturer in a law faculty, which as a practical matter was a function of both objective qualifications and personal connections. While political affiliation was not the cardinal factor taken into account in hiring lecturers in law, it was by the same token not irrelevant, especially with regard to institutions such as the National Cheng Chi University law faculty, which historically had close ties to the KMT. This back door has substantially been closed by the 1992 revision of the Lawyer Law, which now provides that only full-time professors or associate professors who pass a qualifying exam and complete professional internships qualify for admission to the bar by this route.

. . .

Lawyers in Taiwan, like lawyers in Europe, have often had relatively attenuated relationships with clients, focusing on litigation services or documenting transactions. However, in recent decades, as access to the U.S. market became crucial to Taiwan's strategy of export-oriented growth, U.S. legal institutions have become increasingly influential as models for legal change within Taiwan. The ROC legal system was modeled from its inception on the modern German legal system, and as a result, the modern ROC legal profession seems to share certain similarities with the German bar: a relatively large number of lawyers in direct government employment as magistrates or judges and a relatively small practicing bar. As American legal institutions generally have become more influential in Taiwan, the American model of client-centered law practice based on business consulting and lobbying as well as litigation and documentation services seems to be gaining popularity as well.

As private business interests become a more important source of income for lawyers in Taiwan, more lawyers may distance themselves from the interests of the KMT regime. However, it is unclear that a shift in the economic foundation of the legal profession away from the state in favor of private business interests will tend to increase the number of lawyers willing to challenge political or social injustice through the courts. In fact, greater autonomy for the practicing bar, if accompanied by closer connections with local elites or transnational business interests, may actually subvert democratization within Taiwan if autocratic KMT rule is supplanted by control of Taiwan's political economy by economic interests beyond the power of a democratized ROC government to regulate in the public interest.

Reform of the Bar Association

One legacy of authoritarian rule in Taiwan that is only slowly changing as Taiwan makes the transition to democratic rule is central government control of many organizations that would be autonomous, private organizations in Western societies. For example, prior to the repeal of martial law, direct and indirect government control over the activities of unions turned what were ostensibly independent labor organizations into little more than extensions of the state. This dynamic has been often noted and extensively discussed with regard to the P[eople's] R[epublic of] C[hina], where commentators have debated whether the entire notion of civil society or a public sphere is compatible with contemporary Chinese society on the mainland. While there is no question that KMT rule on Taiwan cannot be conflated with Chinese Communist Party (CCP) rule on mainland China, there is nevertheless an interesting resonance in both societies in the hostility of the central administration to granting functional autonomy to many forms of what are considered private associations in Western societies.

Bar associations were among those groups that by Western standards would be presumed to be independent of central government control and organized to represent their members' interests, while in fact in Taiwan these groups often operated as little more than extensions of the KMT regime. Under the terms of the Lawyer Law prior to its revision in 1992, all lawyers were required to join a bar association, but those bar associations were subject to governmental supervision. Revised Article 11 of the Lawyer Law now provides that while lawyers still must join their local bar association, a bar association cannot reject a lawyer's application. In tandem with the relaxation of bar associations' control over their members, the 1992 reform of the Lawyer Law repealed the requirement that a bar association submit its bylaws to the Ministry of Interior for approval. Bar associations are now merely required to report their bylaws to the ministry. Under the old law, cases of alleged attorney misconduct were not within the competence of bar associations to resolve but were referred to a special disciplinary committee composed of five appellate court judges and one lawyer and presided over by the chief judge of the appellate court. Under the 1992 revisions, attorney misconduct cases are heard by a committee composed of three appellate court judges, one prosecutor, and five private attorneys. Appeals are made to a committee of four Supreme Court judges, two prosecutors, and five private attorneys.

The change in the formal regulation of bar associations has been accompanied by a de facto increase in the political autonomy of bar associations in Taiwan. Just as delegates to the National Assembly and Legislative Yuan had been permitted to remain in office without having to run for reelection for over forty years, the ROC Federation of Bar Associations board of directors was permitted to remain in place without being held accountable to its members. The former leadership of the Federation of Bar Associations did not hesitate to express opinions on political issues, such as by denouncing the lawyers who defended the Kaohsiung defendants, discussed below. In 1993, progressive lawyers led [by] Min-sheng Lin assumed control of the Federation of Bar Associations, and many lawyers anticipate that this will promote the independence of the professional bar from KMT control.

In a similar manner, the governance of the Taipei Bar Association (TBA) has recently been reformed. Although there are fourteen local bar associations in Taiwan joined in the ROC Federation of Bar Associations, at least three-quarters of the estimated 2,400 practicing attorneys in Taiwan belong to the TBA. Thus, the TBA's composition and leadership is very significant in determining the political complexion of the practicing bar in Taiwan generally. In 1990, the TBA board of directors was completely replaced, ending decades of political cronyism and ushering in what many of the new directors hope will be a new era of professionalism and political autonomy for the practicing bar. For example, in 1990, the TBA publicly took a position questioning the constitutionality of appointing a general, Hau Pei-tsun, to be prime minister, and questioning the human rights implications of the Social Order Maintenance Act.

Appearance of "Cravath"-Style Law Firms

Some commentators describing apparent correlation between the expansion of global economic competition in recent decades and the expansion of American-style law practice have suggested using the label "Cravathism" for that type of law practice after one of the progenitors of that model of law practice. Even in the absence of any in-depth empirical studies of the organization of the private bar in Taiwan, it is possible to note that the global trend toward large, multipurpose, multinational law firms noted by Trubek et al. (1993) is clear in Taiwan. This is not to assert that large law firms are new to Taiwan: the Lee & Li firm in Taipei has employed scores of lawyers and paralegals, has had highly hierarchical and bureaucratic internal organization, and has pursued a complex corporate law practice for decades, although it was the only firm to do so on such a large scale. Until the recent progress toward liberalizing Taiwan's economy created a sustained demand for corporate law services, most lawyers in Taiwan practiced solo or in small firms, concentrating on litigation with less emphasis on commercial counseling.

One benchmark of how many lawyers in Taiwan have embraced the American model of client-centered business consulting and lobbying law practice is to scan the entries in the international section of Martindale & Hubbell. While this is no substitute for an in-depth study of Taiwan's legal profession, it is a good indication of the number of firms in Taiwan who are self-consciously soliciting U.S. or transnational business. The number of listings for Taiwan rose from 12 firms and 142 entries for legal professionals (of which 49, or about 34 percent, were lawyers admitted in the ROC) in 1984; to 14 firms and 211 entries for legal professional (of which 78, or about 37 percent, were admitted in the ROC) in 1989; to 43 firms and 449 entries for legal professional (of which 184, or about 41 percent, were admitted in the ROC) in 1994. Among those listed who were not admitted to practice in the

ROC were paralegals with legal training in Taiwan, ROC citizens with legal training overseas, and foreign nationals admitted to practice in other countries.

Another indication of the degree to which American norms of law practice are penetrating Taiwan is the number of lawyers trained in the United States. Given the historically abysmally low pass rate for the ROC bar exam, many students with an interest in practicing law in Taiwan attended U.S. law schools and were admitted to at least one U.S. jurisdiction. Many of these ROC citizens returned to Taiwan and, joining with lawyers admitted to practice in the ROC, set up American-style law practices. In addition, many ROC lawyers, prosecutors, and magistrates have also come to study in the United States in recent decades, further expanding the number of ROC legal professionals with exposure to American legal culture.

STRATEGIES OF RESISTANCE AND THE DANGER OF LEGITIMATION

Increased Autonomy for the Judicial Yuan

One necessary condition for the use of litigation to challenge political injustice is a judiciary that is independent of overt political influence. While the appointment of magistrates in Taiwan based on competitive examination and the separation of powers set forth in the ROC Constitution would seem to minimize the possibility of direct political interference with judicial independence, in recent years a growing number of reformist judges and lawyers have criticized several factors that have the effect of subordinating the judiciary to the executive.

Reformist judges and lawyers have been lobbying for greater fiscal independence for the Judicial Yuan. At present, the budget of the Judicial Yuan is drawn up by the Executive Yuan in the process of drafting national budget legislation. Reformist judges are demanding that the Judicial Yuan be given the power to draw up its own budget, removing an important source of indirect political control over the judiciary.

Lawyers in Opposition Politics:
The Kaohsiung Incident and the Founding of the DPP

Although most legal professionals in Taiwan have been and still are politically quiescent, a few lawyers challenged the authoritarian rule that prevailed prior to the repeal of martial law or tackled other politically sensitive issues in contemporary Taiwanese society. The widely publicized trial and conviction of a group of opposition politicians in 1979 was a turning point both in the lives of those on trial and their defense attorneys and in the public perception of the legitimacy of the opposition to KMT rule. While many lawyers active in opposition politics have turned their backs on litigation as a tactic and instead articulated their vision of political change in the forum of mass politics, a small number of lawyers in Taiwan have tried with varying measures of success to use the ROC courts to accelerate the tempo of social reform.

Prior to 1979, there were several largely unsuccessful attempts to establish a political opposition to KMT rule in Taiwan. In 1960, a handful of liberal intellectuals attempted to rally opposition forces with a political journal, the *Free China Fortnightly*, and from an opposition party, the China Democratic Party. The leader of this movement, Lei Chen, was arrested and convicted of sedition by a military tribunal. Notwithstanding the suppression of Lei's nascent political party, an informal group opposed to KMT rule remained active in Taiwan and was known as the *dangwai* (literally, "outside the party," i.e., outside the KMT) because its members were never allowed to form an actual opposition party.

In 1975, Kuo Yu-shin, a participant in the effort to establish the China Democratic Party, ran unsuccessfully for a seat in the legislature. Following his defeat, Kuo brought an action against his opponent based on allegations of vote buying. Although the lawsuit brought by Kuo's attorneys, Lin Yi-shiung and Yao Chia-wen, was unsuccessful, both attorneys became involved in opposition politics as a result of their experience. In 1977, Lin and Yao were elected to the provincial assembly.

On December 10, 1979, the "Kaohsiung Incident" occurred. The *Formosa* magazine, founded by Yao Chia-wen and other *dangwai* politicians, sponsored a political rally to celebrate International Human Rights Day and protest the KMT regime's alleged abuses of human rights. Violence erupted, and while few demonstrators were injured because the police were under orders to limit their use of force, 183 police were injured. It remains unclear if the violence was orchestrated by the authorities to serve as a pretext to suppress the emerging political opposition, or whether the demonstrators were joined by hooligan elements, but in any event, more than one hundred *dangwai* leaders were rounded up, tried and convicted for sedition or inciting the riot, and sentenced for up to life imprisonment. The court-martial of the leaders charged with sedition was plagued with so many irregularities that serious doubts were cast on the validity of their convictions.

Although the Kaohsiung defendants were all ignominiously convicted based on coerced confessions and served terms of varying lengths, the trial became significant as a political event that helped to raise popular consciousness of the objectives of the *dangwai*. Many lawyers who joined together to represent the Kaohsiung defendants were politically radicalized as a result of their experience and went on to help form the leading opposition party in Taiwan today, the D[emocratic] P[rogressive] P[arty].

These lawyers included Yu Ching, who studied law in Taiwan and went on to earn a PhD in law in Germany. In 1981, Yu was elected to the Control Yuan, which is a representative body, and in 1986, he was elected to the Legislative Yuan. In 1989, he was elected magistrate of Taipei County, one of the most populous urban areas in Taiwan. Yu later noted that although the subject of his PhD dissertation was the more theoretical and traditional civil law, during his years of study in Germany he was exposed to many socially progressive ideas in areas such as social welfare law and the regulation of political parties, which influenced his choice of a political career.

One of the defendants was Hsiu-lien Annette Lu, a graduate of National Taiwan University (NTU) law faculty, who had been active in promoting women's rights in the 1970s. After the authorities suppressed her attempt to provide legal assistance to women such as rape victims, Lu went to the United States and received an LLM from the University of Illinois, Urbana-Champaign, and earned a second LLM from Harvard Law School. When she returned to Taiwan, she became active in the *dangwai* and was among the Kaohsiung defendants. Lu was sentenced to twelve years for sedition, but due in part to the intervention of Amnesty International and others, she was released after serving only half her sentence. After further study at Harvard Law School, she returned to Taiwan and in 1992 was elected to the Legislative Yuan.

Su Chen-chang, a graduate of the law faculty of NTU, was a lawyer with 10 years' experience when he represented defendant Yao Chia-wen in the court-martial. He was so galvanized by his perception that Taiwan's legal and political structure were in need of profound reform that he successfully ran for election to the provincial assembly in 1981. In 1989, Su was elected magistrate for Pingdong County, a very populous urban region near Kaohsiung. Likewise, Chen Shui-pian, another graduate of NTU law faculty, later reported that his experience as defense counsel in the court-martial of the Kaohsiung defendants caused him to reappraise his faith in Taiwan's legal system and led him to political life in an attempt to seek needed reforms. Chen was elected to the Taipei City Council in 1983 and to the Legislative Yuan in 1989 and 1992. In 1994, he was elected mayor of Taipei, the first elected mayor since 1967 and the first opposition candidate to hold the office.

Chiang Peng-shien, Chang Chun-hsiung, Hsieh Chang-ting, and Chang Te-ming are also lawyers who represented Kaohsiung Incident defendants who went on to become active in politics. Chiang Peng-shien and Chang Chun-hsiung, both graduates of the law faculty of NTU, were elected to the Legislative Yuan in 1983. Chiang later described how he gradually lost faith in the integrity of ROC institutions. He felt that lawyers could handle routine litigation matters with confidence, but in important matters, lawyers could not predict the outcome of litigation if there were political implications. This was due not only to factors such as the gap between social reality in Taiwan and the formal requirements of the law but also to pressure on judges to influence their decisions. Chiang felt that many magistrates left the bench to enter private practice in order to escape political pressures that limited their independence. Chang also reported that before the Kaohsiung Incident, he believed that law could be used to achieve social change in Taiwan, but that afterward he put his faith in direct political action. Hsieh Chang-tong, a NTU law graduate and holder of an LLM from Kyoto University, was elected to the Taipei City Council in 1983 and to the Legislative Yuan in 1989 and 1992. Chang Te-ming, another Kaohsiung defense counsel, was elected to the Legislative Yuan in 1980. In addition, Chou Ching-yu, wife of Kaohsiung defendant Yao Chia-wen, was elected the county executive of Chang-hwa in central Taiwan, and in December 1994, she was elected to the Taiwan Provincial Assembly.

LAWYERS AND SOCIAL MOVEMENTS

While many lawyers have been driven to advocating democratic reforms through involvement in opposition politics, Taiwan is not without lawyers who have tried to use litigation as a tool for achieving social reform. Some of them have achieved noteworthy results in the areas of labor law, consumer law, and the status of women. However laudable those advances, it nevertheless remains the case that none of those efforts have achieved the high public profile of some of the major civil rights cases in the United States. Even in Japan, which like Taiwan is a society with historically and culturally rooted tendencies not to rely on litigation to effect political change, there have been examples of litigation which have captured the public imagination as a vindication of the rights of ordinary people in the face of apparently overwhelming obstacles.

Workers' rights in Taiwan were until recent years severely restricted pursuant to the Measures for Handling Labor Disputes during the Period of National Mobilization for the Suppression of Communist Rebellion, which effectively denied workers in Taiwan the right to strike, and by labor unions that have effectively been co-opted by management and government interests. Following the lifting of martial law, however, labor unionists became more active and have experienced persecution as a result. Although most lawyers with training in labor and employment law represent management, one attorney, Liu Chih-peng, has recently successfully represented workers dismissed for trying to unionize workers.

The Consumer Foundation was established in 1970 with the assistance of an attorney, Lee Shen-Yi. The foundation has worked for the passage of the Consumer Protection Act in 1988 and has tried to raise public consciousness concerning consumers' rights. As a consequence of these activities, the foundation has found itself repeatedly as defendant in criminal defamation or other tort suits brought by business enterprises it criticized. The foundation has fortunately always been exonerated in these lawsuits.

Although the ROC Constitution and ROC law generally prohibit discrimination based on gender, discrimination against women in economic, social, and legal arenas persists. Annette Lu began her political career by helping start a feminist movement in Taiwan in the early 1970s. Lawyers active in the Women's Awakening Foundation have successfully lobbied for reforms in the law governing employment and the distribution of matrimonial property upon divorce. One lawyer successfully helped a divorced woman retain custody of her child, notwithstanding the overwhelming presumption under ROC family law that the father should always receive custody.

LAW AND LEGITIMACY IN TAIWAN

Under what circumstances may invoking legal proceedings inspire a popular belief that the prevailing social order is morally good and thus merits popular support when such a popular belief is not objectively merited? When do the political activities of reformist lawyers legitimate an unjust regime?

In Taiwan, the work of lawyers committed to liberal democratic reforms may enhance the legitimacy, whether deserved or not, of contemporary Taiwanese political institutions. If political reforms are superficial and partial, injustice may be legitimated. If, however, commitment to liberal democratic reforms is not widely shared in Taiwanese society, the reform efforts of liberal lawyers may be perceived as inappropriate. Furthermore, reformist lawyers' rhetorical invocation of liberal values, when situated within the Taiwanese context, may not necessarily imply an adherence to the idealized procedural notions of justice found in Western political theory.

While the opposition's moral authority to challenge the status quo in Taiwan may have some connection with legal institutions, it is still not clear that perceived moral authority has any connection with such Western liberal democratic ideals as the rule of law. Taiwan is now in the consolidation phase of its recent and still uncertain transition to democracy.

Democratic culture in Taiwan still includes substantial elements of indigenous Taiwanese traditions of political activity shaped by its historical experiences, and it is unclear whether Taiwan will ever evolve a "civic culture" equivalent to that of Western nations. For example, the most popular television program in Taiwan in 1993 dealt with the exploits of Bao Qing-tian, a Song dynasty judge. As with the popularity of programs such as *L.A. Law* in the United States, it is difficult to determine what significance, if any, the broad appeal of a program about the administration of law has in interpreting the popular culture of a country, but it would seem to indicate that there is no necessary contradiction between Taiwanese popular culture and respect for legal institutions, provided those institutions resonate with popular images of justice.

A recent study by *Tianxia Zazhi* (Commonwealth magazine) indicates that while the perception among more educated respondents is that the administration of justice in Taiwan is hopelessly corrupt, respondents with less education voice considerable confidence in the fairness of Taiwan's judicial apparatus. This correlates with the findings of surveys in other countries that members of society who are relatively economically disenfranchised may nevertheless have confidence in the ability of courts to administer justice. Thus, in addition to elite-sponsored law reforms, there may be a popular willingness to support legal institutions that could permit litigation and courts to play a greater role in shaping Taiwan's political development than has been true in the past.

In the absence of in-depth interviews with opposition politicians with training in law, it is impossible to know whether a proclivity toward opposition politics sparked an interest in the study of law, whether the study of law triggered the interest in politics, or whether there is some other explanation for the phenomenon. It is also unclear exactly what the political opposition in Taiwan is seeking. For example, given that membership in the DPP is almost exclusively made up of native Taiwanese (*benshengren*), it is unclear whether DPP leaders' invocation of democratic ideals should be taken literally, or should be understood in part as oblique references to other issues left unstated. Even within the DPP, the factionalism characteristic of Taiwanese politics remains evident, so it is unclear that the DPP can simply be characterized as a force agitating for liberal democracy in Taiwan.

In Taiwan today, it is unclear if lawyers involved in politics are seeking the thorough implementation of Western-style modernizing reforms, or some form of political order that resonates with more traditional notions of polity. With regard to burgeoning enrollments in law schools in China in the 1920s, Blume (1923), the dean of the law school at Soochow University, observed that training in law in Republican China was thought by some to be a surrogate for admission to the then defunct imperial bureaucracy. One key to political legitimacy under the imperial order was the figure of the remonstrating official, who acted from deep moral conviction and great courage, and at great personal peril, to draw problems to the attention of the emperor. The ideal of the virtuous official harmonizing the needs of the people with the conduct of the rulers, while incompatible with many modern notions of representative democracy, is also compatible with a model of competing elites and may offer a compelling vision of political opposition to many in Taiwan.

Within Taiwanese politics generally, it is clear that the KMT has not yet completely surrendered its sovereign power to the people of Taiwan and is unlikely to do so in the very near future because of the unresolved ambiguities involving the ROC's status as a sovereign nation. To the extent that lawyers within the DPP are seeking liberal democratic institutions within Taiwan, their efforts have met with, at best, partial success. To the extent that lawyers within the DPP are seeking the independence of Taiwan, the ultimate success of their enterprise cannot even be estimated from the perspective of present conditions; likewise the danger of co-optation cannot be analyzed.

It is unclear, however, that a committed DPP partisan with legal training is necessarily seeking the full realization of Western-style liberal democracy rather than some modified version of Western democratic institutions that takes account of Taiwan's Chinese cultural inheritance. It is fairly commonplace to note that intellectuals in the PRC invoke the name of democracy, yet seem in fact to be seeking something more akin to the traditional Chinese right of intellectuals to petition the emperor. Likewise, opposition politicians with legal training in Taiwan may actually be seeking a regime whose accountability to the people of Taiwan is maintained not so much by the complex apparatus of liberal democratic institutions as by the willingness of the ruling elite to listen and respond to the appeal of morally upright opponents.

Support for the role of legal institutions in addressing social injustice is not necessarily equivalent to support for the ideal of the rule of law and a procedural concept of justice. In his classic description of the contrasting notions of law and justice in imperial China and the modern West, [Benjamin] Schwartz emphasizes that the traditional Chinese notion of justice looked to moral development, hierarchy tempered by compassion and sensitivity to context. This focus on morality and substantive justice contrasts sharply with the modern liberal ideal of procedural justice, universal norms, and individual rights. If this focus has survived in some form in modern Taiwanese political culture, then lawyers advocating political reform or litigating in support of nascent social movements might be understood as working to ameliorate Taiwanese society by playing a role very different from that played by lawyers who litigated to fight injustice in a Western society such as the United States. The significance of modern Taiwanese rhetoric regarding democratization and the rule of law poses a difficult problem of interpretation, a problem only compounded by the rapid tempo of social and political change now taking place in Taiwanese society.

REFERENCES

Blume, W. W. 1923. Legal education in China. *China Law Review* 1: 305. Reprinted in 1975, Shanghai: Comparative Law School of China, Soochow University; Dobbs Ferry, NY: Oceana Publications.

Trubek, David M., Yves Dezalay, Ruth Buchanan, and John R. Davies. 1993. Global restructuring and the law: Studies of the internationalization of legal fields and the creation of transnational arenas. *Case Western Reserve Law Review* 44(2): 407–98.

5

LEGAL EDUCATION IN
LATE TWENTIETH-CENTURY LATIN AMERICA

Rogelio Pérez-Perdomo

Legal education is part of the legal system and the broader social system (Merryman 1999, 53). Social and political changes have occurred in Latin America in the late twentieth century and the first decade of the twenty-first century: in the 1970s, most Latin American countries were governed by dictatorships; from the 1990s up to the present, the trend has been toward democratization. However, it is not a completely rosy picture: recent troubles in Honduras, Argentina, and Venezuela show that political systems are unstable. Economic crises seem to shake every Latin American country from time to time. But, with all the difficulties, the direction of social change has been clear: increased urbanization, expansion of education, and the persistence of social inequality.

The intensification of cross-border and global interaction is also visible. Capital flows in and out of any country, transnational firms are present everywhere, and Mexican firms invest in Venezuela or Colombia, or vice versa; drug lords do not pay much attention to national frontiers and conduct their business worldwide. These phenomena are not indifferent for the law: new rules and institutions are created, including international institutions that produce legal rules. But even if the law is largely national, law firms have grown and have become more international (Dezalay and Garth 2002). All these changes affect legal education, and in this chapter, we will see both the changes and the permanent features in the area.

LAW SCHOOL AND LAW STUDENTS

Legal education is traditionally done at the universities, and law schools are an important part of the universities. They exist from the colonial past for most countries, or from the early nineteenth-century independence period for Brazil and some Central American countries. Traditionally the law schools have been predominantly the only way to select lawyers, but in some countries bar exams and other requirements have been established.

Taken from Rogelio Pérez-Perdomo, *Latin American Lawyers: A Historical Introduction* (Stanford: Stanford University Press, 2006), with modifications by the author. For more recent data and analysis, see Rogelio Pérez-Perdomo and Julia Rodríguez-Torres, eds., *Formación jurídica en América Latina: Tensiones e innovaciones en tiempos de globalización* (Bogotá: Universidad Externado de Colombia, 2006).

Law schools look like the most traditional part of the legal profession. Their curricula have changed rather little in the last thirty years. The core continues to be courses of constitutional law, civil law, penal law, commercial law, civil procedure, and criminal procedure. The references for these courses are the constitution and the main codes, documents that in their structure and most of their content come from the nineteenth century. In the 1970s there was a movement of renovation of curriculum and teaching methods, usually called "law and development." The more general opinion is that this movement was a failure, and the legal education changed very little. We will discuss this point of view, and we hope to show a more complex panorama. There is more change under the appearance of immobility, but before we analyze these changes in curricula and methodology, we must analyze the demographic trends and their social significance.

Most students enter at approximately age eighteen, immediately after completing their secondary education. University studies usually last for five years. In the predominantly agrarian societies of the past, the fact that law was studied in the university restricted the number of people who could aspire to enter that field. There were few universities, and the cost of moving to and living in the capital or a city with a law school, as well as the opportunity cost of leaving one's agricultural or commercial work, meant that relatively few students entered the university. Despite the fact that law was one of the most desired university degrees and attracted a high percentage of university students, the number of law students in relation to the total population of the country was relatively low.

Development policies altered the scene by promoting urbanization, industrialization, and the expansion of primary and secondary education. In particular, university education expanded enormously. In the 1960s and early 1970s, law students were a few dozen per one hundred thousand inhabitants in most Latin American countries (in 1965, Brazil had 41 law students; Colombia, 29; Mexico, 42; Peru, 40; Venezuela, 70; and, in 1970, Argentina had 124). By 2000 the numbers were closer to two hundred (Brazil, 200; Colombia, 210; Chile, 163; Mexico, 193; Venezuela, 160; Peru, 142; and in 1998, Argentina, 443) (Pérez-Perdomo 2005).

The growth in the number of law students can be explained partially by the expansion of educational systems that generally took place in the latter part of the twentieth century. Around the middle of the century (or a little earlier or later, depending on the country), universities felt the demographic pressure. The response varied by country: restricting entry, increasing the quota, or creating or permitting the creation of new law schools. Frequently, countries simultaneously tried out more than one policy, or changed their policies over time. In any case, growth is related to an appreciable demographic change in the same period as growth of cities and urban populations.

There are a few anomalies, such as the substantial decrease in the number of law students in Peru between 1991 and 2000 (198 in 1991, and 142 in 2000), but this may be related to the different definition of "law students" depending on the source, since the source for 2000 is the National Assembly of Rectors,[1] and UNESCO is the source for 1991.

---

1. For example, in some countries, law students begin with a basic common cycle where the students can also take some courses from the professional cycle that they have selected. Different sources may include, or exclude, these students. The same thing can occur with postgraduate students: they could be included in one statistical study, yet excluded in another. The definition of "university students" also varies, since one of the important changes in the last third of the twentieth century was the growth of institutes of higher education that are not technically universities.

Attributing the increase in law students to the expansion of higher education is obvious in the cases in which the number of university students grew at a higher rate than the number of law students (as in the instances in Brazil, Chile, Ecuador, Venezuela, and, to a lesser degree, Mexico). As opportunities for university study diversified, young people could choose from among a higher number of schools or majors. Thus, the trend is an increase in the number of law students per one hundred thousand inhabitants, but a decrease as a percentage of university students.

The trend, however, is not general. In Argentina, Colombia, and Costa Rica, there has been an increase in law students both in absolute numbers and as a percentage of university students. This indicates that the demographic change and the change in university offerings do not explain everything, since other studies that are as traditional as law (medicine, theology, and philosophy) did not grow in the same proportion and sometimes decreased in absolute numbers. Other studies, nonexistent until midcentury, such as computer science and business, attract a significant number of students. Without a doubt, the perception of job opportunities after graduation is a powerful incentive in choosing a university career.

The growth in the number of students is a manifestation of a much deeper change: the *democratization of education*—that is, access by groups and social classes that were excluded from university education in the past. Thus, women began to have greater access to legal education. The national figures vary considerably, but women went from one-third or fewer of all law students in the 1960s to approximately half around the end of the century. In Mexico, women made up 15 percent of law students in 1965 (UNESCO Statistical Yearbook 1973) and 47 percent in 1997 (López-Ayllón and Fix-Fierro 2003). In Chile, women constituted 23 percent of the 9,308 lawyers in 1992, while of the total of 2,791 graduates between 1995 and 1999, women made up 39 percent. At the University of Buenos Aires in 1964, 34 percent of law students were female; in 1980, 53 percent. At the Central University of Venezuela, women made up 23 percent of law graduates in 1959, while they were 57 percent in 2000.

Also gaining access to law schools were people of lower-income social strata. The racial distribution in Latin America is generally not reported, in part because the ideology of equality and integration means that statistics are not categorized by race or ethnic background. The fact that we have located an article that refers to black students and points out their increase in Brazil reveals not only a trend in the student population but also a disposition to study issues barely looked at until now (Junqueira and Veras 2001).

In short, in relation to earlier periods, not only are there many more students, but also these people have other social and job expectations. This will have repercussions in the changing social function of law schools. As the demand for legal studies has changed in the second half, or last third, of the twentieth century, there is a change in the supply of law schools. New law schools, especially private ones, have been created as a product of the policies of education liberalization. We will look at this later, but we note now that supply and demand are not independent in this matter; in other words, the increase in the number of law schools in recent years could have augmented the demand for legal education. At the same time, the increase in the number of students could cause the strengthening or consolidation of the supply.

Changes in the demography of law students are related to the transformations of Latin American societies and also to their political and social systems. In this sense, the comparison with Cuba is interesting. As we know, in Latin America this is the only country that stayed on the socialist path for many decades. In 1965, when the Cuban Revolution was initiated with great ideological fervor, legal studies almost disappeared: there were 343 law students, who represented less than 2 percent of university students and five out of one hundred thousand inhabitants. In 1995, resulting from an official policy that reevaluated legal studies, the number increased to 1,848 law students. This did not signify a substantial increase in value with respect to its weight in the university, but it meant an increase to seventeen law students per one hundred thousand inhabitants, a figure that, at any rate, is very low compared with the rest of Latin America. In 1995, 70 percent of law students in Cuba were women, and the proportion appears to have increased (data from UNESCO Statistical Yearbook 1997).[2]

The increase in the demand for legal studies partially explains the emergence or strengthening of private legal education. The reasons for its creation may be ideological or commercial, but only the sustained increase in young people inclined to study law made possible the increase in the number of private law schools and the proportion of students in private universities in nearly all of the countries in the region.

Changes in the Programs and in the Teaching of Law

A traditional function of law schools was the training of the political elite. In the nineteenth and early twentieth centuries, it was an expressed function. Legal studies were often called "political science," and parliamentarians, cabinet ministers, and high-ranking public officials were trained there (Falcão 1984; Lomnitz and Salazar 2002; Pérez-Perdomo 1981). Not only did the law curricula include subjects like political economy and sociology, but also many of the students, displaced from their hometowns, met to discuss politics or literature. These networks were later reflected in the political activity and the administration of the state. The legal training as such was complemented by work in the tribunals or in the offices of lawyers.

Around the middle of the twentieth century, legal studies turned more to the law, but its function of training the political elite was preserved in a latent or implicit way. The presence of lawyers in the distinct fields of politics and state administration as well as the informal networks that were formed in the law schools explain this latent function, which was concentrated in certain universities, such as the Autonomous National University of Mexico (UNAM) (Lomnitz and Salazar 2002) and the Central University of Venezuela. The students' political activity, including participation in violent acts, formed part of their political training and establishment of loyalties.

In the last third of the twentieth century, the political function of these large universities came into conflict with their express function of educating lawyers. The intensification of political agitation damaged education at these universities because of the greater frequency of strikes, class suspensions, and acts of violence. The political activity especially affected the large universities of the capitals, which were the principal educators of the political elite. This contributed to the birth or the growth of private universities, and the students who wanted a more continuous course of studies with the possibility of pay migrated to these private schools.

---

2. The very low number of law students and lawyers was a characteristic of the socialist countries (cf. Clark 1999).

The first private law schools, generally created around the end of the nineteenth or the first half of the twentieth century, were in Catholic universities or occasionally, as in the case of the Externado de Colombia and the Escuela Libre de Derecho in Mexico City,[3] were developed for offering a different ideological alternative to the official university. Through the first half of the twentieth century, private universities were few in number and their ideological purpose always present. Nevertheless, the curriculum was very similar to the more traditional schools. In the last thirty years, the number of schools and law programs increased substantially.[4] There were diverse intentions behind the foundation of schools, and now these purposes are reflected in the law curriculum. As a result, someone who wants to study law in any Latin American country now generally has quite a large array of possibilities.

Two types of private universities can be distinguished: those that consider education a business and aspire to provide education to huge numbers of students; and those that try to offer a high-quality education to a smaller number. The latter have attracted the offspring of the economic elite and have begun to stress the training of business lawyers. As a consequence, the law schools of the large, traditional universities lost their standing as the educators of the political elite and their prestige in the training of business lawyers. Likewise, they lost their position as a center of upward social mobility. In the task of training business lawyers, they were quickly substituted by a few private schools; more recently, as business lawyers have gained political power, these schools have also been replaced in the training of the political elite.[5] In short, there has been a shift in the training of the elite from the large public universities to a number of private universities.

At first, there was no difference between private and public education in terms of content and teaching methods. The curricula were fundamentally the same. Around the middle of the twentieth century, legal education concentrated more on the law, not only increasing the number of classes in civil, criminal, and procedural law, but also including new branches of law to be studied, labor and administrative law, among others. The initial change in the law curriculum was therefore an increase in the subjects or fields of study, highly concentrated in the law. As a result, the general education courses lost relative influence and importance. At the same time, universities created departments in economics, sociology, political science, and other social sciences. Society thus had a variety of specializations and disciplinary knowledge at its disposal, and lawyers were more confined to the legal field. We should not,

---

3. The Universidad Externado de Colombia was created in 1886, the Universidad Católica de Chile in 1889, the Escuela Libre de Derecho in Mexico City in 1912, and the Pontificia Universidad Católica del Perú in Lima in 1917.

4. For example, of the forty law schools that existed in Chile by 2000, six were created before 1979, thirteen between 1980 and 1990, and twenty-one between 1991 and 2000. In Venezuela, there were seven law schools until 1980, and in 2001 there were sixteen, of which twelve are private. In Colombia there were few law schools in the 1950s; in 1994, there were thirty-eight. In 2002, there were seventy-four with a total of one hundred thirty programs.

5. Among these schools are the Catholic universities in Santiago, Rio, Lima, and Caracas; the Universidad de los Andes y la Javeriana in Bogota; Libre, ITAM, and Iberoamericana in Mexico City; Diego Portales in Santiago; Belgrano, Torcuato di Tella, and Palermo in Buenos Aires; and Monteávila and Metropolitana in Caracas. The characteristic feature of these schools is that they are private, they recruit the majority of their students from the social elite, and they have made diverse reform efforts in the teaching of law. A new school in Mexico City has been founded with the intent of innovating legal education and educating the elite, but it has two distinguishing characteristics: it is financed by the federal government and it strives to recruit its students (who must pass very rigorous tests) among people of modest income who live in cities in the interior of the country.

then, be surprised that law graduates could no longer claim universal knowledge in the political and social fields and that their preeminence declined.

The accelerated increase in the number of students and the weak social relations of many of the new students meant that the parallel informal education that students traditionally obtained by working in established lawyers' offices, in the courts, or acting in politics in leading roles became more difficult. The increase in subjects of study also reduced the time that students dedicated to these activities, which were extracurricular but important for socialization in politics and the professional milieu. Most law professors only dedicated the necessary class hours to the university, which caused them to limit themselves to repeating what they had learned or reiterating the most important manuals that existed on the subject. Thus, in the 1960s and 1970s, there was a perception among the intellectual leaders of the main law schools that legal studies were irrelevant,[6] and they began various innovation movements.

One of the first reformist voices was Dantas (1955), who called for a quite radical reform to the law curriculum and a reexamination of the methods of legal education. He proposed a flexible curriculum, the incorporation of cases into teaching, interdisciplinary analysis, and an active or participatory method on the part of the students. All of the later reformist agenda was formulated in that formal discourse. Dantas caused an immediate sensation in Brazil (Bastos 2000, 250; Rosenn 1969, 273; Steiner 1971). As we will later observe, his ideas can be seen in the conception of legal studies in the Federal University of Brasilia.

Between 1959 and 1964, there were four conferences of Latin American law schools, which produced an abundant literature and called for substantial reforms, including the introduction of class discussion, seminars, and an interdisciplinary focus (Wilson 1989, 393). These conferences were preceded and accompanied by a reaction against the formalism that has been present in Latin American legal studies since the end of the nineteenth century.

In 1961, the University of Brasilia began to function. Its legal studies were conceived with a distinct curricular organization, and innovations in teaching methodology were also planned (Bastos 2000). The military coup of 1964, which resulted in the arrest of several professors and the resignation of a sizable number of the others, halted this first effort.

LAW AND DEVELOPMENT

In the 1970s, the movement was known as "law and development." The angle that generated most attention was the effort of professors from the United States who, conscious of the important political role of law studies and of the backwardness and poor state of the law schools throughout the region, traveled to Latin America as missionaries of the case method and the interdisciplinary study of law. A much higher number of young Latin American professors and law graduates (especially in Brazil, Chile, Colombia, and Peru) earned master's degrees and doctorates in law, or in some other way familiarized themselves with the teaching of law in the United States (Lynch 1981, 111). A good number of professors began to prepare untraditional instructional materials and made use of "active class," as it was

---

6. At the time, the perception was not necessarily shared by the majority of legal professionals. A study among Colombian lawyers showed that 64 percent were "very satisfied" with their legal education, 24 percent were "satisfied," and only 9 percent were "unsatisfied" (Lynch 1981, 113).

called at that time. A small number were interested in interdisciplinary research. Several of the professors from the United States who participated in the experience considered it a failure, since it did not succeed in changing the Latin American legal culture within a few years, after an investment of approximately five million dollars (Trubek and Galanter 1974).

The view from Latin America is somewhat different. The restlessness for change in legal education predated the presence of U.S. scholars. There was a parallel discussion of the topics considered relevant at the time,[7] and the changes in Latin America continued long after the withdrawal of the American organizations that financed projects and the formal declaration of the cessation of the American programs that Trubek and Galanter's article pronounced.

The case of Venezuela can be significant, since it never formed part of the law and development movement sponsored by the United States; nevertheless, it saw considerable reformist activity both at that time and later. A good number of Venezuelan law graduates received postgraduate education, both in civil law countries and in common law ones, with national, government, and private funds. An important part of these graduates are now professors in the law schools, and a certain number have been innovators in their teaching or in their research. This case should call attention to the important number of law graduates in Latin America who have done postgraduate studies in Europe or, increasingly, in the United States in the last few decades. The Mexican pattern is very similar (Fix-Zamudio 2010).[8]

The changes in legal education have been as much in the teaching of law as in legal academic research. In the 1970s, the teaching changes were very controversial and met with open resistance from the part-time lawyer-professors. In Peru, the innovators were sarcastically called the "Wisconsin boys," and they experienced more than a few conflictual situations. In Colombia, there were important political conflicts within the schools that attempted reform, and some deans and professors lost their jobs in these struggles (Lynch 1981). In Chile, the Pinochet government expelled the reformists from the universities, including the Catholic University. Several suspicious professors, who were part of the political heterodoxy, had to go into exile. We have already noted the Brasilia case.

RECENT TRENDS

Later, changes in teaching came about largely because the private schools that focused on training business lawyers needed to diversify. The innovative schools introduced activities, such as legal clinics, negotiation, and legal writing, and courses, such as law and economics, sociology of law, and human rights. They also placed importance on an education in ethics, which the positivist formalists had banished from law schools. Some professors innovated their teaching methodologies, although there was not a generalized change in this area. The emphasis on which matters are innovated and which stay the same varied from one school

---

7. For a look at subjects in legal education that interested Latin American academics, see Witker (1976). It is important to point out that the type of teaching that uses the class or the professor's lecture as the main instrument has been consistently criticized from different perspectives. Pérez-Perdomo (1974), for example, places it at the root of the practical skepticism and the lack of compromise with the normative order in lawyers. More recently, Torres Arends (1997, 2001) has emphasized that teaching trains abstract reason but does not develop the capacity to tackle problems, and that it produces an inconsistent construction of the concept of law.

8. Hector Fix-Zamudio, personal communication to Rogelio Pérez-Perdomo, Mexico City, Mexico. August 10, 2010.

to another. In the postgraduate programs, which were not regulated by tradition, the variety of subjects and activities was much greater, though we do not know of any evaluation of what happened in this area.[9] Curiously, the large public universities have created the most developed postgraduate programs, while innovations to law curricula have occurred more in a few private schools.[10] The characteristic thing about these reforms is that they have not formed part of a general movement and have tended to be low profile.

By contrast, young law graduates have begun to turn to master's programs in American universities. There, in one year, they familiarize themselves with the language and the problem-solving approach characteristic of legal teaching in the United States. These are abilities that are appreciated in business lawyers today.

The evaluation of law schools by external organizations is a new phenomenon. There is the need, due to the proliferation of law schools and the diversification of programs, but only few experiences are known. In Colombia the Ministry of Justice published an evaluation in 1995. In Brazil, the Ministry of Education and the Ordem dos Advogados, or national bar association, have done the evaluation separately. In Chile in 2001, the magazine *Qué Pasa?* (Dec. 11, 2001) published an evaluation that follows the model of *US News and World Report.* That was the second year that such evaluation had been done.

During the entire period that we are examining, the perception has existed in certain universities that law schools had lost step with social changes and that legal studies had been left behind. This perception may have come from the perceived speed of the social change as opposed to the much slower and more difficult changes in the curricula and teaching methods in law schools. Latin American societies have continued to face severe problems of poverty, marginality, criminality, and police brutality, at the same time that political transformations, which were sometimes quite rapid, a communications revolution, and greater integration into the global economy took place—yet these problems and changes did not seem to affect the majority of law schools, which appeared secluded in a culture of codes and old books (Fuentes-Hernández 2002). Without denying these problems, the argument that we have developed does not correspond with this perception, in the sense that we have shown that legal education has been affected by social change and that the dynamic of reform, driven out through the door, has timidly returned through the window. The perception of stasis probably derives from the desire for law schools to be more proactive and dynamic and from the restrictions to change affecting some schools and a fraction of the students.

---

9. Some examples from different times: in Brazil 1980, there were twenty programs with more than two thousand students (Falcão 1984, 115). In 1975, the Central University of Venezuela renovated its postgraduate program in law and created one in political science. A good number of courses and seminars were interdisciplinary and could be taken equally by people in either of the postgraduate programs. At present there are a dozen postgraduate programs with more than one thousand students. In recent years, the Legal Research Institute of Universidad Nacional Autónoma de México, the Universidad Nacional de Chile in Santiago, and the Externado de Colombia in Bogotá created doctorates in law with an interdisciplinary focus.

10. Mexico seems to be a different case. The law school with the greatest weight in the training of business lawyers (the Escuela Libre) is private and considerably traditional. ITAM and Iberoamericana, two private universities, are also devoted to the training of business lawyers and have made innovations with different degrees of success. The most radical innovation effort is being made in a public school (CIDE) that has barely gotten underway. The characteristic thing about CIDE is its attention to admitting very promising students with scarce resources and providing them with scholarships.

REFERENCES

Bastos, Aurelio Wander. 2000. *O ensino jurídico no Brasil.* 2d ed. Rio de Janeiro: Lumen Juris.

Clark, David S. 1999. Comparing the work and organization of lawyers worldwide: The persistence of legal traditions. In *Lawyers practice and ideals: A comparative view*, ed. J. Barceló III and R. Cramton. The Hague: Kluwer.

Dantas, San Tiago. 1955. A educação jurídica e a crise brasileira. *Revista Forense* 159.

Dezalay, Yves, and Bryant Garth. 2002. *The internationalization of palace wars: Lawyers, economists, and the contest to transform Latin American states.* Chicago: University of Chicago Press.

Falcão, Joaquim. 1984. *Os advogados: Ensino jurídico e mercado de trabalho.* Recife, Brazil: Fundação Joaquim Nabuco y Editora Massangana.

Fuentes-Hernández, Alfredo. 2002. Globalization and legal education in Latin America: Issues for law and development in the 21st Century. Paper presented at the Annual meeting of the American Association of Law Schools. New Orleans, LA.

Junqueira, Eliane, and C. V. Veras. 2001. Estudantes e profissionais negros de direito: Perspectivas para o novo milênio? Unpublished paper. Rio de Janeiro: Instituto de Direito e Sociedade.

Lomnitz, Larissa, and R. Salazar. 2002. Cultural elements in the practice of law in Mexico: Informal networks in formal systems. In *Global prescriptions: The production, exportation, and importation of a new legal orthodoxy*, ed. Y. Dezalay and B. Garth. Ann Arbor: University of Michigan Press.

López-Ayllón, Sergio, and Héctor Fix-Fierro. 2003. "Faraway, so close!" The rule of law and legal change in Mexico, 1970–2000. In *Legal cultures in the age of globalization: Latin America and Latin Europe*, ed. L. Friedman and R. Pérez-Perdomo. Stanford: Stanford University Press.

Lynch, Dennis O. 1981. *Legal roles in Colombia.* Uppsala: Scandinavian Institute for African Studies; and New York: International Center for Law in Development.

Merryman, John Henry. 1999. *The loneliness of the comparative lawyer and other essays in foreign and comparative law.* The Hague; Boston: Kluwer International.

Pérez-Perdomo, R. 2005. Educación jurídica, abogados y globalización en América Latina. *Sistemas Judiciales* 9: 4–14. Buenos Aires: Ediciones del Instituto.

———. 1981. *Los abogados en Venezuela.* Caracas: Monteávila.

Pérez-Perdomo, Rogelio. 1974. *Tres ensayos sobre métodos en la educación jurídica.* Caracas: Universidad Central de Venezuela.

Ranking de Universidades. 2001. *¿Qué Pasa?* (Santiago). December 11.

Rosenn, Keith. 1969. The reform of legal education in Brazil. *Journal of Legal Education* 21: 251.

Steiner, Henry. 1971. Legal education and socioeconomic change: Brazilian perspectives. *The American Journal of Comparative Law* 18: 39–90.

Torres Arends, Irene. 2001. *Cultura jurídica y estudiantes de derecho: Una medición de cultura jurídica en Venezuela.* Prepublication. Caracas: Facultad de Ciencias Jurídicas y Políticas, Universidad Central de Venezuela.

———. 1997. *Educación jurídica y razonamiento.* Caracas: Universidad Central de Venezuela.

Trubek, David, and Marc Galanter. 1974. Scholars in self-estrangement: Some reflections on the crisis in law and development studies in the United States. *Wisconsin Law Review* 1062.

UNESCO Statistical Yearbook. 1997. Blue Ridge Summit, PA: Bernan Press.

———. 1973. Paris: UNESCO.

Wilson, Richard. 1989. The new legal education in North and South America. *Stanford Journal of International Law* 25.

Witker, Jorge. 1976. *Antologia de Estudios sobre la Enseñanza del derecho.* Mexico City: UNAM.

II CRIMINAL JUSTICE

INTRODUCTION

In most modern legal systems, there is a very sharp distinction between the civil and the criminal domains. "Criminal law" has its own special rules and procedures. Socially, too, the two domains are quite distinctive. For example, for most people, there is a real difference between a US$10,000 fine, after conviction for a crime, and paying US$10,000 in damages after losing a contracts case. Conviction of a crime carries with it a stigma that civil liability, on the whole, does not.

In most modern systems, too, the government acts as the plaintiff in a criminal case. The actual victims of the crime do not normally act as plaintiffs, even if the law allows them to play a role in the process. The government is responsible for labeling acts as crimes, and for setting up mechanisms for finding and catching criminals. The government pays the costs, on the whole, for bringing criminals to justice—costs of police, prosecutors, investigating judges, and trials in general. The government also provides the prisons in which convicted criminals may be held. To be sure, the further back you go, the muddier the distinction between the criminal and the civil domain. But in all modern systems, the line is clear and fairly distinct.

Criminal justice—which is the name we give to the whole system, from the laws that define crimes, to the running of the prisons—is the most significant official form of social control. The penal code of a country or state is a catalog of the behavior that criminal law aims to punish. Needless to say, each country has its own particular code. The contents vary over time and differ among cultures and political systems. Currency dealers are rich and respected in, say, France, but dealing in currencies would have been a crime in socialist societies. What are crimes in wartime are not necessarily crimes during peacetime. Democratic societies do not punish sedition, blasphemy, or heresy. Nor do most of these societies punish adultery, or other forms of sexual behavior between consenting adults, but in an earlier period all of these were crimes. Most modern, developed societies have abolished the death penalty. Nobody in Europe can be executed for any crime. Certainly, nobody can be stoned to death or burned at the stake. But there is capital punishment in the United States and Japan. The criminal code of Saudi Arabia and other conservative Muslim countries will be sharply different from the code in Western, democratic countries. And both of these types will differ from the criminal codes in socialist countries like Cuba, or the codes of the indigenous systems that still prevail in parts of Africa.

The legal literature on criminal law, produced by legal scholars, is vast, but most of it does not concern itself with the criminal justice system, and most of it is not empirical. There is, however, a huge social science literature on crime, criminal justice, and social control, and criminology is a recognized subfield of sociology. Some studies on criminal justice and criminology are comparative, for example, Tonry and Frase (2001).

In Part II of this book, we will look at a few of the many issues of theory and research that deal with criminal justice. One issue, which perhaps gets too much attention, has to do with the divide between the common law procedural system, the so-called adversary system, and the civil law, or inquisitorial system. Common law countries emphasize oral testimony. Trials are dramas in which the lawyers for the two sides play starring roles, and there is sometimes a lay jury. The process is more party centered than judge centered. Civil law countries place more stress on written documents, and judges do much more of the work of investigating, gathering evidence, and managing the case. Still, there are probably bigger differences among Japan, Haiti, and Italy (all civil law countries), than there are between, say, Italy and the United Kingdom. Indeed, many traits of common law criminal procedure, such as its emphasis on oral testimony, and on lay participation in the process, have been adopted in France, Germany, Italy, and, more recently, in Latin American countries. In this development, multilateral organizations such as the World Bank, as well as a fast-growing global network of scholars and practitioners, have played a role.

One overtly comparative study is James Whitman's work, *Harsh Justice*, which compares the United States with Europe. An excerpt from this book is Chapter 6 of this section. Notice that Whitman attempts to explain differences between Europe and the United States in terms of cultural traditions—in this case, long-term cultural traditions. Note, too, that the traditions he discusses are not legal traditions (for example, common versus civil law).

Whitman paints with a broad brush; he tries to characterize whole systems. Similarly, in Chapter 7, "The Benevolent Paternalism of Japanese Criminal Justice," Daniel H. Foote tries to characterize the Japanese system as a whole. Whitman also deals with very long time spans. Clearly, however, political forces, especially in open, democratic societies, can have a strong impact on the way the criminal justice system operates. This is the message of a study by Francis Pakes (2004). Pakes shows how the Netherlands, a country that historically had not been obsessed with crime, and where politics was "stable to the point of boring," changed dramatically under the impact of a small number of spectacular crimes and the rise of movements that objected to the new, mostly Muslim, immigrants. The Netherlands then joined the list of countries where law and order, and the war on terrorism, resulted in a sense of crisis that then was translated into harsher laws and increased numbers of people in prison.

Baldwin and McConville's article, which is included in this section as Chapter 8, deals with plea bargaining. In the literal sense, plea bargaining can only occur in countries where there is a guilty plea. England, of course, is such a country, but note that the practice there was not considered legitimate. This article was written in 1979, so it is at least thirty years old, but the practice continues. Plea bargaining also exists in Canada. Indeed, as in England, criminal defendants who go to trial run the risk of "a harsher sentence, commonly known as the 'entertainment tax,' should they be convicted." This is imposed on defendants who are "not seen, in view of a guilty verdict, as being able to justify having entered a plea of not guilty," causing "all of the trouble and expense of a trial" (Lafontaine and Rondinelli 2005, 116).

But, what about civil law systems? According to David T. Johnson (2002), there *is* plea bargaining in Japan. True, there is no guilty plea in Japan, and no right to waive trial. But, under a broader definition, "plea bargaining exists if suspects have a choice between complicated and simple models of case processing," and choosing the simple one is taken to mean "cooperation." Japanese suspects are, indeed, pressured in this way. In this regard, Japan can be said to have plea bargaining.

The material on plea bargaining invites us to consider how legal structures and local cultures impact both procedure and substance in criminal justice systems. Change in criminal justice systems flow from political pressures (as in the case of the Netherlands, according to Pakes 2004), but as to technical details, the work of elite reformers is quite critical. Discontent with criminal justice is fairly widespread. What we might call the Left feels the systems are, in general, too harsh, too prone to oppress. What we might call the Right feels the systems are, in general, too soft, too easy on crime.

Change in recent years has reflected both of these demands, sometimes at the same time and inconsistently. Much depends on actual and perceived crime rates. When people feel fearful and afraid, they tend to demand more toughness in the system and are prone to invest or spend resources in crime prevention or personal protection (Pérez-Perdomo 2005). There may be disjunctures between what ordinary people feel about crime and criminal justice and the opinions of elites (Kotze 2003). It is likely that attitudes toward criminal justice depend on many factors. The actual crime rate is certainly one of them. It is only natural for people in high-crime societies to want more toughness. But this surely does not explain attitudes completely. Much also depends on local culture, including legal culture. An interesting study by Joseph Sanders and V. Lee Hamilton (1992) compared the reactions of people in an American city, two Japanese cities, and a Russian city, toward vignettes that raised questions of crime and punishment.

REFERENCES AND SUGGESTIONS FOR FURTHER READING

Baldwin, John, and Michael McConville. 1979. Plea bargaining and plea negotiation in England. *Law and Society Review* 13: 287.

Doob, Anthony N., and Cheryl Marie Webster. 2006. Countering punitiveness: Understanding stability in Canada's imprisonment rate. *Law and Society Review* 40: 325.

Feest, Johannes, and Erhard Blankenburg. 1972. *Die Definitionsmacht der Polizei.* Dusseldorf, Germany: Bertelsmann.

Foote, Daniel H. 1992. The benevolent paternalism of Japanese criminal justice. *California Law Review* 80: 317.

Friedman, Lawrence M. 1993. *Crime and punishment in American history.* New York: Basic Books.

Garland, David. 2001. *The culture of control: Crime and social order in contemporary society.* Chicago: University of Chicago Press.

Gurr, Ted Robert, Peter Grabosky, and Richard C. Hula. 1977. *The politics of crime and conflict: A comparative study of four cities.* Beverly Hills, CA: Sage Publications.

Johnson, David T. 2002. *The Japanese way of justice: Prosecuting crime in Japan.* New York: Oxford University Press.

Kotze, Hennie. 2003. Mass and elite attitudes toward the criminal justice system in South Africa. *South African Journal of Criminal Justice* 16: 38.

Lafontaine, Gregory, and Vincenzo Rondinelli. 2005. Plea bargaining and the modern criminal defense lawyer: Negotiating guilty and the economics of 21st century criminal justice. *Criminal Law Quarterly* 50: 108.

Lu, Hong, and Terance D. Miethe. 2003. Confessions and criminal case disposition in China. *Law and Society Review* 37: 549.

Miyazawa, Setsuo. 1992. *Policing in Japan: A study on making crime.* Trans. John O. Haley. Albany: State University of New York Press.

Pakes, Francis. 2004. The politics of discontent: The emergence of a new criminal justice discourse in the Netherlands. *Howard Journal of Criminal Justice* 43: 284.

Pérez-Perdomo, Rogelio. 2005. Seguridad y riesgo en tiempos de globalización. In *Violencia, criminalidad y terrorismo.* Caracas: Fundación Venezuela Positiva.

Sanders, Joseph, and Lee Hamilton. 1992. Legal cultures and punishment repertoires in Japan, Russia, and the United States. *Law and Society Review* 27: 117.

Tonry, Michael, and Richard S. Frase, ed. 2001. *Sentencing and sanctions in western countries.* Oxford: Oxford University Press.

Whitman, James Q. 2003. *Harsh justice: Criminal punishment and the widening divide between America and Europe.* Oxford: University Press.

6 HARSH JUSTICE

CRIMINAL PUNISHMENT AND THE WIDENING DIVIDE BETWEEN AMERICA AND EUROPE

James Q. Whitman

INTRODUCTION

At the beginning of the twenty-first century, criminal punishment is harsh in America, and it has been getting harsher. In the year 2000, the incarcerated population reached the extraordinary level of 2 million, roughly quintupling since the mid-1970s. America's per capita incarceration is now the highest in the world, approaching, and in some regions exceeding, ten times the rate in Western Europe. Large-scale incarceration is only part of the story, though. Juveniles have increasingly been tried "as adults"—something that Western Europeans find little less than shocking. New sorts of punishments have been invented over the last twenty-five years, from boot camps to electronic monitoring devices, and old sorts of punishments, from chain gangs to public shaming, have been revived. Some of the new harshness has involved matters almost everybody regards as momentous: in particular, the death penalty, reintroduced in the United States at the very moment that it was definitely abolished in Western Europe. At the same time, some of the new harshness has involved almost laughably trivial matters: "quality of life" policing has landed people in jail, if only for a night, for offenses like smoking cigarettes in the New York subway; and the Supreme Court has declared that police may jail persons for something as minor as driving without a seatbelt. All of these developments, whether trivial or momentous, have been surrounded by jarringly punitive rhetoric in American politics, perhaps best exemplified by the Phoenix sheriff who proudly declares that he runs "a very bad jail."

None of this is news. Everyone who reads the newspapers knows that we have been in the midst of a kind of national get-tough movement, which has lasted for about the last twenty-five years. Still, Americans may not quite grasp how deeply isolated this period has left us in the Western world. Punishment in America is now, as Michael Tonry observes, "vastly harsher than in any other country to which the United States would ordinarily be compared." There are certainly some parts of the world that have turned harsher over the last

Reprinted from James Q. Whitman, *Harsh Justice: Criminal Punishment and the Widening Divide Between America and Europe* (New York: Oxford University Press, 2003). Reproduced with permission of Oxford University Press.

twenty-five years. This is true in particular of some Islamic countries. But among Western nations, only England has followed our lead—and even England has followed us only up to certain point. As for the countries of continental Western Europe, the contrast between their practices and ours has become stark indeed. The Western European media regularly run pieces expressing shock at the extreme severity of American punishment. Meanwhile, continental justice systems have come to treat America as something close to a rogue state, hesitating to extradite offenders to the United States.

To be sure, this era of American harshness will presumably not go on forever, and it may already have slowed. Nevertheless, it is the disturbing truth that we now find ourselves in a strange place on the international scene. As a result of the last quarter-century of deepening harshness, we are no longer clearly classified in the same categories as the other countries of the liberal West. Instead, by the measure of our punishment practices, we have edged into the company of troubled and violent places like Yemen and Nigeria (both of which, like many jurisdictions in the United States, execute people for crimes committed when they were minors—though Yemen has recently renounced the practice); China and Russia (two societies that come close to rivaling our incarceration rates); pre-2001 Afghanistan (where the Taliban, like American judges, reintroduced public shame sanctions); and even Nazi Germany (which, like the contemporary United States, turned sharply toward retributivism and the permanent incapacitation of habitual offenders).

What is going on in our country?

This is the question I want to approach in this book. This is a book about the cultural roots of harsh criminal punishment as it has emerged in contemporary America. Most especially, it is a book about how harsh criminal punishment can develop in a society that belongs to the Western liberal tradition. America *is*, after all, a country that belongs to something it is fair to call the Western "liberal" tradition, elusive though the concept of liberalism may be. Certainly there are many aspects of American culture that seem manifestly to belong to a humane strain of liberalism. Ours, of all Western countries, is the one that is most consistently suspicious of state authority. Ours is the country with the inveterate attachment to the values of procedural fairness. Ours is the country that—unlike Germany or France— never succumbed to any variety of fascism or Nazism. Why, then, is ours not the country with the mildest punishment practices? Certainly, in most respects, Americans define their values by opposition to *illiberal* societies—to the societies of places like China or the Afghanistan of the Taliban or Nazi Germany. How could our patterns of punishment be bringing us closer to them than to the dominant polities of the contemporary European Union?

The answer this book will offer is drawn from history—a comparative history that reaches back to the eighteenth century, to a time before the French and American revolutions. In particular, it is drawn from a close comparative study of the Unites States, on the one hand, and the two dominant legal cultures of the European continent, France and Germany, on the other. There are good reasons to choose France and Germany for such a study. Of all the continental countries, these are the two that cry out most for close comparison with our own, in this era of American harshness. They are large and powerful industrial nations that have been strongholds of humane and democratic Western values since 1945. They are countries that have set the tone for all of the continent for many generations, and that continue to set much of the tone for the human rights jurisprudence of the European Union. Not least, they are the countries that we have measured ourselves against since the time of the American Revolution. Indeed, they are countries that, once upon a time, seemed precisely to lack the humane and democratic values that *America* stood for. France and Germany, as they exist today, are the descendants of the "despotic," state-heavy, hierarchical societies against which we defined ourselves two and half centuries ago. They are also countries that have had recurrent episodes of authoritarian government, from the nineteenth century through the horrific 1930s and 1940s. Yet at the end of the millennium, they are countries that punish far more mildly than ours does. Why?

There is one sort of answer that must be rejected out of hand. This is the sort of answer given by the high-theoretical literature on the sociology of punishment in "modern" society. Sociologists of punishment and "modern" society, from Durkheim to Foucault and beyond, are among the best-known intellectual figures of the day. Their books are widely assigned in college courses, and the sociology of "modernity" is probably the first thing that most educated people think of when the topic is punishment. But theirs is a sociology precisely about punishment in "modern" society in general. The sociology of "modernity" simply does not grapple with the question of how punishment practices can vary—let alone how sharp differences can exist between the "modern" societies of places like the United States, France, or Germany. The sort of "modernity" that Foucault and his followers talk about seems especially beside the point, and especially frustrating to read in the face of recent American developments. Foucault, in his famous *Discipline and Punish*, described modern punishment as the product of an ominous shift from disciplining the body to disciplining the soul. This makes for a dramatic, and sometimes fitting description of *some* aspects of American punishment. But it tells us nothing about how punishment practices could diverge on the two sides of the Atlantic, with America striking off alone on the road to intensifying harshness. Much the same objection applies even to the most sensitive recent work on "modernity." Of course large industrial countries share some "modern" features. But what they share can hardly explain how they have diverged, and these countries *have* diverged. How can any approach that starts by invoking "modernity" explain why?

This book will accordingly avoid talking much about "modernity." We cannot understand American punishment without understanding *America,* and the same goes for the rest of the "modern world." Sensible criminologists have always been ready to acknowledge that different cultures produce different forms of punishment—that, as one pre-Foucault textbook put it, "One learns to react punitively or in some other way just as learns to speak English, German or Japanese." One does indeed. Like other wise scholars, I will accordingly focus on comparative culture: there is something in the American idiom, something in American culture that is driving us toward harsh punishment.

Of course, "American culture" is a vast topic, and I should emphasize from the outset that there are important aspects of American culture that I am not going to explore with any care. It is clear, for example, that American harshness has something to do with the strength of its religious tradition, and especially its Christian tradition. Part of what makes us harsher than continental Europeans is the presence of some distinctively fierce American Christian beliefs. It is also the case that American harshness has something to do with American racism—though, as we shall see, continental European race relations are not noticeably better than American. While I will touch on both these issues repeatedly, I will not discuss either in any detail. Perhaps most important, it is clear that the relative harshness of American punishment has a great deal to do with the prevalence of violence in American society—both because Americans have higher rates of violent crime, and because American patterns of violence also make themselves felt in prisons, policing, and elsewhere. The difference in patterns of violence matters immensely, and it certainly deserves attention beyond what I will give it in this book. Nevertheless, American violence is another problem that I leave for another day.

Instead, leaving race, Christianity, and violence to one side, this book will focus on two quite different aspects of American culture: American patterns of *egalitarian social status*; and American patterns of *resistance to state power*. American society has a deeply rooted tradition of status egalitarianism: a strong dislike for social hierarchy runs throughout American history. American society also displays a recurrent suspiciousness in the face of state power. These are both features of American life that are integral to the American style of liberalism. They are also features of American life that differentiate us unmistakably from the countries of continental Europe. Countries like France and Germany show much more tolerance for traditions of social hierarchy than we do, and much more tolerance for state power as well. As I am going to try to show, these most characteristically "liberal" features of American culture have contributed to making American punishment uniquely harsh in the West.

The bulk of this book will be about the American style of status equality. The notion that the peculiarities of American culture have to do with peculiar American traditions of status equality is nothing new. Tocqueville, in particular, is famous for arguing that the forms of American culture grew out of our historic lack of social hierarchy—out of our lack of what he called the "aristocratic element." This has seemed critically important to many observers of American society ever since, from H. G. Wells to Louis Hartz and Seymour Martin Lipset, and this book too is going to treat it as critically important.

But I am going to offer a very different argument from the kind that Tocqueville offered. To Tocqueville, the absence of an "aristocratic element" implied that America would have *mild* criminal punishment. "Societies become milder," he declared in his *Democracy in America*, "as conditions become more equal": after all, people who are equal can be expected to have more reciprocal empathy and therefore to go easy on each another. America, he thus concluded in 1840, being the most egalitarian country, must inevitably have "the most benign criminal justice system." Nor is Tocqueville the only observer to offer this sort of argument. A kindred idea appeared, a half-century later, in the sociology of Durkheim. To Durkheim, the harshness of punishment in a given society had something to do with its degree of "contractualization." To the extent that market-oriented, contractlike relations governed societies, Durkheim hypothesized, they would tend to have "restitutive" rather than "penal" regulation—they would tend to rely on civil remedies rather than on harsh criminal punishment. This Durkheimian claim had nothing to do with social status as such. Nevertheless, to the extent we associate market forms of social organization with rejection of status hierarchy, we can see real resemblances between Durkheim's arguments and those of Tocqueville. Certainly Durkheim's arguments suggest the same conclusion about America as Tocqueville's: if Durkheim is right, we would expect to observe a link between American styles of market-oriented egalitarianism and mildness in criminal punishment.

Yet, of course, in America there is no such link. Americans display unmistakably deep-rooted patterns of status egalitarianism; Tocqueville was right about that. Yet our punishment is unmistakably harsh. As for market-orientation: it would be hard to point to any society that is more "contractualized," more market-oriented, than ours. Yet ours is the society of harsh punishment.

The main purpose of this book is to explain why—why the American style of status equality should produce results so thoroughly at odds with what these subtle and thoughtful French observers predicted.

The explanation I will offer involves a comparative legal history that reaches well back into the eighteenth century. The key to understanding how Tocqueville and Durkheim went wrong lies, I am going to argue, in understanding the link between traditions of social hierarchy and the dynamic of *degradation* in punishment. Contemporary American criminal punishment is more *degrading* than punishment in continental Europe. The susceptibility to degradation lies at the core of what makes American punishment harsh. And our susceptibility to degradation has to do precisely with our lack of an "aristocratic element."

The literal meaning of "to degrade" is to reduce another person in status, to treat another person as *inferior*, and it is that literal meaning that I will take as my point of departure. We all know intuitively that degradation, in this sense, often plays a significant role in punishment: part of what makes punishments effective is their power to degrade—their power to make the person punished feel diminished, lessened, lowered. Within the world of criminal punishment, such degradation is achieved in the widest variety of ways, from beatings to mutilation to day-glo orange prison uniforms.

Now, contemporary France and Germany are countries, I am going to show, with a deep commitment to the proposition that criminal offenders must not be degraded—that they must be accorded *respect* and *dignity*. The differences between continental and American practices can be little short of astonishing. Some of the most provocative examples come from continental prisons. Prison is a relatively rare sanction in continental Europe, by sharp contrast with the United States, and sentences are dramatically shorter. Nevertheless, there are continental prisons, and there are continental prisoners. But those comparatively few continental offenders who do wind up in prison are subjected to a regime markedly less degrading than what prevails in the United States. Thus continental prisons are characterized by a large variety of practices intended to prevent the symbolic degradation of prison inmates. Prison uniforms have generally been abolished. Rules have been promulgated attempting to guarantee that inmates be addressed respectfully—as "Herr So-and-So" or "Monsieur So-and-So." Rules have also been promulgated protecting inmate privacy, through such measures as the elimination of barred doors. Most broadly, these measures include what in Germany is called "the principle of approximation" or "the principle of normalcy": the principle that life in prison should approximate life in the outside world as closely as possible. Like all ideals in the law of punishment, this one is sometimes realized only fitfully: to study norms of dignity in prison is often to study aspirations rather than realities. France, in particular, lags well behind Germany in implementing these practices, and life in French prisons can be very tough. Nevertheless, the "principle of approxima-tion" does have real meaning, and indeed it has led to some practices that will seem as-tounding to Americans. German convicts, for example, are supposed to work at jobs that are *real* jobs, like jobs in the outside world. This means that they enjoy far-reaching protec-tion against arbitrary discharge, and even four weeks per year of paid vacation (!). All of this is intended to dramatize a fact about their dignity. The lives of convicts are supposed to be, as far as possible, no different from the lives of ordinary German people. Convicts are not to be thought of as persons of a different and lower status than everybody else. As we shall see, these same ideas also pervade European political debate over prison policy. (These are also the continental ideas that most recently came to the fore in European pro-tests over the treatment of the captured prisoners held in Guantanamo Bay after the Amer-ican campaign in Afghanistan.)

Prisons are not the only places where this continental commitment to dignity shows itself. There are many examples that take us beyond life within prison walls. Thus in America we are far less bothered by public exposure for criminal offenders than Europeans are—whether those inmates are being kept behind barred prison doors that expose them to the view of all, or being shown on Internet broadcasts, or being subjected to public shame sanctions, or having their records opened for public inspection. There are other examples, involving de-privation of civil and political rights. The oldest legal form of status degradation—auto-matic deprivation of rights of participation—still survives in America. Convicted American felons are frequently automatically deprived of civic rights—a practice of status degradation that has disenfranchised a substantial proportion of the African American population in some regions. As we shall see, French and German prison systems, by contrast, have pro-grams that encourage inmates to exercise their (almost always unimpaired) right to vote. On the deepest level, American criminal justice displays a resistance to considering the very personhood of offenders. This is a resistance that shows in the triumph of determinate sen-tencing in America, and it is a resistance that is absent in Western Europe.

There are differences of profound significance, I am going to argue, differences that take us a long way toward understanding how American punishment culture has come to differ so much from French and German. Cultures that systematically show respect for offenders are also cultures that are likely to punish with a mild hand; conversely, cultures (like our own) that have no commitment to respect for the offender are likely to show harshness. Where do these differences come from?

"Modernity" obviously has no answer to offer.

That does not mean that sociology has no answer to offer. On the contrary, these are dif-ferences we can only explain if we are grasp some deeply rooted differences in social values and social structure. But the sociology we need is a historical sociology. The continental commitment to "dignity" and "respect" in punishment is something that has grown very slowly since the eighteenth century, and it is a commitment that offers striking evidence of a fundamental connection between degradation in punishment and traditions of social status. For at its core, as I want to demonstrate in this book, it is a commitment to *abolishing historically low-status treatment.*

To understand the differences that divide us from the French and the Germans, we must indeed begin in the eighteenth century. France and Germany are countries in which, two centuries or so ago, there were sharp distinctions between high-status people and low-status people. In particular, there were two classes of punishments: high-status punishments, and low-status punishments. Forms of execution are the most familiar example: nobles were traditionally beheaded; commoners were traditionally hanged. There are many other examples, too: low-status offenders were routinely mutilated, branded, flogged, and subjected to forced labor; all while being displayed before a raucous public, both before and after their deaths. High-status offenders were generally spared such treatment. Forms of imprisonment differed by status as well. Two and a half centuries ago, high-status continental convicts—who included such famous eighteenth-century prisoners as Voltaire or Mirabeau—could expect certain kinds of privileged treatment. They were permitted a relatively normal and relatively comfortable existence, serving their time in "fortresses" rather than in prisons. Their "cells" were something like furnished apartments, where they received visitors and were supplied with books and writing materials. They were immune from forced labor and physical beatings. They were accorded easy and regular visitation privileges. They were permitted to wear their own clothing and to provide their own food; they were permitted to provide their own medical care as well. They were shielded from public exposure, and indeed from all forms of shame. Low-status prisoners by contrast were subjected to conditions of effective slavery, often resulting in horrifically high mortality.

The subsequent development of punishment in these countries can be captured, in its broadest outline, in a simple sociological formula: over the course of the last two centuries, in both Germany and France, and indeed throughout the continent of Europe, *the high-status punishments have slowly driven the low-status punishments out*. Gradually, over the last two hundred years, Europeans have come to see historically low-status punishments as unacceptable survivals of the inegalitarian status-order of the past. More and more offenders have been subjected to the relatively respectful treatment that was the privilege of a tiny stratum of high-status persons in the eighteenth century. In particular, what used to be the privilege of relatively respectful imprisonment has slowly been extended to every inmate. This is a generalization that can only be made in broad outline: I speak of tendencies that, while always present, are never fully realized. What has happened, has happened only within the limits of the possible. There is no way that every ordinary inmate can really be accorded all the accommodations and comforts that an imprisoned Voltaire or an imprisoned Mirabeau once enjoyed. It has happened, in part, only recently: the full-scale abolition of low-status punishments has occurred only over the last twenty-five years, and it is indeed still in the process of occurring. Nevertheless, it has happened. The old "honorable" forms of imprisonment have driven the "dishonorable" forms out: within the limits of the possible, everyone in a continental prison is now treated in the way only aristocrats and the like were once treated, and norms of dignified and respectful treatment have become generalized. This is a development that is, moreover, entirely typical of continental European law: as I have argued elsewhere, in almost every area of the law, we see the same drive toward a kind of high-status egalitarianism—of an egalitarianism that aims to lift everyone up in social standing. These countries are the scene of a *leveling-up* egalitarianism—an egalitarianism whose aim is to raise every member of society up in social status.

High social status for everybody: this is the drive in continental Europe. This drive has caught the attention of continental observers from Rudolf von Jhering in the nineteenth century to Norbert Elias and Pierre Bourdieu in the twentieth. All of these continental authors see the same deep desire among their countrymen to eliminate the vestiges of low status and bring everyone up in social rank. It is a desire that has profoundly affected the continental approach to punishment. High social status for everybody has come to mean high social status even for criminal offenders.

Nothing of the kind has happened in the United States, by contrast, and this reflects the fact that the history of social status in the American world is very different. Our traditions of punishment do not begin the way continental traditions do: with an eighteenth-century practice of making sharp distinctions between high- and low-status punishment. The common law world does not have the same long history of legally guaranteeing high-status treatment for some. In certain ways, in fact, English status differentiation had already begun to break down in the later Middle Ages and sixteenth century. Certainly by the mid-eighteenth century the contract between the continental and Anglo-American worlds was very striking: by around 1750, special high-status treatment had already begun to vanish in both the British colonies and in metropolitan England. Over the course of the nineteenth century, this historic tendency became consistently stronger in the United States, as special high-status treatment was regularly attacked. The consequence is that our large sociological tendency ran in a direction opposite from that of continental Europe. Where nineteenth-century continental Europeans slowly began to *generalize* high-status treatment, nineteenth-century Americans moved strongly to *abolish* high-status treatment. From a very early date, American showed instead, at least sporadically, a typical tendency to generalize norms of *low*-status treatment—to level down. The tale of this American development is, as we shall see, exceedingly complex. Most important, it is bound up with the history of American slavery in ways that have to be carefully traced and carefully weighed. What matters though, for my purposes in this book, is principally what did *not* happen. Americans never displayed the European tendency to maintain and generalize older high-status patterns of treatment.

In this, the law of punishment is, once again, simply typical of the law more broadly: Europeans live with the memory of an age of social hierarchy and feel a corresponding horror at historically low-status punishments. To tolerate the infliction of degrading punishments, for Europeans, is to tolerate a return to the bad old world of the ancient regime, when ordinary people had to fear flogging, mutilation, and worse. We do not live with memories of that kind in the United States (despite our history of slavery), and the European urge to replace low-status punishments with high-status ones is an urge that we do not feel. We can revive old-style public shaming, for example, without feeling any European qualms: humiliating and degrading offenders, for us, does not smack of social hierarchy. We have not learned to think of humiliation and degradation, in the way that Europeans do, as inegalitarian practices.

The connection between traditions of social hierarchy and degradation is my main topic, but it is not my only one. I will also spend some time on another aspect of American liberalism: our traditions of resistance to state power.

Here, too, there is a long tradition of interpretation that seems simply wrong when tested against the American case. At least since Montesquieu, people have believed that harsh punishment is produced by strong states, with relatively unbridled power. Durkheim stated it as nothing less than a "law": the intensity of punishment, he held, depended not only on the complexity of a society, but on the "absolute character" of its state power. This is an idea that is still taken perfectly seriously by scholars, and it is an idea that most ordinary Americans undoubtedly find completely congenial. Following this idea, one would imagine that the countries that punished harshly were what Montesquieu called the "despotic" ones. In particular, one would predict that American, home of a powerful antistatist tradition, would punish mildly. And indeed, most Americans assume that our traditions of resistance to state power, and especially our traditions of procedural protections against prosecution, make our country uniquely liberal in its criminal justice. Yet, despite our unmistakably libertarian traditions, ours, among Western countries, is the one with distinctively harsh punishment.

This, too, is a puzzle for any of us attached to the values of liberalism. Part of the solution to the puzzle is that Americans overestimate the distinctiveness of their traditions. Europeans have procedural protections too, as we shall see. Indeed, they have been actively extending their procedural protections over the last quarter-century. (What is more, even the historical difference is not as sharp as Americans imagine: it has been argued, for example, that the privilege against self-incrimination, far from being an Anglo-American innovation, was borrowed from the continent.)

But this issue goes beyond procedural protections. It is my aim to show that traditions of state power can make for *mildness* in punishment, in ways that our scholarship has not fully grasped—ways that have to do primarily with two aspects of state power: the exercise of systematic mercy, and the tendency toward bureaucratization.

Mercy is the most important of the aspects of state power that I will discuss. Mercy is complex concept. In part, it is a concept that assumes, once again, relations of status hierarchy. Mercy comes *de haut en bas*: superiors accord it to inferiors. In this, mercy is akin to degradation: when we show a person mercy, we confirm his inferior status—more gently, but just as surely, as when we degrade him. A society with a strong tradition of acknowledging and enforcing status differences will thus often be a society with a tradition of mercy.

There is more to the concept of mercy than that, though. Mercy involves respecting individual differences. A merciful justice looks down on the offender, and asks: What is it that might entitle this offender to milder punishment than others who have committed the same offense? In this sense, mercy involves individualization of justice—a willingness to distinguish between more deserving and less deserving persons. The contrary of mercy, as understood in this sense, is formal equality: a system that operates by the principle of formal equality is a system that aims to treat all persons exactly alike, extending no special mercy to anyone. Kant is the most famous advocate of a species of formal equality that excludes mercy, and his best-known passage presents his view with a kind of Old Testament fury: "The law of punishment is a categorical imperative, and woe to him who creeps along the serpent paths of the theory of social welfare hoping to turn up some argument that makes it seem like good policy to release him from his punishment, or diminish it." When we reject mercy, in the spirit of this slightly terrifying passage, we refuse to countenance any special treatment for any offender.

As we shall see, the values of mercy have shown themselves to be much stronger in French and German justice, over the last quarter-century, than in American justice. This is partly because practices of mercy that date back to the eighteenth century, and beyond, have never died in continental Europe: both France and Germany still dispense general amnesties, just as the royal and princely government of the eighteenth century did. But it is not just a matter of the literal survival of ancient regime practices of mercy. It is also that a vaguer spirit of mercy pervades continental justice. Individualization of punishment, and a concern for individual deserts, run throughout both French and German law. American law, by contrast, is much more hesitant to individualize. To be sure, there is plenty of mercy in America, as we shall see. Nevertheless, the strong tendency of the last twenty-five years has been toward a formal equality of nearly Kantian severity, and there is no doubt that America differs dramatically from continental Europe by this measure. Unlike the French or the Germans, we display a powerful drive to hit every offender equally hard.

Why are the values of mercy so much stronger in continental Europe?

Part of the answer that I will give takes us back once more to the European history of status hierarchy. Mercy does indeed come *de haut en bas*, and a long continental tradition of condoning grace can still be detected in the law of today. Moreover, traditions of status-oriented thinking have conditioned continental jurists to think in terms of distinctions between persons in a way that is relatively alien to American legal thought. Making distinctions between persons has been the stuff of continental law for centuries: French and German jurists have always resisted the idea that everybody is exactly alike. One consequence is that today both French and German justice are much readier than American justice to make individualizing distinctions among offenders. Formal equality is just not at home in continental Europe. Traditions of status are not the only source of the strength of the values of mercy in continental Europe, though. Those values have another taproot too, and one that is of fundamental importance for understanding the shape of continental criminal justice: France and Germany are countries with much stronger states than ours.

What we mean by a "strong" state is, of course, no simple matter; the proposition that France and Germany have stronger states calls for some real care in definition. For my purposes here, I will mean two things when I describe continental states as "strong": Germany and France have state apparatuses that are both relatively *powerful* and relatively *autonomous*. They are powerful in the sense that they are relatively free to intervene in civil society without losing political legitimacy. They are autonomous in the sense that they are steered by bureaucracies that are relatively immune to the vagaries of public opinion. The relative power and autonomy of these continental states, I am going to argue, has done a great deal to keep the values of mercy alive in continental society and promote other forms of mildness in criminal punishment as well.

The connection between state power and mercy is clearest in the survival of amnesties, and in the various ways in which the old practice of pardoning has persisted in modern practices of "individualization." The power of the continental states has also produced another, especially important, form of mildness: both Germany and France display a notable tendency to define many acts, not as *mala in se*, but as *mala prohibita*—not as acts evil in themselves, but simply as acts the state may choose to prohibit through the exercise of its sovereign power. This capacity to define forbidden acts as merely forbidden, not evil, has been of great important for the establishment of relatively mild orders of punishment in contemporary Europe. The contrast with the United States in stark: as I will try to show, contemporary American law has a strong tendency to define all offenses as inherently evil and consequently to punish them harshly. And as I will suggest, the capacity to define offenses merely as *mala prohibita* is a capacity that European states enjoy largely because the exercise of state power has much more untroubled legitimacy in continental Europe than it does in the United States.

State power, in short, has made for mildness, in continental punishment. This is a claim that will seem exceedingly paradoxical to Americans. We have a very long tradition of resisting state power, and many protections for offenders that involve guarantees of due process. (Indeed, in general Americans tend to have procedural protections where Europeans have substantive ones.) Moreover, it is certainly the case that state power does not always breed mildness in continental Europe. There are undeniably aspects of continental justice in which the application of state power comes down hard—most importantly in investigative custody, the preconviction form of imprisonment that is the focus of the worst problems in continental incarceration. But these differences do not alter the picture of the divergence of the last quarter-century. If continental Europeans have a weaker tradition of procedural protections, it is nevertheless the case they have been working to improve their procedural protections over the last twenty-five years. In this too, the continental tale is a tale of a deep structural drive toward increased mildness. Indeed, even with the problems of investigative custody taken into account, the strength of continental states has, I am going to try to show, made the application of the power to punish far more sparing than it is here at home. State power has turned out, in northern continental Europe, to make for mild punishment.

Much mercy comes, in fact, from the *power* of continental states. Much mercy comes from their *autonomy* too. This is partly for a reason that is obvious—indeed, a reason that has captured the attention of every thoughtful commentator on the American punishment scene. American punishment practices are largely driven by a kind of mass politics that has not succeeded in capturing Western European state practices. We have, as many commentators observe, "popular justice," and indeed populist justice. The harshness of American punishment is made in the volatile and often vicious currents of American democratic electioneering. Calling one's opponent "soft on crime" has become a staple of American campaigning—even in judgeship elections, whose candidates were longtime holdouts for norms of decorum, and this has had a powerful, often spectacular, impact on the making of harsh criminal legislation in the United States. Even practices that have nothing directly to do with election campaigns are part of a momentous American pattern—a pattern in which public officials use garish punishments as a way of grabbing political publicity. Prosecutors, in particular, have been making political hay all over the country through actions such as leading Wall Street executives out of their offices in handcuffs or televising the names of the busted clients of prostitutes.

Politicians in continental Europe do sometimes try to play to the same public instincts that American politicians play to. For the most part, though, American-style politics has failed to exert an American-style influence on German or French criminal justice, as we shall see. Part of explaining why France and Germany are different involved explaining why this kind of politics has not made any headway in those countries, and that, in turn, involves exploring the relative autonomy of German and French state apparatuses. Manifestly, the weakness of the politics of harsh punishment in Germany and France reflects the autonomy of the state in both countries: what is at work in both countries is a basic tension identified long ago by Max Weber; the tension between democratic politics and bureaucratic control. In both Germany and France, bureaucrats have succeeded in keeping control of the punishment process, without becoming subject to decisive pressure from a stirred-up public. The success of bureaucratic control also has some other consequences for continental punishment, as we shall see: consequences such as the careful effort to define and train prison guards as civil servants.

There is, in fact, an intimate nexus between the politics of mass mobilization, unchecked by bureaucracy, and the making of harshness in criminal punishment, and that is a fact that should raise some uncomfortable questions for any of us who like to think of ourselves as committed to the values of democracy. Part of what I want to do, in this book, is to weigh those questions and to ask how uncomfortable they should make us.

. . .

As this summary suggests, my argument will take some complex turns. Nevertheless, at the end of the day, my claim will be a simple one, and one that I think ought to have special resonance in America. Criminal punishment is milder in continental Europe today largely because Europeans have been shaped by social and political traditions that we in the United States have vigorously rejected. The continental Europe of today is recognizably descended from continental Europe of the eighteenth and even the seventeenth centuries. It is a world of strong, condescending states, with a close historical connection to norms of social hierarchy.

It is, in short, the world whose values the traditions of the American Revolution condemned. Americans already feared strong states and strong traditions of social hierarchy in the eighteenth century; and most of them undoubtedly still associate strong states and strong traditions of social hierarchy with all that is harsh and nasty in human relations. Yet, in the long run, I am going to try to show, the traditions of the continent have developed into the milder traditions, at least in the law of punishment.

This is thus partly a book about the legacy of the American Revolution. I also hope it will be read as a book about the character of criminal punishment more broadly. Our parting of the ways with Europe, over the last twenty-five years, should force us to confront some fundamental, and hard, questions about the workings of criminal justice. Degradation matters in ways that our philosophies of criminal punishment have neglected. There are unexpected facets of the exercise of state power that matter in neglected ways as well. Most of all, social and political traditions matter. Criminal punishment is not something that can be analyzed in abstract and general terms. It differs deeply from society to society, and it differs in ways that reflect fundamental divergences in social and political values.

One final preliminary word, and one methodological caveat, before I begin. The preliminary word: in making my argument, there is one seemingly obvious explanation for the differences between the United States and continental Europe that I will downplay. This is the explanation that holds that continental justice is milder today because the continental countries experienced fascism and Nazism. German and French lawyers can often be heard making this claim: their countries, they say, learned the lesson of fascism in the 1930s and 1940s, and that is why they have turned to humane practices today. This claim is by no means entirely false, and I will try to do justice to it. Nevertheless, it is by no means entirely true either. The place of the fascist period in European development is much more ambiguous than this frequently repeated explanation would suggest. Moreover, the historical roots of the differences are far older than the fascist period, and indeed far older than the twentieth century.

The methodological caveat: the characterizations of both American and continental European systems that I offer in this book are not offered as true characterizations in the absolute sense. This is a study in *comparative* law, and accordingly my claims will be comparative ones and not absolute. This is nothing to be apologetic about. It is precisely the capacity of comparative lawyers to identify relative differences that gives comparative law its special value. No absolute descriptive claim about any legal system is ever true. Human society is much too complex for that; there are always exceptions. If we make the absolute claim, for example, that American law is committed to the values of the free market, we are saying something false: there are many exceptions. On the other hand, if we claim that American law is *more* committed to the values of the free market than are those of comparable legal systems, we are saying something that is both true and extremely important. As this example suggests, relative claims can be a good bit more revealing than absolute ones. Therein lies the unique strength of comparative law. It is precisely because they deal in relative claims that comparative lawyers can walk the high road to the understanding of human legal systems, as they have been trying to do since Montesquieu.

At the same time, comparative lawyers always run the risk of creating false impressions—of seeming to claim more than they should. Let me therefore emphasize that my claims in this book *are* relative ones. I do not mean to argue that American punishment is always and everywhere harsh and degrading, and I certainly do not mean to argue that German or French punishment is never degrading or never harsh. I do not mean to deny that there are regional differences in America—just as there are regional differences in Germany and France. What I mean to say is that American punishment is often more degrading and often harsher—and that where we find these relative differences, we can detect the intermittent strength of some real, if subterranean, differences in fundamental values that are widely shared in each of the three societies that I discuss.

THE BENEVOLENT PATERNALISM OF
JAPANESE CRIMINAL JUSTICE

Daniel H. Foote

INTRODUCTION

Japan's criminal justice system has been widely praised both within Japan and abroad as both highly efficient and generally lenient. There is much truth to these characterizations. Japan's clearance rate—the percentage of reported crimes that are solved—is among the highest in the world, and its conviction rate stands at more than 99.8 percent. Yet fewer than 5 percent of the adult suspects considered by police to have committed Penal Code offenses are sentenced to prison; those who are sentenced to prison serve a median sentence of under two years.

Some commentators, however, remain skeptical of Japanese criminal justice. Takeo Ishimatsu, a former High Court judge who handled criminal matters for most of his forty-year career, recently generated shock waves within Japan by flatly asserting that prosecutors and not the courts conducted the real trials of Japanese criminal defendants. A leading criminal procedure scholar and former president of Tokyo University, Ryūichi Hirano, went so far as to label Japan's criminal justice system "abnormal," "diseased," and even "hopeless."

MODELS OF CRIMINAL JUSTICE

Commentators have long recognized two recurrent themes in the American debate over the criminal justice system: an emphasis on repression of criminal conduct, on the one hand, and a "solicitude" for the rights of the individual, on the other. Herbert Packer neatly synthesized these themes and labeled them the "crime-control" and "due process" models, respectively.

The crime-control model, as Packer described it, "is based on the proposition that the repression of criminal conduct is by far the most important function to be performed by the criminal process." The key to achieving that end, he concluded, is "the efficiency with which

Reprinted from Daniel H. Foote, "The Benevolent Paternalism of Japanese Criminal Justice," *California Law Review* 80: 317 (1992). Permission courtesy of the University of California Berkeley School of Law.

the criminal process operates to screen suspects, determine guilt, and secure appropriate dispositions of persons convicted of crime." Applying that model to the United States—where, as he noted, a wide range of behavior is treated as criminal, the amount of crime is very high, and increases in the quantity and quality of resources devoted to crime suppression are unlikely—Packer described several additional attributes of the model necessary for it to operate successfully. The model, according to Packer, "must produce a high rate of apprehension and conviction." The combination of high crime and limited resources requires an emphasis on "speed and finality." In turn, the desire for speed leads to an emphasis on both informality and uniformity: by preferring such informal processes as interrogation at a police station to formal examination in open court, the "facts" can be established more quickly, and by treating cases in a uniform, basically administrative manner pursuant to "[r]outine, stereotyped procedures," the process can move to a prompt, "successful" conclusion.

Packer's due-process model, by contrast, "stresses the possibility of error" and places great weight on avoiding mistakes. In place of the crime-control model's confidence in administrative fact-finding, the due-process model "insist[s] on formal, adjudicative, adversary fact-finding processes in which the factual case against the accused is publicly heard by an impartial tribunal." In addition to this emphasis on reliability rather than efficiency, the due-process model is also premised on the complementary concepts of "the primacy of the individual and ... limitation on official power." Motivated by a concern over the potential for abuse of power, the due-process model establishes numerous restrictions on administrative fact-finding and vindicates those restrictions through the criminal process itself by excluding evidence and reversing convictions even in cases in which the evidence strongly points to guilt.

The Battle Model and the Family Model

Packer claimed that his two models embraced the entire range of value choices underlying the criminal process. [John] Griffiths took issue with that characterization, arguing that Packer's two models in fact represented only two aspects of a single model—what Griffiths labeled the "battle model"—and that one could imagine other possible models, most notably the family model. Griffiths noted that Packer assumed a fundamental irreconcilability between the interests of the state and the interests of the individual. The basic goal of the state, as Griffiths interpreted Packer, is "to put a suspected criminal in jail"; the goal of the individual is, presumably, to stay out of jail. Both the crime-control and due-process models, suggested Griffiths, share a common conception of implacable hostility between the individual and the state: the models differ only in where they place the balance in the battle between the adversaries. Thus, Griffiths concluded, "[w]hat [Packer] gives us is a single Battle Model with two possibilities of bias."

Griffiths suggested that one can imagine an alternative criminal justice system premised not on "disharmony, fundamentally irreconcilable interests, a state of war," but rather on "reconcilable—even mutually supportive—interests, a state of love." Taking as his template the institution of the family, Griffiths offered a number of attributes for this family model. First and foremost, the system would be based not on punishment as such, but on seeking to reform the offending member, keeping that individual's best interests at heart.

In Griffiths' formulation, this approach in turn would have a wide variety of implications for the criminal process. Among the most notable of these would be a "basic faith in public officials," without which the family model "could not exist": "[E]veryone would assume . . . that if a public official has a particular role or duty, he can be expected to carry it out in good faith and using his best judgment."

Griffiths seemed to envision a system that would entail very little intrusion on the personal autonomy of individuals. He stated that the family model would "minimize social intervention by limiting such intervention to situations in which an individual has failed to exercise the required self-control." In addition, he claimed that under the family model the "change in our attitude toward criminal defendants would bring with it a thoroughgoing respect for their rights and their dignity and their individuality, going far beyond the purely formal respect which now attaches to the defendant." This thoroughgoing respect, he suggested, would carry with it a notion of protection for the integrity of the persons and homes of the guilty as well as of the innocent. Ultimately, Griffiths seemed to imagine a world in which criminal justice authorities leave everyone alone unless someone commits a transgression necessitating intervention, at which point they respond with love and respect, maintaining the rehabilitation of the individual as their key goal.

The Benevolent-Paternalism Model

Griffiths expressly acknowledged that his family model was nowhere directly applicable; he was simply "set[ting his] mind free to wonder" about possible alternatives. One could just as easily imagine an alternative, however, that would display concern for rehabilitation and reform of the offender but would lack the family model's respect for the personal autonomy of the individual. This alternative, which I refer to as the benevolent-paternalism model, would also be characterized by great faith in public officials. Yet this model would not only permit, indeed it would expect, public officials to maintain careful watch over the members of society. At least in cases in which individuals are suspected of misbehavior, moreover, the benevolent-paternalism model would entrust public officials with the authority to intrude on the personal autonomy of suspects to the extent deemed appropriate both for clarifying the nature of the individual's conduct and for determining the most suitable means of achieving reformation. The authorities would be given a relatively free hand to uncover whatever information they considered relevant, but after uncovering that information they would be expected to treat the suspect in the manner most suited to rehabilitation and re-integration into the community.

JAPAN'S CRIMINAL JUSTICE SYSTEM

Historical Overview

Before turning to an examination of criminal justice in Japan today, a brief historical excursus may be useful. During the Tokugawa era (1600–1868), members of the public bore a broad duty to assist investigative officials in reporting crimes. A further key source of information on crime was the so-called *meakashi*, private persons whom shogunate officials paid to uncover crime and arrest suspects. Apparently, however, offenders often paid *meakashi* not to reveal crimes. Given widespread reports of these and other abuses, the level of respect for *meakashi* probably was not high. The collection of evidence and close questioning of suspects by *meakashi*, however, along with intensive pretrial questioning by shogunate investigators, permitted shogunate officials to guard against the possibility of an acquittal at the ultimate trial stage. The occurrence of such an acquittal was regarded as a disgrace that might undermine respect in the shogunate officials themselves.

Confessions played a central role in the Tokugawa criminal process, and torture was an accepted and carefully codified means of obtaining them. Confessions were regarded as the best evidence of truth and reportedly also played an important role in maintaining public trust in the shogunate criminal justice process by ensuring that those accused of crime had submitted to public authority. There is little to suggest, however, that confessions served a rehabilitative purpose, at least during the first half of the Tokugawa period. On the contrary, during that period the emphasis was squarely on general deterrence, achieved through the public imposition of harsh penalties, such as parading the heads of offenders. Even during the last half of the Tokugawa period, Japan's criminal justice system continued to be characterized by stiff penalties. As late as 1873, five years after the Meiji Restoration, more than nine hundred people were executed in a one-year period in Japan.

Nonetheless, during the long era of peace and stability in Tokugawa Japan the criminal justice system increasingly became characterized by elements of specific prevention. The authorities regularized the use of pardons with explicit emphasis on rehabilitative goals and established a system for putting some offenders to work at hard labor, again with expressly rehabilitative objectives. Spurred at least in part by Western influence, this trend accelerated in the Meiji era. By as early as 1885, Justice Minister Yamada was urging limiting the use of imprisonment for minor crimes—in part to save money, but in part to avoid recidivism. And in 1914 Procurator General Hiranuma sharply rejected the notion that all offenders must be punished, instead urging the widespread use of oral exhortations and admonishments in cases in which those steps would be sufficient to prevent future wrongdoing. This trend toward specific prevention also received strong theoretical support from Japanese adherents of the so-called "new school" of criminal justice. Influenced by the thinking of European scholars, this school, which gained considerable strength in Japan early in this century, emphasized that criminal behavior was the result of identifiable causes, and that the primary role of penalties therefore should be to eliminate these underlying causes through education, rehabilitation, and specific deterrence.

Western-influenced reforms of other aspects of criminal procedure following the Meiji Restoration included a prohibition of torture and elimination of the requirement that convictions be based on confessions. As a practical matter, however, confessions remained the centerpiece of most proceedings. Investigators used a wide variety of tools, including intimidation and physical abuse, to procure confessions from unwilling suspects. Yet in keeping with the trend toward specific prevention described above, there are clear indications that sincere confessions came to be regarded as playing an important role in the rehabilitation of suspects and their reintegration into society. The most celebrated such example was the "conversion" (*tenkó*) of thousands of leftists who repudiated their communist ideology and in turn received complete forgiveness from governmental authorities.

During the period through the end of World War II investigators had broad authority to conduct searches and seizures. In keeping with the continental model on which the Japanese criminal justice system was based, a "preliminary judge" conducted a second, preliminary investigation after police and prosecutors completed their initial investigation. The results of that judge's preliminary investigation, which included further questioning of the suspect, were set forth in a dossier that in principle contained all the files relating to the case. The trial consisted primarily of a confirmation of the findings of the preliminary investigation based on a review of the written record and questioning of the defendant.

Following World War II, the Allied Occupation sought to achieve "fundamental change of the criminological attitude" in Japan. This task demanded basic changes in numerous aspects of Japan's criminal justice system through the establishment of a broad set of constitutional protections as well as statutory revisions. The Occupation reforms included strengthening the warrant requirements for both arrests and searches and establishing broad limits on searches and seizures. Particularly important was a set of interrelated constitutional and statutory provisions designed to restrict opportunities to obtain confessions and to limit prosecutorial reliance on confessions. The reforms erected a constitutional privilege against self-incrimination, a statutory right to refuse to answer questions (coupled with a duty of investigators to notify the suspect of that right), and both constitutional and statutory prohibitions against admission at trial of coerced confessions. The Occupation also sought to foster a vigorous adversary system and to ensure that the formal trial itself would be the key step in the criminal justice process. To this end, the new procedure abolished the preliminary judge's examination of suspects and established strict rules against the use of hearsay evidence.

Current Practice

Investigation: Thorough and Careful

The postwar reforms might appear to have placed Japan's criminal justice system squarely within the due-process model.

In actual practice this has not been the case. Because the specific language of the Constitution and Code of Criminal Procedure is narrower than the rhetoric of the Occupation might suggest, and because courts have interpreted these written provisions narrowly, the current criminal justice system in Japan provides wide discretion to the investigative authorities. There is considerable potential for intrusion on personal autonomy.

The organization of the police force and its manner of patrolling bring the Japanese police into much closer contact with individuals and the community than is currently the case in the United States. Although this might in part be an inevitable result of the fact that Japan has far less land than the United States, Japan also has considerably fewer police per capita than does the United States. What brings the police into closer contact with the community is the stationing of police in local police boxes (*kōban* and *chūzaisho*) within each neighborhood or town, coupled with regular patrolling through neighborhoods on either foot or bicycle. A considerably higher level of contact also arises from twice-yearly residential surveys, in which police are supposed to visit every residential unit and inquire about such matters as the name and age of each resident, employment or other activities, automobile ownership, and the like. This information is kept on file at the police box and may be used for criminal investigations (and, presumably, other purposes as well). Furthermore, at least in certain areas in Japan, fixed cameras not only regulate traffic but also provide routine surveillance. In various ways, therefore, the authorities keep close watch on individuals.

When an individual comes under suspicion of criminal conduct, the authorities have wide discretion to investigate. As mentioned above, among the postwar reforms was the establishment of a new set of limits on searches and seizures. Article 35 of the Constitution provides that "[t]he right of all persons to be secure in their homes, papers and effects against entries, searches and seizures shall not be impaired except upon warrant issued for adequate cause and particularly describing the place to be searched and things to be seized." The Code of Criminal Procedure provides for an exception to the warrant requirement for searches incident to arrest. As interpreted by the courts, searches pursuant to this exception extend quite far. The Supreme Court has upheld the warrantless search of an entire house by four policemen who were waiting for the suspect to arrive home so that they could arrest him.

The courts have also limited the reach of the warrant requirement by construing narrowly the concept of a "search." In rather baffling language from one leading case, the Supreme Court indicated that police officers who, acting without a warrant, had unzipped a bowling-ball bag over the objections of the two suspects, had not conducted a search. Rather, the Court held that such action was permissible as a "measure incident to the stop and questioning" of the suspects—who were shortly thereafter arrested for armed bank robbery when the police discovered some of the stolen money inside the bag.

For Japanese investigators, however, the questioning of suspected criminals is considerably more important than searches and seizures. Notwithstanding the elaborate postwar reforms in the area of interrogation and confessions, Japanese police and prosecutors possess broad powers for preindictment interrogation. Police may request individuals to cooperate voluntarily in questioning and to "voluntarily accompany" them to the police station for such questioning. As interpreted by the Japanese courts, this police power to suggest voluntary accompaniment may be quite broad indeed. In the most extreme reported case to date, the so-called Takanawa Green Mansion Case, four police officers met a murder suspect at his company dormitory one morning and, without arresting him, asked him to accompany them to the police station in their police car. At the station, officers questioned the suspect throughout that day and late into the evening. The questioning continued for three more days; on each of the intervening nights, officers placed the suspect in a nearby hotel room where he could be kept under observation. Finally, the suspect's mother came to Tokyo and signed a form asking the police to release her son into her custody. A divided panel of the Supreme Court concluded that the police had not exceeded the bounds of voluntary accompaniment.

When the police have probable cause and choose to arrest a suspect, that arrest will trigger a period of up to twenty-three days that may be utilized in whole or in part for questioning. Under the current Code of Criminal Procedure, the police must decide whether to release or refer a suspect to the prosecutors within forty-eight hours after arrest. The prosecutors then have another twenty-four hours within which to decide whether to release the suspect or go to court to seek a warrant for the suspect's detention. The initial detention warrant authorizes detention for ten days; the prosecutors are then entitled to seek a ten-day extension of the detention period before they must decide whether to indict the suspect. In practice, police refer more than 90 percent of the suspects they arrest for Penal Code offenses to the prosecutors, and the prosecutors request detention for approximately 85 percent of those suspects (with ten additional days of detention for about one-third of them). Under the Code, prosecutors normally must show a fear of flight or destruction of evidence in order to obtain a detention warrant. They obviously have little trouble doing so: requests for such warrants (whether for the initial ten days or the extension) are granted more than 99.7 percent of the time.

Some scholars have argued that, in light of the limited statutory purposes for detention, the detention period should not be used for interrogation. That position has never been accepted, however. On the contrary, other statutory language dating from the Occupation reforms expressly contemplates the questioning of suspects who are under arrest or detention. Prosecutors freely acknowledge their use of the detention period for interrogation, even stating that the key purposes of preindictment detention are "questioning the suspect, demanding a confession, and pursuing other crimes."

Under the Code, the suspect has the right to remain silent during questioning and must be informed of this right. A literal reading of the Code, however, supports the inference that a suspect who is under arrest or detention has no right to leave the interrogation room, and there is no requirement that investigators break off questioning if a suspect asserts the right to silence. In practice, therefore, these standards have resulted in the so-called duty to submit to questioning—the duty to sit in the interrogation room and listen to the questions or comments of the investigators—during the period of up to twenty-three days while the suspect is under arrest or detention.

Of course investigators do not have time to question each suspect throughout all that time, but they do consider obtaining a confession to be a vital part of each case. And they usually succeed: approximately 90 percent of Japanese cases involve full confessions, and in most of the remainder the defendant confesses to all but certain elements of the crime (such as intent).

For Japanese investigators, however, obtaining a confession signifies more than just getting the suspect to admit to having committed the crime. It entails obtaining a thorough account of all relevant details of the crime and the personal background and circumstances of the suspect, including possible involvement in other crimes. Obtaining a confession also means getting the suspect to accept moral responsibility. Yet despite the importance of confessions, the confession statement itself need not include a verbatim account of the suspect's words. To the contrary, it is a standard and court-approved practice for investigators to prepare summarized confession statements following—sometimes long after—the conclusion of one or even several interrogation sessions. These summarized confession statements typically form the heart of the evidence introduced at trial. Furthermore, the constitutional and statutory prohibitions on use of involuntary confessions have been construed narrowly. As a practical matter courts almost always focus their attention on questions concerning the reliability, rather than the voluntariness, of confessions.

Another right strongly promoted by the Occupation was the right to counsel. In practice, though, the role of defense counsel has proven to be quite limited. Counsel are never permitted to attend interrogation sessions. Moreover, even when the suspect has access to and can afford counsel, the Code of Criminal Procedure permits investigators to impose conditions on meetings between the suspect and counsel. Investigators are not shy about using this authority. According to various estimates, meetings with counsel may be limited to fifteen minutes once every four or five days in complex or difficult cases, and a suspect in detention is unlikely to have much opportunity to meet with counsel until the prosecutors have finalized their case. Fewer than one-quarter of defendants are released on bail, and for the remainder, meetings must occur at the detention facility.

The role of the adversary process—and even the formal trial itself—remains highly circumscribed. Japan has few lawyers and fewer still who take criminal cases. In the view of many prosecutors, defense counsel often display low levels of skill and effort. From the standpoint of defense attorneys, the superior strength of the prosecutor's investigative powers can make criminal cases seem hopeless. There is also the perception among defense counsel that contesting cases, rather than simply confessing and showing remorse, can result in harsher penalties.

Furthermore, despite the Occupation's goals of invigorating both the adversary process and the trial itself more along a U.S. model, most Japanese trials in fact are dominated by a written file, prepared not by a preliminary judge but by the prosecutors. The trial consists primarily of confirming the results of the investigation as reported in this file. This prosecutorial dominance has led to widespread characterizations of Japan's criminal justice system as "prosecutorial justice" (*kensatsukan shihō*) and "trial by dossier" (*chōsho saiban*). And it is this aspect of Japanese criminal justice in particular that Judge Ishimatsu was focusing on when he asserted that "criminal defendants in Japan do not receive trials by judges." In Ishimatsu's view, "criminal trials ... are conducted in closed rooms by the investigators, and the proceedings in open court are merely a formal ceremony [to confirm the conclusions of the investigators]."

Prosecution of Cases: Benevolence at Work

The Police: Bizai Shobun Japanese police boast one of the highest rates for clearing reported crimes of any system in the world. Even excluding cases involving professional or gross negligence causing death or bodily injury by traffic accident (all of which were reported as cleared), the 1988 official overall clearance rate for Penal Code offenses was 59.8 percent. Yet police arrested fewer than 20 percent of the adult Penal Code suspects they themselves identified. Does this mean that the police were wrong more than 80 percent of the time? That there was no more than minimal intrusion on the personal autonomy of the unarrested 80 percent? Apparently neither.

In Japan, a crime may be treated as cleared even if police have not arrested a suspect for it. Only a relatively small percentage of those identified as suspects are later deemed to have had nothing to do with the crime in question, and 80 percent of all identified suspects are not arrested. Yet the substantial majority of those not arrested are nevertheless subject to prosecution on what is frequently referred to as an "at-home basis." In other words, these suspects are not arrested and legally have no duty to present themselves to the authorities for questioning, but their cases are sent on to the prosecutors for further proceedings.

Even before referral, however, a substantial minority of the cases—nearly 40 percent of adult Penal Code offenders in recent years—are closed by the police as petty offenses. In principle, this option, known as *bizai shobun* (disposition of trivial crimes), is reserved for a specified list of minor offenses, including assault, theft, fraud, embezzlement, and gambling. Given the breadth of several of these offenses, police have considerable discretion over what to treat as minor. Suspects in this category are not punished in a formal sense. Yet neither are they cleared from the system free from any consequences whatsoever. On the contrary, pursuant to official investigation standards, if police release a suspect on the basis of *bizai shobun* they must take certain steps. Police are required to counsel the suspect sternly and admonish him or her not to commit crimes in the future. Accordingly, suspects can expect to be questioned carefully and given a lecture by police. They may also be required to sign an apology and pledge not to engage in inappropriate behavior again. The investigation standards also instruct police to call in a member of the suspect's family, the suspect's employer, or some other such responsible individual, counsel that person to keep close watch over the suspect in the future, and even have that person undertake in writing to provide such ongoing supervision. Finally, police are required to persuade the suspect to provide restitution, to make an apology, or to take other appropriate measures for the victim. In addition, a record of the *bizai shobun* will be kept, which presumably will affect decisions on leniency in the event of future wrongdoing.

Thus, for relatively minor crimes in the category of *bizai shobun*, police have discretion to withhold formal sanctions and avoid substantially disrupting the life of the suspect. In an effort to deter any future misbehavior, police nonetheless seek to impress upon the suspect the gravity of the situation and its potential consequences as a means of deterring any future misbehavior. As a group, police are undoubtedly the most deterrence-minded among criminal justice authorities in Japan. Yet in handling cases of this sort and in recommending that the prosecutors deal leniently with suspects who have "shown sincere repentance," police give considerable weight to interests of rehabilitation and specific prevention.

There are at least two broad categories of cases in which police decline to arrest a suspect but still refer him to the prosecutors on an at-home basis. If police have received a formal complaint of crime from a victim or other person, the Code of Criminal Procedure requires the police to refer the matter to the prosecutors. Thus, even if the police feel that a complaint is groundless or that the matter is insignificant, they must refer the case to the prosecutors, but in such cases they are unlikely to arrest anyone. Many other at-home referrals fall into a second category, however. These involve relatively serious offenses, with substantial evidence that a particular suspect is guilty. In such cases, even if there has been a formal complaint, the police may nonetheless conclude that there is no need for a formal arrest if factors such as the nature of the crime and the suspect's personal circumstances so indicate. Again, this does not mean that the suspect is not questioned by the police. On the contrary, this latter category of cases is composed almost entirely of suspects who voluntarily cooperate in the investigation, and such "voluntary" questioning can be lengthy and intense. But in cases in which they refer suspects to the prosecutors without arresting the suspect, the police are implicitly determining that the interest in maintaining order does not necessitate arrest and that the interest in reforming the suspect would best be served by minimizing disruption in the suspect's life. At least in the case of moderately serious crime, police almost certainly will take this approach only if the suspect provides a full and apparently sincere confession and displays true remorse.

The absence of a formal arrest requires further comment. Although there are other, more severe types of stigma in the Japanese criminal justice system, I am convinced that arrest is in practice the most important. In part, this reflects the practical consequences: an arrest carries with it the prospect of physical confinement for at least forty-eight hours and potentially much longer. The first such confinement, presumably, has the greatest psychological and symbolic impact on the individual. More importantly, despite the existence of a presumption of innocence under Japanese law, upon arrest a suspect is widely regarded by the media and the public as guilty. The arrest record can also have a significant effect on employment, community attitudes, and other social relations.

The powerful stigma of arrest, I believe, helps to explain in part why Japanese courts have been willing to relax greatly the standards for voluntary accompaniment. The courts seem inclined to let police use considerable "persuasion" to convince suspects to consent to accompaniment and questioning, rather than force the police to take the formal and stigmatizing step of arrest. Other factors, however, provide the primary rationale for the broad license that courts have recognized in the area of voluntary accompaniment. These include great deference to the perceived needs of investigators and, apparently, a feeling that such police intrusions are not unreasonable.

One further observation is in order. Although the Japanese policy of limiting arrest can avoid stigma for some suspects, the relaxed standards on voluntary accompaniment have the further effect of insulating police from constitutional and statutory limitations on arrest and questioning. So long as questioning is "voluntary," the warrant requirements do not come into play, nor does the clock begin to run on the time period for referral to the prosecutors.

The Prosecutors: Suspension of Prosecution   At the next stage of the criminal process, prosecutors have broad discretion over both investigation and disposition of cases. The prosecutors can and, for suspects who have been arrested, usually do seek warrants for at least ten days of detention. As noted earlier, prosecutors request detention for about 85 percent of the arrestees referred to them and, across nearly every category of warrants, such requests are granted more than 99 percent of the time. In addition, for those suspects referred to the prosecutors on an at-home basis, cooperation remains the rule.

Although prosecutors investigate other evidence and question other witnesses, the centerpiece of the investigation is ordinarily the interrogation of the suspect. During this interrogation, the investigators seek to gather all relevant details of the crime. In addition, however, they carefully explore the suspect's motives, family background and other personal circumstances, and involvement in any other crimes. As should be apparent from its breadth, interrogation plays a major role not only in proving the crime but also in determining the manner in which the prosecutors will treat the suspect. Moreover, the authorities regard close one-on-one questioning as their most important tool for leading suspects to accept full moral responsibility for their misdeeds and for setting them on the road to rehabilitation.

In addition, prosecutors normally interview the victim or the victim's heirs not just for evidence relating to the crime but also regarding such matters as restitution and the victim's feeling toward the suspect. The prosecutors may also obtain information about the suspect's character and background from the suspect's family and employer and from other members of the community.

All of this information is relevant to prosecutors in determining how to dispose of cases, a determination that is heavily influenced by the goal of specific prevention. Approximately 6.5 percent of suspects referred to the prosecutors for nontraffic-related Penal Code offenses are not prosecuted because of insufficient evidence or other weaknesses in the prosecution's case. A somewhat larger group of nontraffic-related Penal Code offenses, approximately 15 percent, is closed through uncontested summary proceedings—not available for major crimes—in which the maximum penalty is a fine of ¥200,000 (about US$1,500 at current exchange rates).

A much larger group of suspects, covering the entire spectrum of criminal behavior, falls into the "suspension of prosecution" category. The doctrine of suspension of prosecution has existed since the 1880s and was formalized by statute in 1922. It expressly permits prosecutors to refrain from prosecuting a case about which they conclude that, despite solid evidence of guilt, prosecution would not be in the interests of justice. Although suspension of prosecution initially was used only for minor crimes, in much the same manner as *bizai shobun* today, by around 1900 prosecutors had begun to use the system for more serious crimes.

As the suspension-of-prosecution doctrine has been interpreted and applied since early in this century, moreover, the emphasis has been squarely on seeking to reform offenders and ensure their reintegration into the community. The doctrine seeks to obviate the stigma of indictment and conviction and the potentially detrimental impact of incarceration.

This emphasis on specific prevention remains a central element of suspended prosecutions. A recent study by five Ministry of Justice researchers characterized suspension of prosecution in the following way:

> Recently, "avoidance of labeling" is frequently cited as one of the reasons, from the standpoint of criminal justice policy, for suspended prosecutions. Yet the avoidance of labeling simply follows from the guiding principle of suspension of prosecution. Prosecutions are not suspended in order to avoid labeling. Rather, the avoidance of labeling occurs as a consequence of suspending prosecutions for the purpose of rehabilitating offenders.

In analyzing the goals of this system, the authors concluded:

> Japanese prosecutors have two primary missions. One is that of the strict prosecutor who does not let the evil sleep and who cries along with the victims. The other is that of the prosecutor who devotes efforts to the reform of offenders so that they will not return to crime, a role that at times entails crying along with the offenders. . . . Suspension of prosecution is a key tool for prosecutors in achieving this [latter] mission.

Factors influencing prosecutors in the decision whether to suspend prosecution include the character and personal circumstances of the suspect, prior criminal record, age, family situation, and employment status; remorse and acceptance of responsibility; restitution to the victim; the views of the victim; and the gravity of the crime. The suspect's chances of obtaining suspension of prosecution can be enhanced by statements from family, employers, or even other members of the community demonstrating that support will be available to the suspect.

Some of these factors, in particular the attention paid to the gravity of the crime, reflect general deterrence concerns. Certain crimes are regarded as so serious that prosecution is essential in order to send a message to other potential offenders and to society in general, although highly mitigating circumstances can still result in suspension of prosecution. Other factors, including the role played by the views of the victim, reflect a retributive function, although forgiveness by the victim can also be seen as playing an important reintegrative and restorative function. Yet specific prevention, which lies at the heart of Japan's benevolent paternalism, is by far the dominant objective of the suspension-of-prosecution doctrine.

Suspension of prosecution promotes specific prevention in a number of ways. Although a suspension of prosecution will normally terminate prosecution for the crime in question, without any explicit conditions placed upon it, as a practical matter preconditions may include remorse, the existence of solid family relationships, and secure employment or other evidence of support mechanisms—all factors that might help protect against renewed offenses. As a positive mechanism to guard against recidivism, a government-financed system exists to provide limited financial assistance and aid in obtaining housing, education, and employment for suspects whose prosecutions have been suspended. An implicit negative sanction also exists to help deter misconduct by suspects whose prosecution has been suspended: suspension of prosecution is regarded as a first bite at the apple of leniency, justifying harsher penalties in the event of subsequent wrongdoing.

Suspension of prosecution is not regarded as special, isolated, or experimental in nature. To the contrary, it is a firmly established, nationwide program utilized as a key component of the criminal justice system. In 1988, suspension of prosecution was granted to nearly two out of every five adult Penal Code suspects referred to prosecutors; nearly half of theft suspects and even 6 percent of the murder suspects were granted suspensions.

Trials: Suspended Sentences and Short Sentences Approximately 40 percent of the adult Penal Code suspects referred to prosecutors go to full trial. Given the conviction rate of more than 99.8 percent, virtually all of them can expect to be convicted. This does not mean that considerations of specific prevention, including rehabilitation, are at an end, however, or that the judgments of prosecutors no longer play a role.

The Penal Code and other statutes specify very broad sentencing ranges. The range for murder, for example, is from three to twenty years, or life, or the death penalty. If extenuating circumstances are found, courts can reduce the minimum sentence by half. Moreover, for those who have not been imprisoned within the past five years, sentences of up to three years may be suspended. Given the ability to halve the minimum sentences for extenuating circumstances, sentences can be suspended for all but a very small handful of crimes.

Within these broad statutory ranges, the determination of sentences is left to the discretion of the courts. Prosecutors file sentence requests, however, which are usually accorded considerable weight. In addition, fairly clear sentencing standards for major classes of crime have developed through internal judicial practice. Not surprisingly, considerations of specific prevention heavily influence those standards.

Such considerations appear to play an especially strong role for courts deciding whether to suspend a sentence. The history of the suspended-sentence doctrine bears striking similarities to that of suspended prosecution. When it was first introduced in 1905, the system of suspended sentences was intended to eliminate problems associated with short-term confinement, presumably including both overcrowding of facilities and the potentially corrupting influence of hardened criminals on minor offenders. Over time, however, the system progressively came to be used for explicitly rehabilitative purposes; it was expanded to cover a broader range of crimes and began to be utilized much more frequently.

In addition such factors as family relationships, working habits, assurances from sureties and employers, and type of friends play an important role in determining whether sentences are suspended. The attitude of the defendant at trial also carries great weight: a sincere confession evidencing acceptance of moral responsibility and the sincere desire to reform is crucially important. Although under the Constitution and the Code of Criminal Procedure the defendant has the right not to testify at trial, judges clearly expect defendants will testify. Also because the fact-finding and sentencing phases are merged into a single proceeding, a defendant who does not testify at trial and who is subsequently convicted cannot then confess at the sentencing stage. When suspects do testify, an attitude of true remorse may result in a lighter sentence, whereas continued denials and a refusal to take responsibility are likely to result in harsher treatment. This outcome is based on the view that a sincere confession and acceptance of moral responsibility are essential elements in the reformation of the offender.

Suspended sentences are widely utilized in Japan. Nearly 60 percent of adults convicted of Penal Code offenses are granted suspended sentences. Of that total, fewer than 15 percent are placed under supervision; the remainder need not report to any probation officer. Apart from having gone through the additional steps of indictment, trial, and conviction, this group might appear to be in a similar position to those whose prosecutions have been suspended; indeed, the same factors influence each decision. One important reason for deciding to prosecute and then to recommend a suspended sentence stems from general deterrence and retribution: some crimes are so grave that it is regarded as essential to prosecute formally in order to deter others and reaffirm the community sense of seriousness. The suspended sentence has a further role in specific deterrence. Unlike the vague "first bite at the apple" aspect of suspended prosecution, the consequence of a subsequent violation by one on a suspended sentence is clear: incarceration.

The second key aspect of sentencing is, of course, the term of the sentence itself. Here, too, courts appear to place considerable weight on rehabilitative goals. This is reflected primarily in relatively short sentences. The great majority of those entering prison in 1988 received sentences of two years or less. As one might expect, multiple-repeat offenders—those who had been in prison nine or more times before—received, on balance, the longest sentences, but nearly 65 percent of even that group received terms of no more than two years. At the other end of the spectrum, out of nearly seventeen thousand offenders sentenced to actual time in prison for Penal Code offenses in 1988, only eighty-four were sentenced to terms of more than fifteen years. Virtually all offenders receiving the longer sentences were convicted of murder or felony murder, yet even for those categories the average sentence was well under ten years.

The key focus in Japan is on keeping individuals out of prison in the first place. After going through successive screenings based to a greater or lesser extent on the individual characteristics of the suspect, fewer than 5 percent of the adults originally identified as suspects actually serve time in prison. For that 5 percent, studies have suggested that the determination of sentencing length is influenced most heavily not by the defendant's personal characteristics but by the nature and gravity of the crime itself. This in turn suggests that criminal justice in Japan does not concern itself solely with specific prevention. In the case of crimes above a certain level, and when dealing with offenders deemed to have advanced criminal tendencies, general deterrence and retribution become highly relevant. Nonetheless, judges also take rehabilitation into account in determining the length of sentences. One judge, discussing the trend throughout much of the period since World War II toward progressively lighter sentences for many crimes, remarked that Japanese judges "tend to give more lenient sentences so that defendants would be impressed with the generosity and thus encouraged to rehabilitate themselves."

Sentencing occurs within a rather narrow spectrum. With the sentences as low as they are, any term more than ten years seems long indeed; less than 1 percent of all prisoners receive—much less serve—terms of more than ten years. For all but the most serious offenses and most hardened criminals, the objective is to get offenders, even multiple-repeat offenders, out of prison and back into the community quickly. The notion that deterrence requires sentences of 50, 150, even 600 years is simply unfathomable (nor are such sentences even possible under the Penal Code).

The most notable exception to this sentencing approach is the death penalty, which still exists in Japan but use of which has declined sharply in the past century. The number of executions has dropped from more than five hundred per year in the early Meiji era to an average of about twenty-five per year as late as the 1950s, and to an average of only two per year in the past five years. In one sense, the death penalty is simply the ultimate sanction of a system based on specific prevention. In this view, execution would be appropriate only when the individual is found to be completely beyond redemption. As a recent decision reveals, however, the Japanese Supreme Court continues to see the death penalty in terms of general deterrence. The Tokyo District Court had found one Norio Nagayama guilty of four murders, each committed in cold blood, and sentenced him to death. On appeal, the Tokyo High Court noted various extenuating circumstances and concluded that the defendant had undergone a "remarkable" transformation. That court reduced the sentence to life imprisonment, finding that under the circumstances "it is too harsh to apply the death sentence to defendant, and is more appropriate to have him devote the rest of his life to atoning for his offenses and praying for the repose of the victims' souls." The Supreme Court reversed, explicitly referring to the relevance of general deterrence and retribution in imposing the death penalty. As that decision reflects, benevolent paternalism and the emphasis on specific prevention might not apply everywhere, but they remain vital themes for most aspects of the criminal justice system.

The Postconviction Corrections Process   Although maintaining order is a high priority for Japanese correctional officials, public pronouncements by such officials tend to stress the value of institutional rehabilitation. This public emphasis receives more than merely rhetorical support. The most important aspect of the prison experience is vocational training and work: more than 93 percent of all inmates work forty-four-hour weeks. Japanese prisons, although Spartan, do indeed resemble "factories with fences." Primary categories of employment include maintenance, metalworking, tailoring, and woodworking. Labor union and other opposition to use of prison labor does not exist, and numerous private industries contract to have work performed by prisoners in or out of the prison facility. A number of other rehabilitative programs exist, including basic education courses, correspondence courses, and visits by volunteer groups.

In Japan, the granting of parole is entirely up to the discretion of the criminal justice authorities. The inmate has no right to file an application for parole, nor is automatic good-behavior credit awarded. Rather, the superintendent of the prison must initiate the process by requesting a regional parole board to grant parole for one or more specified individuals. In practice, superintendents request parole for more than 60 percent of adult inmates, typically after they have served at least two-thirds of their sentences. The parole boards grant more than 95 percent of such requests. As one would expect, the key factors influencing the grant of parole include the inmate's progress toward rehabilitation as well as the conditions in the family and community to which the inmate will return.

The Voluntary Probation Officer (VPO) forms a link between the offender's home environment and the criminal justice system. A VPO visits the home of the inmate at the outset of incarceration and, if conditions exist that would impede reintegration of the offender, seeks to improve those conditions before the inmate's release. That is one of numerous functions played by VPOs, a group of nearly fifty thousand individuals who serve under a staff of approximately eight hundred professional probation officers responsible for the supervision and aftercare of released offenders. The VPOs are generally financially stable, well-respected members of the community; they come from established families with close ties throughout the community. In contrast to the professional probation officers, who have an average caseload of nearly one hundred fifty parolees and probationers at any given time, VPOs are responsible for an average of less than two people. They smooth the way for the offender's return to the community by seeking to arrange employment and alternative housing where no family exists to receive the offender, and by visiting the offender and family regularly during the parole or probation period. In addition, VPOs undertake the more general function of carrying the "philosophy of rehabilitation to individual neighbors or the public as a whole [and working for the] eradication in cooperation with the community residents of environmental conditions generating crime."

The wide network of VPOs reflects the support and involvement of the community in the criminal justice system's goals of specific prevention and rehabilitation. This involvement is seen as "foster[ing] the reintegration of offenders into the free community." The VPOs' efforts at postconviction rehabilitation, moreover, represent only one aspect of much broader community involvement in crime reduction. VPOs often serve in local volunteer Crime Prevention Associations, with responsibility for organizing community crime-prevention programs. In that role, their regular contact with prior offenders presumably aids in prompt detection of any new offenses.

THE "BENEVOLENT-PATERNALISM" MODEL REVISITED

Skeptics might argue that the system's "benevolence" is largely an illusion. They could argue that, even for those suspects who have committed an offense and are released without being indicted, the experience of being investigated is by no means pleasant. Investigation can entail detention under strict conditions, accompanied by long periods of tough interrogation and perhaps even abuse. Nor would such an experience seem benevolent to one who was wrongly suspected of a crime. For those who are indicted, moreover, detention pending trial is the norm, rather than the exception. And for those who are convicted and incarcerated, prison life will involve long hours of work, accompanied by a Spartan regimen. Finally, such critics could question whether the statistics really support the conclusion that Japanese practices relating to indictment and sentencing are so much more lenient than those in the United States (which is by no means a model of leniency). They might note, for example, that, notwithstanding highly publicized sentences of one hundred years or more in the United States, more than 30 percent of those convicted of felonies in the United States are not incarcerated at all and approximately another quarter are sentenced to terms of less than one year.

There is considerable truth to many of the skeptics' arguments, a number of which I will discuss in the context of due-process rights. As for incarceration, however, a closer examination of the statistics reveals a far more lenient approach in Japan than in the United States. Japan's incarceration rate of 45 per 100,000 people ranks among the lowest in the world; it is only about one-tenth the rate of the United States, which at 426 per 100,000 is reportedly the world's highest. That statistic, of course, relates in part to Japan's lower overall crime rate. Yet even looking at incarceration rates for only those actually convicted at trial, nearly 60 percent of Japanese found guilty of Penal Code offenses do not go to prison for their crimes.

If one takes into account other levels of benevolence, the relative leniency of the Japanese system becomes even more pronounced. Prosecution is suspended in nearly 40 percent of the cases referred to the prosecutors—in all of which the prosecutors have, in principle, found conclusive evidence of guilt. Ultimately, less than 5 percent of those formally identified as suspects actually go to prison in Japan, as compared to more than 30 percent of those arrested in the United States.

DOES BENEVOLENT PATERNALISM WORK?

It seems appropriate to examine the effectiveness of the system on its own terms. Accordingly, the key initial inquiry relates to recidivism, especially the success of the various mechanisms designed to reintegrate the offender into society with a minimum of disruption and stigma. To the best of my knowledge, there are no statistics available that address recidivism by offenders who have been cleared from further formal proceedings by *bizai shobun*. On a number of occasions, however, the Ministry of Justice has undertaken studies of recidivism by those in the suspension-of-prosecution and other categories. In the most recent and comprehensive such study, researchers tracked recidivism within a three-year period for all individuals whose prosecutions were suspended throughout Japan during the two weeks from September 16 through September 30, 1980. The study also tabulated all persons sentenced to fines, sentenced to imprisonment but with the sentence suspended, released on parole prior to completion of their sentences, and released upon completion of their sentences during the calendar year 1980.

Apart from the *bizai shobun* category, one can identify at least six levels of sanctions in the Japanese system. The determination of the appropriate level of sanction depends on both the gravity of the crime and a judgment about the likelihood of the offender's successful reintegration into the community. In ascending order from the least intrusive, those categories are as follows: suspension of prosecution; fine; simple suspension of sentence (without supervision); suspension of sentence with probation (and supervision); release on parole; and release only upon completion of full sentence. Within the suspension-of-prosecution category, one important additional factor is whether the suspect was referred to the prosecutors on an at-home basis or was arrested.

The recidivism statistics show almost precisely what one would have predicted for the system from its underlying theoretical bases. Offenders deemed most likely to achieve full rehabilitation with the least intrusive level of sanctions—that is, first-time offenders whose prosecutions were suspended and offenders referred to the prosecutors on an at-home basis whose prosecutions were suspended—display by far the lowest levels of recidivism (5.1 percent and 7.8 percent, respectively). Next comes the suspension-of-prosecution group as a whole (11.5 percent). Recidivism rates for other categories rise progressively in tandem with the degree of severity of the sanction imposed, peaking with those offenders who are sentenced to prison and never granted parole, for whom the recidivism rate is nearly 60 percent.

These figures do not reflect all instances of recidivism, but they appear to provide a fairly reliable measure of relative rates of recidivism for the various categories of disposition. The statistics strongly suggest either that the criminal justice authorities are very good at predicting recidivism or that the benevolence at the early stages of the system is highly effective in achieving rehabilitation and specific prevention. Unfortunately, from this study it is impossible to tell which. Nor have other studies attempted to test this proposition by, for example, utilizing control groups and deliberately dealing in different ways with cohorts of apparently like-situated suspects. It seems probable that the recidivism rates reflect a combination of both good prediction and successful specific prevention. Yet even assuming that good prediction is the predominant factor, on the basis of these statistics one would scarcely expect Japanese criminal justice authorities to want to change their basic approach to sanctions. Ever since the Meiji era it has been a fundamental policy of Japanese justice officials to keep lesser offenders out of prison and away from the adverse influence of hardened criminals. These statistics suggest that, for whatever reason, in the Japanese setting that approach has worked. Lenient sanctions correlate closely with low recidivism rates. Moreover, this leniency has evidently not undermined general deterrence.

REFERENCES

Griffiths, John. 1970. Ideology in criminal procedure or a third "model" of the criminal process. *Yale Law Journal* 79: 367–71.

8 PLEA BARGAINING AND PLEA NEGOTIATION IN ENGLAND

John Baldwin and Michael McConville

INTRODUCTION

Underlying the common law theory of evidence and procedure in criminal cases is an assumption that guilt will be determined by means of a formal adversarial process in which evidence is presented to an impartial jury. It has long been recognized, however, that courts and legal practitioners, in both England and the United States, operate according to a quite different assumption: that the right to be tried by jury will only exceptionally be exercised and that the great majority of cases will be settled by a plea of guilty. The available statistics for both countries show that this latter assumption is well founded. In England, about 85 percent of defendants charged with indictable criminal offenses plead guilty, and in the United States it would seem that the proportion is even higher (see, for example, Newman 1966; Blumberg 1967; President's Commission 1967). The recognition of the importance of the guilty plea has led American researchers to devote considerable attention to examining the factors that cause defendants to plead guilty and to exploring the procedural safeguards that should surround pretrial plea discussions as well as those that ought to be available on appeal. The American evidence clearly demonstrates that a large majority of guilty pleas are the result of some kind of out-of-court bargaining. By comparison, researchers in England have displayed little interest in guilty pleas, and the courts themselves have been reluctant to acknowledge that a plea of guilty can by anything other than a full, free, and voluntary decision by the defendant. More specifically, the idea of plea bargaining, or the notion that pressures may be brought to bear upon defendants to induce them to plead guilty, has traditionally been regarded as repugnant to the English legal system. This has fostered the belief that such bargains or pressures do not exist. The validity of this belief, and the consequences to which it gives rise, represent the central concern of this paper.

It must immediately be recognized that certain features of the American criminal process that give an impetus to negotiated pleas are absent in the English system. Furthermore, the English Court of Appeal has firmly pronounced against the development of plea-bargaining practices on a number of occasions. Indeed, one of the central features of the English judicial system is the extent to which trial judges have been able to retain their sentencing discretion. With very few exceptions (the principal one being murder), offenses in England, unlike those in many jurisdictions in the United States, do not carry fixed sentences. Two consequences follow from this: the pressure to mitigate the harshness of the law by means of informal procedures is much less intense; and the trial judge's discretion over sentence makes it difficult for the prosecution to offer the defense any promise with respect to the sentence. A second important difference between England and the United States concerns the role of the prosecutor. In the United States, the prosecutor wields considerable power: he decides whether to proceed with a prosecution; he may agree to reduce a particular charge; and he can recommend a particular sentence to the court. In England, on the other hand, criminal prosecutions are not usually conducted by professional prosecutors at all. In the Crown Court, prosecutions are conducted by barristers who commonly appear for the Crown in one case and for the defense in another. Moreover, the barrister does not have an unsupervised power to manipulate charges, and a specific sentence recommendation by prosecuting counsel would be quite unethical. In short, the dominance of the English judge in the trial system and his control over prosecutorial and sentencing discretion limit the use that can be made of informal settlement procedures in criminal cases.

Nor are the restrictions on plea negotiations in English courts indirect. When the Court of Appeal was confronted with some of these very questions in the leading case of *Turner* (54 Crim. App. R. 352, 1970), it sought to check, if not eradicate, the development of plea bargaining. Turner was charged with theft and pleaded not guilty. In the course of the prosecution's case, his barrister advised him in strong terms to plead guilty, telling him that if he did so he might well receive a noncustodial sentence, whereas if he persisted in pleading not guilty, there was a risk he would be sent to prison. Turner refused to take this advice but eventually pleaded guilty after his barrister had discussed the matter in private with the trial judge and thereafter repeated the earlier advice. Turner was fined but appealed against conviction on the ground that his plea has been involuntary because he had believed that counsel had been expressing the view of the judge. On the first point, the Court of Appeal took the view that counsel had not exceeded the bounds of his duty or deprived Turner of a free choice of plea. On the second point, however, the appeal succeeded because, once it was shown that Turner believed that the views about sentence had emanated from the judge, it was idle to think that he had a free choice. In the course of its judgment the Court attempted to clarify the confusion surrounding the practice of plea bargaining and to lay down strict rules that would reduce the judicial role to a minimum. The Court did not rule out the possibility that barristers might discuss cases with judges informally prior to trial but insisted that any such discussion must involve counsel for both defense and prosecution. However, the Court said, in vague and elliptical language, such discussions should take place "only when really necessary," and it emphasized that importance of justice being administered in open court. Counsel must be free to give advice to his client, in strong terms if need be, and this might well include the advice that a plea of guilty, showing an element of remorse, could lead to a reduction of sentence. But the Court stressed that counsel must not advise a defendant to plead guilty unless he had committed the offense, and that the defendant must have complete freedom of choice as to his plea. The judge's role in any pretrial discussion was also heavily circumscribed. He could not indicate to counsel the sentence he had in mind, unless it would take a particular form regardless of plea. In conclusion, the Court observed that, where some informal meeting had involved the judge, defense counsel should disclose this to the defendant and inform him of what had taken place. Given the very restricted nature of judicial involvement in such discussions, it has been widely assumed that the scope for plea bargaining in England has all but been eliminated.

It is therefore not surprising that researchers in England have shown little interest in the subject of guilty-plea negotiation. Only two empirical studies have investigated the practice in any depth. The more detailed study was conducted by McCabe and Purves (1972), who examined ninety Crown Court cases (involving 112 defendants) in which there had been a late change of plea to guilty. Although they uncovered a considerable amount of evidence to suggest some kind of plea bargaining in many of these cases, they concluded that the outcomes served the interests of all parties, including the defendants. They found no evidence that any defendant had changed his plea as a result of excessive or improper pressure (although they did not interview defendants). On the contrary, it appeared to them that the changes of plea were the result of a realistic and practical approach by all concerned, with the defendants openly confronting the harsh realities. As Purves has noted, "It can at least be concluded at this stage that the plea-bargaining process . . . does ease the administration of justice and . . . does so without either prejudicing the rights of innocent men or occasioning real injustice to the guilty." The second study, which examined the subject of plea bargaining in much less detail, was carried out in Sheffield by Bottoms and McClean. They, too, found considerable evidence of last-minute changes of plea, often the result of advice given to the defendant by his own barrister. Unlike McCabe and Purves, however, they were not so convinced that these pleas were always in the interest of the defendant.

> These defendants have for many weeks expected to plead not guilty. This intention has been supported by their solicitor—after all, a trained professional. Then, out of nowhere appears a barrister, usually on the morning of the trial, strongly suggesting a change of plea. It is hardly surprising if defendants acquiesce, faced with this predicament; it is also hardly surprising if some of them subsequently resent having acquiesced to last-minute pressure. (Bottoms and McClean 1976, 130)

It was against this background of empirical findings and judicial pronouncements that we began our research into late guilty pleas in 1975. It appeared that the scope for informal settlements of plea in England was limited: the criminal justice system lacked certain features that had proved conducive to plea bargaining in the United States; the courts were openly hostile to such arrangements; and the limited empirical data suggested not so much bargaining for sentence as late changes of plea resulting from a realistic, if reluctant, acceptance of the actual situation.

PLEA NEGOTIATION IN THE BIRMINGHAM CROWN COURT

Our interest in plea negotiation arose more by accident than design. In 1974, we began an inquiry into the outcome of jury trials in the Birmingham Crown Court. For various technical reasons we wished to identify, some time before trial, those cases that would be contested before a jury. It soon became clear, however, that many of the cases that we (and the Crown Court authorities) confidently anticipated would be tried by jury ended suddenly with the defendant pleading guilty. Many defendants appeared to change their minds abruptly, only deciding to plead guilty literally minutes before their cases were due to begin in court. Cases of this kind were so common that we decided to ask defendants the reasons for this apparent *volte-face*. We therefore selected a sample of 150 defendants, whose cases were tried in a fifteen-month period in 1975 and 1976, and succeeded in interviewing 121 (81 percent). The interviews, which usually lasted between one and two hours, were tape-recorded and subsequently transcribed verbatim. We shall use some of the quotes derived from these interviews as illustrative case material in this paper.

Before the findings are discussed, it is necessary to indicate their limitations. The sample of defendants was drawn from those who appeared for trial at the Birmingham Crown Court, one of the largest court complexes in England. It follows that our study is not concerned with the way in which pleas are settled in the lower criminal courts. Nor can it be stated with certainty how far this sample is characteristic of the mass of individuals who plead guilty at the Crown Court. It is likely, however, that the pressures that defendants in the sample experienced are typical of those in other Crown Court centers, although the intensity may vary regionally. The other important qualification to make is that our research is primarily concerned with informal negotiating procedures as seen from the defendant's perspective. Although it would clearly be foolish to take what defendants say at face value, there are good reasons to believe that defendants' accounts of what happened to them are often essentially true. As will become apparent, there is corroborative evidence independent of the defendant interviews, but the important point in the present context is that it is the defendants' *perception* of events that ultimately explains the decision to plead guilty. We return below to the question of the reliance that can be placed on defendants' accounts of their experiences.

It soon emerged from the interviews we conducted in Birmingham that the picture of plea bargaining (or its absence) traditionally accepted in England was largely mythical. Not only did we find that informal plea negotiation was common, but it was also clear that virtually all defendants were exposed to a variety of pressures calculated to induce them to plead guilty. The view put forward by legal commentators that plea bargaining operates to the advantage of all concerned was not shared by many defendants in our sample. Some had benefited considerably, but very many were dissatisfied with or angry about the shabby treatment they felt they had received.

Less than one-third of the defendants said that their guilty plea reflected culpability and had been entered without any pretrial negotiations. We shall not pursue those cases here (as far as we could ascertain they did not differ qualitatively from others in the sample), but shall concentrate on the remaining defendants, many of whom described experiences that scarcely tally with the official view on plea negotiation.

Though it is quite clear that there is no highly organized *system* of plea bargaining in England, in the sense in which such a system is to be found in many courts in the United States, many defendants in Birmingham seemed to have been involved in a process that resembles plea bargaining more closely than has been hitherto appreciated. The essence of plea bargaining is the offer of a specific sentence concession in return for a guilty plea; in all but three of the twenty-two cases of explicit negotiation, the defendant said that the bargain had taken this form. Sometimes the defendant had been told of a specific sentence he would receive if he pleaded guilty; in other cases, the offer was in more general terms. The following are two examples of the bargains described by defendants:

> The barrister wanted to get it over with. He went to see the judge with the other barrister and told me that if I pleaded guilty I would get a suspended sentence but if I fought the case I'd be done for wasting the court's time and would get 3 years' imprisonment or, if I was lucky, a suspended sentence. He left it up to me—so I pleaded guilty and got a suspended sentence. [Case 13]

> The barrister looked at the witness statements and said, "I don't think you've much hope. If you authorize me to see the judge, I might learn a lot." With the barrister saying that I thought, "Well, he must know." He went to see the judge and when he came back he said, "If you plead guilty, the most you will get is probation, but if you don't plead guilty, the judge will have to impose a stiffer sentence." He also mentioned that if I pleaded not guilty the trial would be reported in the newspapers, and I thought of the effects this would have on my family, so I pleaded guilty and got probation. [Case 104]

In nine of the twenty-two cases, the stories related by the defendants seemed to indicate that the judge in question, by holding out a precise offer to the defendant, was in breach of the guidelines laid down in the *Turner* case. Those guidelines, it will be recalled, permit a judge to discuss a case with counsel but stipulate that he must never indicate the *quantum* of the sentence, only its form, and then only when he is in a position to say that the sentence will take that form whatever the plea. The following case, in which we had the views of both the defendant and his solicitor, represents a clear illustration of this point:

> DEFENSE SOLICITOR: The judge indicated to counsel for the defense in chambers that he would not imprison the defendant in the event of a guilty plea. This is what caused the defendant to plead guilty.

> DEFENDANT: The judge sent for my barrister and the prosecution barrister and said, "As the case stands at the moment, I'll be more inclined to give your defendant a suspended sentence but if he goes on pleading not guilty he will go to prison." So when the barrister told me this, I pleaded guilty. [Case 128]

Whether such cases are within or outside the rules, however, is largely beside the point. We encountered several in which the judge and lawyers appeared to have behaved impeccably from a legal standpoint, but we remained unconvinced that the defendant's guilty plea was truly voluntary. We would argue that once the judge becomes involved in pretrial discussion of this nature it is meaningless to talk about a defendant's plea being voluntary. As many defendants in this situation see it, the judge has made up his mind about their guilt and is already discussing with counsel the question of sentence. Once he has received some intimation on sentence, the defendant, understandably, may well feel that he has no realistic alternative but to plead guilty.[1]

We entertain similar doubts about the voluntariness of the actions of the forty-eight defendants who said that they had pleaded guilty in response to the advice of their barristers. It is the barrister who is seen by defendants as the major influence on their decisions as to plea. In the usual case, the defendant meets his barrister for the first time on the morning of the trial and the pretrial discussions must inevitably be brief and hurried. This fact alone often gives the defendant the impression that the barrister's prime concern is to have the case dealt with as quickly as possible. As noted above, the barrister is permitted to put pressure upon his client to plead guilty and may if necessary advise him "in strong terms," but how much pressure counsel may properly apply, and what "strong terms" he may use, have not been made explicit by the courts. Nevertheless it is clear that many defendants in our sample saw the barrister's advice as nothing short of coercive. The following two examples illustrate how the nature of the advice given may in some cases be seen to be coercive in effect:

> My barrister compelled me to plead guilty. He threatened me, saying: "You will go to gaol for three years if you plead not guilty; the case will go on for a long time and you will have to pay all the expenses, which will come to £400. But if you plead guilty you will just get a fine." He wouldn't listen to what I had to say; he compelled me to plead guilty. [Case 60]

> My barrister came to see me just before the trial and said, "Hello, what are you doing?" When I said I was pleading not guilty, he said, "Oh," and he threw a fit—I could see it in his face. Maybe he wanted to get home early, but he just didn't want to know. He hadn't even bothered to look at the case papers. [Case 114]

Many defendants said that they were given no real alternative but to plead guilty and that their barristers had "instructed," or "ordered," or "forced," or even, on one occasion, "terrorized" them into pleading guilty. It may well be, of course, that this did not really happen, that the barrister scrupulously observed his code of professional conduct. But we would argue that the way the defendant *perceived* the advice of his barrister is critical to understanding how he came to plead guilty. The perception of many defendants that their barristers were behaving in an overbearing or domineering manner is the more disturbing because *Turner* makes clear that only in extreme cases will the defendant be able to argue that counsel's advice was such as to destroy the voluntariness of the plea. Both judges and legal advisers often seem slow to recognize that some defendants are weaker and more compliant than others, and that what may be vigorous persuasion to a lawyer may appear coercive to a layman.

---

1. Whether the bargains struck were favorable or not is often a matter of opinion and an interesting glimpse of differing perspectives is given by the following case.

DEFENSE SOLICITOR: The judge met counsel privately after the trial had started. As soon as defense counsel informed the defendant that the judge was not intending to send him to prison if convicted [of the lesser charge], my client changed his plea to guilty. He was as pleased as punch with the final outcome.

DEFENDANT: My barrister told me to plead guilty to [the lesser charge]. The judge talked to the barrister and solicitor and they begged me to plead guilty. The two of them said the judge had guaranteed that I'd walk out of court [that is, receive a noncustodial sentence], so eventually I pleaded guilty to please my solicitor, not to please myself. (Case 29)

THE QUESTION OF INNOCENCE

It is evident that, contrary to popular belief, the English criminal justice system effectively secures a large number of guilty pleas by means of covert negotiating procedures. Although these procedures raise many problems, some commentators view the situation with little unease since they believe that present practices discriminate accurately between guilty and innocent. We do not share this view; indeed, the results of our research suggest that some defendants who perhaps were innocent, and a larger group who probably would have been acquitted had the case gone to trial, were nonetheless induced to plead guilty. No fewer than 58 percent of the defendants interviewed made some claim (if often a weak one) that they were innocent of some or all of the charges they faced. Of course this is not, in itself, a reliable measure of innocence though it is worth recording that we ourselves, as interviewers, did encounter certain cases where the protestations of innocence were convincingly expressed and could not be lightly dismissed.

The difficulties involved in testing guilt or innocence suggested, at the outset of the research, that we should examine instead the probabilities of conviction or acquittal had the case gone to trial. In England, all cases to be tried in the Crown Court begin with committal proceedings in the lower court in which the prosecution evidence is presented to magistrates in the form of committal papers containing witness statements and depositions. Because we thought it important to gain some independent assessment of the strength of the prosecution case on the basis of these committal papers we obtained copies from the Crown Court in each of our cases and had them examined separately by two persons highly experienced in criminal trials: a former Chief Constable of Police and a retired solicitor. These experts were asked to predict the likely outcome of each case on the assumption that the case would ultimately be contested, to specify the degree of certainty with which they made the prediction, and to assess whether, on the evidence contained in the committal papers, the decision to prosecute was justified. These predictions do not have any direct bearing upon the question of innocence: establishing whether the prosecution is likely to prove its case at trial is not by any means the same as judging whether a defendant is innocent or guilty. But the exercise is important for it provides an opportunity of determining the extent to which a defendant was justified in claiming that his case was arguable and affords an independent assessment of the likelihood of conviction or acquittal at trial. Moreover, and directly relevant to the question of plea negotiation, it offers a test for deciding whether there was sufficient evidence to warrant a guilty plea.

The results of these independent assessments clearly indicate that the system of "negotiated justice" we have described distinguishes only crudely between those likely to be convicted at trial and those likely to be acquitted. Although the two experts anticipated a conviction with some certainty in 79 percent of the cases, they were uncertain as to the likely outcome in the remaining 21 percent or else expected an acquittal. Two examples of the assessor's views are given below:

> [Both assessors strongly predicted an acquittal.] There is a complete absence of evidence to support either charge. . . . There is a faint possibility that the jury will convict because of [the defendant's] statement but it is unlikely. [Case 97]

[A conspiracy charge] I think that this case will not get off the ground. I have never read such inconsequential evidence. Taken in the context of the case as a whole, I do not consider that there was any offense committed. . . . I consider that the time of the court should not be taken up with this rubbish. [Case 138]

As is clear from these forthright comments, a few cases were seen by the assessors as so weak that the prosecution should not have been brought in the first place. Even here, the defendants in question had said that they pleaded guilty only under pressure.

That these independent case assessments should not be dismissed is shown by a related study. As was mentioned earlier, our main research concerned an investigation of contested trials in the Crown Court; the assessors conducted a similar exercise as part of that investigation. Altogether, they examined the committal papers of almost one thousand defendants who pleaded not guilty over a two-year period in the Crown Court. The predictions were made without knowledge of the actual outcome in all cases, and in most in advance of trial, thereby permitting a test of their accuracy. When the assessors said that the prosecution was not justified in putting a defendant on trial, over 80 percent of the cases resulted in acquittals. This is strong evidence that certain cases in the negotiated guilty plea sample would have ended in acquittals had they gone to trial and suggests that the defendants involved may well have been wrongly advised to plead guilty and were justified in claiming that their cases ought to have been heard by a jury rather than being settled hastily outside the courtroom. To what extent innocent people are induced to plead guilty by these out-of-court procedures is difficult to determine accurately. In our view, the evidence is compelling that innocent persons are frequently placed at risk and that, on occasion, the weaker and less knowledgeable are wrongly persuaded to plead guilty.

THE FACTORS THAT PROMOTE NEGOTIATED PLEAS IN ENGLAND AND THE RESPONSE OF THE COURTS

We noted above that, although certain features of the American system conducive to bargaining are absent in England, nonetheless negotiated plea settlements do occur with some frequency. The paradox is more apparent than real. There are inherent pressures within the English criminal justice system that combine to stimulate the informal disposition of cases outside established courtroom procedures. For example, the English sentencing system customarily awards a reduction in sentence in return for a plea of guilty; in some recent cases the reduction has been massive (for example, *Hall*, 52 Crim. App. R. 528, 1968). Today there is considerable uncertainty whether such a reduction should be offered only to those who show remorse (as the Court of Appeal has *frequently* maintained), or whether it is an automatic reward for all who plead guilty. Recent judicial pronouncements, which have created a good deal of confusion and ambiguity, indicate a shift from the traditionally accepted view. A startling example is the case of *Cain* in which it was bluntly stated that:

it was trite to say that a plea of guilty would generally attract a somewhat lighter sentence than a plea of not guilty after a full-dress contest on the issue. Everybody knew that it was so, and there was no doubt about it. Any accused person who did not know about it should know it. The sooner he knew the better.

Though there may be ambiguities of principle, the practice is clear enough. Defendants in England who plead guilty can expect a substantial discount in sentence virtually as a matter of course. The truth is that English courts do not ordinarily embark on a search for remorse in a defendant. One indication of this is that the defendant who pleads guilty in the Crown Court is almost never asked by the judge (or by anyone else) if he wishes to say anything before sentence is passed. The conclusion we draw is that the guilty plea itself is generally taken by the courts to be strong, if not conclusive, evidence of remorse. On the other hand, our own research (and that of other writers) tends to show that few defendants who plead guilty are truly contrite. Indeed, the great majority of defendants to whom we spoke in Birmingham assumed that they had received a reduced sentence by pleading guilty, yet very few made any pretense at contrition about their behavior. The very fact that more than half were still protesting their innocence (in whole or in part) when they spoke to us is evidence of this. It seemed to us that, for these defendants, the guilty plea reflected bitterness and cynicism far more than genuine remorse. Yet there can be little doubt that the great majority received substantial reductions in sentence. In conversations with English judges, we have come to recognize a wide range of views on the reduction that a guilty plea justifies: some would reduce the sentence by as much as one-third in most cases, whereas others view any reduction as wholly conditional upon evidence of contrition. But a separate study of sentencing patterns in Birmingham showed that reality differs greatly from such expressions of intent. We tried to measure the extent to which a sample of defendants who pleaded guilty received reductions by comparing their sentences with those of a matched group of defendants who had unsuccessfully contested their cases. The result was extremely interesting. Stated badly, it was that many of those who pleaded guilty received a massive discount in sentence. Indeed, taken as a group, those who pleaded not guilty and were convicted received custodial sentences (and longer custodial sentences at that) one and half times as frequently as those who pleaded guilty.

We were inescapably driven to the conclusion that it was the powerful and pervasive inducement to plead guilty provided by the so-called discount principle that created many of the defects of "negotiated justice" described in this paper. The operation of the principle can scarcely be squared with justice: it exists primarily because of administrative expediency. In recent years the Crown Court system in England has had to cope with a considerable increase in work and has kept pace only with great difficulty. Everyone who works within the system suffers from the burden of this caseload, a burden that is considerably lessened for all officials by the guilty plea. It might well be thought fanciful to argue for the elimination of sentencing discounts, or even for a reappraisal of the premises upon which they are based, but there should at least be public recognition of the severe pressures that they inflict upon all defendants—innocent and guilty alike. Indeed, the greater the disparities (or more accurately, the anticipated disparities) between sentences imposed following pleas of guilty and not guilty, the greater the risk that innocent defendants will plead guilty. Furthermore, we would argue that the mere existence of substantial discounts for guilty pleas lends legitimacy to unfair pressures exerted on defendants by lawyers. Such pressures produce outcomes that can then be justified (if by reasoning that is clearly circular) as realistic and pragmatic, even though morally they are scarcely defensible.

But this is not the only problem. There seem to us to be other defects in the criminal justice system that lie at the root of many of the problems of negotiated guilty pleas and with which the courts seem reluctant to grapple. One, in particular, stands out: the complaint by many defendants in our sample that counsel seemed unwilling to contemplate challenging police evidence in court. Of course allegations of brutality and fabricated evidence are frequently leveled against the police by defendants, and the present sample was no exception. There was no way in which we could ascertain the truth—but then neither could the barrister. That abuses of police power occur is indisputable; the only question is the frequency with which the police concoct evidence or secure confessions by illicit methods. But the unhappy truth, as we have been told by several barristers (including a good number of our most vocal critics), is that to challenge police evidence in court or engage in any kind of defense that resembles mudslinging will generally be ill-advised. The police, rather than the defendant, *will* almost always be believed in court and a heavier sentence is a likely consequence of an unsuccessful defense based upon allegation of police misconduct. This is a disturbing situation, the more so because there will usually be no way of ascertaining which party is telling the truth. In England, the questioning of suspects by the police is largely unregulated in practice, and as most police officers readily concede, the existing rules are routinely honored only in the breach. For a barrister to be placed in the position of having to advise a defendant to plead guilty after he has been interrogated in these unsatisfactory circumstances is, in our view, insupportable, though once again such advice may well be realistic and even prudent. Though the courts in England have discretion to exclude evidence illicitly obtained by the police, it is widely recognized that judges tend to wink at infractions. The upshot is that the defendant can easily be convinced by counsel that his position is hopeless and abandons all thought of acquittal, pleading guilty even though he may believe himself to be innocent.

As we have already hinted, the response of the courts has been far from reassuring. They appear determined to ensure, by means of a general sentencing policy, that all defendants are subjected to some pressure to plead guilty, and they have shown no real willingness to control what takes place during police interrogations. Their early response to the problems of negotiated pleas demonstrated, at the least, a lack of appreciation of realities. A good illustration of this occurred in the case of *Peace* ([1976] *Crim. L. Rev.* 119), where a defendant had pleaded guilty after his barrister told him that failure to do so would lead to a heavy prison sentence and possibly to prosecution of his alibi witness for perjury. Subsequently, evidence came to light exonerating the defendant, and he was granted a free pardon. Despite this, the Court of Appeal refused to treat the plea as a nullity on the grounds that, although he might have pleaded guilty "unhappily and regretfully," he could not be said to have lost his power to make a voluntary and deliberate choice. Since the publication of *Negotiated Justice* (Baldwin and McConville 1977), the Court of Appeal appears to have become more willing to intervene in cases involving negotiated pleas in order "to preserve the good face of justice" (*Bird* [1978] *Crim. L. Rev.* 237, 238; see also *Atkinson* [1978] *Crim. L. Rev.* 238;

Howell [1978] *Crim. L. Rev.* 239). It is hardly sufficient, however, for the Court to proceed on this ad hoc basis: what is required is a thorough examination of the basis of the discount principle and the place, if any, of negotiated plea settlements in the English system. Unless and until this is done, the remedies available to those who have been wrongly induced to plead guilty will remain both arbitrary and ineffective.

THE REACTION OF THE LEGAL PROFESSION

If the results of our research pointed to deficiencies in the operation of criminal justice in England, the response of the legal profession scarcely encourages optimism that these deficiencies will be rectified. From the outset, it was clear that the leaders of both branches of the legal profession were fundamentally hostile to the publication of our report. Indeed, even before publication, a concerted attempt was made not merely to discredit the findings publicly but also to create serious doubts about our professional integrity. These activities did not abate once the report was finally published, after several delays, in September 1977. The thorough public airing that we hoped our book would receive took a form we could scarcely have anticipated. Its academic merits are obviously for others to judge; indeed, whether its hostile reception is justified turns, in part, on whether the research has made any contribution to an understanding of the English criminal justice system. It nevertheless remains the case that many of the comments and repeated slurs broadcast by senior figures are very important in themselves since they exemplify the stance adopted by the profession in England when delicate questions about plea bargaining are raised. Hence the very ferocity of the reaction that the book provoked among lawyers is of an interest in its own right and requires some explanation.

To superficial observation, the response of the legal profession may appear to be outrage at the suggestion that plea negotiation, traditionally assumed to be virtually nonexistent in England, occurs with some frequency. Yet one of the most interesting aspects of the reaction to *Negotiated Justice* has been the complete absence of any denial that plea bargaining is fairly widely practiced. Quite the contrary: even the chairman of the Bar has publicly stated that "plea bargaining is a very useful part of the system of English criminal justice." Furthermore, several practicing lawyers in England have now gone on record as saying that the findings of our book are entirely unexceptionable. Nor can there be any great secret about this. Informal plea settlements have acquired a special language, and a casual visitor to any Crown Court can readily overhear barristers, defendants, and police referring to the "deals" that have been struck, the anticipated contested trials that have "folded," and the "knife-and-fork" or "carve-up" cases that are being informally settled. It seems likely, therefore, that the shrill (one might almost say hysterical) reaction of the senior ranks of the profession can be satisfactorily explained only in terms of a deliberate attempt to divert public attention from the sensitive issues underlying plea bargaining.

A campaign has been conducted by the legal profession, both privately and publicly, to suppress publication of the book. This campaign—unprecedented even in England where there has always been an uneasy relationship between researchers and the legal profession—culminated in the chairman of the Bar writing to the home secretary, urging him to intervene to prevent publication of the report which would be, he said, "directly contrary to the public interest." The home secretary's response was as swift as it was unpleasant. First, a letter was sent to the vice chancellor of our university seeking his support in discouraging publication of the report; second, three months before publication, the home secretary gave a lengthy comment about our report in Parliament stating that, though he did not wish to suppress publication of the book, he nevertheless regarded the conclusions as "questionable" (932 H.C. Debates col. 169 [Written Answers] May 18, 1977). Our vice chancellor, Sir Robert Hunter, mindful of the long-term interests and reputation of the university, was greatly disturbed by the public furor and press speculation about the findings of the research. He decided to carry out his own assessment of whether the methods we had adopted were those that others in the discipline would regard as sufficiently sound to support the conclusions we had drawn. In the event, our approach was vindicated, and the vice chancellor offered to contribute a foreword to the book making this point explicit.

We were very much taken aback by the way the campaign against publication was conducted and, on several occasions, wrote to individuals (both privately and through the columns of national newspapers) to correct serious misstatements of fact and quite unfounded allegations made against us. Indeed, the allegations were on one occasion of so grave a nature that we considered them to be defamatory and a full public apology was eventually made. But perhaps the most depressing aspect of the various outbursts has been the underlying attitude that leaders of the profession have shown toward those charged with criminal offenses. It is no exaggeration to say that their comments on the statements of convicted defendants that we cited have been contemptuous. They have completely refused to place any credence in what defendants have had to say—their views, opinions, and complaints about the system have been summarily dismissed as worthless. How far the views of defendants should be taken seriously is clearly a contentious issue and one discussed at considerable length in the first chapter of our book. Suffice it to say here that the complaint by many defendants in our sample that they had received cursory attention from their legal representatives is rendered the more credible if the reaction by leaders of the legal profession to their views can be taken as any guide.

CONCLUSION

Plea bargaining is a fact of life in the English criminal justice system. It is not practiced on the same scale as it is in the United States, and its true dimensions are only now beginning to emerge. Although openly and avowedly opposed by English appellate courts, plea bargaining thrives in a climate actually determined by the principles and procedures approved by the Court of Appeal itself. The unwillingness of the courts publicly to acknowledge what goes on has stultified the development of appeals procedures, so that the honoring of promises held out to defendants is problematic. The Court has given superficial attention to the question of plea bargaining and, more generally, to the voluntariness of a defendant's plea. The blind indifference of judges and lawyers to the effects of "back-stairs" agreements and discussions can only reinforce an informal system that, with some frequency, rewards the complaint at the expense of justice.

REFERENCES

Baldwin, John, and Michael McConville. 1977. *Negotiated justice: Pressures to plead guilty.* London: Martin Robertson.

Blumberg, Abraham S. 1967. *Criminal justice.* Chicago: Quadrangle Press.

Bottoms, Anthony E., and John D. McClean. 1976. *Defendants in the criminal process.* London: Routledge and Kegan Paul.

McCabe, Sarah, and Robert Purves. 1972. *By-passing the jury.* Oxford: Basil Blackwell.

Newman, Donald J. 1966. *Conviction: The determination of guilt or innocence without trial.* Boston: Little, Brown.

President's Commission on Law Enforcement and the Administration of Justice. 1967. *Task force report: The courts.* Washington, DC: Government Printing Office.

III   LEGAL CULTURE AND LEGAL STRUCTURE

INTRODUCTION

In Western cultures, the idea of law is commonly linked to the image of a blindfolded Roman goddess holding a sword and a weighing scale. Another picture that often comes to mind is that of old, leather-bound books or antique scrolls that contain sets of immutable rules that dictate how we all ought to behave and how society should operate. Another common legal image is the picture of an imposing court building, with marble columns and high ceilings. In almost every modern society, the idea of a legal system also brings to mind a chamber where "justice" is imparted and laws are mechanically applied by elegantly dressed judges and lawyers, who operate in a sterile environment completely insulated from any outside influence. Despite this powerful symbolism, and the sense of tradition and nostalgia that it evokes, the living law is quite different.

Law is not a collection of fossilized institutions, or rigid and isolated rules emanating from some ancient and mysterious source and serenely passed on to us by tradition. The legal system is a living organism, and its concepts are in constant process of revision and change, as the system interacts with the larger social context from which it emerges, and which it is meant to serve. The law and its different elements do in fact follow certain traditions and the system does have its hierarchies, but all of this fundamentally depends on the role of law within an ever-changing society. Particular aspects of law emerge as a response to specific demands from social groups, or as a reaction to certain cultural or social phenomena. Law is never static, but the linkage between law and culture is permanent and indestructible.

The point is that the legal system does not exist in a vacuum. It is in constant interaction with the multiple layers that form society, and it is both cause and effect of social phenomena. It is under the direct influence of the general culture and also the influence of external forces and events in society.

For example, many key legal changes in the Western world during the nineteenth and twentieth centuries, in labor relations, public health, and urban development, stemmed directly or indirectly from the Industrial Revolution that took place during the eighteenth and nineteenth centuries. In a similar fashion, the various civil rights and feminist movements of the 1960s in the United States and parts of Europe, shifted attention toward subordinated groups and changed the ways in which ordinary citizens interacted with the laws and legal institutions of those societies. More recently, the rapid expansion of technology, such as the rise and expansion of cyberspace, the development of biotechnology, stem-cell research, and the manufacturing of nano-materials, or the emergence of transnational drug cartels and sophisticated networks of organ traffickers, all have prompted legal changes to deal with the problems and opportunities of the contemporary world. In sum, each major technological or medical advance has had an impact on the law. And quite generally, pressures and demands of various social groups, acting in accordance with their own values or norms, ideas, attitudes, perceptions, and expectations have determined the role to be played by the law and led to the transformation of legal institutions. Markets and the configuration of physical spaces also act as constraints of individual and collective behavior, thus affecting how the legal system operates (Lessig 1999).

In this section, we discuss the important role played by legal culture and its influence on the emergence and transformation of law and its institutions, processes, and mechanisms (legal structure). We have selected a few works that use the concept of legal culture, in an attempt to understand how the legal system works and what place it holds in society. These readings also address the connections between culture and structure, as represented by legal institutions, processes, and mechanisms that decode the social forces that constitute its raw material.

As some of us have argued elsewhere (Friedman 1969, 1975, 1994, 2001; Friedman and Pérez-Perdomo 2003), legal culture is a very useful concept, but at the same time a difficult one to pin down. Over the years, scholars have come up with many definitions and interpretations of what they think constitutes legal culture (Merry 1988; Gessner, Hoeland, and Varga 1996; Nelken 1997; Blankenburg 1998). Others have proposed calling the phenomena that some call legal culture by quite a different name (Cotterrell 1997), or have equated legal culture with other notions such as legal consciousness, legal values, or legal ideology (Gibson and Caldeira 1996; Silbey 1998; Ewick and Silbey 1998; Couso 2010). From a broader standpoint scholars have debated whether to use legal culture as an "analytic concept within a more developed theory of social relations," or simply "as concrete, measurable phenomena" (Silbey 2009).

Part of what makes the task of definition so difficult rests on the fact that legal culture refers to a range of overlapping and sometimes conflicting mental processes (Galanter 2005), lumped together into a multifaceted, open-ended, umbrella term (Friedman 1997). The concept, as we understand it, refers to a general set of ideas, images, opinions, beliefs, and perceptions that people hold about the law and its institutions. Legal culture is not exclusive to judges, lawyers, and public officials. To the contrary, it is something that everybody has, regardless of their social and economic status, race, nationality, political affiliation, gender, and occupation.

In one sense, legal culture is specific to each individual, because no two people (even identical twins) have the same perceptions, values, or opinions about the law, or view their position with respect to the legal system in the same or even similar terms. In this sense, legal culture resembles a fingerprint. But as is true of fingerprints, similar individual traits or characteristics may be aggregated and classified, and some generalizations can be drawn from them. This process of collecting similar opinions, ideas, or values is what allows us to talk about a legal culture of lawyers, of government officials, and of teenagers; or the legal culture of France as opposed to the legal culture of Japan; or more generally, about an internal and an external legal culture; or a popular legal culture, just to mention a few useful categories. Depending on their connection to an identifiable stratum or social group and their position with respect to the legal system, their shared experiences, common history, and comparable economic or political status, individuals may share similar perceptions or ideas about the law, and as a result their legal cultures (or some of its elements) may be placed in the same cluster, at least for analytical purposes.

What has earned legal culture a central place among law and society scholars is the fact that it refers to phenomena that can be empirically observed and measured, and this is particularly helpful if we want to understand how the legal system works, or why individuals or groups of individuals behave differently when facing the same incentives-structures (Couso 2010). For example, in a study about parking violations by diplomats in New York City, Fisman and Miguel (2006) observed that diplomats from countries that had negative views about the United States, or who came from societies with high levels of overall corruption, tended to violate parking rules more often than individuals from less corrupt countries, or who came from nations that had closer affinity with the United States. In other words, their behavior was molded by the cultural image that they had about official law and its institutions.

The use of legal culture as a variable also helps explain why antidiscrimination laws are not followed by Toba Batak people in Indonesia (Ihromi 1994); why Amish people tend to avoid the use of formal legal institutions (Kidder and Hostetler 1990), or how "litigation masters" served as power brokers between ordinary citizens and the state in late imperial China (Macauley 1999).

The term legal structure refers to the institutions, rules, and processes that serve as the skeleton that supports and gives shape to the legal system. The presence of a structure also provides stability and gives people guidance about which norms and values have been generally accepted by society, and what laws they are expected to follow. However, as a social product itself, the legal structure does not stand apart from the legal culture. Its presence is conditioned by the prevailing attitudes, perceptions, and opinions that people have about the law and its institutions. In this sense, we can say that institutions are permeable and porous, and that the legal structure is susceptible to penetration and influence from the prevailing legal culture.

Legal structures seem relatively stable, yet legal structure, certainly in the long run, is a functioning and dynamic mechanism. Rules, institutions, and processes may seem static compared to more dynamic elements—actors, perceptions, and values. Indeed, part of the function of legal structure is to promote, monitor, or hinder change. In so doing, it embodies and helps disseminate the values embedded in those institutions, rules, and processes. Yet, ultimately, structure and culture are related and interact with one another. It is, however, also possible for there to be a certain disconnect between structure and culture. Take, for example, the numerous instances of failed legal transplants and the problems of recent agendas of judicial reform (Dezalay and Garth 2002).

In short, there is an endless cycle of change and development in the legal system. Structure and culture shape each other and are shaped by each other. They are, at the same time, cause and effect, raw material and end-product. Their relationship is far from linear or single-stranded; rather, it is one of mutual interdependence or symbiosis.

REFERENCES AND SUGGESTIONS FOR FURTHER READING

Appelbaum, Richard P., William L. F. Felstiner, and Volkmar Gessner. 2001. *Rules and networks: The legal culture of global business transactions.* Oxford: Hart Publishing.

Blankenburg, Erhard. 1998. Patterns of legal culture: The Netherlands compared to neighboring Germany. *The American Journal of Comparative Law* 46: 1–41.

Couso, Javier. 2010. The Transformation of Constitutional Discourse and the Judicialization of Politics in Latin America. In *Cultures of legality: Judicialization and political activism in Latin America,* ed. J. Couso, A. Huneeus, and R. Sieder. Cambridge: Cambridge University Press.

Chiba, M. 1989. *Legal pluralism: Toward a general theory through Japanese legal culture.* Tokyo: Tokai University Press.

Cotterrell, George. 1997. The concept of legal culture. In *Comparing legal cultures,* ed. D. Nelken. Aldershot, England: Darmouth.

Dezalay, Yves, and Bryant Garth, eds. 2002. *Global prescriptions: The production, exportation, and importation of a new legal orthodoxy.* Ann Arbor: University of Michigan Press.

Ewick P., and Susan Silbey. 1998. *The common place of law: Stories from everyday life.* Chicago: University of Chicago Press.

Feldman, Eric A. 2006. The tuna court: Law and norms in the world's premier fish market. *California Law Review* 94: 313.

Fisman, Raymond, and Edward Miguel. 2006. *Cultures of corruption: Evidence from diplomatic parking tickets.* Cambridge, MA: National Bureau of Economic Research.

Friedman, Lawrence M. 2001. Some comments on Cotterrell and legal transplants. In *Adapting legal cultures,* ed. D. Nelken and J. Feest. New York: Hart Publishing.

———. 1997. The concept of legal culture: A reply. In *Comparing legal cultures,* ed. D. Nelken. Aldershot, England: Darmouth.

———. 1994. Is there a modern legal culture? *Ratio Juris* 7: 117–31.

———. 1975. *The legal system: A social science perspective.* New York: Russell Sage Foundation.

———. 1969. Legal culture and social development. *Law and Society Review* 4: 29.

Friedman, Lawrence M., and Rogelio Pérez-Perdomo, eds. 2003. *Legal cultures in the age of globalization: Latin America and Latin Europe.* Stanford: Stanford University Press.

Galanter, Marc. 2005. *Lowering the bar: Lawyer jokes and legal culture.* Madison: University of Wisconsin Press.

Gessner, Volkmar, A. Hoeland, and C. Varga. 1996. *European legal cultures.* Aldershot, England: Darmouth.

Gibson, James L., and Gregory A. Caldeira. 1996. The legal cultures of Europe. *Law and Society Review* 30: 55.

Gómez, Manuel A. 2010. Political activism and the practice of law in Venezuela. In *Cultures of legality: Judicialization and political activism in Latin America,* ed. J. Couso, A. Huneeus, and R. Sieder. Cambridge: Cambridge University Press.

Ihromi, T. Omas. 1994. Inheritance and equal rights for Toba Batak daughters. *Law and Society Review* 28: 525.

Kidder, Robert, and John A. Hostetler. 1990. Managing ideologies: Harmony as ideology in Amish and Japanese societies. *Law and Society Review* 24: 895–922.

Lessig, Lawrence. 1999. The law of the horse: What cyberlaw might teach. *Harvard Law Review* 113: 501.

Macauley, Melissa A. 1999. *Social power and legal culture: Litigation masters in late imperial China.* Stanford: Stanford University Press.

Meyerstein, Ariel. 2007. Between law and culture: Rwanda's gacaca and postcolonial legality. *Law and Social Inquiry* 32: 467.

Merry, Sally. 1988. Legal pluralism. *Law and Society Review* 22: 869–96.

Nelken, David, ed. 1997. *Comparing legal cultures.* Aldershot, England: Darmouth.

Nelken, David, and Johannes Fest. 2001. *Adapting legal cultures.* Oxford: Hart Publishing.

Pérez-Perdomo, Rogelio. 2009. *Derecho y cultura en Venezuela en tiempos de revolucion (1999–2009).* Caracas: Fundacion Garcia Pelayo.

Sarat, Austin. 1976. Studying American legal culture: An assessment of survey evidence. *Law and Society Review* 11: 427.

Silbey, Susan. 2009. Legal culture and cultures of legality. In *Sociology of culture: A handbook*, ed. J. R. Hall, L. Grindstaff, and M. Lo. New York: Routledge.

———. 2001. Legal culture and legal consciousness. In *International encyclopedia of the social and behavioral sciences*, 8623–29. Amsterdam: Elsevier Science, Ltd.

———. 1998. Ideology, justice, and power. In *Justice and power in law and society research*, ed. B. Garth and A. Sarat. Evanston, IL: Northwestern University Press.

Verweij, Marco. 2000. Why is the river Rhine clearer than the great lakes (despite looser regulation)? *Law and Society Review* 34: 1007.

9 | THE TUNA COURT

LAW AND NORMS IN THE WORLD'S PREMIER FISH MARKET

Eric A. Feldman

INTRODUCTION

Based on a detailed analysis of Japanese traders at the Tokyo Central Wholesale Market's tuna auction (hereinafter Tsukiji, the name of the neighborhood where the market is located), this article utilizes the case-based method that provided earlier studies with their analytical and rhetorical bite. It interrogates the claim that norms will trump law within particular types of groups by looking at a small, close-knit, specialized merchant community, trading a product (tuna) with cultural resonance, within a marketplace inscribed by local values, in a nation where recourse to formal legal institutions is often discouraged. Under this set of conditions, existing theories would expect norms to flourish. Through its investigation of conflicts among Tokyo's tuna traders, this article makes five distinct contributions to the literature on law, norms, and dispute resolution in close-knit business communities.

First, the article offers the only analysis in English or Japanese of how merchants at the world's biggest tuna auction handle conflict. Second, and contrary to previous case studies, the article demonstrates that members of close-knit groups may turn to law rather than norms because legal rules and institutions can be breathtakingly fast and inexpensive. Conflicts over auctioned tuna are brought to Tsukiji's Tuna Court (the more technical term is Jiko Kensa-sho, or "Accident Inspection Place"), which was created and is controlled by the government. Third, the evidence in this article indicates that the Tsukiji marketplace is rife with disputes between merchants whose work brings them into daily contact. Yet in contrast to the view that frequent face-to-face conflict is likely to undermine future dealings and is thus studiously avoided, market relationships remain strong. Fourth, by comparing conflict over auctioned tuna in the United States and Japan, the article highlights the superficiality of generalizations about American litigiousness and Japanese aversion to conflict, as well as other myths about transcendent differences between the two legal systems. American tuna traders rarely complain about the quality of their purchases, and U.S. tuna auctions do not

Reprinted from Eric A. Feldman, "The Tuna Court: Law and Norms in the World's Premier Fish Market," *California Law Review* 94: 313 (2006). Permission courtesy of the University of California Berkeley School of Law.

provide a formal mechanism for resolving disputes. Japanese buyers, by contrast, formally dispute the price of almost 2 percent of all auctioned tuna, and there is a formal mechanism to adjudicate their claims. To explain that contrast, the article uses an analytic middle ground between hard-nosed economism and rootless culturalism. It accepts the view that Americans and Japanese will both articulate and pursue grievances when it is in their interest to do so. But it treats such interests as highly contextual, depending on individual and social values, the availability of particular dispute-resolution mechanisms, and the existence and power of financial incentives, among other factors. The article employs carefully tailored analysis rather than broad generalization to unravel the different approaches to tuna defects in the United States and Japan. Fifth, the success of the Tuna Court indicates that thoughtfully designed and focused courts may outperform the informal norms of close-knit commercial groups. California cattle ranchers, New York diamond dealers, and Tokyo tuna traders all had the option to use formal legal procedures to resolve their disputes, but only the tuna traders invoked law rather than norms to settle their differences.

AUCTIONING TUNA AT THE TOKYO CENTRAL WHOLESALE MARKET

The chain of events that leads to a claim about the quality of auctioned tuna starts in the early morning, when trucks filled with fish unload at the Tsukiji marketplace. Although it is located in central Tokyo just steps from the upscale Ginza district, Tsukiji is built on the water's edge. In the past, boats plying the Pacific entered Tokyo Bay and moored on the market's docks.

These days, almost all tuna that reaches the auction floor is flown to Tokyo and driven from the airport to the market. Most of the tuna comes to Japan from overseas—some are farmed in Mexico; others are shipped from suppliers in Indonesia, Sri Lanka, and Taiwan; still others are initially caught in fishing boats off the coast of Spain and elsewhere. Most of it arrives frozen, since tuna boats often remain on the water for extended periods and have flash-freezing facilities on board. Some arrive fresh, packed on ice and shipped in large boxes called coffins. Only a small portion of the tuna at Tsukiji comes from Japanese suppliers, but it includes the most highly prized catch—bluefin tuna from Japan's northern coast, many weighing more than five hundred pounds and arriving at Tsukiji by truck.

Because of the size and structure of the Japanese tuna market and the internationalization of tuna fishing, auctioning tuna at Tsukiji involves a variety of parties. The market is owned and operated by the Tokyo Metropolitan Government (TMG), and city officials are involved in every aspect of the auction, from the arrival of fish at the marketplace to their display, sale, processing, resale, and shipping. Fish suppliers are also essential to the operation of Tsukiji. Although they are not a physical presence in the marketplace, they own and operate fishing vessels worldwide and send their catch to the market. Because few of the suppliers are based in Tokyo, they entrust their products to *oroshi*, or sellers/brokers/wholesalers, who are responsible for getting the tuna onto the auction floor and for operating the auction. *Oroshi* rarely own the tuna that they sell. Instead, they profit by taking a commission on whatever they auction, at a TMG-mandated rate of 5.5 percent of the sales price.

Prior to the auction, generally at 3 am, sellers (I will refer to the five *oroshi* companies and their employees as sellers, auctioneers, and *oroshi*) arrange their daily "catch" on the cement floor of the auction house. The tuna have their bellies gutted, tails cut, major fins removed, and are sometimes displayed with their heads removed. Once the fish are arranged, generally an hour or two before the start of the 5:30 am auction (5:00 am during the busy end-of-year period), buyers arrive and inspect them.

Because both buyers and sellers at Tsukiji are extremely knowledgeable about tuna, their ability to detect even minor and subtle differences between fish is finely tuned. In fact, interviews with tuna experts in the United States make clear that Japanese tuna buyers are accorded the highest degree of respect.

BRINGING DISPUTES TO THE TUNA COURT

As buyers and sellers work their way through the day's supply of tuna, the auction begins to wind down and activity shifts to the wholesale stalls within the market. Buyers are determined to quickly split open their "catch" and slice it into sellable pieces because their customers will soon arrive and they want to display their goods in the most attractive manner possible. But they have an additional motivation for immediately carving their catch: they want to look inside the fish to see whether it conforms to their expectations of quality. Until a whole tuna is sliced open, there is a risk that the poking and prodding of the preauction inspection may have failed to reveal a defect that could diminish the value of even the most highly prized and priced fish. So buyers quickly eviscerate their purchases because if there is a problem with internal quality they may want to complain. And complaining means that they must bring their fish to the Tuna Court on the same day that it was purchased.

From 7:30 to 7:45 every morning, and for three additional sessions lasting fifteen minutes at 8:15 am, 9:15 am., and 10:30 am, the Tuna Court convenes to adjudicate the claims of unhappy tuna buyers. The operation and jurisdiction of the Tuna Court is spelled out by a TMG ordinance, passed in 1972 under authority delegated to the TMG by the Ministry of Agriculture, Forestry and Fisheries. It provides for the resolution of conflicts over the quality of auctioned tuna, but it makes clear that buyers cannot simply throw caution to the wind and recklessly bid for poor-quality fish with the expectation that they will later be compensated. Instead, it requires that sellers allow preauction inspection and makes buyers responsible for whatever problems have been discovered through it. The Court's focus, therefore, is on problems that are akin to what one might think of as no-fault complaints, since they involve a gap between a buyer's expectations and the actual quality of a purchase resulting from defects that even the most conscientious and highly skilled tuna expert would not have discovered. The buyers who bring claims to the Tuna Court will prevail only if they can show that the seller is at fault for a particular problem (like misrepresenting the weight of a fish), or if the problem with the quality of their tuna could not have been known without bringing it back to their stall and opening it up. Although the Court has jurisdiction over different types of claims, the vast majority involves no-fault complaints.

To initiate a claim at the Tuna Court, buyers must attend an adjudication session on the same day as their purchase and bring at least one-quarter of the allegedly damaged fish, for which they must have paid at least ¥ 120 per kilo. In addition to an official from the TMG, who is required to supervise every meeting of the Court, there are five judges charged with examining each tuna and determining the degree of damage. Not surprisingly, judges are not members of the national judiciary, nor do they have any legal training. Instead, they are registered tuna auctioneers who work for the Tsukiji tuna brokers (*oroshi*) in the specialized tuna and swordfish division. Each company supplies a judge for every adjudication session.

Although the announcement of the initial verdict is generally met with silence, occasionally a buyer will emit a loud groan or rhetorically say, "Are you kidding?" "What, only 15 percent for this kind of serious problem?" or "Unbelievable." On rare occasions, perhaps once or twice a year, a buyer is so dissatisfied with the initial determination and the resolution of the appeal that he decides to press his case even further. The provisions of the TMG ordinance are murky in terms of how they apply to such situations because they do not distinguish between the first and subsequent appeals. Nonetheless, when a case boils over and a buyer is deeply dissatisfied with the actions of the Tuna Court, other parties get involved and help broker a solution. Despite the infrequency of such problems and the absence of written records, the comments of tuna traders suggest that in contentious cases the judges, buyer, representatives from the Tuna and Swordfish Buyers Association (Omono Gyokai), and sometimes another experienced and respected tuna buyer will meet, examine the fish, and try to find a solution that involves increasing the price reduction offered to the buyer by a mutually agreeable amount.

NORMS, LAW, AND THE TUNA COURT

The tuna market at Tsukiji provides an opportunity to evaluate the claim that members of close-knit merchant communities will rely on efficient, informal norms rather than on legal rules to order their relationships and manage conflict. Applied to Tsukiji's tuna traders, that claim suggests that merchants are likely to reject formal legal rules because informal norms will offer a faster, cheaper, and simpler way of handling disputes.

But the reluctance of Tokyo's tuna dealers to pull their fish carts through the streets of Tokyo in order to assert their claims at the Summary Court or District Court does not represent a rejection of state-sponsored law. Like all wholesale markets in Tokyo, Tsukiji is built on land owned by the TMG, and its overall operations are regulated by the Ministry of Agriculture, Forestry and Fisheries, which has jurisdiction over all Japanese fish, vegetable, and livestock markets. National legislation is far too blunt to take into account the many differences in locales and products that are germane to such locally embedded institutions. Consequently, the detailed regulation of regional markets is left to local government, and in the case of Tsukiji that means the TMG. Among the TMG's many ordinances that set standards for the operation of Tsukiji is the one from 1972 outlining a process for compensating buyers who purchase a damaged tuna. Tuna traders have therefore turned their backs on the government's centrally administered system of courts, but in its place they have embraced another form of government involvement in their relations—a TMG-created dispute-resolution mechanism that I call the Tuna Court.

Of course, one's willingness to conceptualize the system at Tsukiji as a court depends at least in part upon how "court" is defined. Clearly, the Tuna Court does not conform with what Martin Shapiro calls the "prototype" of courts—institutions where independent judges apply preexisting legal norms after hearing adversary proceedings, with the goal of making a dichotomous decision that one party is legally in the right and the other is legally in the wrong. But as Shapiro argues, the prototype fails to describe the vast majority of institutions that we call "courts." Instead, courts exist on a spectrum; beyond a common dispute-resolution logic that entails the use of third parties to resolve conflicts, they take many forms and incorporate a variety of features. Marc Galanter and John Lande have pointed to an array of features that make courts more or less "public" or "private," with "public" resembling the prototype critiqued by Shapiro. To distinguish between the publicness and privateness of courts, they offer criteria that include access to and location of the proceedings, as well as personnel, funding, review, substantive norms, and procedures.

Using these definitions and criteria as a matrix, what is the best way to classify Tsukiji's dispute-resolution institution? On the one hand, the TMG ordinance is quite specific in detailing the operation of the Tuna Court. It prohibits buyers from bringing claims that involve fish that cost less than ¥ 120/kilo and requires that when buyers make claims they must cut their fish into at least four pieces before presenting it to the judges. It prescribes a system for selecting judges and outlines the supervisory authority of the TMG. It provides the substantive rules that control the proceedings, limiting price reductions to between 11 and 50 percent. It offers a system of appeal. Like most courts, it occupies a specific location on government land, and precedent matters. The rules for handling disputes at Tsukiji are thus state law, which is interpreted and imposed by a specialized public court.

On the other hand, the Tuna Court incorporates a number of features that are more typical of private courts: only certain types of parties have access to the Tuna Court, the proceedings are not open to the public, the industry-supplied judges are paid by private parties, and there are no public records. If one's definition of a court is limited to the prototype described and rejected by Shapiro, then the Tuna Court is a different kettle of fish. There are obvious differences between Tsukiji's dispute-resolution forum and courts like the United States or Japanese Supreme Court, just as there are between the Tuna Court and standard trial courts. But if one accepts that there are many different types of courts that manifest a variety of features, including public courts like supreme courts, housing courts, and small-claims courts, as well as the range of institutions that Galanter and Lande call "private courts" (court-annexed arbitration, rent-a-judge systems, "embedded tribunals" like the NCAA's Committee on Investigations, and others), then the question is not whether the Tuna Court is a court, but rather what kind of court it is.

· · ·

The intertwining of the formal and the informal is well illustrated by Tsukiji's dispute-resolution mechanism. Just as the avoidance of national courts does not signify the rejection of public law, the embrace of the TMG's Tuna Court does not mean that informal norms are unimportant in the resolution of conflict between tuna merchants. One can identify a variety of norms that affect the operation of the Tuna Court. Buyers, for example, are invariably polite to each other. They never try to make a case for a high price reduction by comparing their (worthy) claim with another buyer's (frivolous) claim. They avoid bringing tuna with marginal problems. They defer to the initial decisions of judges, which greatly limits the frequency of appeals. Numerous norms also shape the behavior of judges and administrators. Although the TMG ordinance does not specify how Court decisions are to be communicated, for example, a norm of openness has developed, and judges shout each verdict so that all who are present can hear the decision. Norms are also important to the determination of price reductions. The chief judge is given wide latitude in reaching a final judgment so that he can try to find a number that "feels right" rather than strictly following the ordinance and averaging the judges' scores.

Moreover, the Tuna Court's very existence likely depends on social norms. Although it is difficult to verify, for instance, the principle that the risk of latent defects should be borne by both buyers and sellers may have started as a market norm and been formalized as a legal rule in the TMG ordinance. And norms that bear on trust and reputation help to keep buyers and their disputes within the market's dispute-resolution mechanism.

Along a number of important dimensions, therefore, the government-controlled dispute-resolution process at Tsukiji resembles a public, formal court; however, like many courts, it is interwoven with community norms. Contrary to the view that informal norms and formal rules are mutually exclusive, Tsukiji's Tuna Court is an expression of both. The Tuna Court thus defies predictions that members of close-knit merchant groups will reject formal, public courts and laws in favor of informal group norms. Instead, formal law-bound procedures play a central role in the interactions of tuna traders and govern their management of disputes; compared to ranchers and diamond dealers, tuna traders have opted for a high degree of legal formality. Yet the presence of formal legal rules is compatible with many norms that inevitably shape their behavior.

There is an additional way that the Tuna Court challenges past scholarship on close-knit merchant communities. Although there is considerable disagreement among scholars of the Japanese legal system about how best to explain Japan's low litigation rate, one rare area of consensus is that the assertion of rights and the resort to formal means of resolving disputes is particularly infrequent among repeat players with regular future interactions. In fact, that claim is commonplace among American law and society scholars. Stewart Macaulay's widely cited work on Wisconsin businessmen argues that their desire to maintain a future relationship leads them to rely on informal methods of resolving disputes, and Marc Galanter's study of U.S. litigation patterns emphasizes that parties with continued dealings avoid using formal legal rules to resolve disputes because it risks severing their relationship. Such views have been repeated and amplified by other sociolegal scholars, particularly anthropologists and sociologists who have studied conflict in discrete American communities.

Such well-considered analyses are contradicted by the fact that Tsukiji's tuna traders have adopted a system that encourages buyers to assert a right to compensation in the approximately seven thousand claims they bring each year. It is crucial to note that tuna traders are not required to bring their complaints to the Tuna Court. If they desired, buyers and sellers could resolve their conflicts privately. They could agree, under the auspices of their trade associations, to avoid the market's Tuna Court by imposing the cost of poor-quality fish on buyers. Or they could make sellers wholly responsible for quality problems. If they considered informality critical to positive future business dealings, they could avoid the TMG's formal court proceedings and opt for a different approach to dispute resolution. Yet tuna traders have come to depend upon a system that is more formal and rule oriented than many alternatives, and which involves clear, persistent, and direct disputing. They do so, I claim, for two reasons. First and most apparently, the Tuna Court is an efficient way of handling problems with the quality of auctioned tuna. Second, it plays a critical role in creating and preserving order in the marketplace.

WHY A TUNA COURT?
EFFICIENCY AND THE CREATION OF COMMUNITY

Studies of business dealings within close-knit commercial groups emphasize the efficiency of resolving conflict by means of informal norms. Such claims do a poor job of explaining the dispute-resolution process at Tsukiji. The most distinctive characteristic of the Tuna Court is its legal formality. Although the Tuna Court in part owes its existence to the norms of tuna traders at Tsukiji, traders did not choose to rely only on the unwritten practices and values of their profession that had been created and reshaped over generations. Tuna traders' informal norms undoubtedly influenced their approach to dispute resolution—even the shared acknowledgment that there was a problem in need of a solution reflects the influence of trade norms. But when it really mattered, they turned to the government for rules and structures that could facilitate the resolution of conflict. In effect, they turned their backs on informal norms (perhaps because they were inadequate, or contested, or for some other reason; the historical record is insufficient to say), and moved away from what some scholars suggest is a particularly efficient way of handling conflict. Instead, they dragged the state into their conflicts, just as they drag their tuna to the Tuna Court.

The government-administered Tuna Court imposes certain costs on the parties. To make a complaint, buyers—generally the owners of small, family-operated companies—must take thirty to forty-five minutes away from their wholesale stalls during peak market hours to bring their fish to the Tuna Court and await a decision. Sellers, namely the five Tsukiji tuna auction houses, adjudicate the cases, so they must provide personnel who might otherwise spend more time on more obviously profitable activities. Market administrators oversee every claim, record the decisions, and inform all parties of the adjusted price; this requires extensive paperwork and consumes staff hours.

Nonetheless, such costs are modest when compared to what the Court provides. Buyers who bring their damaged fish to the Tuna Court obtain a rapid and almost automatic price reduction of between 11 and 50 percent. The entire process takes much less time than the average Tokyo commute. No lawyers or representatives are needed, there are no case-filing fees, and the only relevant evidence is a single fish (and the price that the buyer paid for it). Fact finding involves nothing more than five judges who inspect the disputed tuna, and their skill at doing so enables buyers to feel confident that they are being treated fairly. In short, Tsukiji's tuna traders appear to be engaged in a highly efficient system for resolving conflict, even though it is dominated by formal legal rules and procedures. They use the Tuna Court because they believe that the rewards considerably outweigh the costs.

The finding that Japanese disputants will turn to the legal system when they think that they have something to gain confirms the claims of others who have studied conflict in

Japan. Whether relying explicitly on a rational-choice perspective or taking a broader po-litical or sociological approach, recent scholarship consistently emphasizes that individuals in Japan have no inherent hesitation about bringing their claims to court. Indeed, the Tuna Court is exactly the type of court that one would expect litigants to favor. Its ability to re-solve disputes quickly and efficiently makes it more attractive than alternative dispute-resolution techniques, so that even the predictability of its decisions (almost half of all cases reach the same 11 percent result) has not led tuna merchants to resolve their claims in the shadow of Tuna Court law.

But the promise of a fast and inexpensive solution to the problem of overpaying for a poor-quality fish is not the only reason for the frequent use of the Tuna Court. Tanase Takao, an influential legal academic, echoes the views of some American legal analysts in expressing skepticism about the social consequences of rights assertion and conflict. As he puts it, "Appeals to rights interrupt the flow of everyday social interaction and create ten-sions in social relationships [in Japan] . . . rights talk inevitably constructs subjects into abstracted identities lacking a communitarian ethos." By focusing on the corrosive effect of formal disputing on the bonds of community, however, Tanase underemphasizes an alter-native understanding of rights, conflict, and community. The Tuna Court at Tsukiji is an example of the centrality of rights and conflict in the creation of social order. By facilitating buyers' assertions of rights and airing of disputes; providing mild, community-preserving remedies rather than all-or-nothing, punitive, existence-threatening judgments; and down-playing the potentially divisive consequences of too much "rights talk," the Tuna Court serves to strengthen the ties between tuna traders that are essential to the successful opera-tion of the market. Rather than splintering relationships and incurring unjustifiable costs, the process at Tsukiji neutralizes the negative feelings that often accompany litigation in the United States and instead is essential to the maintenance of an ordered marketplace. Stated differently, the formal rules for resolving conflict over defective goods at Tsukiji, embodied by the Tuna Court, succeed in diffusing a variety of tensions that would otherwise inhibit the operation of the tuna auction. Tsukiji's Tuna Court thus fulfills a number of functions. Not only does it serve to resolve discrete disputes, but it also fosters positive relationships between tuna traders and enables goods to rapidly flow through the marketplace.

The effectiveness of Tsukiji's Tuna Court in creating and maintaining order does not suggest the absence of personal animosity or the suppression of competition among tuna traders. Those are inevitable and enduring features of any complex marketplace. Instead, "order" refers to a set of qualities that enable the auction to operate in a way that best serves the interests of all parties. Among the qualities that constitute order, trust is notable. With-out trust, buyers would be less willing to rely on the seller's preauction grading of tuna; they would be suspicious of how auctioneers conducted the auction; and sellers would lack con-fidence in the behavior of buyers engaged in tuna inspection and in other circumstances. Such concerns would affect the overall atmosphere of the market, and they would also slow its operation. And in a business where the freshness of the product is crucial to its value, getting tuna quickly from the auction floor to the table is of the utmost concern.

. . .

The most common Japanese word for court, *saibansho*, has a decidedly official, judicial meaning. Unlike the liberal use of the word "court" in English to refer to a variety of different types of dispute-resolution mechanisms, *saibansho* clearly references one of the hierarchically organized bodies administered by the Supreme Court Secretariat. The TMG ordinance that established the Tuna Court does not use the word for court, and Tsukiji's tuna traders disclaim the association between the Tuna Court and a "real" court, at least in part because it would be misleading in Japanese to call Tsukiji's dispute-resolution body a *saibansho*, since it clearly exists outside of the Secretariat's administrative domain. Consequently, the tuna traders have the best of both worlds—they can legitimately deny that their dispute-resolution institution is a court but at the same time enjoy the benefit of an efficient government-run, conflict-resolving body, which saves them from the potential complications of private bargaining.

In that way, the Tuna Court provides traders with an elegant solution to their conflicts. By offering an in-house system for adjudicating claims, it eliminates the time and trouble of bringing their cases to the official courts and, at the same time, obviates the potential discomfort of having to find more personal, private solutions to their disputes. By keeping their claims local, tuna traders can defang the existence of face-to-face conflict and instead define their disputes as simply routine discussions of technical "accidents" that are necessary to arrive at the appropriate price adjustment. Likewise, the pursuit of a price reduction is not articulated as the assertion of a right to compensation but rather as a mutual quest for consistent results. In essence, the Tuna Court enables tuna traders to deny the existence of frequent disputing in their workplace and instead allows them to emphasize their membership in a cohesive trading community, where the inherent nature of the product brings about certain problems with quality that are nobody's fault and that can be quickly and consensually resolved. Packaged in nondisputatious terms, the Court poses a minimal threat to the social order of the tuna traders and instead highlights the informal, consensual, and personal nature of market relationships. This further stabilizes the tuna marketplace.

"The Shasta County evidence," writes Ellickson, "indicates that people are aware that the legal system is a relatively costly system of dispute resolution and therefore often choose to turn a deaf ear to it." In contrast, the Tuna Court is in almost perfect harmony with the needs of market participants. The Court's durability and vitality cuts against the grain of theories predicting that overt conflict between closely linked parties shatters relationships. At Tsukiji, the airing and resolving of disputes is critical to the connections binding tuna merchants. Moreover, in contrast to the received wisdom that members of close-knit merchant communities generally find informal norms of managing conflict more efficient than formal legal rules, Tokyo's tuna traders use formal rules and institutions to resolve their disputes. The heavy reliance on the formal, state-created Tuna Court neither obliterates the possibility of long-term cooperation nor inhibits the flow of tuna through the marketplace. To the contrary, it provides evidence that in Japan and perhaps elsewhere, carefully designed, highly specialized, government-operated courts may be an effective way of handling conflict that arises in distinct merchant communities. As the operation of the Tuna Court makes clear, such courts can quickly and inexpensively handle a high volume of cases and, at the same time, contribute to the maintenance of an ordered marketplace.

REFERENCES

Ellickson, Robert C. 1991. *Order without law: How neighbors settle disputes.* Cambridge, MA: Harvard University Press.

Galanter, Marc, and John Lande. 1992. Private courts and public authority. *Studies in Law, Policy and Society* 12: 298–99.

Takao, Tanase. 2006. Rights and community. Untitled manuscript on the Japanese legal system on file with author.

10 THE LEGAL CULTURES OF EUROPE

James L. Gibson and Gregory A. Caldeira

The concept "legal culture" figures often and prominently in the scholarship of the diverse disciplines of sociolegal studies. Political scientists, for example, use the concept to account for variation in the permissible legal delay in trials and in the behavior of judges and lawyers, as well as to explain differences in rates of litigation. Sociologists have found the concept useful for analyses of the ethics and practices of legal organizations. And anthropologists, using a more holistic approach, have characterized the legal cultures of entire societies. Indeed, this notion "legal culture" is one of the most general and ubiquitous concepts in the study of law and society.

Yet much too often scholars invest the concept "legal culture" with little rigorous meaning: indeed some have questioned whether culture is viable as an analytical construct for scientific analyses of law. Formal definitions, to the extent they are proffered, vary tremendously across disciplines and scholars. It is not clear, for instance, whether legal culture may be thought of as a unidimensional or multidimensional concept. Perhaps most important, we can point to only a few attempts in the literature to operationalize legal culture as a directly measurable variable. All too often, legal culture is a term used to account for that which cannot be accounted for in any other way—that is, culture becomes the beneficiary of the residual term in explanatory equations. If we are to use the concept to test important hypotheses about the connections between law and society, we must attach rigorous operational meaning to legal culture. Few scholars have attempted this important task.

We wish to accomplish four specific goals here. First, we offer a multidimensional conceptualization of legal culture. Although we conceive of legal cultures as a broad *syndrome* of values, we focus here on three particular subdimensions: the valuation people attach to individual liberty, their support for the rule of law, and their perceptions of neutrality in law. Second, we operationalize these subdimensions of legal values and present evidence on the distribution of these attitudes within and across several Western European nation-states. We also investigate the interrelationships among these beliefs, focusing in particular on whether perceptions of the neutrality of law are associated with normative commitments to obey universalistic law. Third, we explore the correlates of legal values at both the micro (individual) and macro (nation-state) levels. Finally, we speculate about how rigorous studies of mass legal culture might move beyond our limited efforts to begin the process of testing important hypotheses about the role of culture in the operation of law.

This analysis focuses on the values of residents of the member states of the European Union [EU] as revealed during a survey conducted in the fall of 1993. The EU is an especially important venue for studying variation in mass legal cultures since such a wide variety of countries is represented in the community, ranging from Great Britain, to Portugal, to Greece. Moreover, European cultures are largely unexplored territory; the limited extant work on cultural aspects of law focuses almost exclusively on the United States (but see Ehrmann 1976). And as more and more nations from Scandinavia (Finland and Sweden voted in 1994 to enter the EU) to Central and Eastern Europe (Austria entered in 1994 as well; others, perhaps later), and perhaps even to the eastern outskirts of Europe (for example, Poland, Turkey) seek to join the European Union, the question of the diversity of legal values becomes all the more important for transnational legal policy. Furthermore, the structures of formal European legal systems vary; for example, the system is common law in Britain and Ireland, civil law in France and most of the Continent, with important (even if subtle) differences among those systems stemming from civil law traditions. Thus, it seems quite likely that the cultural values underpinning these systems differ as well. Although ours is only an initial foray into the structure of legal values in Europe, the importance of the issue may well justify the tentative nature of our efforts.

THE CONCEPT "LEGAL CULTURE"

Specifically, we are interested in the structure of the values held by ordinary citizens on important issues concerning the nature and operation of law. These broad values are important because they structure more specific opinions and expectations toward legal institutions, including the willingness to turn to legal institutions for the management of essentially private conflicts. We do not focus on more ephemeral opinions on issues of the day but instead attempt to measure more stable and more deeply held legal values.

Dimensions of Legal Values

But exactly what sort of values are important within legal cultures? Here we distinguish among three sets of orientations: (1) *legal consciousness*, which refers to specific attitudes toward legal issues and institutions; (2) *legal cultural values*, by which we mean more general values relevant to the legal system but not necessarily closely connected to it; and (3) more *general cultural values*, such as a preference for individualism over collectivism, trust in people, and so forth (cf. Putnam 1993; Bierbrauer 1994). We believe all these values, attitudes, and opinions are important, but legal values especially warrant consideration since they have clear, if not necessarily proximate, implications for the operation of the legal system, and at the same time they are general enough to (*a*) structure a variety of opinions and (*b*) be comparable across different legal systems.

In particular, we investigate here three components of mass legal values—attitudes toward the rule of law, perceptions of the neutrality of law, and the relative valuation attached to individual liberty. This set of attitudes, of course, does not exhaust the panoply of values that constitute a legal culture, but surely these are three central dimensions of any definition of legal culture. It is useful to explicate these values a bit further before turning to the data and empirical analysis.

Support for the Rule of Law

Willingness to tolerate exceptions to the law is an attitude of some importance in the operation of a legal system. At the extreme, of course, nearly everyone agrees that there are some circumstances under which law must be put aside in favor of justice or self-interest or the need to craft immediate solutions to pressing political and legal problems. At the opposite end of the continuum, nearly everyone also believes that, in general, laws ought to be followed, that citizens and rulers have a normative obligation to abide by the rule of law, and that under most circumstances the universal and equal application of the law should prevail. But between these two extremes, there is a great deal of latitude, and it is this variability that is of most interest to us. We hypothesize that individuals differ in the rigidity with which they believe law ought to be adhered to. Some believe that law ought to prevail unless there are severe exigencies to the contrary; others believe that law is something to be manipulated or ignored in pursuit of one's own self-interests (variously defined). This continuum has been dubbed "universalism versus particularism" in some earlier research (for example, Levin 1972, 1977; Wilson 1976). The extent to which citizens believe that they ought to adhere rigidly to law is one aspect of legal values, and it is quite likely that nations differ significantly on this dimension.

Perceptions of the Neutrality of Law

Various people may well perceive the role of law in society in quite different lights. For some, law is no doubt thought of as a rather neutral force, perhaps embodying consensually held social values. Those who view law in this way are likely to value it as a liberating force, either because it creates or reinforces a desirable social order, or because it serves other interests of the entire citizenry. This view of law as consensual and neutral is common within a variety of types of legal scholarship (for example, "neutral principles" for constitutional interpretation, "jural postulates," and so forth).

Others, however, may perceive law as an external, repressive, and coercive force. Instead of embodying a broad social consensus to which nearly all citizens subscribe, law may be seen as an instrument of social control, as a means by which others advance their contrary political interests. By this view, law is not neutral in the sense that it represents the values of the entire society, but instead it is seen as representing the specific values of hegemonic groups and interests. This view of law as an instrument of political struggle, of political conflict, stands in sharp contrast to the perception that law represents the consensual interests of society.

We therefore propose a continuum ranging from the view of law as a largely neutral, consensual, liberating institution to the perception that law is a biased, repressive institution representing the interests of dominant social and economic groups. In the largely legitimate political and legal systems of Western Europe, it is reasonable to expect that most ordinary people embrace the view that law in general represents the interests of the entire society and that few will express a fundamental alienation toward law and legal institutions.

Conceptually, we distinguish between support for the rule of law and the perception that law is a neutral institution. Empirically, however, we expect a fairly close connection between the two concepts. Those who view law as neutral, we anticipate, will be more willing to embrace the universalism of the rule of law, to be willing to endorse a more absolutist view of the need for compliance with law (cf. Tyler 1990). Conversely, we expect the view that law is a repressive institution, representing the interests of the few rather than the many, to be associated with skepticism about the necessity of following law. Thus, although we do not necessarily posit a causal relationship between the two concepts (and even if we did, the nature of this relationship would be difficult to disentangle given our cross-sectional data), we do hypothesize at least a moderate intercorrelation between the measures.

Valuation of Individual Liberty

Earlier research has argued that a basic distinction among people is in their willingness to tolerate disorder for the benefit of individual liberty, or, conversely, their willingness to sacrifice liberty for the sake of social order (Gibson, Duch, and Tedin 1992; Caldeira and Gibson 1992). This seems to be a basic social attitude, one stable over time and closely associated with a variety of other political beliefs. Moreover, struggles over the extent of individual liberty constitute the very heart of most legal systems. Since in the abstract everyone favors both individual liberty and social order, we have posed to the respondents items that present a conflict between these two desired states. Their choices under these conditions reveal the relative valuation they attach to individual liberty and to social order. We hypothesize that those who value liberty are more likely to favor the universalistic application of the rule of law and are less likely to view law as an instrument of repression and social control.

RESEARCH DESIGN

We base our report on data from two major surveys of mass opinion within the European Union, conducted in 1992 and 1993.

The 1992 Eurobarometer Survey

The first survey was conducted in each of the member states of the European Community between September 21 and October 15, 1992. We commissioned several questions concerning the European Court of Justice, and they were asked as part of the Eurobarometer 38.0, the semiannual mass survey of the Commission of the European Communities. The Eurobarometer surveys are representative of the populations of the respective nationalities, aged fifteen years and over, in each of the countries.

The 1992–1993 Panel Survey

In the fall of 1993 we were also able to reinterview subsamples of the respondents in the 1992 Eurobarometer. The reinterviews were by telephone, except in Ireland, Portugal, and East Germany, where telephone penetration was not sufficiently high to ensure representative samples. We excluded Northern Ireland from the panel reinterviews, and since national law made it impossible to reinterview the Danish respondents, we drew a fresh sample in Denmark and interviewed them by telephone. For most of the analysis reported here, we rely on data from the second wave of the panel because they are more complete.

Results

The data reveal significant cross-national variability in attitudes toward law. Consider first the items on attitudes toward the rule of law. To anticipate the factor analysis results ... the best indicator of attitudes toward the rule of law is the third item: "If you don't particularly agree with law, it is all right to break it if you are careful not to get caught." This is a cynical statement that in essence cedes no moral authority to law. According to this item, the most law-abiding people are clearly the British—nearly 93 percent of the respondents disagree or disagree strongly with the statement. Similarly, in Italy, the Netherlands, Ireland, Denmark, West Germany, Spain, and East Germany, we find widespread disapproval of the idea that it is legitimate to break laws. Conversely, respect for law is lowest in France, Luxembourg, and Belgium, where roughly one-quarter of the respondents agree or agree strongly with the statement (Portugal follows closely behind). There is certainly considerable cross-national variation within the EU in attitudes toward the rule of law.

There are comparable differences in perceptions of the neutrality of law. In West Germany and the Netherlands, more than 60 percent of the respondents reject the proposition that "My interests are rarely represented in the law; usually law reflects the views of those who want to control me." In Denmark, a majority of the respondents also rejects the statement; near majorities disagree with it in Great Britain, Ireland, and France. On the other hand, a majority of the respondents in Greece (and a near majority in Belgium) view law as a repressive force. In all our countries, sizable minorities, at least, assert that law reflects the interests of those who would control them. Thus, these perhaps surprising results suggest that belief in the neutrality of law is not necessarily widespread in Europe and illustrate significant cross-national variability.

Finally, consider attitudes toward individual liberty. On this subdimension of legal values, we find much more consensus. The best indicator of these attitudes—responses to the statement "It is better to live in an orderly society than to allow people so much freedom that they can become disruptive"—does *not* so clearly divide the countries of Europe as do the other items. In fact, the citizens of most of the countries endorse social order over potentially disruptive liberty. More than three-quarters of the respondents favor order in Portugal, Great Britain, and Ireland (and perhaps Luxembourg and East Germany as well). Only in the Netherlands, Italy, and Spain do we find at least 20 percent of the respondents expressing support for liberty on this item.

CROSS-NATIONAL DIFFERENCES IN LEGAL ATTITUDES

Are there cross-national differences in these attitudes? Certainly there appears to be considerable variability across the member states in citizens' commitments to these three values, at least as reflected in the mean scores on the various indices. For instance, at one extreme stands Greece, where legal alienation is widespread, support for the rule of law is limited, and there is a slight tendency toward favoring order over liberty. At the other extreme is Denmark, where alienation is uncommon and support for liberty and the rule of law is relatively strong. Overall, however, "nation-of-residence" is *not* an especially strong predictor of attitudes. Eta indicates that there is considerable within-nation variation in attitudes, even if the difference across the mean scores on each of the indices is statistically significant.[1] As would be expected from any study of the member states of the EU, there is important inter-national variability, but there is also great intra-national variation. Germans are different from Greeks, but neither all Germans nor all Greeks are similar.

Through analysis of the interrelationships among the mean scores on each of the subdimensions of legal values, we discovered that support for the rule of law is very strongly related to perceptions of the neutrality of law ($r = .83$), which of course is compatible with the microlevel findings reported above. In fact, at the aggregate level, we might just as well collapse these two subdimensions into one. The correlations between these values and the valuation attached to liberty are not as strong but are still substantial—with legal neutrality, $r = .45$; with rule of law, $r = .48$. Polities committed to individual liberty also tend to support the rule of law and to reject the notion that law is a repressive instrument of social control. Had we been able to develop measures of the valuation of liberty that more finely distinguish the countries, these coefficients would probably rise. But generally the correlations suggest strong interrelationships among the three indicators of legal values.

The summary indicator of legal values suggests three major clusters of countries within the EU. At one extreme we find Greece, Belgium, Luxembourg, Portugal, and East Germany. In these countries, regard for the rule of law is not strong, support for individual liberty is weak, and alienation from law is fairly common. Then, at the opposite end of the continuum lie Denmark, the Netherlands, West Germany, and Great Britain. The peoples of these countries tend to value individual liberty, to support the rule of law, and to reject the proposition that law is an external, repressive force. In the center, the cluster of Spain, Italy, France, and Ireland, somewhat mixed views prevail. Although there are important differences within these three clusters, we have some confidence that beliefs about law differ across these three major groupings of countries.

The differences between the halves of the united Germany deserve special attention. West Germans seem to look favorably on law and are at least somewhat positively oriented toward individual liberty. The East Germans, contrariwise, tend not to view law as neutral, value liberty less, and are not strong supporters of the rule of law. Like virtually all elements of the "unified" German system, there are substantial differences between East and West.

Just how stable are these so-called legal cultural values? Although we do not have a strong test of the hypothesis that these are enduring attributes of the cultures of the member states, we can compare these findings with similar questions asked of the same respondents in the first wave of the panel in 1992. In that survey, six items measuring the three subdimensions

---

1. Eta is a statistic that compares the within of sum-of-squares (within-nation variability) to the between of sum-of-squares (across-nation variability) and is equivalent to R2 from regressing the dependent variable on a set of country dummy variables. One would never expect either of these statistics to be very large because all variability within the country is treated as error variance.

of legal values were asked (the 1993 survey included one new measure of perception of legal neutrality and one new rule-of-law question). Comparison of the national mean scores for 1992 and 1993 reveals a great deal of stability. Fully 84 percent of the variance in the 1993 legal neutrality scores can be explained by the 1992 scores. For the other two subdimensions, the relationships are not quite so strong, but the correlations are still remarkable—63 percent of the variance in rule-of-law attitudes in 1993 can be explained; for attitudes toward individual liberty, 67 percent of the variance can be explained. Thus, it seems that our measures capture a stable attribute of the cultural values of these polities.

It appears from this analysis that there are important cross-national differences in legal values. Yet, as we noted above, there is also important *within-country* variation in attitudes. Especially since one of the most trenchant criticisms of cultural analyses is that they *assume* cultural homogeneity rather than testing for it (cf. Sarat 1993; but see Tyler 1994; Lind, Huo, and Tyler 1994; Rasinski 1987), it is prudent to explore subcultural differences in legal values. It is to that task we now turn.

SUBCULTURAL DIFFERENCES IN LEGAL ATTITUDES

To what degree are these national differences a function of the composition of their respective populations? After all, the standard deviations of the indices employed above are substantial, indicating that there is important within-culture variance to explain (cf. Tyler 1994; Lind, Huo, and Tyler 1994). We can investigate this problem by considering whether these legal attitudes are predictable by standard sorts of demographic variables. Here we focus on differences in legal values potentially associated with social class (including level of education), gender, age, religion, and ideology. To simplify the analysis, we focus on the summary indicator of legal values (from the second-order factor analysis).

The data are absolutely conclusive on one of these variables—ideology. At least as measured by ideological self-identification, ideology is completely unrelated to one's legal values. This finding may reflect in part the continuing deterioration of the utility of the terms "Left" and "Right" in contemporary European politics, at least as ordinary people understand them.

The findings for the remainder of the variables are much more significant, although they are complicated as well. In most countries, there are very strong effects of level of education on legal values. Those who are more educated tend to support the rule of law more, favor individual liberty more, and to believe in the neutrality of law. This is not true in Belgium, Denmark, Ireland, and Luxembourg, although in all countries except Luxembourg *either* education or social class has a significant (and in most instances strong) impact on legal values. Only in France and Great Britain do we observe significant independent effects of both education and social class.

Education is a variable that may characterize different processes. It can represent the acquisition of cognitive abilities, or it may simply stand for the amount of social learning (socialization) the individual has acquired. Although we are unable to disentangle the specific process involved, the better educated tend to view law in more liberal and universalistic terms.

Neither age, gender, nor religion has much substantial or consistent impact on legal values. In Denmark, Italy, and Luxembourg, older respondents tend to have less liberal and universalistic legal values, but that is not true in the other ten countries. Only in Portugal and Great Britain are there gender differences, and in both countries women tend to have slightly more liberal and universalistic legal values. Religion is significant only in the two halves of Germany, but in both, Catholics tend to be *more*, not less, committed to the rule of law and individual liberty and to believe in the neutrality of law. In West Germany, there is also a significant, similar effect of those from minority religious groups. Elsewhere within the EU, religion does not seem to divide the mass public, at least when it comes to attitudes toward law.

In general, from this analysis, we conclude that differences in legal values are rooted mainly in social class. In virtually all countries, the combination of social class and level of education provides relatively good purchase on the sorts of attitudes people hold toward law. To some extent, it is those who profit from the existing socioeconomic structuring of society who tend to view law as a beneficent institution.

CONSEQUENCES OF LEGAL CULTURE

So far, although we have spoken about the correlates of legal culture, we have focused on the potential sources of this syndrome. Ultimately, though, we are all interested in how, if at all, legal culture shapes the operation of the legal and political systems, the actions of individuals, and the behavior of officials. Here, too, we are not in a position to go very far in addressing these questions, but we can offer a couple of tidbits about the correlates and perhaps consequences of legal culture in the member nations of the European Union.

One of the biggest issues in any legal system is compliance. Do citizens, organizations, and officials obey the law? Do they obey in conflictual situations? We do not have measures of the compliance or noncompliance of individuals. But we do have data on the compliance of European governments with the treaties of the European Union. The transnational character of the EU makes compliance an especially salient issue; accordingly, the EU relies on a number of procedures to bring about obedience to European law. Together with the Court of Justice, the European Commission [EC] serves as a bulwark of the integrity of the treaties, working to ensure compliance with the various forms of European law. Under Article 169 of the EC Treaty, the Commission initiates proceedings against national governments for "infringement" of the treaties. This procedure involves several steps: the Commission files a letter of notice; the member state responds; the Commission investigates further and then issues a reasoned opinion; and then, if the member state does not comply, the Commission may bring the question to the ECJ. The infringement procedure is one of the most critical mechanisms of European integration, and, naturally, the EU has kept a careful record of the performance of member states in this regard. Here we use the number of notices of infringement filed against nations by the Commission as a national indicator of law-abidingness (on the EU and infringements, see Nugent 1994, 112–17). There is some ambiguity about this measure, but it gives us a rough-and-ready indication of which nations have shown a propensity to go against the laws and treaties of the Union.

Following the logic of our arguments about the correlates of the rule of law and legal neutrality, we expect to find a strong association between this pair of subdimensions of legal culture and our measure of noncompliance. For the neutrality of law, the relationship is strong ($r = -.55$); for the rule of law, it is significant but weaker ($r = -.37$). The stronger the commitment to the rule of law and neutrality of law as principles in a nation, the less extensive the noncompliance with the European law. Thus, it appears that legal values have at least some connections with broader legal and political policies.

DISCUSSION

In this inquiry into the legal values of Western Europeans, we have made several important discoveries. First, the member states of the European Union do indeed differ in the legal values their citizens hold. Significant differences in attitudes toward the rule of law exist, as do perceptions that law is a neutral, benevolent institution. Lesser but still important differences can be found in attitudes toward individual liberty and social order. These various attitudes cluster into discernible groups, and we have presented a classification of each member state according to its legal culture.

We have also made some progress in identifying the sources of these legal values. At the microlevel, we found that social class made a substantial difference in virtually every society. Indeed, some of the explanation of cross-national differences is surely connected to the nature of the class cleavages within the societies. We do not wish to overstate our findings, but it appears that law is often bound up with class struggles in the states of Western Europe. Working people in Western Europe do not easily embrace the view that law is neutral, that the rule of law ought to prevail, or to value individual liberty as highly as social order. We also found some important nonrelationships—legal values rarely vary according to ideology, gender, age, or religion.

At the macrolevel, legal culture flows from differences in levels of modernity, in the degree of fractionalization of society, and, to a lesser degree, in the extent of individualism within the broader social culture. In many respects, the macro- and microlevel findings lead to the same conclusion. To the extent that politics is driven by traditional, class-based cleavages, law is perceived as an instrument of political advantage rather than of social consensus. Where societies are more modernized, law is perceived as less repressive.

We do not contend that the legal values of the mass public are the only important influence over the operation of the legal system. Indeed, we accept [Erhard] Blankenburg's argument that, under some circumstances, the objective incentives offered by legal institutions are sufficient to explain the behavior of citizens within the polity. Certainly, rules and institutions do matter and culture cannot be expected to determine legal practice irrespective of objective conditions.

Nor do we wish to overemphasize the role of the mass public. Many patterns of behavior are determined not by the mass public but by elites. The mass public occasionally sets the broad parameters within which political decisions are made; it rarely commands its leaders to take particular courses of action. The legal values of the mass public are certainly only a single strand in the broader fabric of law and politics. But we nonetheless contend that mass legal values play some role in the functioning of the legal system and that whether citizens are committed to the rule of law, for instance, has something to do with the way that legal decisions are made and implemented within the political process, and we have adduced some empirical evidence of this connection.

We have not been able to demonstrate directly the behavioral consequences that flow from these cultural differences. We suspect that there are important differences across the systems in the degree to which individual citizens flout the law or seek to manipulate it to their own self-interests, but we have presented no data on this point. Moreover, there is likely a myriad of consequences—for both the performance of legal institutions and the behavior of individual citizens—that flows from these values but which is extremely difficult to demonstrate in a rigorous, scientific way. We do not despair that it is impossible to conduct such analysis, but we have not yet figured out how to do so.

Finally, we return for a moment to the European Union. The EU, in large part a creation of law, now faces important issues of decentralization through the concepts of subsidiarity and federalism. It is of course a fiction to assert that there has ever been consensual acceptance of the universalism and supremacy of EC law over national law and national cultural beliefs and practices. But given the new impetus toward decentralization, we fully expect that differences in legal cultures will play an even greater role in the ways in which EC law gets implemented within each of the member states. The interaction between law and culture, as we noted in the introduction, becomes all the more momentous within the context of an expanding EU, especially to the extent that formerly authoritarian systems and perhaps even Islamic states are considered for admission to the Union. In light of the substantial variations we have documented within the current structure of the EU, the differences throughout the remainder of Europe may take on increasing importance. Consequently, more systematic and broader explorations and explanations of legal cultures should certainly be a high priority in the research agenda of the field.

REFERENCES

Bierbrauer, Gunter. 1994. Toward an understanding of legal culture: Variations in individualism and collectivism between Kurds, Lebanese, and Germans. *Law and Society Review* 28: 243.

Caldeira, Gregory A., and James L. Gibson. 1992. The etiology of public support for the Supreme Court. *American Journal of Political Science* 36: 635.

Ehrmann, Henry W. 1976. *Comparative legal cultures*. Englewood Cliffs, NJ: Prentice-Hall.

Gibson, James L., Raymond M. Duch, and Kent L. Tedin. 1992. Democratic values and the transformation of the Soviet Union. *Journal of Politics* 54: 329.

Levin, Martin. 1977. *Urban politics and criminal courts*. Chicago: University of Chicago Press.

———. 1972. Urban politics and judicial behavior. *Journal of Legal Studies* 1: 193.

Lind, E. Allan, Y. J. Huo, and Tom R. Tyler. 1994. . . . And justice for all: Ethnicity, gender, and preferences for dispute resolution processes. *Law and Human Behavior* 18: 269.

Nugent, Neill. 1994. *The government and politics of the European Union*. 3d ed. Durham, NC: Duke University Press.

Putnam, Robert D. 1993. *Making democracy work: Civic traditions in modern Italy*. Princeton, NJ: Princeton University Press.

Rasinski, Kenneth. 1987. What's fair is fair—Or is it? Value differences underlying public views about social justice. *Journal of Personality and Social Psychology* 53: 201.

Sarat, Austin. 1993. Authority, anxiety, and procedural justice: Moving from scientific detachment to critical engagement. *Law and Society Review* 27: 647.

Tyler, Tom R. 1994. Governing amid diversity: The effect of fair decisionmaking procedures on the legitimacy of government. *Law and Society Review* 28: 809.

———. 1990. *Why people obey the law.* New Haven, CT: Yale University Press.

Wilson, James Q. 1976. *Varieties of political behavior.* New York: Basic Books.

BETWEEN LAW AND CULTURE

RWANDA'S *GACACA* AND POSTCOLONIAL LEGALITY

Ariel Meyerstein

INTRODUCTION

This article uses the Rwandan *inkiko gacaca* (*gacaca*) and Amnesty International's (AI) criticism of them as a lens through which to reflect on contemporary human rights praxis. Though what follows relates most closely to debates in transitional justice over the rule of law in postconflict societies, the ramifications of the discussion may apply with equal force to more quotidian human rights violations that occur on a smaller scale. Postgenocide Rwanda does present an extreme situation, but the challenges the country faced in rebuilding itself are unfortunately not unique among postconflict situations throughout the world, particularly in developing states. This article, then, is about Rwanda and its struggles, but it is hoped that its experiences will serve as an adequate reflection of broader global phenomena.

The *gacaca* are a state-administered system of approximately ten thousand community-based judicial forums established by the Rwandan government to process its massive population of suspected *genocidaires* (those who participated in the 1994 genocide) through a blend of retributive and restorative justice. The word *gacaca* is Kinyarwandan, referring to the lawn where community members traditionally gathered to arbitrate minor disputes among close relations or neighbors. Though based on the traditional practice of *gacaca*, the contemporary *inkiko gacaca* have additional features not present in the restorative mechanisms once used throughout the country to settle local property disputes and other conflicts. Most significantly, the government modified the traditionally restorative form to accommodate a retributive aspect with a strong emphasis on a plea-bargaining mechanism and community service.

The Rwandan government turned to the *gacaca* after years of watching the Western-styled national courts fail to process the suspect population adequately, which at its height reached one hundred twenty thousand detainees languishing in jails outfitted for fifteen thousand. After deliberations with members of civil society, international donors, and NGOs, in 2001, the government established the *gacaca* with the aim of speeding up its processing of genocide suspects. The international community supported the Rwandan government's attempts at maximum accountability through extensive prosecution—as opposed to granting blanket or conditioned amnesties or simply doing nothing at all (A[mnesty] I[nternational] 2002, sec. II). However, despite this satisfaction with the approach to justice taken, human rights groups like Amnesty International nonetheless remain discontent with the *form of justice* the Rwandan government has chosen.

Noting that these *gacaca* differ significantly from the precolonial version of the justice mechanism, AI and others in the global North insist on holding the *gacaca* to the international standards for due process and find them lacking (A[mnesty] I[nternational] 2002, sec. VII; A[mnesty] I[nternational] 2004). Human rights advocates argue that the *gacaca* fail to satisfy the demands of Article 14 of the International Covenant on Civil and Political Rights (ICCPR), governing the right to a fair trial, including the right to be presumed innocent, the right to equality of arms, and the right to impartial judges. Amnesty International grounds its criticism in the state-administered nature of the new *gacaca* jurisdictions, arguing that this apparent centralization of justice has radically transformed the traditionally decentralized local process, increasing the need for safeguards for the accused (A[mnesty] I[nternational] 2002, sec. VI).

In an interesting turn of events, the Rwandan Supreme Court responded to Amnesty International's criticism, offering a different interpretation of international human rights standards and, indeed, a different jurisprudential logic for approaching international human rights. The Rwandan Supreme Court's response expresses a form of weak or "soft" cultural relativism: it does not deny the existence of universal norms outright (indeed, it would be difficult for it to do so, since Rwanda has ratified the ICCPR and the African Charter of Human and Peoples' Rights), but at the same time, finds nothing inherently wrong with the due process offered by the *gacaca*. The Rwandan Supreme Court claims that respecting human rights does not demand blind obedience to overly detailed positive law, but rather is fundamentally about "respect[ing] [of] the value of human dignity" (Supreme Court of Rwanda 2003, 2).

The Rwandan Supreme Court also exposes the central inconsistency inherent in absolutist expressions of these standards in light of Rwanda's particularized circumstances, namely, the mass participatory nature of the genocide and the material reality of Rwanda's underdevelopment. This situation, the Court argues, juxtaposes competing universal human rights norms against one another (for example, the prohibition against indefinite detention versus the bundle of rights involved in ensuring a fair trial) in a seemingly irreconcilable paradox. Finally, the Court argues from the standpoint of resources, indignantly remarking that the *gacaca* present the best possible solution given the near-impossible context of a mass participatory genocide in a developing country, and [the Court] welcomes any "miracle solutions" the human rights group would propose (Supreme Court of Rwanda 2003, 5).

The *gacaca* have become emblematic of a larger global contestation over norms of justice and human rights and the continuing global experiment constituting the field of transitional justice. This article seizes on the case of the *gacaca* as a lens through which to bring these issues into sharper focus in an effort to understand what they mean for human rights praxis. By being attentive to the counterhegemonic impulse displayed in the Rwandan Supreme Court's reply to the international NGO critique, this article responds to Jose Alvarez's call for more thinking about how international law can "look to the bottom" (Alvarez 1999, 474; Rajagopal 2003). Entertaining this soft cultural relativist perspective challenges the faith exuded by the "international legalists"—international lawyers and other human rights practitioners in the global North (Alvarez 1999)—hopefully exposing some of the assumptions and problems of their approach.

I argue that AI's overly legalistic approach to the *gacaca* forces them into a Western-court paradigm, even as they acknowledge the *gacaca*'s complex origins. Comparing the *gacaca* to the standards of fair trial set out in international human rights law, the AI critique finds them deficient substitutes for Western justice. The *gacaca* are threatening to the universalizing, homogenizing human rights imaginary, which lashes out to squash cultural difference and legal pluralism by criticizing the *gacaca* for failures to approximate canonized doctrine. This "jurispathic" gesture (Cover 1983) places the AI critique within the broader framework of the Western will to power through categorization of knowledge, a form of symbolic violence that has had profound effects in the past (Said 1978; Fanon 1965; Mbembe 2001; Mamdani 2001). By complicating the view of the *gacaca* with insights from the extensive fieldwork of another international NGO, Penal Reform International, the article tries to show how AI's heavy-handed critique obstructs efforts of understanding the *gacaca* as *gacaca*. Rather than try to force them into a Western model of a court, they should be appreciated as a truly hybrid form emerging from Rwanda's postcolonial condition that is perhaps uniquely capable of responding to the problem of mass atrocity produced by collective violence.

. . .

As this article is as much or more about the human rights community as it is about communities in Rwanda, I have relied on a "paraethnographic" method (Riles 2006, 57). I did not do extensive fieldwork of my own, directly observing the *gacaca* or interviewing the human rights advocates to whom I refer. Rather, I pay close attention to the rhetorical strategies and approaches of the human rights advocates as they represent them through their reports and other documents. Riles points out that such documents are integral to ethnographies of NGOs and international organizations and should themselves be treated as "ethnographic artifacts" (Riles 2000). Observations and data on the *gacaca* and Rwandan society are culled from direct observational studies done by others and from daily monitoring of the national Rwandan press and international press coverage of the *gacaca* and political developments in Rwanda.

What hopefully emerges is a "vertical slice" (Nader 1974, 1980) of a particular episode in which actors battle out their competing visions of global norms of human rights and justice. A vertical slice is an attempt to "study up"—to link the localized effects of a particular set of practices and knowledge production back to the sites of power wherein this knowledge is articulated and implemented. Importantly, the vertical slice approach also allows us to give voice to the Rwandans, rather than allowing the conversation—much like the authoring of the "universal" human rights treaties themselves—to continue solely among "ourselves," namely, privileged legal elites in the West (Merry 2006).

THE *INKIKO GACACA*

Background

We lack extensive information about the cultural practice of *gacaca* in precolonial Rwanda. Traditionally, respected members of the community, *inyangamugayo* (literally, "those who detest disgrace"), would serve as judges in a community-wide process of resolving civil matters, that is, disputes pertaining to inheritance, civil liability, failure to repay loans, thefts, and conjugal matters, arising between family members or close neighbors (Tully 2003, 395; Waldorf 2006, 48; Karekezi et al. 2004, 73). The community considered guilt for transgressions to extend to the accused's entire family. Sanctions resulting from disputes typically involved compensation for damaged or stolen property. Payment signified recognition of the seriousness of the offense while still allowing for the eventual reintegration of the offender into the community (Tully 2003, 396). The *gacaca* shared many qualities typically associated with "informal" conflict resolution mechanisms: parties with direct links to one another; litigation viewed as a communal concern—rather than merely between aggrieved or affronted individuals; a victim-centered trial; litigant's participation motivated primarily through soft social pressure as opposed to official state coercion; flexible procedures; and finally, a goal of social harmony (Karekezi et al. 2004, 73).

Though there is not much empirical work on the continuing prevalence of *gacaca* in the postcolonial era, the practice did survive colonization (Waldorf 2006, 49). Foreign observers reported various communities across the country making recourse to the *gacaca* in the immediate aftermath of the genocide and the legal vacuum it precipitated, though it is somewhat disputed as to whether this was motivated by spontaneous grassroots demands or imposed by local officials (ibid.). The *gacaca* were available, though perhaps not pervasively so, when the Rwandan government found itself searching for solutions to its judicial impasse following the genocide.

After stopping the genocide, the Kagame regime executed twenty-two Hutu extremists in public stadiums and arrested tens of thousands of people, creating a prison population of over one hundred and twenty thousand inmates held in prisons designed to hold a maximum of fifteen thousand prisoners (Drumbl 1998, 571–76). Large numbers of people were imprisoned on scant evidence, often turned in by opportunistic neighbors (Waldorf 2006, 41; Des Forges and Longman 2004, 56; Schabas 2005, 880). Starting in 1996, twelve national specialized courts began processing the inmates, rendering judgment in 9,700 cases as of December 2003 (Waldorf 2006, 44). At that pace, it would have taken over eighty years to try all of the accused (Schabas 2005, 888).

These trials, moreover, which worked as Western courts, were heavily criticized by international human rights advocates for shortcomings in due process, particularly the inadequate defense offered the accused (Schabas 2005, 886). Schabas, who observed early trials himself, insists that the severity of the criticism varied with whether those observing were common law-trained or civil law-trained lawyers (887). Lars Waldorf insists the positive assessments were "overly positive" but concedes that fairness has improved over the years (Waldorf 2006, 44–46).

Structure

Given this incredible situation, the Rwandan government began searching for alternatives. The decision to pursue the *gacaca* came out of a series of "meetings of reflection" (Karekezi et al. 2004, 71) held between May 1998 and March 1999, which aimed at creating a discussion about postgenocide reconstruction among leaders of government, civil society, and industry. After debates and redrafting, the Transitional National Assembly adopted the Organic Law establishing the *gacaca* courts on October 12, 2000.

The official goals of the *gacaca* are: (1) to reveal the truth about what has happened, (2) to accelerate the genocide trials, (3) to eradicate the culture of impunity, (4) to reconcile the Rwandans and reinforce their unity, and (5) to prove that Rwandan society has the capacity to settle its own problems through a system of justice based on Rwandan custom. Specifically, the *gacaca* jurisdictions were to process the genocide suspects by categorizing them according to the four categories created by a previous Organic Law passed in 1996, which had established domestic jurisdiction over the crimes of genocide and crimes against humanity. It was in fact the first domestic genocide law passed in the world (Waldorf 2006, 43).

Each *gacaca* court consists of a General Assembly (comprised of all cell inhabitants over eighteen years old, requiring no fewer than one hundred people for a quorum), and a Bench consisting of nine judges (and five alternates). The Organic Law prohibits individuals with specific governmental or political affiliations from being elected to the Bench or being selected as a delegate to the General Assembly of a superior jurisdiction. Though there is a strong emphasis on impartiality in the Organic Law itself, this has proven one of the greatest challenges to their successful implementation.

All *gacaca* hearings are to be held in public (except when held *in camera* for reasons of public order or good morals). While Bench deliberation is confidential, all judgments are made public, and trial details are supposed to be documented in full. The *gacaca* Benches have the power to summon individuals to testify before the tribunal, to issue search warrants, impose criminal sanctions, and confiscate property. The Bench can also sentence those who refuse to testify, who omit testimony, or who make false accusations to one- to three-year prison terms.

CURRENT STATUS OF THE *GACACA*

Though a central purpose of the *gacaca* jurisdictions is to deal with the significant prison population that the national courts were failing to process quickly enough, they have in fact *added* considerably to the number of total suspects. By the end of the pilot phase, 63,447 additional suspects were implicated, leading the government to make the crude prediction that as many as 761,448 persons could eventually be prosecuted nationwide (National Service of Gacaca Jurisdictions 2006). Accurate statistics are difficult to find ... but as of February 2007, more than 818,564 people had been implicated as participants in the genocide, more than 50,000 had been tried, and more than 152,000 had confessed. Of those accused,

47,000 are judges, 15 of whom are currently detained (Hirondelle News Agency 2007; National Service of Gacaca Jurisdictions 2006). We can get a sense of the distribution of these suspects across the categories based on figures released in October 2006. Suspects were categorized as follows: 72,539 in Category 1; 397,103 in Category 2; and 296,847 in Category 3 (Hirondelle News Agency 2007). The *gacaca* should process these additional suspects much faster than the twelve specialized national courts could have processed a similarly sized population, but it seems unlikely that they will complete their work by 2008, the timeline suggested by national officials.

THE HUMAN RIGHTS CRITIQUE OF THE *GACACA*

Amnesty International's Due-Process Concerns

In the introduction to its report, "*Gacaca*: A Question of Justice," AI makes a clear distinction between the traditional community dispute resolution form of *gacaca* indigenous to Rwandan society and the new, "legally established judicial bodies . . . re-invented and transformed" by the Rwandan government, which "merge customary practice with a Western, formal court structure" (A[mnesty] I[nternational] 2002, I). The report notes the hybridity of the *gacaca* almost in passing, failing to appreciate fully the significance of this unique juridical form, and instead, choosing to treat the *gacaca* as if they were simply Western courts.

Amnesty International makes several recommendations to Rwandan authorities on how to improve the due process of the *gacaca*. Defendants should be held in adequate detention facilities meeting international standards; defendants should be given information regarding the reasons for arrest and detention and provided prompt information as to charges against them; defendants should be provided with lawyers; defendants and lawyers should have access to appropriate information, including documents, and be given adequate time and facilities necessary to the preparation of their defense; trials should be postponed if they have not had enough time or materials to prepare their defense; defendants must be able to call and examine witnesses on their behalf and examine those against them; judicial advisors should have a clear mandate regulating their intervention in *gacaca* proceedings; defendants should have the right to appeal; and compensation for bodily harm or property loss should be paid (ibid., sec. IX[1]).

These recommendations—adding defense lawyers, extending preparation time before trial, and so forth—are mostly all quite impossible goals for Rwanda to achieve. More importantly, implementation of these recommendations would slow the processing of the accused to the rate at which the national courts were working, meaning that several decades or more would pass before the authorities tried the last case. In other words, meeting Amnesty International's checklist for what constitutes a fair trial—Article 14 of the ICCPR—would mean turning the *gacaca* into Western courts.

THE COUNTERCRITIQUE: RWANDA RESPONDS

The rhetoric from Paul Kagame on the eve of the national election of *gacaca* judges stands in sharp contrast to the human rights critiques. Kagame urged Rwandans to realize that *gacaca* represents a uniquely Rwandan solution to the problems of the country and added,

"If the *Gacaca* Courts function as we anticipate, it will be an important contribution to the understanding and advancement of international law" (Githae 2004). Overreaching statements like these reinforce the reactions of some observers of the *gacaca*, which find them, like other experiments in "local justice," to be invented traditions intended to "promote social control and political ideologies" (Waldorf 2006, 6).

Such bold assertions . . . could also be described as falling into line with the standard denial of human rights abuses among developing world governments or the claims made by Asian countries in response to outside criticism of their human rights records that any criticized practices exhibited "Asian values" (Wilson 1997). While it is beyond dispute that the *gacaca* are a state-administered hybrid form that taps into traditional forms of dispute resolution, whether they are a means of social control or a forward-looking attempt to rebuild the country is an empirical question that cannot be so readily resolved. It is, in any case, still worthwhile to indulge the Rwandan response for what their perspective might add to global discussions of human rights.

GACACA AS GACACA

The "truth" about the *gacaca*, and the adequate measure of their capacity to respond to the social rupture caused by the genocide, lies somewhere between these two accounts. The challenge confronting the human rights practitioner is to straddle these versions and arrive at practical solutions that can improve on overall human flourishing relative to respective starting positions. This kind of advocacy is one of incremental change, drawing strength and ingenuity from recognizing and accepting its own conceptual limitations and the prevailing material and sociocultural constraining factors. In this case, one such conceptual limitation is the liberal legal model of the law and the expectations it generates among human rights advocates. Its basic assumptions about law's neutrality—if they are ever true—certainly are placed under great strain in the socially immersed *gacaca* courts. Material and sociocultural constraining factors emerge from Rwanda's underdevelopment; it powerfully shapes their daily lives and the functioning of the *gacaca*. Thus, any human rights intervention must take these salient factors into account. Perhaps above all else, the choice the human rights practitioner makes as to how to make his or her intervention should be guided by a principle of humility and a willingness to suspend one's own conceptions as to how things naturally work and, in his or her view, *must* work.

The particular form of the *gacaca* and the defense of them present distinctly cultural responses to the Nuremberg model that has dominated transitional justice. The *gacaca* both accept and resist the dominant international legalist model but do so from a standpoint of culture, rather than sovereignty. Moreover, this particularized form is attentive to the needs of postcolonial society in the developing world and in its emphasis on communal development and reconstruction driven by local, informal processes. The *gacaca* are in this way perhaps a more appropriate form of justice for the Rwandan postgenocide than AI credits them to be. Concern about the social and economic well-being of the polity—development—takes precedence over the narrow focus on individual civil and political rights, as the liberal legalists and human rights activists tend to do, despite the impracticality of such interventions in postconflict situations.

Rwanda has not rejected the basic notion of universal jurisdiction, either in its own national prosecutions or in its initially begrudging but ultimately productive cooperation with the International Criminal Tribunal for Rwanda [ICTR]. On the contrary, it has adopted the "maximum accountability" approach, becoming the first country in the world to pass domestic legislation creating jurisdiction over the crime of genocide (Waldorf 2006, 43). It has applied this paradigm selectively, thus far, in not making RPF [Rwandan Patriotic Front] acts subject to the *gacaca* proceedings, but the ICTR, which relies on the Rwandan government's cooperation for its continued operation, has yet to investigate RPF crimes either. The Rwandan government's response to AI's criticism presents an argument about what the universality of human rights really means in practice and simultaneously demands respect for the particular forms of justice it employs.

While trying not to essentialize Rwandan culture, I contend that this rejection of the idealized conception of the rule of law is different from [Slobodan] Milosevic's imperialism arguments or the legalistic constructions of the Latin American courts. Rather, the Rwandans' protests found themselves on an assertion of culture, albeit a weak one: they appeal to an idea of Rwandan culture and identity that can be conceived of as precolonial or as postcolonial but drawing on precolonial forms. In either conception, the practice the Rwandans are defending has its roots in a political moment that is presovereign by definition (in the strictly Westphalian sense). It reaches back to a time that predates the imposition and subsequent removal of colonial orderings that redefined Rwandan political space in accord with the structures of sovereignty under international law. In short, the Rwandan Supreme Court is quibbling with the details of what justice means from a standpoint of cultural difference.

In sum, the internal logic of the *gacaca* is a truly hybrid postcolonial cultural form—borrowing both from the retributive logic of the Belgian penal codes and the international criminal paradigm, while maintaining fidelity to and marshalling the power of the restorative justice of its indigenous roots and directing it toward a modern state-driven development enterprise. Though it does not purport to articulate a theory of justice per se, the Rwandan government clearly sees the *gacaca* as central to the country's redevelopment, and, thus, a notion of "development as justice" seems an apt description. Such a theory of justice, however, does not sit easily with the international legalists and human rights advocates because they see its communal and informal processes as sacrificing attention to the sanctity of individual rights and the imperative to prosecute every individual wrongdoer. The hybridity of the *gacaca* threatens the universal vision of human rights espoused by the legalists, and so AI's attempts to impose the homogenizing universal ideals of the human rights normative regime on the *gacaca* can be seen as an effort to stamp out the legal pluralism they represent, understandably generating the countercritique.

REFERENCES

Alvarez, José. 1999. Crimes of state/crimes of hate: Lessons from Rwanda. *Yale Law Journal of International Law* 24: 365–483.

Amnesty International. 2004. Rwanda: The enduring legacy of genocide and war. http://web.amnesty.org/library/index/engafr470082004

———. 2002. Rwanda-Gacaca: A question of justice. http://web.amnesty.org/library/index/engafr 470072002

Cover, Robert M. 1983. Foreword: "Nomos and narrative." *Harvard Law Review* 97: 4–68.

Des Forges, Allison, and Timothy Longman. 2004. Legal responses to genocide in Rwanda. In *My neighbor, my enemy: Justice and community in the aftermath of mass atrocity*, ed. Eric Stover and Harvey Weinstein. Cambridge: Cambridge University Press.

Drumbl, Mark. 1998. Rule of law amid lawlessness: Counseling the accused in Rwanda's domestic genocide trials. *Columbia Human Rights Law Review* 29: 545–638.

Fanon, Frantz. 1965. *The wretched of the Earth.* New York: Grove Press.

Githae, Muturi. 2004. Gacaca courts undertaking to hasten trials. *The New Times*, October 1.

Hirondelle News Agency. 2007. Rwanda/Gacacas-2006: General opening of the semi-traditional tribunals. January 1.

Karekezi, Urusaro Alice, Alphonse Nshimiyimama, and Beth Mutamba. 2004. Localizing justice: Gacaca courts. In *My neighbor, my enemy: Justice and community in the aftermath of mass atrocity*, ed. Eric Stover and Harvey Weinstein. Cambridge: Cambridge University Press.

Mamdani, Mahmmod. 2001. *When victims become killers: Colonialism, nativism, and the genocide in Rwanda.* Princeton, NJ: Princeton University Press.

Merry, Sally Engle. 2006. New legal realism and the ethnography of transnational law. *Law and Social Inquiry* 31: 939–95.

Mbembe, Achille. 2001. *On the postcolony.* Berkeley: University of California Press.

Nader, Laura. 1980. The vertical slice: Hierarchies and children. In *Hierarchies and society: Anthropological perspectives on bureaucracy*, ed. G. M. Britan and R. Cohen, 31–44. Philadelphia, PA: Institute of the Study of Human Issues.

———. 1974. Up the anthropologist—Perspectives from studying up. In *Reinventing anthropology*, ed. Dell Hymes. New York: Random House.

National Service of Gacaca Jurisdictions. 2006. Gacaca jurisdictions: Achievements, problems, and future prospects. http://www.inkikogacaca.gov.rw/En/EnIntroduction.htm

Rajagopal, Balakrishnan. 2003. *International law from below: Development, social movements, and third world resistance.* Cambridge: Cambridge University Press.

Riles, Annelise. 2006. Anthropology, human rights, and legal knowledge: Culture in the iron cage. *American Anthropology* 108: 52–65.

———. 2000. *The network inside out.* Ann Arbor: University of Michigan Press.

Said, Edward. 1978. *Orientalism.* New York: Pantheon.

Schabas, William A. 2005. Genocide trials and gacaca courts. *Journal of International Criminal Justice* 3: 879–95.

Supreme Court of Rwanda-Departement des Jurisdictions Gacaca. 2003. Mise au point au sujet du rapport et differentes correspondances d'Amnesty International [Developments on the subject of the report and different documents of Amnesty International].

Tully, L. Danielle. 2003. Human rights compliance and the Gacaca jurisdictions in Rwanda. *Boston College International and Comparative Law Review* 26: 385–414.

Waldorf, Lars. 2006. Mass justice for mass atrocity: Rethinking local justice as transitional justice. *Temple Law Review* 79: 1–87.

Wilson, Richard A. 1997. Introduction. In *Human Rights, culture, and context: Anthropological perspectives.* Cambridge: Cambridge University Press.

12 | LEGAL CULTURES IN THE (UN)RULE OF LAW

INDIGENOUS RIGHTS AND JURIDIFICATION
IN GUATEMALA

Rachel Sieder

INTRODUCTION

Tate and Vallinder, writing about the judicialization—which they define as the global expansion of judicial power, make a distinction between "the judicialization of politics" and a second, distinct phenomenon, namely, the "less dramatic instance of the expansion of judicial power, or judicialization, [that is] the domination of nonjudicial negotiating or decision-making arenas by quasi-judicial (legalistic) procedures" (Tate and Vallinder 1995, 5).

In this chapter I focus on this aspect of judicialization, which I refer to here as juridification. Discussion of the phenomenon of juridification has traditionally focused on advanced capitalist economies and welfare states rather than on the developing economies and fragile democracies of Latin America. Rather than the spread of regulation per se, I suggest here that in many parts of Latin America, juridification instead involves the strategic invocation of legal instruments and the adoption and appropriation of lawlike discourses and practices by different social actors.

My principal focus in this chapter is not on the actions of plaintiffs, lawyers, or judges within the formal structures of the courts. Rather, I consider processes of juridification whereby indigenous people's social movements stake their rights claims to greater autonomy, not simply or principally by resorting to the tribunals but by mimicking the state and constituting alternative "(para)-legalities." More broadly, this chapter seeks to reflect on the relationship between dominant legal cultures and social movement engagements with legality within a broader context of legal pluralism. As I discuss later, addressing the specific case of Guatemala, indigenous people in Latin America have contested the exploitation of natural resources in their territories by resorting to symbolic representations and alternative practices that invoke international legal principles and, specifically, their collective rights to prior consultation. New forms of social protest and resistance combine local cus-

Reprinted from Rachel Sieder, "Legal Cultures in the (UN)Rule of Law: Indigenous Rights and Juridification in Guatemala," in *Cultures of Legality: Judicialization and Political Activism in Latin America*, ed. Javier Couso, Alexandra Huneeus, and Rachel Sieder (Cambridge: Cambridge University Press, 2010). Permission courtesy of Cambridge University Press.

toms and communal authority structures (customary law) with global rights discourses, as well as international instruments and institutions.

In addition to judicializing their rights claims before the courts, indigenous peoples' juridification of social protest signals the ways in which their contemporary forms of collective action draw on both local and transnational understandings of entitlements, obligations, and rights. In effect, a dominant legal and political environment that is hostile to expanding or protecting citizens' rights encourages certain categories of citizens to constitute alternative legalities and to attempt to secure their claims by "lawlike" actions outside the courts. These subaltern (para) legal cultures can be understood as a response to current patterns of economic and legal globalization, and to the law's failure to guarantee basic human rights to security and subsistence for the majority of the population. Yet by mimicking and appropriating formal legal instruments and institutions, these forms of claim-making both challenge and legitimate law with potentially far-reaching consequences for counterhegemonic organization.

INDIGENOUS PEOPLE, LEGAL PLURALISM, AND JURIDIFICATION

Legal pluralism is not new in Latin America: indigenous forms of law preceded the emergence of the modern nation-state and continue to coexist alongside state law. Today, the absence, inaccessibility, ineffectiveness, and discriminatory nature of state law in much of the region, particularly for the poorest sectors of the population, mean that many of the region's indigenous people continue to look to their community authorities, rather than to the national courts, to protect their interests and resolve disputes. However, across Latin America, new "legal cultures" and forms of political engagement developed by indigenous people are increasingly common, often consciously linked to global rights discourses (Brunnegger forthcoming; Rappaport 2005; Sawyer 2004; Rodríguez-Garavito and Arenas 2005). These symbolic representations of claims as legal issues appeal to a range of international instruments or institutions and can be understood as expressions of the highly globalized legal pluralism described by Boaventura de Sousa Santos (2002), where legal institutions, codes, norms, and discourses are constantly intermixed.

This form of juridification responds to a number of different factors: first, the increasing recognition of indigenous peoples' collective rights during the 1990s and 2000s within Latin American state constitutions and international law and the failure to enforce those rights in practice. A second contributory factor is the limited but important official sanctioning and promotion of community-based forms of justice that has occurred across the region.

Third, current patterns of economic globalization, particularly surrounding the exploitation of natural resources, and associated patterns of legal globalization—including legal guarantees for investors' interests and reform of domestic legislation to favor transnational capital—have spurred indigenous communities and organizations to try to secure, control, and protect their historic territories. Fourth, the acute deficiencies of the rule of law across the region, the unresponsive and exclusive nature of many countries' dominant legal cultures, and the acute asymmetries of power relations between indigenous people and national elites have also encouraged a phenomenon whereby social movements resort to law outside formal legal institutions.

INDIGENOUS RIGHTS: MULTICULTURAL CONSTITUTIONALISM

Indigenous peoples' rights and claims became increasingly politicized in Latin America throughout the 1990s. Governments across the region responded to indigenous demands and their own legitimacy deficits by constitutionally recognizing the existence of indigenous peoples, a trend Donna Van Cott (2000) referred to a decade ago as "multicultural constitutionalism." New or reformed constitutions enumerated a series of recognitions and collective entitlements of indigenous peoples living within states' borders, such as rights to customary law, collective property and bilingual education. A range of different policies were subsequently implemented to advance the new multicultural model.

The degree to which indigenous rights were formally incorporated within the region's constitutions varied. For example, in Guatemala, a constitutional reform to strengthen indigenous rights provisions in the 1985 Constitution was promised as part of the peace settlement, concluded in December 1996. However, the constitutional reforms were ultimately rejected in a popular referendum held in 1999. Some mention is made of indigenous peoples in two articles in the 1985 Constitution, but their rights are not specifically enumerated in such a way as to make them easily actionable in the courts. This partly explains the relatively limited evidence of such judicialization to date in Guatemala.

COMMUNITY JUSTICE REFORMS

An additional feature that has encouraged juridification is the tendency for judicial reforms across Latin America to endorse experiments in community-based justice. Following the first wave of multicultural constitutional reforms, the recognition of legal pluralism became part of the public policy agenda across the region (Faundez 2005). In practice, this tended to interact with broader international trends in reforming justice systems toward "de-judicializing" certain areas of social conflict. This involves a greater role for mediation, conciliation, and arbitration mechanisms and an increase in the role of nonprofessional civil society actors in the provision of justice. Initiatives involving hybrid, quasi-communal/quasi-state fora such as indigenous community courts, community conciliation services, and lay justices of the peace have been promoted in recent years. These function, in effect, as courts of first instance or alternative dispute resolution (ADR) mechanisms for petty crimes, misdemeanors, and familial or intracommunal conflicts.

Such tendencies, in effect, endorsed greater lay participation in the business of law—previously perceived as a highly technical and specialized domain. In some instances, indigenous organizations have worked with the new officially promoted multicultural justice mechanisms, reappropriating and resignifying them (Sierra 2004). In others, indigenous organizations have denounced initiatives such as *juzgados de paz indígena* as a means to supplant indigenous law and curtail the autonomy of traditional authorities. Certainly efforts by indigenous peoples' social movements to secure greater political and legal autonomy have been opposed bitterly by governments and the private sector, particularly when the territories in question contain valuable natural resources.

GUATEMALA: THE (UN)RULE OF LAW

The ways in which indigenous people interact with and mobilize around legal norms and spaces ultimately depend on the nature of the states and social movements in question, and on the legal and political opportunity structures specific to each context. In Guatemala, the possibilities for judicializing rights claims are acutely limited: it constitutes an extreme case of judicial dysfunctionality and lack of accountability in the region. Although the country has been a constitutional democracy since 1985, civil rights continue to be routinely violated, and judicial redress for even the most serious crimes is virtually nonexistent. For much of its recent history, Guatemala was characterized by restricted, semiauthoritarian forms of government (and outright military dictatorship between 1978 and 1984), and extremely high levels of systematic state violence used against the civilian population.

Consultas Populares: The Juridification of Social Protest

In 2004 and 2005 indigenous community activists in the western Guatemalan department of San Marcos mobilized to call on the government to annul a concession for open cast gold and silver mining and processing, known as the Marlin project (Fulmer, Godoy, and Neff 2008). The license for exploration was granted in 1996 to Montana Exploradora S. A., a subsidiary of Canadian mining company Glamis Gold, but the company only began operations in San Marcos in 2004. Although the license was approved after the National Congress had ratified I[nternational] L[abour] O[rganization] Convention 169, the indigenous Maya Mam and Sipakapense communities of the directly affected municipalities of San Miguel Ixtahuacan and Sipakapa were not consulted about the proposed mining development.

The Marlin project was denounced as an antidemocratic imposition and demands grew for development priorities for the municipality and surrounding areas to be decided by local people. Once Marlin's prospecting operations began, protests gained pace and drew support from environmentalists, the Catholic Church, and indigenous and popular organizations in other parts of the country.

The municipal authorities of Sipakapa then announced that they would hold a public consultation on the mining operations. This was to be held via open community assemblies in different villages according to "indigenous customary law." Although community activists defended such communal assemblies as part of their traditional forms of indigenous law and governance, Montana Exploradora immediately tried to impede the vote, submitting a legal injunction in an attempt to force the municipal authorities to suspend proceedings. In the end, pressure from the company forced the municipal mayor to back down. However, the local community development council, a relatively new body set up as part of the ongoing process of municipal decentralization, was the institutional space through which the community consultation was finally held on June 18, 2005. In all, eleven out of thirteen villages voted against the mining development, one in favor and the other abstained. Approximately 2,564 people voted in total, 95 percent of whom rejected the mining development (Central America Report 2005). The Ministry of Energy and Mines submitted an injunction to the Constitutional Court, claiming that the popular vote was unconstitutional. Nevertheless, the Court upheld the villagers' right to vote, citing ILO

Convention 169 and Article 65 of the 2002 Municipal Code, which states that when an issue particularly affects the rights and interests of indigenous communities, municipal councils will carry out consultations at the request of the indigenous communities or authorities. In effect, the Court's specific mention of the municipal councils was interpreted by some as an attempt to limit the sphere of consultation to existing official administrative structures and legal frameworks.

The Sipakapa *consulta popular* (community plebiscite) provides a clear example of juridification in response to the failure of the government and the national legal system to guarantee internationally recognized indigenous rights. In addition, a series of judicial and administrative actions against the Marlin mining concession were filed outside the country by Guatemalan popular organizations and NGOs.

Subsequent to the Sipakapa community plebiscite, other indigenous communities throughout Guatemala organized similar consultation processes in opposition to proposed projects to exploit natural resources, encouraged by growing social opposition to mining. Between 2005 and October 2009, in total thirty popular consultations or plebiscites concerning exploitation of natural resources were carried out in indigenous communities, involving more than half a million people. Two-thirds of these plebiscites related to mining concessions; the rest focused on proposed hydroelectric projects (Central America Report, October 2, 2009). In the majority of cases the consultations were organized through local indigenous municipal authorities (including community development councils); in others however, villagers organized their deliberations in communal assemblies in the face of widespread opposition from the local municipal authorities (Central America Report 2008, 2007). Together, these *consultas* signaled the increasing juridification of indigenous claims to prior consent, irrespective of whether the procedures and outcomes were legally recognized by the national or local authorities.

These "soft law" and paralegal engagements by indigenous social movements and their allies represent a watershed in indigenous people's fight to defend their natural resources and territories. Juridification involving community plebiscites is part of a wider process whereby indigenous law is being strengthened, revitalized, and reinvented in Mayan communities across the country (Rasch 2008; Sieder forthcoming).

Through the community plebiscites, indigenous people are effectively transforming local processes of participation, appealing to indigenous custom—such as deliberation in community assemblies, the importance of reaching a collective consensus, and invoking internationally enshrined collective rights to autonomy and consultation to challenge the prevailing economic model and the government's failure to take their views into account.

CONCLUSIONS

The recognition of indigenous peoples' collective rights by states and within international law, combined with the failure of states to uphold those rights in practice, has led social movements to promote processes of judicialization and juridification in favor of indigenous claims across Latin America. This is, in part, a consequence of an increasingly complex and globalized legal pluralism whereby people, territories, and commodities are subject to multiple overlapping legal regimes, and poor peoples' livelihoods are increasingly threatened by patterns of economic globalization. Under prevailing global conditions, law continues to be one of the principal tools of colonial power, even as the kind of judicialization and juridification processes described here signal the counterhegemonic uses of law. In Guatemala, juridification has occurred in the absence of a significant or strong process of judicialization. Social movements do resort to actions before the courts to defend indigenous rights, but very often with little hope that their petitions will find a hearing, or that successful challenges before the courts will translate into effective policies to guarantee their rights. I have argued here that this is partly because of the weak constitutionalization of indigenous rights and the weakness of support structures for counterhegemonic legal mobilization, and partly because of the highly dysfunctional nature of the rule of law, and the elitist, authoritarian, and violent character of the government. The relationship between processes of judicialization before the courts and the juridification of social protest in contexts of strong legal pluralism is undoubtedly an area for further comparative inquiry.

In this chapter I have indicated how the combination of a new awareness of indigenous rights, as enshrined in ILO 169 and promised by the peace accords, and the lack of due process and adequate consultation of indigenous people over mining and hydroelectric projects has produced innovative processes of juridification and paralegal engagements around the *consultas populares*. In Tate and Vallinder's words, "nonjudicial negotiating or decision-making arenas" have come to be dominated by "quasi-judicial (legalistic) procedures" (1995, 5). Through new kinds of informal, highly transnationalized justice practices involving cultural appropriation and reappropriation, Mayan activists and communities challenge the state's traditional monopoly on the production of law and publicly state their claim to being sources of legal norms and practice. Ultimately, juridification can be understood as a symbolic means by which indigenous social movements seek to stake a claim for sovereignty and for alternatives to dominant conceptions of development and democracy.

Yet powerful interests are stacked up against recognition of greater legal autonomy for local communities. Other areas of law, such as those related to foreign investment and intellectual property rights are effectively extraterritorialized or denationalized via free-trade agreements and the legal processes associated with global economic integration, often with minimum or zero transparency. Within such a context of legal fragmentation, poor and marginalized indigenous people have framed a powerful critique of hegemonic forms of development and globalization by juxtaposing internationally sanctioned collective human rights of indigenous peoples with the failure of governments to deliver on those rights in practice. However, the emancipator potential of such developments and of legal mobilization more broadly remains open to question.

REFERENCES

Brunnegger, Sandra. Forthcoming. Justice and culture in Colombia: Negotiating indigenous law. *PoLAR, The Political and Legal Anthropology Review.*

Central America Report, biweekly news bulletin. Infopress Centroamericana. http://infopressca. com/CAR/

Faundez, Julio. 2005. Community justice institutions and judicialization: Lessons from rural Peru. In *The judicialization of politics in Latin America*, ed. R. Sieder, L. Schjolden, and A. Angell, 187–210. New York: Palgrave McMillan.

Fulmer, Amanda, Angelina Snodgrass Godoy, and Philip Neff. 2008. Indigenous Rights, Resistance, and the Law: Lessons from a Guatemalan Mine. *Latin American Politics and Society* 50(4): 91–121.

Rappaport, Joanne. 2005. Intercultural utopias. *Public intellectuals, cultural experimentation, and ethnic pluralism in Colombia.* Durham, NC: Duke University Press.

Rasch, Elisabet. 2008. Representing Mayas: Indigenous authorities and the local politics of identity in Guatemala. PhD thesis, Department of Anthropology, University of Utrecht.

Rodrıguez-Garavito, Cesar, and Luis Carlos Arenas. 2005. Indigenous rights, transnational activism, and legal mobilization: The struggle of the U'wa people in Colombia. In *Law and globalization from below: Towards a cosmopolitan legality*, ed. Boaventura De Sousa Santos and Cesar Rodriguez-Garavito, 241–66. Cambridge: Cambridge University Press.

Santos, Boaventura de Sousa. 2002. *Towards a new legal common sense.* London: Butterworth/Lexis-Nexis.

Sawyer, Susanne. 2004. *Crude chronicles: Indigenous politics, multinational oil, and neoliberalism in Ecuador.* Durham, NC: Duke University Press.

Sieder, Rachel. Forthcoming. Constructing Mayan authority: The "recuperation" of indigenous law in postwar Guatemala. *Law and Society Review.*

Sierra, Maria Teresa, ed. 2004. *Haciendo justicia: Interlegalidad, derecho y genero en regiones indigenas.* Mexico: CIESAS.

Tate, C. Neal, and Torbjörn Vallinder. 1995. *The global expansion of judicial power.* New York and London: New York University Press.

Van Cott, Donna Lee. 2000. *The friendly liquidation of the past: The politics of diversity in Latin America.* Pittsburgh, PA: Pittsburgh University Press.

13 THE TRANSFORMATION OF CONSTITUTIONAL DISCOURSE AND THE JUDICIALIZATION OF POLITICS IN LATIN AMERICA

Javier Couso

INTRODUCTION

Implicit in the assertion of a connection between *legal culture* and the *judicialization of politics* in Latin America is the notion that both concepts relate to relevant practices in this area of the world. As it turns out, however, neither is uncontroversial. Some scholars do not recognize the notion of legal culture as a meaningful or useful category because they reduce social reality to rationally motivated individual actors operating under the constraint of different structures. Others dismiss the idea of a judicialization of politics in Latin America as unsuitable to the region. Building on the growing body of literature that has documented the emergence of judicialization of politics in Latin America (Rios-Figueroa and Taylor 2006; Taylor 2006; Sieder, Schjolden, and Angell 2005; Gloppen, Gargarella, and Skaar 2004; Domingo 2004; Smulovitz 2002; Helmke 2005), this chapter takes legal culture to be a useful analytical category to make sense of the behavior of judges, lawyers, and even society at large. It then proceeds to explore the connection between judicialization and legal culture in the region. Furthermore, it suggests that in addition to structural factors such as the introduction of constitutional courts, the grant of judicial review powers to high courts, or the emergence of support structures, important changes in the internal legal culture of the region have been crucial for the emergence of judicialization of politics in Latin America. Specifically, the chapter traces the role that legal scholarship—in particular, constitutional theory—has played in transforming the region's legal culture.

The focus on legal scholarship as a factor contributing to the shape of the legal cultures of Latin America derives from the conviction that it represents one of the most important sites for the configuration of an understanding of the nature, sources, and role of the law, as well as conceptions about the judiciary and legal interpretation.

This is particularly the case in a region where—like other places with a civil law back-ground—legal scholarship, or *la doctrina*, is considered a formal source of law, and where it plays a critical role in socializing students into the legal field. Not all scholarship on law carries this formal status; only scholarship that specifically interprets and develops legal doctrine. Thus, as will be further elaborated later on, when I refer to legal scholarship in this chapter, I refer to the narrower meaning encompassed by the civil law understanding of *la doctrina*. Thus, in what follows, an effort is made to trace the evolution of the constitutional scholar-ship of Latin America as it has played out in Chile, a country with a long and rich history of legal scholarship. This exercise reveals that constitutional discourse experienced a revolution-ary transformation over the last few decades. I argue that this dramatic shift facilitated the introduction of processes of judicialization of politics in the region by changing traditional understandings of the status of legislated law and the role of the courts in a democracy.

LEGAL SCHOLARSHIP AS LEGAL CULTURE

The very idea of culture questions approaches that see social reality as exclusively driven by rational individuals pursuing their self-interest under the constraint of structures. Indeed, any appeal to culture implies that shared meanings and understandings can move people to act in ways not determined by either their self-interest or structural features. The power of culture becomes apparent when an observer is confronted with situations in which actors facing similar incentive-structures nonetheless exhibit radically different behavior. To make sense of such disparate ways of acting in the presence of the same options, it seems appro-priate to search for other explanatory factors beyond incentive-structures. This residual is often labeled as culture, a notion that most people take to refer to deeply rooted conceptions of the self, what is deemed right and wrong, and so forth.

As is the case with other complex concepts, even when it is accepted, the idea of legal culture resists a simple definition. Thus, some equate it to notions like legal consciousness, legal values, or legal ideology. Given the complexity and indeterminacy of this concept, it is important to stipulate as clearly as possible the way in which such terms will be used in this chapter. I take *legal culture* to express the conceptions of the law, the legal system, and their relationships with politics, held by both individuals repeatedly exposed to it (internal legal culture), as well as by those who have more distant or occasional relationship with the legal system (external legal culture). The conception of legal culture adopted here is meant to capture the symbolic representation of things legal by both the central actors of the legal process (judges, lawyers, jurists) as well as by people with a less direct relationship to it. Furthermore, the ideas and representations just mentioned translate into patterned prac-tices. As cultural artifacts do, legal culture helps to stabilize expectations through the con-straint of the behavior of the relevant actors, in this case, legal actors.

Once a definition of legal culture is stipulated, the problem is to identify indicators or elements in which the legal culture expresses itself. However, this is not an easy matter. One strategy is to make use of surveys and other techniques of this type to inquire about the conceptions of the law and the legal system held by representative samples of the general population or of the legal actors. Another possible path is the kind of qualitative research common within ethnography, which emphasizes in-depth interviews of relevant actors and participant observation of legal practices.

However, here I use the lens of legal scholarship to examine the changing legal culture of Latin America, in particular constitutional scholarship, which represents a particularly valuable way to get at the internal legal culture of the region because of the relevance that it has both in the training of lawyers and judges and within legal practice.

By *legal scholarship* I refer to the form of legal discourse that is elaborated to clarify the meaning of legal norms and decisions made by the courts. In countries with a civil law tradition, legal scholarship is produced through a systematic conceptualization of legal materials such as codes, constitutional clauses, statutes, and judicial decisions. The relevance of legal scholarship in the legal life of countries associated with the Continental European legal tradition (such as those of Latin America) derives from the fact that it is one of the most important factors shaping the conceptions of the law and the universe within which legal actors operate.

. . .

Legal scholarship in civil law countries is not merely a heuristic tool but—more importantly—a way of shaping the representation that legal actors maintain concerning the very nature of the enterprise of law. This is typically implicit because—while explaining the law of the country—jurists help to constitute a discourse about the very nature of law and of the legal system. This discourse is then transmitted to judges, legal academics, and litigants through the medium of legal education, which in civil law regimes makes an intensive use of legal scholarship as a pedagogical tool.

In spite of its relevance for the legal culture of Latin America, recent comparative scholarship on law and politics has made surprisingly little use of legal scholarship. Instead, it is common to encounter studies that claim to be analyzing legal culture, but that do this through analyses of the number of lawyers or degree of litigiousness in a given country, factors that are better conceptualized as either sources or consequences of changes in the legal culture, but not elements of it. The lack of attention to legal scholarship in the field of Latin American judicial politics is a reflection of the little consideration that law in general gets in the numerous studies that have been published on the judicialization of politics in the region.

In spite of its relevance for sociolegal studies, however, legal scholarship has so far failed to capture the attention of most scholars working on Latin America. One of the reasons for such neglect might lay in the presumption that there is not much of it to study, and that of the little there is, most merely reproduces European and North American scholarship. Such an approach, however, ignores the fact that in peripheral countries jurists do engage in doctrinal work aimed at guiding the actions of the rest of the members of the legal domain. Indeed, although much of the *doctrina* articulated in the region represents a mixture of misreadings and appropriations borrowed from more prestigious jurisdictions, it plays an important role in the configuration of the legal ideology of Latin America.

Having said this, it is of course true that paying attention to the evolution of legal culture through the study of legal scholarship does not preclude the need to be fully aware that—as it happens with other rhetorical practices—they often have little connection with what happens on the ground. This danger, however, should not prevent us from exploring the ways in which legal scholarship can shape the representations of law and the legal system in ways not predicted by those who ushered it in.

THE TRANSFORMATION OF CONSTITUTIONAL SCHOLARSHIP IN LATIN AMERICA

From Marginality to Centrality

As stated earlier, to make sense of transformations within the legal culture(s) of Latin America, which are relevant for the emergence of judicialization of politics, we need to focus on changes at the level of the constitutional scholarship of the region because of the connections between constitutional discourse and judicialization processes.

Furthermore, constitutional scholarship is particularly well suited to make sense of the legal culture(s) of a given place because one of its main tasks is precisely to draw the limits and relationships between law and politics. When looking at Latin America's constitutional scholarship, the first element that stands out is the sea change that it has experienced in the last two to three decades, both in terms of its status within the legal field and of its content. Indeed, after more than a century in which it paled in comparison with private law, constitutional scholarship has become the most important and vibrant legal subject in the region, to the point that it has started to colonize other legal subjects, in what some jurists call the "constitutionalization of law" (Aldunate 2009; Bauer 1998).

Although the new preeminence of constitutional discourse in Latin America is most apparent in countries such as Colombia, Costa Rica, and Argentina—which are at the frontline of judicialization of politics—it can also be noticed in other countries of the region with more limited processes of judicialization. Thus, for example, in Chile the status of constitutional law has experienced a dramatic rise when compared with twenty years ago. The increased relevance of constitutional discourse in Chile can be first appreciated from the academic production of books on this subject, which has been booming over the last two decades (more than three hundred books were published in the period 1989–2009, compared to less than a hundred in the much longer period of 1924–89). This sharp increase in the publication of constitutional law books is all the more significant in a context in which the elaboration of works in other legal subjects has remained relatively constant. Second, there was a sharp increase in the number of journals dedicated to constitutional scholarship, from just two before the 1970s to ten in 2007.

In addition to the increment in the number of works published in the field of constitutional law, the subject has become far more prestigious. An indicator of the growing status of constitutional law within the Chilean legal field can be ascertained by the unprecedented numbers of deans of law schools who are constitutional law scholars. In fact, whereas in the first century of university-level legal education constitutional law scholars were elected to a deanship only once, it is now fairly common to see scholars from this field being promoted to lead law schools.

Another indicator of the new relevance attained by constitutional scholarship in Chile is the sharp growth in the number of research projects that get funding from the National

Commission for Scientific and Technological Research (CONICYT). Whereas up to the mid-1990s constitutional law projects represented around 10 percent of all law-related projects funded, by the late 2000s they had doubled that level (to around 20 percent of the total), a sign of the current academic prestige and sense of relevance attained by constitutional law.

As the data of this section suggest, the traditional marginality of constitutional discourse has been completely transformed in the last two decades, to the point that it has become one of the most vibrant subjects in the legal field, attracting the best and the brightest scholars and students.

The Sources of the Doctrinal Revolution

Parallel to becoming more productive and prestigious, constitutional discourse in Latin America was experiencing a revolutionary transformation that would completely transform its outlook in the space of just a few years. Consequently, the traditional paradigm prescribing a formalist interpretation of law and a complete subordination of judges to legislation was substituted by another encouraging a value-oriented jurisprudence exerted by activist judges and characterized by the notion that legislated law should be subordinated to the courts' interpretation of the Constitution (Landau 2005). This paradigm shift owes much to the reception in Latin America of a global doctrine affirming that human rights constitute the central category of constitutionalism. Furthermore, it is also the result of the importation to the region of doctrines legitimizing judicial control of the constitutionality of law, either in its Continental European version (that is, through the introduction of constitutional courts), or in its American version (which gives that power to the regular courts). In the case of the reception of the European model, the borrowing was to some extent natural, as the latter had been the regular source of doctrinal change in Latin America. In the case of the U.S. model of judicial review, the inspiration came from the scores of Latin American legal academics who started to pursue graduate training in law in the United States in the late 1970s, where they were socialized by their liberal North American law professors into the virtues of the legendary Warren Court (Couso 2007).

Moreover, the new constitutional theories started to penetrate the legal field as most of the countries in Latin America were leaving behind the wave of brutal military regimes that had affected the region in the 1960s and 1970s. This coincidence made the reception of the new constitutional theories all the more feasible because the very formalism and judicial deference to legislated law that characterized the previous paradigm was being blamed for the passivity exhibited by the judiciaries in the face of the massive human rights violations perpetrated during the authoritarian wave. Thus, the antiformalism and judicial activism promoted by the new constitutional paradigm encountered little opposition from those scholars who had invested in more traditional understandings of constitutional law.

For all the previous facts, and in spite of the radical change that it implied, the new constitutional orthodoxy was soon consolidated to the point that it became dominant.

The unprecedented academic contact between constitutional scholars from the region and prestigious scholars from Europe and North America helped to cement adherence to the new constitutional creed among Latin American constitutional scholars. One important site of confluence was (and continues to be) the conferences regularly organized since 1981 by the International Association of Constitutional Law (IACL), an organization that gathers some of the most prominent constitutional scholars of the world.

As we have seen, the transformation of Latin American constitutional doctrine signaled the abandonment of the strong legal formalism that had dominated throughout the previous century and a half. The traditional insistence on the superiority of codified and statutory law and the prescription of a modest role for the judiciary (to apply the law without scrutinizing its fairness) was suddenly replaced by a constitutional discourse emphasizing the relevance of human rights, constitutional principles, and value-oriented judges. To illustrate this remarkable transformation, in the next section I analyze constitutional textbooks and treatise before and after this momentous change.

The Old Constitutional Discourse

The roots of Latin America's adherence to legal formalism and the notion of the supremacy of legislated law lie in the reception in the early nineteenth century of the French Revolution's mistrust of judges. These ideas were embraced and disseminated throughout the region by Andrés Bello, who was the most influential legal scholar in the region. The Civil Code Bello drafted for Chile (which was also adopted by Colombia, Ecuador, El Salvador, Venezuela, Nicaragua, and Honduras) emphasized the role legislated law played in the life of a republican system as well as the imperative that each and every person obey it. This call to submit to legislation was directed not only to the public or the government, but especially to the judiciary itself. Given his insistence in the majesty of legislated law, Bello's Civil Code explicitly denied any legal value to the judicial decisions.

The emphasis that Bello gave to the supremacy of legislation and the subordination of the courts would have a long-lasting effect in the region. Following this theory, Luis Claro Solar, a highly influential Chilean legal scholar writing a few decades after Bello toward the turn of the century, fully embraced the formalist and deferential paradigm introduced by Andrés Bello.

The hegemony of this traditional constitutional theory was not confined to legal treatises. In fact, it was the working theory embraced by members of the judiciary as well. This is apparent in a study conducted in the late 1980s on the perception of law and its relationship with the political system among high court judges (Cuneo 1980). The study, which was based on public speeches by the head of the Supreme Court during the period 1971–79, found that the legal conceptions of the justices expressed "the most primitive sort of formalist legal positivism" (Cuneo 1980, 18), especially regarding their notion that codified and statutory law was so clear as to make interpretation superfluous. Furthermore, the justices' public statements reproduced to the letter the modest role prescribed for the judiciary by constitutional theory:

> The mission of the Court is to defend the current legal order. We lack—as is evident—the power to alter the latter through interpretation. . . . The renovation of the legal order can only be pursued through new legislation. Therefore the violation—directly or indirectly—of legality is unacceptable, because without law there is no justice. . . . Judges ought to act strictly within the framework of existing Legality.

What is interesting about these statements by Chile's top court is that they were consistent amidst a period of unprecedented political conflict, that is, the government of Salvador Allende (1970–73) and the military dictatorship that followed it. The main features of this discourse were a formalist attitude toward legal interpretation (textualism, originalism, and so forth), accompanied by a strong opposition to judge-created law. This last point was consistent with an understanding of the theory of separation of powers that translated into judicial deference to the legislative branch. Finally, the theory had a clear preference for procedural values over substantive justice, in spite of the occasional statement defending— in the abstract—the importance of natural-law theories.

The formalist character of the constitutional theory prevalent in Latin America for most of the twentieth century explains that the syllabus of constitutional law courses were mostly devoted to the treatment of what was called the "organic" section of the Constitution (that is, those establishing the different branches of governments, their powers, and their recipro-cal relationships), while the treatment of the "dogmatic" section of the Constitution (that dealing with individuals' rights) was reduced to a mere enumeration of the Bill of Rights, without much analysis.

Summing up this point, the analysis of the relatively scarce literature on constitutional theory available up to the 1980s shows that the dominance of legal positivism and a defer-ential understanding of the role of the courts vis-à-vis the political system was absolute.

The New Orthodoxy: From Legal Formalism to Neoconstitutionalism

Given the hold that formalism traditionally had in Latin America's legal scholarship in gen-eral—and in constitutional discourse in particular—the dramatic transformation of con-stitutional theory over the last two decades represents nothing short of a conceptual revolu-tion. Although it is impossible to date it precisely, it is clear that by the late 1980s the new orthodoxy was rapidly penetrating the region's constitutional scene.

The works of scholars such as [Carlos] Nino, [Carlos] Peña, and others introduced into Latin America what Alec Stone Sweet (2000) has labeled "higher-law constitutionalism"; that is, a theory that regards the Constitution as embodying universal principles (human rights) deemed to be above any statutory law and susceptible to be directly applied by the judiciary, even at the cost of trumping the sovereign decisions of the democratically elected branches of government. This approach, continues Stone Sweet, amounts to a postmodern version of natural-law thinking.

The radical departure from the past implied by the adoption of "higher-law constitu-tionalism" benefited from the fact that the constitutional discourse of France and Spain (the countries that had historically been most influential in the development of Latin American legal theory) were themselves finishing their own conversion to the new orthodoxy, which took the label of neoconstitutionalism in Spain.

A good indicator of the prevalence achieved in recent years by the new constitutional orthodoxy is the sudden popularity within Latin America's constitutional academic com-munity of three important global exponents of higher-law constitutionalism: Ronald Dworkin (from the Anglo-American academic world); and Robert Alexy and Luigi Ferrajoli (from the Continental European one). The interesting aspect of the prominence of these authors among Latin American constitutional scholars is that it suggests that a kind of natural-law perspective is permeating the region.

A final indicator of the rising influence of neoconstitutionalism in Latin America can be seen in the enormous interest that public interest law has sparked in some of the most prestigious law schools of the region. These programs, which have received financial support from U.S.-based foundations, have built a powerful network that regularly publishes works that combine constitutional theory and human rights with different aspects of the public interest law agenda in Latin America.

Given this bleak diagnosis, proponents of this approach to legal action and teaching openly embraced the U.S. model of constitutional discourse and practice, which most of them had experienced firsthand as Master of Laws LLM students. At this point it is relevant to point out that the transformation of Latin America's constitutional scholarship has not been confined to public law. In fact, it has affected the general outlook of legal theory. One example of the effect of the growing acceptance of higher-law constitutionalism is the decline on the degree of formalism exhibited by the judges of the region.

Related to this, in the new constitutional orthodoxy the value of legal certainty has been substituted by that of substantive justice, developments that would have shocked any legal theorist in the region just two or three decades ago.

CONCLUSION

In the last two decades, so-called processes of judicialization of politics have made their mark in Latin America. With instances of great success in some countries and some setbacks in others, courts have reconstituted themselves as relevant political actors in the region. Although most social scientists account for this remarkable development solely in terms of structural reforms, incentive-structures, strategic-interaction, and other material causes, in this chapter I have aimed to complement those explanations with a cultural one, namely, the role of constitutional scholarship.

As we have seen throughout the chapter, the change in the constitutional discourse of Latin America has been radical, going from a strict adherence to a formalist legal positivism hostile to judge-created law and routine interference with the elected branches of government, to a kind of natural-law approach ("neoconstitutionalism"), based on the preeminence of human rights and constitutional principles over legislated law, as well as an activist conception of the role of courts in a democracy. This new constitutional orthodoxy, in which the human rights provisions of the Constitution—and even international human rights law—can be invoked to void legislation by judges empowered with the power of judicial review, represents a crucial cultural factor encouraging the judicialization of Latin American politics.

We are, of course, very much aware that even a revolutionary transformation of constitutional doctrine is not enough to explain the emergence of judicialization. Having said this, it is an important factor in the supply-side of the story because it socializes key legal actors (judges, lawyers, and law students) into new understandings of the nature and status of the Constitution, the courts, and the role of the judiciary in a democratic regime. This change in the constitutional ideology of the legal elite can, in turn, be mobilized to respond to demands of individuals and groups attempting to use the courts to further their policy preferences.

REFERENCES

Aldunate, Eduardo. 2009. Neoconstitucionalismo: Aproximacion a una etiqueta y discussion de contenidos. Unpublished manuscript on file with the author.

Bauer, Carl. 1998. Derecho y economia en la Constitucion de 1980. *Perspectivas en Politica* 1(2): 23–47.

Couso, Javier. 2007. The seduction of judicially triggered social transformation: The impact of the "Warren Court" in Latin America. In *The global impact of the Warren court*, ed. H. Sheiber, 237–63. Lanham, MA: Lexington Books.

Cuneo, Andres. 1980. La Corte Suprema de Chile, sus percepciones acerca del derecho, su rol en el sistema legal y la relacion de este con el sistema politico. In *Universidad de Costa Rica, La administracion de justicia en America Latina*, 71–83. San José, Costa Rica: Universidad de Costa Rica.

Domingo, Pilar. 2004. Judicialization of politics or politicization of the judiciary: Recent trends in Latin America. *Democratization* 11(1): 104–26.

Gloppen, Siri, Roberto Gargarella, and Elin Skaar. 2004. *Democratization and the judiciary: The accountability function of courts in new democracies.* London: Frank Cass Publishers.

Helmke, Gretchen. 2005. *Courts under constraints: Judges, generals, and presidents in Argentina.* Cambridge and New York: Cambridge University Press.

Landau, David. 2005. The two discourses in Colombian constitutional jurisprudence: A new approach to modeling judicial behavior in Latin America. *George Washington International Law Review* 37: 687–744.

Rios-Figueroa, Julio, and Matthew Taylor. 2006. Institutional determinants of the judicialization of politics in Brazil and Mexico. *Journal of Latin American Studies* 38(4): 739–66.

Sieder, Rachel, Line Schjolden, and Alan Angell. 2005. *The judicialization of politics in Latin America.* New York: Palgrave McMillan.

Smulovitz, Catalina. 2002. The discovery of the law: Political consequences in the Argentine experience. In *Global prescriptions: The production, exportation, and importation of a new legal orthodoxy*, ed. Y. Dezalay and B. Garth. Ann Arbor, Michigan: Michigan University Press.

Stone Sweet, Alec. 2000. *Governing with judges: Constitutional politics in Europe.* Oxford: Oxford University Press.

Taylor, Matthew. 2006. Courts, policy contestation, and the legitimation of economic reform under Cardoso. In *Statecrafting monetary authority: Democracy and financial order in Brazil*, ed. L. Sola and L. Whitehead, 205–36. Oxford: Centre for Brazilian Studies.

LITIGATION AND DISPUTE RESOLUTION

INTRODUCTION

For decades, the interest in exploring disputing behavior and the different ways to process it has occupied the attention of a broad range of social scientists. Since the early twentieth century, for example, anthropologists have been studying the social conditions that motivated the emergence of disputes, how different social groups coped with conflict, and how they utilized the various institutions available to them. Malinowski (1926) and Hoebel (1940) are canonical studies in this area and have served as the basis for further development in the field. Throughout the rest of the century, anthropologists' contribution to the study of conflict and dispute resolution continued to be substantial (Collier 1973; Nader 1990). Social psychologists have also explored disputing behavior, but the work has tended to examine individual action without considering the impact of external social forces; in particular, there is a vast literature on procedural justice (Lind and Tyler 1988; Thibaut and Walker 1971, 1975, 1978).

Dispute resolution, strictly speaking, refers to a process by which disputes are handled and sometimes resolved. General interest as well as scholarly work in this field has grown during the last three decades. This expansion has resulted in part from the popularity of the alternative dispute-resolution movement, which also helped to shift attention from litigation and other state-sponsored mechanisms to a broad array of informal and private processes that include different forms of mediation, arbitration, and the like.

In broader terms, the term "dispute resolution" goes beyond the study of *how* disputes are channeled to include also the exploration of *what* gives meaning to disputes. That is, it relates to the study of disputes themselves as social constructs, including the causes and the forces that shape the transformation of claims or incidents into actual disputes (Friedman 1989).

The dispute-resolution field is also interested in those institutions that administer a variety of processes that deal with disputes, ranging from those that are official and formal, to those that are unofficial and informal. Whether disputants use these institutions, or not, and *how* they use them, are two important themes that are dealt with here. In this section, we focus on the scholarly research that deals with these three interrelated dimensions: disputes, processes, and institutions.

Disputes are social constructs (Felstiner, Abel, and Sarat 1973), cultural events (Merry and Silbey 1984), normal—and often inevitable (Sarat 1976)—occurrences in everyday life (Koch, Sodergren, and Campbell 1976). Disputes also imply a form of social relationship (Abel 1973), although usually there are negative aspects to the relationship underlying the dispute (Merry and Silbey 1984); since the mere existence of the dispute suggests that a rule has been violated, that a duty has been breached, or that someone's right has been challenged or ignored. In very broad terms, disputes come out of a process in which some person or institution sees an event or situation as wrong or grievous, and as a violation of some rule or law or normative order. It is hard, however, to define and measure disputes in any given society, and the fact that in complex societies there are many different normative orders adds to the difficulty.

Whether some event will be labeled as a grievance, and then turn into a dispute, depends on the social context, and varies from society to society. A conduct or behavior regarded as grievous by members of a particular social group may be acceptable and undisruptive to others. Take, for example, so-called honor killings in some societies, or the practice of polygamy. It is often suggested, too, that certain cultural traits of a particular group (the Japanese, say) make members of the group less inclined to voice their grievances and bring disputes, compared to people in other societies or social groups, who are perceived as more *litigious*. Legal structure also has a powerful influence on legal behavior. Certain situations or claims are labeled as *rights*, and redress mechanisms are established for the enforcement of these rights; this may occur, even when the "right" is not socially accepted; conversely, if no mechanism is established, there may be no structural way to enforce norms even though they are widely accepted in society.

Another important theme in the study of dispute resolution deals with the question of *how* disputes are processed (Gomez 2008). Once a grievance has ripened into a dispute, the parties may either be compelled or voluntarily choose to react in different ways (Collier 1973). They may simply avoid processing the conflict altogether, or they may try to negotiate or enlist others to help in the negotiation. The parties might also try to impose their will by force or violence or through any other method that enables them to "square their accounts with others" (Ellickson 1987). In taking action, disputants may seek the intervention of a third party whose role may be that of a decision-maker with authority to decide and enforce his or her ruling, or a mediator capable of assisting the parties in reaching an outcome amenable to both. In some instances, disputants may even appeal to the supernatural (Felstiner 1975) hoping that this will help them find a solution to the quarrel.

This is, of course, only a very rough account of the different attitudes and strategies that individuals may take toward conflict, since there are many, many possibilities. However, most processing models fall into two major categories, depending on the presence or absence of a third party. A dispute process in which a third neutral party is involved is called *triadic*, and when the contending parties or disputants are the only ones involved in the process, we talk about a *dyadic* model.

The path of choosing the appropriate method to handle a dispute often follows a pattern, beginning with some low-cost, less formal approach, and then (if this fails) moving on to more expensive, structured, and formal means. Litigation is situated for the most part at the formal and structured end of the spectrum.

In a broad sense, the term "litigation" refers to the process by which a legal dispute is handled within the official court system. As a result, litigation implies the involvement of legal professionals, some of whom may act as brokers, agents, or intermediaries (lawyers, prosecutors) between the interested parties (usually, ordinary citizens) and the courts. Others (judges, magistrates) may perform the role of adjudicators or referees, either by making decisions geared to help the parties reach some sort of outcome or closure, or by more formally deciding the case and imposing a decision on the parties.

Only a small fraction of disputes will ever reach the point of being transformed and encoded into the formal legal system in the form of litigation. The formal resolution of disputes is the typical function of litigation, but it is certainly not the only one. Litigation may sometimes have implications for society that go far beyond its meaning for the parties directly involved. In this sense, litigation may serve as a tool to facilitate access to justice, to achieve social change (Rabin 1975; Rosenberg 1991), shape social policy (Hensler 2001), or as a vehicle for mobilizing political resources (Sellers 1995). Litigation can also be utilized as a device to harass and force someone into a particular solution (Savaiano 1979), or as a negotiation tool (Goodpaster 1992).

The law and society literature also explores the question of litigiousness, as a trait of national legal cultures (see Part III, on legal culture and legal structure). Kawashima's seminal work presented Japan as a society averse to litigation, perhaps due to its Confucian tradition (Kawashima 1963). His finding has been challenged with regard to Japan (Haley 1978; Miyazawa 1987; Ramseyer 1988), but some recent research continues to stress, in some countries, a culture of litigation avoidance (Engel 2005; Blankenburg 1994). The United States is often labeled as a litigious society; a more nuanced view, espoused by Robert Kagan, has identified what he calls a system of adversarial legalism (Kagan 2001). A great deal of the public discussion of this issue has proceeded without the benefit of hard data (Galanter 1993). Nevertheless, it is undeniable that some countries use litigation more than others. Blankenburg (1994), for example, compared the Netherlands with that portion of Germany bordering the Netherlands. The German area has a much higher litigation rate, even though the two regions are quite similar in terms of culture and level of economic development. The proclivity or aversion of certain categories of individuals to litigate has also been explained in terms of certain traits such as level of education (Posner 2002), or the dynamics of social relationships (Macaulay 1963; Ellickson 1991). Other research has focused on the advantageous position of certain groups with regard to outcomes in litigation (Galanter 1974), or on the connection (or lack thereof) between litigation and economic performance, as part of the larger question about the autonomy of the legal system (Toharia 1974, 1987).

An individualistic, secular, and claims-conscious culture might produce an increase in litigation and in litigiousness, or at least this seems plausible. But has this really happened? As some of the studies selected for this volume suggest, litigation rates depend on many factors. One factor might be legislative change, which judicializes—or dejudicializes—whole categories of conflicts or matters. New rules and doctrines have made it possible for more lawsuits to be brought in the United States against doctors, manufacturers, governments, schools, and universities; for similar reasons, there has been an increase also in lawsuits brought by consumers, women, and minorities. In many countries, the numbers and importance of lawyers and judges have been increasing, and politics is increasingly judicial-ized (Pérez-Perdomo and Friedman 2003; Sieder, Schjolden, and Angell 2005; Rios-Figueroa and Taylor 2006). More lawyers mean more written contracts, arguably an increased legal-ization of business relations, and perhaps eventually more claims and litigation. The volume of empirical data on these trends is not great, and the tendencies are not entirely clear. Liti-gation rates and litigiousness, their causes and consequences, continue to be live issues in the law and society literature.

A common feature of modern legal systems is the existence of state-sponsored institu-tions (official courts) where the handling of disputes takes place. The operation of these institutions rests in the hands of a professional bureaucracy (judges) vested with authority to render binding decisions on the matters brought to them and with power to ensure the enforcement of their verdicts according to official legal rules.

The processes that take place in public courts tend to be formal and often require the intervention of lawyers and other professionals, who possess specialized knowledge that enables them to understand how the system works and who act as middlemen between ordinary citizens and the state apparatus. Official courts, however, have also enforced social or extrastatutory norms as a way of contributing to the maintenance of social order (Lanni 2009). The official courts of a given country are collectively known as "the judicial system" or "the judiciary." The judiciary, together with the executive and legislative branches, forms one of the pillars of the modern state.

The official system of justice is not always the product of a peaceful and steady evolution. Sometimes it has a history of cultural or political clashes, out of which the system arises. In many colonial settings, for example, the colonial power has imposed a formal system of justice through violent means, and the coexistence between the formal justice system and other ways of handling conflicts has not always been pacific. Formal justice has also been associated with Western values and the national power over indigenous communities (Peña Jumpa 1998) and comes from above, saturated with an image of civilization and progress, as opposed to the "primitive" and old-fashioned (Merry 1999).

Even though the handling of legal disputes is formally portrayed as the exclusive business of the official courts, it is a generally admitted fact that, in reality, only a small fraction of those disputes reaches the courts, as we have said (Galanter 1981). The vast majority end up being channeled through alternative and often unofficial means, or simply remain unpro-cessed. In addition to their role as dispute-processing facilities, official courts also carry out a number of administrative tasks such as performing marriages, overseeing probate pro-ceedings, handling evictions, and keeping civil records (Friedman and Percival 1976).

Conversely, some institutions, both within and outside the state apparatus, routinely perform dispute-settlement functions, even though they are not called "courts." A long list of commissions, public agencies, and panels could be included here. In a similar fashion, professional organizations, trade unions, and chambers of commerce also perform dispute-processing functions, and their operation often involves the application and interpretation of legal rules and the use of formal procedures sometimes even requiring the interven-tion of lawyers and judges or arbitrators (Feldman 2006 [also included here as Chapter 9]; Galanter and Lande 1992). Take, for example, the case of arbitration among diamond traders as described by Bernstein (1992) and Richman (2004). In some institutions, though independent of the state, rely on the coercive power of public courts for the enforcement of their rulings. One prime example of this can be found in commercial arbitration, which in spite of its characterization as an unofficial mechanism, seems to be increasingly dependent on the official courts for its effectiveness.

If we look further away from the state, in preliterate and modern societies alike, we will find other social structures, in which dispute processing takes place and rules are enforced, but through extralegal means that include community pressure, threats of exclusion from certain economic benefits, social isolation, and shaming.

The following chapters touch on some key issues in the definition of disputes, on dispute-resolution mechanisms, private and public, formal and informal, and on the role played by the institutions that host these mechanisms in legal systems around the world.

REFERENCES AND SUGGESTIONS FOR FURTHER READING

Abel, Richard. 1973. Dispute institutions in society. *Law and Society Review* 8: 219, 227.

Bernstein, Lisa. 1992. Opting out of the legal system: Extralegal contractual relations in the diamond industry. *Journal of Legal Studies* 21: 115.

Blankenburg, Erhard. 1994. The infrastructure for avoiding civil litigation: Comparing cultures of legal behavior in the Netherlands and West Germany. *Law and Society Review* 28: 789–808.

Blegvad, Britt-Mari. 1990. Commercial relations, contract, and litigation in Denmark: A discussion of Macaulay's theories. *Law and Society Review* 24: 397.

Burman, Sandra, and Wilfried Schärf. 1990. Creating people's justice: Street committees and people's courts in a South African city. *Law and Society Review* 24: 693.

Collier, Jane Fishburne. 1973. *Law and social change in Zincantan.* Stanford: Stanford University Press.

Ellickson, Robert C. 1991. *Order without law: How neighbors settle disputes.* Cambridge, MA: Harvard University Press.

———. 1987. A critique of economic and sociological theories of social control. *Journal of Legal Studies* 16: 67, 76.

Engel, David M. 2005. Globalization and the decline of legal consciousness: Torts, ghosts, and karma in Thailand. *Law and Social Inquiry* 30: 469.

Feldman, Eric A. 2006. The tuna court: Law and norms in the world's premier fish market. *California Law Review* 94: 313.

Felstiner, William L. F. 1975. Avoidance as dispute processing: An elaboration. *Law and Society Review* 9: 695.

Felstiner, William L. F., Richard Abel, and Austin Sarat. 1973. The emergence and transformation of disputes: Naming, blaming, claiming . . . *Law and Society Review* 15: 631.

Friedman, Lawrence. 1989. Litigation and society. *Annual Review of Sociology* 15: 17–29.

Friedman, Lawrence M., and Robert Percival. 1976. A tale of two courts: Litigation in Alameda and San Benito counties. *Law and Society Review* 10: 267, 270.

Galanter, Marc. 1993. News from nowhere: The debased debate on civil justice. *Denver University Law Review* 71: 77.

———. 1986. The day after the litigation explosion. *Maryland Law Review* 46: 3.

———. 1981. Justice in many rooms. *Journal of Legal Pluralism and Unofficial Law* 19: 1–25.

———. 1974. Why the "Haves" come out ahead: Speculations on the limits of legal change. *Law and Society Review* 9: 95–160.

Galanter, Marc, and John Lande. 1992. Private courts and public authority. *Studies of Law, Politics, and Society* 12: 393.

Gómez, Manuel. 2008. All in the family: The influence of social networks on dispute processing (A case study of a developing economy). *Georgia Journal of International and Comparative Law* 36: 291.

Goodpaster, Gary. 1992. Lawsuits as negotiations. *Negotiation Journal* 8: 221.

Guo, Haini, and Bradley Klein. 2005. Bargaining in the shadow of the community: Neighborly dispute resolution in Beijing hutongs. *Ohio State Journal on Dispute Resolution* 20: 825.

Haley, John Owen. 1978. The myth of the reluctant litigant. *Journal of Japanese Studies* 4: 359.

Hensler, Deborah R. 2001. The new social policy torts. *De Paul Law Review* 51: 493.

Hoebel, E. Adamson. 1940. The political organization and law-ways of the Comanche Indians. *American Anthropological Association Memoir* 54: 110.

Kagan, Robert A. 2001. *Adversarial legalism: The American way of law.* Cambridge, MA: Harvard University Press.

Kawashima, Takeyoshi. 1963. Dispute resolution in contemporary Japan. In *Law in Japan: The legal order in a changing society*, ed. Arthur Taylor Von Mehren. Cambridge, MA: Harvard University Press.

Koch, Klaus-Friedrich, John A. Sodergren, and Susan Campbell. 1976. Political and psychological correlates of conflict management: A cross-cultural study. *Law and Society Review* 10: 445.

Kritzer, Herbert. 1991. Propensity to sue in England and the United States of America: Blaming and claiming in tort cases. *Journal of Law and Society* 18: 400.

Lanni, Adriaan. 2009. Social norms in the courts of ancient Athens. *Journal of Legal Analysis* 1: 691–736.

Lind, E. Allan, and Tom R. Tyler. 1988. *The social psychology of procedural justice.* New York: Plenum Press.

Macaulay, Stewart. 1963. Noncontractual relations in business: A preliminary study. *American Sociological Review* 28: 1.

Malinowski, Bronislaw. 1926. *Crime and custom in savage society.* London: Routledge and Kegan Paul.

Merry, Sally. 1999. *Colonizing Hawai'i: The cultural power of law.* Princeton, NJ: Princeton University Press.

Merry, Sally, and Susan S. Silbey. 1984. What do plaintiffs want? Reexamining the concept of dispute. *Justice Systems Journal* 9: 151, 157.

Miyazawa, Setsuo. 1987. Taking Kawashima seriously: A review of Japanese research on Japanese legal consciousness and disputing behavior. *Law and Society Review* 21: 2.

Nader, Laura. 1990. *Harmony ideology: Justice and control in a Zapotec mountain village.* Stanford: Stanford University Press.

Peña Jumpa, Antonio. 1998. *Justicia communal en los Andes del Perú: El caso de Calahuyo.* Lima: Pontificia Universidad Católica del Perú.

Pérez-Perdomo, Rogelio, and Lawrence M. Friedman, eds. 2003. Latin legal cultures in the age of globalization. In *Legal culture in the age of globalization: Latin America and Latin Europe.* Stanford: Stanford University Press.

Posner, Richard. 2002. *The problematics of moral and legal theory.* Cambridge, MA: Harvard University Press.

Rabin, Robert L. 1975. Lawyers for social change: Perspectives on public interest law. *Stanford Law Review* 28: 207.

Ramseyer, Mark J. 1988. Reluctant litigant revisited: Rationality and disputes in Japan. *Journal of Japanese Studies* 14: 111.

Richman, Barak. 2004. Firms, courts, and reputation mechanisms: Towards a positive theory of private ordering. *Columbia Law Review* 104: 2328, 2330.

Rios-Figueroa, Julio, and Matthew Taylor. 2006. Institutional determinants of the judicialization of policy in Brazil and Mexico. *Journal of Latin American Studies* 38: 739–66.

Rosenberg, Gerald N. 1991. *The hollow hope: Can courts bring about social change?* Chicago: University of Chicago Press.

Sarat, Austin. 1976. Alternatives in dispute processing: Litigation in a small claims court. *Law and Society Review* 10: 339.

Savaiano, Dominick W. 1979. Excessive discovery in federal and Illinois courts: A tool of harassment and delay? *Loyola University Chicago Law Journal* 11: 807.

Sellers, Jeffrey M. 1995. Litigation as a political resource: Courts and controversies over land use in France, Germany, and the United States. *Law and Society Review* 29: 475.

Sieder, Rachel, Line Schjolden, and Alan Angell, eds. 2005. *The judicialization of politics in Latin America.* New York: Palgrave-McMillan.

Thibaut, John, and Laurens Walker. 1978. A theory of procedure. *California Law Review* 66: 541, 551.

———. 1975. *Procedural justice: A psychological analysis.* Mahwah, NJ: Lawrence Erlbaum Associates Publishers.

———. 1971. An experimental examination of pretrial conference techniques. *Minnesota Law Review* 55: 1113.

Toharia, Juan-José. 1987. *"Pleitos tengas!" Introducción a la cultura legal española.* Madrid: Centro de Investigaciones Sociológicas.

———. 1974. Cambio social y vida jurídica en España. *Cuadernos para el Diálogo* 12. Madrid: Edicusa.

14

COMMERCIAL RELATIONS, CONTRACT, AND LITIGATION IN DENMARK

A DISCUSSION OF MACAULAY'S THEORIES

Britt-Mari Blegvad

INTRODUCTION

Stewart Macaulay's examination of the effects of continuing relations on the mobilization of law has been a starting point for studies of dispute resolution and remains an important source of insights for contemporary research. More than a quarter-century has passed since the publication of Macaulay's article on noncontractual relations in business (1963), yet surprisingly few theoretical advances have been offered that extend, refine, or deepen Macaulay's analysis of continuing relations and law, termed "preliminary" by Macaulay even at the time (but see the special 1985 issue of the *Wisconsin Law Review* commemorating the publication of Macaulay's article). In particular, little research has considered the continuing relations hypothesis in the setting in which it was originally described, namely, commercial transactions between business firms. This essay will report further consideration of Macaulay's continuing relations hypothesis in light of the formation of contractual relations by decision-makers in larger firms.

THEMATIZATION OF BUSINESS RELATIONS

In his 1963 article, Macaulay conceived of transactions and disputes in commercial relations as *actor* problems. To understand why business relations follow certain patterns, one must grasp the reasons that underlie a manager's decisions to do business, to make a claim, or to litigate a dispute. Thus, the task for the researcher is to understand why a particular frame of reference has been chosen for decisions made in the course of business dealings.

Niklas Luhmann, a major European sociologist, called this process of framework selection *thematization*. Thematization is a potentially useful concept in the study of dispute resolution, for it describes a process that includes both the identification of an event as

Reprinted from Britt-Mari Blegvad, "Commercial Relations, Contract, and Litigation in Denmark: A Discussion of Macaulay's Theories," *Law and Society Review* 24: 397 (1990). Copyright © 1990 *Law and Society Review*. Reproduced with the permission of Blackwell Publishing.

relevant to interaction between particular actors and the linking of that event to special resources and rules that seem appropriate for use in the interaction. Thematization includes the formation of initial perceptions of an event by a single actor, but more importantly it also includes the subsequent communications and interactions with others by which the event takes on meaning and becomes part of the flow of events between actors or between firms. Thus, in thematizing business relations, the manager's professional ideology, experience and organizational role, the management structure, the interactions with the other businesses in the exchange, and the legal and economic cultures of the society all play a part.

There is a relationship between different types of thematization and the use of different types of rules for dispute resolution. Through thematization a transaction is linked to special resources and rules, including a particular type of dispute resolution. In this regard, consider the differences between legal thematization and economic thematization. The thematization of a business relation in classic legal terms leads to the relationship being formed in light of applicable contract law. Thematization in an economic framework leads to structuring the relationship through such economic means as ongoing adjustment of performance to achieve economic goals. Further, legal thematization implies that a dispute arising from the transaction would activate the legal system with its institutional resources and sanctions. A dispute arising from a transaction thematized in economic terms, on the other hand, would activate economic reasoning and involve use of resources which draw on economic power relations.

THEMATIZATION OF CONTRACTUAL RELATIONS
IN THE BUSINESS FIRM

Macaulay's description of the role of the manager in a firm's economic transactions may be refined in two ways, both inspired by his original article. First, Macaulay addressed the question of how transactions were structured from the perspective of the individual manager. If we are to take a conceptually more sophisticated approach to understanding this behavior, we should think in terms of the complex organization of the firm rather than in terms of the individual manager. While it is beyond the scope of this article to detail how this might be done, here I will set forth a few of the issues raised by this approach. In particular, I will argue that the thematization of content and form in business transactions occurs through the influence of at least two closely related structures within the firm: managerial role, and interdepartmental organization.

Second, while Macaulay carefully considered the reasons why managers employed or failed to employ contract doctrine as the model for the formation and maintenance of business transactions, the broader question is how any content or form is given to a transaction. In particular, not only must the manager determine the appropriate substance of a transaction; he or she must in addition establish its *governance structure*—the means selected by the parties for maintaining their relationship over time. The range of possible governance structures is great, and the issue may be not whether to consider formal contract terms and remedies but rather which of many alternative means—legal, economic, or mixed—to employ. Contract law itself is now broader than the classical contract doctrine that served as the reference point for the 1963 article (MacNeil 1985; Williamson 1985; Macaulay 1985).

Managerial Role

The manager's job is to establish meaning in a situation mostly characterized by information overflow. In a potential sales situation, for example, the manager must sort out, filter, and organize communications from other firms and from within the manager's own firm; the manager, alone or in concert with others, also must fashion meaning from them (MacCall and Kaplan 1985). The manager may use a network of internal contacts to obtain a range of alternative choices or to obtain a rationale to use as a basis for his decision.

The manager's professional experience and role (MacNeil 1980, 40) will exert a strong influence over these decisions. Macaulay (1963) describes the influence of a manager's professional role on the decision to employ contract law as an orienting framework for a commercial transaction. For example, sales managers will favor an interpretation and an ongoing structure that maximizes the opportunity for continuing sales relationships, while financial managers will want to maximize fiscal accountability within each transaction, and lawyers will prefer a structure that maximizes successful dispute resolution and defense of rights in transactions. Managers who have different training and perform different functions will favor normative structures that place priority on different types of transaction outcomes. In the thematization process, actors draw on their *knowledge and ability* to activate relevant available *resources* and *rules* from the organization or the society at large (Luhmann 1981).

Internal Organization of the Firm

But it would be misleading to focus on decisions by business firms as if they were the decisions of individuals. The manager's position within the firm is crucial. The position itself may call for activating different ways of thematizing transactions. The selections made initially by the single manager link the decision to other roles in the firm. The selection of frame of reference is then discussed—thematized—in a reference group, communication that may be structured by both formal and informal organization within the firm.

The internal organization of a firm influences the power and relative priority given to particular goals and modes of acting with respect to other firms. The managers initially in charge of decisions may be motivated by the possibility of interference or oversight by a hierarchy of other managers in the firm. This, in turn, may influence their willingness to take risks in business dealings and, once a business relationship has been established, their readiness to acknowledge conflict or disputes with other firms (Macaulay 1977; Kurczewski and Frieske 1977). Relations between departments will depend in part on how such relations are structured; for example, whether the firm has in-house or outside counsel will be important, and the formal and informal channels created between offices will affect the influence of each over decisions about transactions. Macaulay reports, and the Danish pilot study confirmed, that while sales managers in many firms may cooperate with lawyers—mostly with house counsel—counsel will rarely participate in the economic negotiations. This may be the result of the way decision-making authority has been structured within the firm. Also, as Macaulay (1963) notes, the house counsel learns to survive in the economic system by allowing the sales manager to take the lead.

TRANSACTION GOVERNANCE STRUCTURE

In a study of forms of governance incorporated into private economic transactions, Williamson (1979, 1985) has suggested that a third important influence determining the form of governance is the structure of the transaction itself.

Williamson suggests a fourfold typology of forms of transaction governance. *Market governance* corresponds to classical contract models in which the substance of a transaction is determined entirely by referring to the terms of the contract. Alternatively, parties may specify a *trilateral governance* structure, which allows for later redetermination of key terms of a transaction in light of future contingencies by reference to a supplemental third-party process such as arbitration of, for example, a price term. A third alternative is a flexible *bilateral governance* structure, which leaves open vital terms that must be negotiated but with recognition that both parties want a continuing economic relationship. A fourth type is *unified governance*, in which no terms are specified in advance of a transaction, thereby providing maximum flexibility, but terms are set for each transaction by one party on behalf of both. Unified governance is appropriate where decisions are internal to a single organizational entity.

THE DANISH PILOT STUDY

We have found evidence supporting both Macaulay's theories and Williamson's reasoning about the relationship between transaction type and governance structure in the practices of firms examined in a pilot study of Danish business firms. For example, *Firm #1* of the Danish pilot study has a yearly production of 3,200 machines, 85 percent of which are exported. Sales are conducted by agents; in 1985 the annual gross sales amounted to 60 million Danish kroner.

In *Firm #1* 98 percent of all transactions are based on framework agreements. These are based on quarterly forecasts with a right to change the order one month before the delivery and with a running possibility to adjust the yearly forecasts. If a deal is based on a long-term contract, the parties meet at regular intervals for a discussion of prices, costs, and forecasts. The general attitude is that "if the deal cannot carry such discussion, both parties shall have a possibility of getting out of it" (Case Report 1986, 1: 4).

The built-in possibility for quantity adjustments in a long-term agreement with no other enforcement than the parties' mutual interest in a long-term relationship is an example of employing a *bilateral* governance structure in such situations.

In routine, discrete transactions, such as debt collection, *Firm #1* uses lawyers and a more traditionally contract-oriented approach. But even in such short-term relations the firm starts with negotiations, and litigation is rare.

Firm #2 is a subsidiary of a large American firm manufacturing various kinds of computers. The Danish firm functions primarily as a trading company for goods produced in the United States. There are three different Danish units: a software trading department where 50 percent of the products are made in Denmark and the rest imported; a development center that produces programs and systems; and a central computer unit that provides services. In 1985, the annual gross amounted to 314 million Danish kroner.

Some of the trading might be regarded as part of a *unified* governance structure, that is, transactions are removed from the market and organized within the firm. The organizational structure of *Firm #2* shows a purposely centralized system with little relation to the other subsidiary firms in Europe but with vertical channels transmitting information up to the parent company, which, in its other relations, has a quite authoritarian structure.

While the internal relationship between *Firm #2* and its parent firm represents a unified governance structure, the external relationships with buyers may have bilateral relational or trilateral governance structures.

Firm #1 previously used a standardized contract which had too many limitations. The subsidiary firm therefore established a project group with the mandate to draft a more reasonable contract. The group included a representative from the marketing department, the administrative manager, and two people from the systems development company. After this group had formulated a draft of a new contract, this was sent to the house counsel for comments (Case Report 1986, 2: 7).

Like *Firm #1*, *Firm #2* uses counsel for formal debt collection but only as a last resort. *Firm #3* operates in the graphics industry and functions as part of a cartel that includes eight other independent firms. In 1985, the annual income was 130 million Danish Kroner. *Firm #3* uses a standardized contract for routine, nonspecific (goods/services) sales. This was drafted by one of the two "house" counsels. The form is rather brief and contains a confirmation of the order but reserves the power to increase the price until delivery takes place.

For large, specific sales/services contracts one of the two "house" counsel is used. The sales department, however, usually starts out on its own and reaches an agreement that covers the economic aspects. And the lawyer then is brought in and usually clarifies the legal aspects in cooperation with his opposite number in the other firm. A large contract always passes the desk of the top manager—otherwise these documents are signed by the sales manager (Case Report 1986, 3: 4–5).

Like the other two firms, *Firm #3* uses legal counsel for routine debt collection. Within each of the three firms studied one finds examples of transactions with different structures and different forms of governance. The question is by what process is a particular transaction thematized as discrete, trilateral, bilateral, or unified within each of these firms? Williamson argues that characteristics of the transaction itself determine the most efficient form of governance. The Danish pilot study shows that there is a correspondence between transaction type and governance structure (cf. Daintith 1986, 1988). Long-term relationships between firms involved trilateral or bilateral governance. The relationship between a subsidiary and parent took the form of a unified structure, while classical contract or market mechanisms were reserved for the most nearly discrete economic relationships, namely, debtor/creditor transactions.

There is play in the selection of governance mechanisms, however, and room for elements of the internal structure of the firm to have their effect. For example, the manager's particular legal/economic orientation toward business transactions may influence assessment of the desirability of longer-term commercial relations with another firm. Such individual perceptions are likely to play an important part at the initiation of a relationship before others on the management team are involved and before exchanges between firms begin to give form to a relationship. Further analysis of data from the Danish pilot study shows how the selection of governance mechanisms is modified by the internal organization of the firm in specific cases.

The internal structure of the firm may have an important effect as well. For example, access to direct communication is an essential factor during the life of a long-term, relational contract. A constant, two-way flow of information, of consultation and advice, will also be necessary as part of ongoing bilateral governance. This calls for a managerial structure that will seek and use the various types of information needed and that has the flexibility to allow the relationship to evolve. It is essential that the parties commit themselves *"one after the other*, so that each can base his actions on those of the other" (Luhmann 1981, 250). This process creates a basis for mutual understanding of the rules of the relationship. Successful maintenance of a bilaterally governed relationship thus depends on the firms' ability to develop a relationship through this form of economic diplomacy. Further, a transaction characteristic that points to Williamson's distinction between appropriate types of governance is the dimension of uncertainty—the risk that a transaction might result in a costly failure. A firm's internal structure may determine its capacity to tolerate or reduce uncertainty or risk in a flexible economic relationship.

CONTRACTUAL RELATIONSHIPS AND
GOVERNANCE PATTERNS OVER TIME

A corollary to Macaulay's discovery that classical contract doctrine was of marginal importance in business transactions was his finding that litigation was likewise of little importance in resolving conflicts. Macaulay also discovered, however, that litigation was not random, but was strongly correlated with the relative power of the parties and their interest in maintaining continuing business relationships.

From this discussion of thematization of economic relations within the firm and of the Danish pilot study, what can we conclude about litigation in business relations? First, the Danish pilot study confirmed that Danish firms employ a variety of types of economic relations. The range of commercial relationships may include new types and greater variation than when Macaulay first wrote. As Macaulay and Williamson recently noted, the new forms that have emerged reflect interest in sometimes maintaining long-term economic relationships, even at the price of autonomy. The formation of such relationships demonstrates a strong preference for economic as opposed to legal structure and for private rather than public governance. If anything, the emergence of these forms of economic relationships should reduce the incidence of certain types of business litigation.

There is some evidence of a shift in litigation in Denmark. The categories of *commercial transactions* (including actions for damages in sales of goods), *marketing and trademarks*, and *transportation* represent actions arising out of bilateral governance where a discretionary aspect of a party's performance has failed and the court is asked to provide a rule to govern the transaction. The litigation statistics reveal a mix of trends that might be consistent with increasing numbers of bilaterally governed relationships. But the evidence is incomplete, and there is no suggestion of increasing preference for the more privatized outcomes of litigation such as out-of-court settlement. However, the time period covered by these statistics is short, and at this stage of analysis we do not have a sufficient breakdown of case types to draw further conclusions.

Of equal importance is the way in which the Danish court system has adapted to a world in which private governance of economic relations is strongly favored by the business community. In Denmark, as in the United States, there has been a strong movement toward forms of private governance of commercial relationships that reduce the need for court involvement at all. Even if this movement is not reflected clearly in the short-term fluctuations in litigation statistics we have collected thus far, the interesting point is that the Danish court system has deliberately developed techniques for settlement other than judgment. It is legally institutionalized that a court shall settle a case if possible. This has taken the form of a "notification" formulated by the judges, which then is used as a basis for the settlement. The notification follows an in-court hearing, further procedure, and the exercise of discretion by the court. It is then presented orally to the parties. The judges here function as mediators in the sense that they offer a solution to the problem at hand. It is up to the parties, or rather their lawyers, to use the notification as a basis for settlement.

The adaptation of the court system demonstrates that the business communities' practices that disfavor litigation have had a long-term influence on legal institutions. Some of the reasons for this are apparent from the foregoing discussion of decisions within the firm. Litigation is expensive. Businesses and society have become more cost-conscious. Litigation has also become more time consuming, as the cases are more complex today than in previous times. But as our examination of the firm suggests, litigation is avoided for reasons other than cost. The zero-sum decisions the legal statutes entitle a party to are not what the manager, the financier, the legal agent, or the franchise owner need. What all these relatively new actors in the economic field need are solutions built on a basis other than legal rationality. In this context one finds both parties using economic rationality and economic policy arguments. Daintith (1986) speaks of an "intimacy" between the parties. More and more problems are discussed and treated in a "mixed" (legal/economic) way.

What is often desired in modern business is not application of a past-oriented rule granting a legal entitlement but a future-oriented solution where the disputing parties are defined as parties to a shared situation and where cooperative means rather than legal constraints are needed. If this description is plausible, it is easier to understand the present role of the Danish Maritime and Commercial Court. The Court continues to serve the societal need for regulation. Dispute settlement based on the *relations* between the parties has become the core of its work, displacing to a degree dispute settlement based on formal rules. Equity, rather than predictability of outcome, will be given pride of place and compromises will be the result.

The discussion of management of business relations by business firms has shown that private governance is an important source of new norms for relationships and for dispute resolution. The evolution of the court's procedures suggests that economic norms may come to replace some official or public legal norms. This development raises profound questions about the long-term relationship between public order and private governance. In particular, are we witnessing the displacement of law by other types of norms, private and/or economic? Or do laws on the books (even if they are not invoked), or the deeply rooted legal culture that they symbolize, cast a more subtle shadow over business dealings?

Luhmann (1983) argues that unless private and economic norms are legalized, the domain of law will be reduced. Earlier studies, like the Danish pilot study, indicated that at the very least the integration of the economic and the legal systems into a "mixed" system leads to such a reduction in the domain of law. But law may not be displaced in all relations between parties to economic transactions. Consider a system where the financing aspects are covered by law. The existence of the legal debt collection system is, at least, a "shadow" resource, for example, to a seller in his creditor role, because he can fall back on legal remedies if he needs them.

Other aspects of a transaction, say, delivery of goods, where the parties have a mutual interest in maintaining flexible relations, illustrate a need for norms based on economic rationality. The question, therefore, is whether the integration of the legal system into a "mixed system" that includes other systems will diminish the role of the legal system. Or will the role diminish because of a refined parallel use of all three possibilities (legal, economic, or "mixed") based on the advantages of each system for each party under the circumstances at hand (Jacobsson 1988; Macaulay 1963, 1988; Williamson 1985). Economic rules may in such situations acquire greater importance and be regarded not merely as rules that fill out the existing legal system but as norms that rank with law.

The short-term trends in frequency and outcome of litigation before the Danish Maritime and Commercial Court suggest that a complex relationship exists between governance of contractual relations and legal process. The model of intrafirm decision-making sketched in this essay may suggest some reasons for these complex changes in litigation patterns and may thus contribute to our understanding of the continuing role of law in business relations as well as to our understanding of the growing presence of private governance.

While the changing distribution of business relationships may favor bilateral governance and reduced reliance on legal interpretation and enforcement of contracts, it is clear from the foregoing discussion that the success of bilateral governance depends on the firm's organizational capacity to manage risks involved in building a continuing relationship with another firm. The internal organization of business firms will, of course, affect this capacity. Economic relationships and the structure of transactions are affected by the evolution of management ideologies and internal business firm structures (Nobel 1977). Further, new ideas spread. New forms of economic relationship may emerge through collective "learning" by managers in an industry.

Many external changes will interact with the firm's capacity to form long-term relationships that require a degree of mutual trust, such as changes in business climate that extend or reduce planning horizons, or in the terms offered by the financial institutions underwriting a continuing relationship, or in business planning necessitated by a wave of takeover threats, or in regulation that increases the risks of cooperative undertakings (for example, changes in tax, banking, patent, or antitrust laws). Each of these changes in the environment of decision-making by business firms may increase the uncertainty of mutual understandings about continuing or ending a bilateral relationship. Thus, understanding the thematization of business relations requires a careful analysis of the factors that affect managerial decisions and the capacity of a firm to absorb risk efficiently.

It remains open whether, even in light of the widely acknowledged trend toward private governance, the emergence of important new forms for economic relationships in the business community represents a long-term trend away from law. Bigger businesses have meant bigger stakes and bigger, if perhaps less frequent, lawsuits. Businesses seem to have continued to employ law when other forms of governance of economic relationships have failed. Thus, law is still an important source of power in the business community, and, as Macaulay noted in his early essay, power and litigation go hand in hand. This and the observation that the law and legal culture continue to cast a complex shadow over many events in society leave many important questions for future exploration.

15

CREATING PEOPLE'S JUSTICE

STREET COMMITTEES AND PEOPLE'S COURTS IN A SOUTH AFRICAN CITY

Sandra Burman and Wilfried Schärf

A wide variety of nonstate courts operate in the African townships of South Africa. Contrary to current popular mythology in South Africa's non-African population, this is not a new development. A dual system of colonial state (or formal) and noncolonial state (or informal) courts existed in the rural areas from the arrival of the first magistrates in African territories, although the magistrates sometimes opposed and often much disliked the non-state courts. With urbanization and the growth of political movements and of other forms of organization in the townships during the twentieth century, the variety of informal court models proliferated, many based on the informal courts of the rural areas. During the recent political conflict yet another type of informal court, known as people's courts, joined the plethora already operating in the townships, although people's courts are now largely inactive. In this article we use informal courts in Cape Town to address a number of questions about informal justice and, in light of our answers, to suggest some elements of informal justice that may be useful in considering the infrastructure of the court system in a post-Apartheid South Africa.

Many of the questions we will address regarding South Africa have been raised in various other contexts (for example, Santos 1977; Abel 1979; Galanter 1981; Channock 1982). Among them are: What stimulated and has sustained the variety of courts in South Africa? What does the history of the courts we are examining show about the relationships between adjudication, enforcement, and policing structures? What does it show about the roles of courts as generators, as opposed to instruments, of those in power? What does it suggest about the relationships between communities and the justice their informal courts dispense? To what extent must informal court justice reflect community values, and how far can it be used to change those values without sacrificing either legitimacy or effective enforcement? In particular, how far can the claims of women and the young to a greater say in their own fates be reconciled with conservative community values? What mechanisms of control can communities or groups have over the informal courts which they have set up? What effect might social disruption have on the type of justice informal courts dispense? What, if any, is the informal court's role in challenging the state's control of communities?

METHODOLOGY AND RESEARCH CONSTRAINTS

Our interest in informal courts in Cape Town sprang from different sources and involved different courts. One of us (S.B.) had worked on the political implications of the early competition for clients between colonial and indigenous courts and has been accumulating information on contemporary informal courts in her current work. The sociolegal investigation of family breakup in twentieth-century Cape Town has revealed that domestic cases are being—and have for many years been—referred to informal courts called, in Cape Town, street committees. The other author (W.S.) became increasingly interested in informal courts as two strands of his current criminological work, on the youth and on formal and informal policing, found a common focus in the development of people's courts, first established in Cape Town by the youth in 1985.

We were interested in the relationship between these two forms of informal courts as well as their effects on each other and on the communities they purported to serve. Inherent in this, of course, were questions about the quality of the justice they purported to dispense, the satisfaction this gave their clientele, and their relationship with the state. Given our patchy historical and anecdotal information on informal courts in Cape Town, we set out more systematically to investigate the relationship between political power and these judicial services, together with consequent likely developments.

STREET COMMITTEES

Today in Cape Town street committees are the primary informal courts in the townships' networks of informal local community courts. Although the main type of informal court is the street committee, many other bodies set up by such groups as gangs, political parties, and even sports teams (Hund and Rammopo 1983; Burman 1983) operate simultaneously, hearing complaints and making settlements in special circumstances. The people's courts, recently established by the youth, are one such body. Cape Town's African population is currently estimated by bodies which work in the townships to number more than one million. While some Africans, primarily those from upper-income groups, have little or no contact with informal courts, for a large sector of Cape Town's African population, the formal rather than the informal courts of South Africa are peripheral. Indeed, Galanter suggests that it is by no means uncommon, even in first world settings, that informal ordering is the "primary locus of regulation" (1979, 20).

The Origins of Street Committees

Street committees are the lowest level of a loosely constituted three-tiered system of informal local rule in the townships. In certain areas they are known as "section committees" or "headmen's committees," but they exist in all the established townships and squatter camps of Cape Town. Street committees serve several streets, with the number of houses or sites covered varying from a score to almost a hundred. Above them are the executive committees, sometimes also rather confusingly known as "civics." Both these types of committees are directly elected by adults and operate at grassroots level to settle disputes and attend to the daily affairs of the township. Above these is an umbrella body called the Western Cape Civic Association, where all the executive committees meet. However, it is not clear how often this forum meets and whether the issues about which it meets relate to the cases of the two lower structures.

Type of Cases Heard

From the interviews it does not appear that street committees see their judicial functions as a different type of activity from their other problem-solving roles. When asked to explain the role of street committees, they usually included dealing with domestic disputes between spouses or between parents and children, disputes with neighbors, and disputes over custody of children, assisting unwed mothers who were unable to support their children, reporting to the administration board (and its successors) on the arrival of new residents or the departure of old ones, reporting on deaths (but not murder cases), and, in some cases, street cleaning. Some have retained their burial society functions, described to us as arranging for burials and having prayer meetings to console the families. In [the area known as] KTC the nature of the squatter camp has also led street committees to deal with such issues as rents and which residents qualify for a site or a shack. In addition, the street committee members are obviously called on for less formal assistance: for example, interviews from the family breakup sample revealed that, in the frequent instances of domestic violence, women fleeing drunken or enraged husbands had on occasion sought refuge in the home of the nearest street committee member.

A number of diverse women's committees, based either in the community or in political party-type organizations, operate parallel to the street committees. When we asked members what their functions included, they all told us that they took up issues that affected the community, family, or individual, and that they were concerned with mediation, not punishment.

The Process and Problems of Adjudication

Most street committees met once a month or whenever a problem was brought to them, and they usually met in a member's home since committees generally did not have their own buildings. Ideally the committee would secure the attendance of both parties in a dispute, but our cases show that this did not always occur, particularly where the attendance of teenagers and others classified as "youth" (that is, unmarried) was required—a trend that predated the 1985 political turmoil.

When all parties were assembled, considerable time was devoted to hearing both sides of the case. Descriptions by the interviewees indicated that the emphasis was on mediating between the parties and seeking acceptable solutions, often by dint of combining face-saving solutions and exerting social pressure.

Where facts are in dispute, committees will often go further than conventional courts to try to obtain all the facts and ensure that the parties concur with the court's decision.

We would not, however, suggest that the impartiality of the committees is beyond dispute. Although they hear a large number of family-related matters, women are almost entirely absent from the committees. Those on committees do not hold office except occasionally as secretary. Some committees quite specifically state at elections that only men may be elected, and we were told, "generally people know that the committee should be composed of men—that is a traditional trend." When questioned about this, committee members expressed variations of the opinion that women would not have enough time to deal with the issues, as "traditionally the place of a woman is at the kitchen and she is there to look after the children and the household in general." We were told that it was not unusual to exclude from discussion even those women who were on committees by the ploy of asking them to make and serve tea when the discussion stage was reached, while the discussion continued unabated. The effect of such masculine bias on cases was reflected repeatedly in interviews.

To avoid a distorted view of women's influence, however, it should be borne in mind that some cases involving women do not reach the street committees; instead, they are settled by mediation or other action by a local women's committee.

Enforcement of Judgments

An ability to enforce its decisions would seem to be highly advantageous if a court is to retain its credibility. We therefore examined the methods used by the street committees for this purpose.

Under the law of the land, street committees cannot impose physical punishments or fines, but the police are unlikely to intervene unless a charge is laid. The topic is obviously sensitive, and it was therefore unclear whether denials of the use of force were always strictly correct. The answers to questions on this topic are revealing. All of the members of the eight first-tier street committees from the three old established townships and New Crossroads denied that they used physical punishment at all for adults, though members of two said they gave lashes to youths with their parents' or guardians' permission. In the squatter camps and new townships, however, the picture appeared to be different, despite the denials already mentioned from New Crossroads. An executive committee member from New Crossroads said that the committee had the power "to give punishment to whoever deserves it" (interview, December 1–2, 1987). A headman (committee chairman) from the KTC squatter camp said that he and his committee had the right to punish the party they judged guilty, though he may have been referring to eviction, as the executive member from KTC interviewed said that headmen did not have this right. In Khayelitsha interviewees from both the core housing and the site-and-service areas said that they could use physical punishment on adults and that parental consent was not required for such punishment of children.

Informants from Nyanga told us that their committees had the power to "fine" people found guilty in certain circumstances, by ordering them to replace a broken object within a stipulated time.

Appeals from Street Committee Decisions

Street committees, as has been indicated, are linked to the two other structures above them: the executive committees and the Western Cape Civic Association. However, the linkage to the latter is very tenuous.

Executive committees usually insist that cases go first to the street committees, though in New Crossroads we were told that cases involving youths that the youth committee could not solve were referred directly to the executive committee, the youth committee being empowered to provide counseling, attempt reconciliation, or punish its members. In some areas at least, executive committees will also hear cases at first instance between parties from different street committees. It is indicative of the ethos of street committees' judicial functions that the explanation always given of why cases which had already been heard at the lower level came before executive committees was that the street or youth committee had not managed *to settle* the dispute and the case had therefore been referred to the executive committee. The executive committees' procedures, methods, and criteria in settling a case did not appear to differ from those of the street committees, and cases were fully presented all over again, often with the street committee that had originally heard the case present. Executive committees each also had their own views on which types of cases they would exclude from their hearings. However, as mentioned above, it appeared that in some areas at least, the executive committee had to ratify eviction orders before they could be executed and in other areas only the executive committee could use force to ensure that judgments were implemented.

PEOPLE'S COURTS IN SOUTH AFRICA

The idea of collective justice in the form of people's courts is not a new one in South Africa or in other countries in a state of intense conflict (Santos 1979, 1982; Fitzpatrick 1983; Spence 1982). They became a prominent feature of the political scene in South Africa from the beginning of 1985 until they (and most news and views about them) were silenced by the power exercised by the police in terms of successive emergency regulations. The courts sprang up with remarkable rapidity in many African townships throughout the country (as outlined in the case of *State v. Mayekiso*, Supreme Court of South Africa) as part of a community initiative to combat the growing crime rate caused by members of the townships exploiting political turmoil. Major extraparliamentary political movements decided to try to create disciplinary structures for other reasons too. The consumer boycotts, which had begun during the first few months of 1985 (South African Institute of Race Relations 1985), stimulated calls for policing efforts, but the United Democratic Front and its affiliates, which opposed the Apartheid state, could not resort to state courts and police forces. Members of these political movements also wished to demonstrate to the township residents that the movements were capable of running most aspects of township life, including the administration of justice.

But more than these utilitarian reasons influenced the formation of "people's courts." They were ideally conceived as both courts and places where a moral vision of a desired future South Africa could be communicated to the residents. They were also intended to be a way of involving all residents in political structures. The people's courts were thus—in some cases at least—an attempt to experiment with prefiguring the lowest rungs of a post-Apartheid adjudicative infrastructure. Unfortunately, as fledgling structures in an experimental phase, they inevitably varied markedly across regions, not only in their makeup and practices but also in their deviations from the standards of justice that they had set for themselves. Moreover, in regions where the political organizations were not strong enough to gain, or keep, control of people's courts, they could be diverted from their original goals and used to promote the interests of those who usurped them (such as street gangs).

CONCLUSIONS

Some tentative conclusions and unanswered questions emerge from this preliminary account of our work. The first is that at no stage since the establishment of the colonial state has there been a single, generally accepted adjudicative and enforcement infrastructure that accommodated the needs of the indigenous population. This milieu led to a plurality of both adjudicative and policing structures and practices, which developed and coexisted with varying degrees of compatibility and friction. Galanter (1981) has pointed out that to understand the formal justice system, the full range of informal justice structures and practices must be known.

Our material also suggests various tentative answers to questions about the nature of informal courts in South African urban settings such as Cape Town, and their consequent probable future existence. We asked whether informal courts are likely to continue or will recur if suppressed. If so, are they likely to provide a form of justice acceptable to the communities they purport to serve? And what role might they play in local power politics? It is clear that in selecting a forum for settling their disputes, people will try to avoid discredited or impotent courts. Those seeking power in an area where the state courts have been discredited may therefore attempt to attract and hold followers by bringing into existence nonstate, informal courts if they do not already exist or, if they do, by trying to take over existing courts or providing additional courts to hear special cases. The history of Cape Town's informal courts again emphasizes that the whole process of adjudication and enforcement is intimately linked to the process of acquiring and exercising political power. Groups will compete to gain and maintain a following, and thereby secure local power. Where the courts serve small, fairly tightly knit and established communities, the competition between groups may well focus on trivia or personalities, since basic values are not at issue. In such cases the courts tend to concentrate on mediation to enable disputing individuals to continue to coexist, and so are more likely to be conservative than innovative in the value systems that they apply. They are also likely to favor established families rather than the youth when there is a conflict between these two groups' value systems.

However, when there is a lack of agreement on basic ideals in a society, as when new values are being generated, competition for followers is likely to take the form of offering alternative sets of values. In Cape Town the values and tactics of the street committees, which included a strategy of cooperation and negotiation with the state to further the power of the committees, became unacceptable after the uprising of 1985–86 had challenged old modes of operation. Contributing to this challenge was the significant change in the power relations between the generations, leaving the youth with a feeling of empowerment and a desire to attack the way in which informal justice had been exercised. Their courts emerged as a result.

Since domestic disputes form a sizable part of a community's problems, any court established to provide a service (even if to attract followers) will tend to include the settlement of domestic disputes if such work is not already adequately provided for by existing informal courts. Furthermore, a court must offer acceptable remedies and be able to enforce its judgments if it is to keep its credibility as a possible forum. Informal courts in urban areas that cannot rely on a continuing community consensus are much better able to provide some remedies, such as physical punishment, than those that require regular supervision. Some courts may not be able to obtain such remedies as regular maintenance payments or probation-type supervision. Therefore, even courts established by political movements to hear political offenses will, since the movements want followers, probably soon provide a dispute settlement service for all types of disputes, including domestic, unless a satisfactory forum already exists. But political courts, particularly in a context of generational and political divisions, may well be unable to count on community pressure as a means of enforcing their judgments in nonpolitical cases. They are therefore likely to resort to one-off remedies, such as physical chastisement, confiscation, or a fine. They may soon get a reputation for this and begin to attract mainly cases which are best solved by such means.

. . .

Even where informal courts *can* be linked to political movements, the adequacy of such links for ensuring justice needs to be examined. It may be debatable whether control by political parties is a *necessary* condition for justice to be achieved by the courts; our data, however, indicate that it is definitely not a *sufficient* condition. Neither group or community support for a court, nor mediatory methods of settling disputes, guarantee that minorities (or even voiceless majorities) will be spared having imposed on them a form of justice they find unacceptable; additional safeguards are required.

Although the performance of neither street committees nor people's courts can be admired uncritically, it must be asked what lessons they can teach us for the future. The street committees performed an extremely important role in settling disputes and advancing the values in which their members believed. The very conservatism of these values led them to insist on maintaining the supportive network of the African family. It was a desperate and most necessary defense against the multitude of pressures which threatened to tear apart those networks in a deeply hostile environment. The emerging political groups could provide no substitute for what was obviously felt to be a very real need. On the credit side of any account of Cape Town's people's courts, it must be noted that in its early phases the people's court of the Youth Brigade showed some potential for shaping a new set of ideals of post-Apartheid society and a more progressive notion of punishment. There was obviously a need for courts that administered justice informed by the values each generation supported. It is therefore likely that, whatever their shortcomings, a plurality of different types of adjudicative and enforcement structures will persist, ranging from state-supported squatter leadership which has been persuaded to opt for the patronage and power that flows from cooperation and even co-optation, to politically motivated groups in search of pre-figurative justice, each drawing support from different sectors of society.

Thus planners seeking to formulate a future judicial system face a complex task, although not one without hope, as evidenced, for example, by the fact that all the courts operate on a basic pattern of majority vote. As Abel has cogently argued (1973), there is a tension be-tween, on the one hand, the desire to allow local groups and communities full democratic expression and, on the other, the need to subject them to those controls that will allow them to be incorporated into national or regional organizations, whether state or party. The first option implies free operation of local courts, untrammeled by central controls; the second implies the existence of some controls by the larger unit. The dangers in leaving local courts unsupervised center on the vulnerability of weaker groups. The dangers of the imposition of some measure of uniformity revolve around the way local courts are inextricably linked to particular forms of local power and local norms: intervening in them will inevitably produce many changes, some unpredicted and not necessarily for the better, as Abel (1979), Ladley (1982), and Santos (1984) have warned. But, more important, if a central power obliges a local court to implement norms for which there is too little consensus in the local community, the court is unlikely to implement them very thoroughly or effectively. The central power, whose credibility is thus challenged, may then face the choice between hu-miliatingly public ineffectiveness or enforcement of those norms by its own enforcement arm. Unless these dangers are avoided in post-Apartheid South Africa, the judicial system will yet again be in peril of foundering without legitimacy.

REFERENCES

Abel, Richard. 1979. Theories of litigation in society. In *Alternative rechtsformen und alternativen zum recht*, ed. E. Blankenburg, E. Klausa, and H. Rottleuthner. *Jahrbuch für Rechtssoziologie und Rechtstheorie*, vol. 6. Opladen: Westdeutscher Verlag.
———. 1973. A comparative theory of dispute institutions in society. *Law and Society Review* 8: 217.
Burman, Sandra B. 1983. Beyond apartheid courts: Reaping the whirlwind. Paper presented at the Conference of the Research Committee on the Sociology of Law, International Sociological Asso-ciation. Antwerp: Belgium.
Channock, Martin. 1982. Making customary law: Men, women, and courts in colonial Northern Rho-desia. In *African women and the law: Historical perspectives*, ed. M. J. Hay and M. Wright. Boston University Papers on Africa, VII. Boston: Boston University.
Fitzpatrick, Peter. 1983. Law, plurality, and underdevelopment. In *Legality, ideology, and the state*, ed. D. Sugarman. London: Academic Press.
Galanter, Marc. 1981. Justice in many rooms: Courts, private ordering, and indigenous law. *Journal of Legal Pluralism* 19: 1.
———. 1979. Legality and its discontents: Some preliminary notes on current theories of legaliza-tion and delegalization. In *Alternative rechtsformen und alternativen zum recht*, ed. E. Blanken-burg, E. Klausa, and H. Rottleuthner. Jahrbuch für Rechtssoziologie und Rechtstheorie, vol. 6. Opladen: Westdeutscher Verlag.

Hund, John, and Malebo Kotu Rammopo. 1983. Justice in a South African township: The sociology of Makgota. *Comparative and International Law Journal in Southern Africa* 16: 179.

Ladley, Andrew. 1982. Changing the courts in Zimbabwe: The customary law and primary courts act. *Journal of African Law* 26: 95.

Santos, Boaventura de Sousa. 1984. From customary law to popular justice. *Journal of African Law* 28 (1 and 2): 99.

———. 1982. Law and revolution in Portugal: The experiences of popular justice after the 25th of April 1974. In *The politics of informal justice*, vol. 2, ed. R. L. Abel. New York: Academic Press.

———. 1979. Popular justice, dual power, and socialist strategy. In *Capitalism and the rule of law— from deviance theory to Marxism*, ed. B. Fine et al. London: Hutchinson.

———. 1977. The law of the oppressed: The construction and reproduction of legality in Pasargada. *Law and Society Review* 12: 5.

South African Institute of Race Relations. 1985. Survey. Johannesburg: SAIRR.

Spence, Jack. 1982. Institutionalising neighbourhood courts: Two Chilean experiences. In *The politics of informal justice*, vol. 2, ed. R. L. Abel. New York: Academic Press.

16

ALL IN THE FAMILY

THE INFLUENCE OF SOCIAL NETWORKS ON DISPUTE PROCESSING (A CASE STUDY OF A DEVELOPING ECONOMY)

Manuel A. Gómez

This article constitutes an effort to describe the influence of social networks on how individuals choose to process their legal disputes. The objective is to explain how social connections shape the ways in which conflict is processed within formal institutions. Using the social context in which the Venezuelan business sector operates as a framework, this research tries to draw a real-life picture of how dispute processing occurs in society, which in turn is important in understanding how different systems of social control can function.

Studying the Venezuelan business context offers a tremendous opportunity to discover dispute-processing choices in an environment that combines many features that are typically seen in technologically advanced, modern, and affluent societies and, at the same time, discover some of the characteristics that sociolegal scholars attribute to societies considered to be primitive, indigenous, or traditional. This interesting contrast allows me to explore how the different mechanisms of social control interact within a specific social and cultural context, and how the social network paradigm can facilitate its study.

THE SOCIAL NETWORK PARADIGM

The term "social network" denotes a set or group of individuals who are related or connected to each other by a social relationship based on friendship, cognatic kin, professional or work collegiality, economic linkage, religious affiliation, or some other form of affinity. Social networks are present in every society regardless of its level of modernity, economic affluence, political structure, or prevailing cultural norms. Nonetheless, the degree of cohesiveness among network participants—the network's salience, and the ways in which these structures interact with official institutions—differs from one society to another and is conditioned not only by the existing cultural and social norms, but also by the presence of institutional and legal constraints that are present in the social settings in which those networks operate.

Reprinted from Manuel A. Gómez, "All in the Family: The Influence of Social Networks on Dispute Processing (A Case Study of a Developing Economy)," *Georgia Journal of International and Comparative Law* 36: 291 (2008). Permission courtesy of *Georgia Journal of International and Comparative Law*.

As a result, there are societies, or clusters within societies, in which interpersonal networking is deemed so important that most aspects of ordinary life depend exclusively on the norms that emerge from the group or clan. Many of these social networks have also taken part in the organization of social structures that help monitor compliance and enforcement of rights; hence, these become a substitute for the official legal order.

The salience of social networks in these environments results from the fact that its members are usually linked through multiplex relationships (for example, by having kinsmen in common, sharing the same cultural traits, living in the same neighborhood, having attended the same schools, and sharing intergenerational friendships), and that the social distance between them is usually less than the social distance between those who live in larger and more complex environments.

In contrast, there is another type of society (generally, larger ones), in which social networks are still important, but their overall influence seems to be less apparent as a result of social, cultural, economic, and legal constraints. Members of these large societies tend to interact with many more people than their counterparts from small ones. Their social circles may be larger, too, but their exchanges tend also to be briefer and more superficial. The complexity of life in large and generally urban environments also generates more social and geographical mobility, which in turn works toward creating less cohesive networks where the difference between insiders and outsiders is more difficult to notice.

. . .

The social network approach can help obtain a more complete picture by considering context as an important element. To this end, social network analysis may be used as a vehicle to explore the way in which individuals cope with interpersonal conflict within social group settings, to understand the ways in which group norms are effectively enforced in the absence of a centralized formal authority (for example, enforcement of incomplete contracts), and most importantly, to explain the influence of the social context on individual choices for dispute-processing mechanisms and fora, in a way that goes beyond the traditional dichotomy that views societies as either traditional or modern. Ultimately, such analysis could also shed light on the understanding of the role of conflict in the transformation and maintenance of social structures.

ALL IN THE FAMILY: SOCIAL STRUCTURE, NETWORKS, AND THE VENEZUELAN BUSINESS SECTOR

To this day, Venezuela is still the third-largest oil producer in the world. As a founding and a very proactive member of the Organization of the Petroleum Exporting Countries (OPEC), the international oil cartel created in 1960 whose members are mostly Middle Eastern oil-rich nations, Venezuela has been a key player in the global trade of natural resources for several decades. Though the industry employs less than 2 percent of the labor workforce, oil revenues have traditionally represented more than 90 percent of the country's revenue from exports and at least one-fifth of Venezuela's gross national product (GNP).

By being blessed (or cursed) with such a significant source of wealth from oil and other natural resources, the different administrations that ruled the country during the second half of the twentieth century found themselves in the position of playing a major role in shaping the economy. The government was not only the richest investor but also an important benefactor. This, in turn, motivated the private sector to organize and mobilize politically so it could benefit from oil rent distribution. In addition, members of the business community were expected to pledge allegiance to the ruling political party as is common in relationships based on "clientelism."

As the state apparatus grew exponentially and started intervening in most areas of the economy, it became paramount to those who wanted to succeed in business to cultivate the "proper" connections. Obviously, certain groups achieved more power than others, and as a result, they were more successful in their business activities, often at the expense of others.

Some areas within the business sector still appear to be controlled by groups of a common ethnic background, but the larger community is able to form into a relatively cohesive group of people who are bound by multiplex social relationships where families are members of the same social clubs, children attend the same private schools, and they travel to the same places for vacation. Social networks have influence over most aspects of business life, and the processing of disputes is not an exception.

Whenever legal conflicts arise, the first move on each side is usually to resort to the network. Since business relationships are so intertwined with personal ties and the degree of social cohesiveness is high, it is common for disputants to sort out their differences with the intervention of other members of their social group, which may also be part of their family. When conflicts get out of hand, and the contending parties are not members of the same social group, or the intervention of official institutions is deemed necessary for any other reason, disputants utilize the official fora, but still through their social networks. In this sense, lawyers have become important players within the business sector because they are the ones who usually interact with official institutions and serve as liaisons or brokers between different social groups.

To an outsider, the Venezuelan business sector appears to enjoy a level of modernity typically found in industrialized and affluent societies. But after a closer look, this modernity reveals itself to be a facade for two reasons: first, family and social relationships still have more weight than individual merits and, second, the success of most corporations and individual businesspeople depends more on their political and social connections than on their capacity to compete and innovate. In other words, the know-who is much more important than the know-how.

Dispute Processing, Networks, and the Courts: From the Tribes to the Judicial Revolution of the Twenty-First Century

An average business disputant in Venezuela knows that the first step before filing a lawsuit is to identify a well-connected lawyer, a friendly court, a familiar judge, and, of course, be open to gratify court employees for "being diligent." Judges regarded as friendly to the business community are usually labeled by executives as "decent" and "competent," even if their diligence is clearly tilted in favor of one side.

Also, business lawyers have traditionally been judged not only for "what they know" (their particular legal skills) but more importantly, for "who they know" (their social connections); as a result, legal professionals have become brokers in the real sense. The stereotypical image of a network within the Venezuelan legal environment is that of a group of lawyers with political power and influence, who together with some judges and other public officials, form close-knit and strong chains known as "judicial tribes" (*tribus judiciales*). These networks became popular approximately fifty years ago, portray an extreme form of judicial clientelism, and have largely influenced the way in which the courts operate in Venezuela.

The origin of these judicial tribes can be traced back to the early 1960s, when the national government took direct action to suppress the flourishing leftists' guerrilla movements that were seen as a threat to the young Venezuelan democracy. The government's reaction to the growing activity of these rebel groups was to prosecute them in military courts, as these fora were easily controlled by the executive. However, as some cases had to be tried in ordinary criminal courts, the executive decided to expand its sphere of influence and moved in order to expand its political control over those courts as well.

The process of appointing judges was one of intense negotiations among political actors. It was an unwritten rule that those who wanted to enter into the judiciary needed a political sponsor (*padrino*), which produced a relationship of subordination between the candidate and his or her supporter in case the first got appointed. Among the usual backers there were influential politicians, some of whom were connected with lawyers who in turn were key members of the judicial tribes. Leaders of the business community were, to a certain extent, members of these networks of power, which translated into clear benefits for them.

The tribes were clanlike structures led by private lawyers who had been involved in politics or were fundraisers for political campaigns and therefore had connections with important political parties or the government. Some tribes were actually led by retired judges who after leaving the bench decided to go back to private practice and to keep their influence on some courts. Some groups had spheres of influence in particular areas (for example, criminal courts) or levels (for example, trial courts, Superior Courts, or the Supreme Court itself) while others were known for having control over a certain jurisdiction.

The main purpose of these networks was to manipulate the courts in order to get favorable decisions for their clients, to speed the handling of judicial processes, or to simply counteract the negative influence of another clan favoring the other side. Each of these tribes had a law firm as a facade. The firm would offer its clients the guarantee of a speedy trial, with a favorable decision, and would often assure clients of positive results on possible appeals and even, if necessary, at the Supreme Court level. The lawyers of the firm would usually set their fees very high since they had to include the "work" of others.

The firm also served as a hub to all members of the network, and a small group of lawyers (brokers) centralized the communication with judges, clerks, and other public officials. Some active judges were permanently tied to particular tribes, while others were known to freelance by collaborating with several different groups on a case-by-case basis. Business lawyers were also part of these webs, and although many of them maintained a very low profile, their reputation as effective professionals largely depended on how close they were to the heart of the network. Lawyers not only used the networks to process cases in courts, but also to get help bypassing regulatory processes, dealing with government authorities, and negotiating disputes outside the formal system.

. . .

The mid-1990s witnessed a crisis among the traditional political parties who lost legitimacy and therefore their traditional power and influence within the political arena. After the two failed coups d'etat of 1992, the Venezuelan political elite became increasingly fragile, which also affected their spheres of influence on the judiciary. About the same time, high-profile corruption cases involving judicial networks were denounced by the media, which made the judicial tribes weaker and eventually led to their demise. The pacts according to which the leading political parties had shared their control over the courts slowly eroded; remaining members were left on their own. A number of retired judges who had amassed some power during the previous years became leaders of their own small-scale corruption rings, thus becoming judicial entrepreneurs of a sort. These judges were only capable of cutting deals involving cases being tried in their own former courts or in others in which they still had connections. The network-based system became less efficient due to the fact that participants were only tied by one-dimensional, single-stranded, and relatively weak relationships.

With the advent of the "Bolivarian Revolution" that started in 1998, the existing political structures suffered an important change. Newly in power, President Hugo Chávez, a leader of the first 1992 coup attempt, vowed to undertake a complete overhaul of the state institutions plus a deep legal reform process, including the drafting of a new constitution.

Almost six years after the judicial emergency was declared, Venezuela now has an overtly politicized judiciary in which new cartels and close-knit groups have emerged under the shadow of the president's political project. The big difference now is that only those who have connections within the ruling political party can take advantage of the influential cartels that have permeated the courts. The system is more loyalty-based than in the past, and business disputants are still able to find their way around.

THANKS, BUT NO THANKS: THE MODEST ACCEPTANCE
OF ADR PROVIDING ORGANIZATIONS IN VENEZUELA

Reform advocates in Latin America have stressed that the true demand for alternative mechanisms at the domestic level is high, but the lack of a modern legal framework has acted as a barrier, thus confining disputants to conform themselves with the allegedly malfunctioning courts. This had led to the belief that the implementation of modern alternative dispute resolution (A[lternative] D[ispute] R[esolution]) legislation, the investment of resources in training, and the sponsorship of institutional providers can contribute to meeting such needs.

Following this idea, both the Venezuelan government and the private sector embarked on a crusade to advocate the promotion of ADR mechanisms, also believing that it would help decongest the ill-functioning courts, in addition to allowing citizens to address their legal disputes in an expeditious, inexpensive, and efficient manner. This, advocates believe, is the trend in modern nations where ADR mechanisms have become very popular and have also proved to be efficient tools for solving many problems related to the administration of justice.

Strong governmental support for ADR became evident with the passage of several laws providing for the use of mediation and arbitration in different areas such as labor, consumer rights, insurance, and family law. As a corollary, the Constitution, approved in 1999, made the promotion of alternative mechanisms part of a state policy.

Thanks, But No Thanks

Notwithstanding the enormous efforts and resources invested, and the apparent positive image that ADR centers have among members of the business community, these institutions have not been truly embraced by its potential beneficiaries. Instead, disputants continue to prefer processing their conflicts in the same traditional ways that have always been available to them, and consequently, the new ADR centers are still among the least used paths.

With very few exceptions, the executives and corporate lawyers interviewed had a positive image of mediation and arbitration and were generally in favor of its promotion. Indeed, the private sector has offered financial and institutional support to the new arbitration centers. At the time of the interviews, many business executives—mainly from multinational corporations—were also familiar with ADR processes and had been trained in negotiation and problem-solving techniques. Business lawyers, on the other hand, were not only acquainted with the legal framework of arbitration and mediation but in many cases had attended ADR workshops and were knowledgeable about the leading literature in the field. Interestingly, they also reported using mediation very often.

However, the mediation that most of these lawyers and executives employ is not the one offered by the ADR centers in an institutionalized form. The mediation they reported using often takes place after golf or tennis matches at the local country club, during dinner parties, weddings and other social engagements. Prominent lawyers whom both parties respect and know well tend to act as neutrals.

CONCLUSION

As this research demonstrated, the decision to use a particular mechanism (formal versus informal) or procedural approach (adjudicatory versus conciliatory, dyadic versus triadic) depends on the social context and not necessarily on the intrinsic characteristics of each mechanism. Venezuelan lawyers, for example, do not use judicial processes because of their intrinsic value as impartial adjudicatory mechanisms, but rather because they occur in a forum where disputants feel comfortable. By the same token, business disputants seem to use ADR processes not because of ADR's ability to ensure distributive justice, but instead because it takes place in a familiar social context. In other words, the choice of mechanisms follows from the perceived advantages of the forum to those who actually use it.

Dispute processing among Venezuelan business actors takes place in a context where interpersonal relations are paramount and social networks have permeated private and public institutions. This characteristic has allowed social networks to become stronger and to maintain a leading role in the operation of the business sector. It has also strongly influenced the way in which its members process their disputes.

The two examples offered in this article of procedures and procedural choices embedded within the larger case study of the Venezuelan business sector demonstrate how disputants' choices are heavily influenced by the social context in which they interact.

In the first place, the research demonstrates how reliance on social networks drives business parties in Venezuela to use the courts voluntarily in spite of the conventional wisdom—among judicial reform advocates—that disputants avoid using the judiciary at all costs. Second, the research demonstrates how social networks are also relied on for mediating and arbitrating disputes that arise among businesspeople and paradoxically, how this has discouraged potential use of the recently established ADR centers.

17

BARGAINING IN THE SHADOW OF THE COMMUNITY

NEIGHBORLY DISPUTE RESOLUTION IN BEIJING HUTONGS

Haini Guo and Bradley Klein

This study aims at adding a needed perspective to the existing literature by examining dispute-resolution practices in a far different environment: the traditional neighborhoods of urban China. Unlike the environments examined in prior studies, Hutong neighborhoods are economically underdeveloped and subject to an institutionally deficient legal system, a nondemocratic political regime, and a distinctly illiberal postwar cultural experience. The extent to which dispute-resolution practices in ancient Beijing Hutong neighborhoods track those prevalent in the modern Western world has great implications for the law and society literature of the last decade.

Are the norm-based systems documented over the last ten years a truly universal human phenomenon, or are they a more distinct product of practices and intuitions unique to developed liberal market societies? Are there unique practices or institutional arrangements in radically dissimilar cultural settings that can help enrich—and place in proper perspective—our understanding of more familiar dispute-resolution mechanisms? Are there valuable lessons that we in Western academia can learn?

In fact, our research did reveal that residents of Beijing Hutongs rely primarily on informal social norms in determining individual entitlements and resolving disputes among themselves. Private bargaining between individuals according to community social norms is the default option for residents who have grievances against their neighbors. Recourse to formal legal channels is viewed as too costly, socially disruptive, and unpredictable to be an efficient option in all but the most serious disputes. In these respects, our findings corroborate the general thrust of recent law and society scholarship on dispute resolution in more developed countries. The main point of divergence in general orientation is the Hutong residents' view of formal legal institutions as fundamentally unpredictable and untrustworthy, as opposed to simply too expensive. This finding derives directly from the underdeveloped nature of the Chinese legal system and thus may be common to dispute-resolution regimes across the developing world.

Reprinted from Haini Guo and Bradley Klein, "Bargaining in the Shadow of the Community: Neighborly Dispute Resolution in Beijing Hutongs," *Ohio State Journal on Dispute Resolution* 20: 825 (2005). Permission courtesy of the authors.

Yet, even within this familiar norm-based orientation, novelties emerge as Hutong communities use some unique institutional arrangements to manage norm-based dispute resolution. When disputes between neighbors prove intractable, Hutong residents engage in a set of unique, middle institutions we term "nonlegalistic public authorities." Comprised of the local Residents' Committees and specialized Neighborhood Police, these institutions lie somewhere between the domains of formal law and informal social norms. They are institutions expressly tied to the community that act as neutral mediators for Hutong residents. They are commissioned by the Beijing municipal government and receive salaries from public funds, but they do not apply formal legal rules in mediating disputes and have no coercive or punitive powers. Instead, they act as specialized custodians of community social norms, resolving disputes as those norms dictate and relying on the community's collective informal sanctioning of intransigents to enforce their mediated solutions.

Through these institutions, Hutong residents benefit from the cost, flexibility, and convenience advantages of norm-based solutions while also securing some of the benefits of institutional specialization and standardization. Thus, our results suggest that, while social norms are certainly the informal creation of the community, formal institutions can actually play a vital role in upholding and administering a norm-based social regime, often achieving results preferable to purely informal, decentralized modalities.

The solutions mediated by these nonlegalistic public authorities are in turn enforced informally by the community through direct physical reprisals or group social punishments against norm-violators. In this process, residents' reputation and status within the community is a vital consideration, and many of the residents appear to be maximizing social status as much as economic efficiency in upholding norm-based dispute resolutions. This result implies that, at least for premarket communities, social status may be just as important as material wealth in individual dispute-resolution calculations.

BACKGROUND ON THE HUTONG RESIDENTIAL ENVIRONMENT

From *Siheyuan* to *Dazayuan*: A Brief History of Beijing Hutongs

Beijing's numerous Hutongs have served as long-standing residential institutions for generations. The word "Hutong" refers to the lanes or alleyways that connect the traditional living quarters of Beijing residents, known as *siheyuan*, or quadrangles.

The close physical proximity of the Hutong residences and the inevitably daily interactions among neighbors create a strong need for mutual dependence and reciprocal cooperation. Such bonding social capital has become an essential part of the Hutong way of life to the residents. This is of especially great value to lower-class working residents who have few outside resources, either economic or administrative, on which to rely. Further, the harsh economic situation many residents face today renders the social capital invested in their immediate neighborhood communities even more important. Despite their frequent friction over mundane issues, residents have a strong sense of sharing both benefits and burdens with their neighbors. While the lack of distance and space deprives residents of their personal privacy, it also furnishes a formidable public supervision system that contributes to public safety and promotes mutual adjustment and cooperation. In short, the extensive interdependencies among the Hutong residents cause the residents to view responsibility-sharing as a part of life.

Poverty and interpersonal friction thus coexist with extensive cooperation and social bonding every day in Hutong neighborhoods, providing a perfect environment for the study of extralegal dispute-resolution methods.

RESEARCH METHODS

We pursued our research primarily through face-to-face interviews with Hutong residents, Residents' Committee mediators, and Neighborhood Police officers in the summer of 2002. In all, we conducted interviews with sixty-five residents of the Hou Hai, Jianguomen Wai, Liu Li Chang, Yabao Lu, Taiping Jie, and Qianmen Hutong areas of Beijing. We met with eight Residents' Committee mediators from the Jianguomen Wai and Yabao Lu Hutong neighborhoods and examined their records of resident disputes and mediation activities covering the time period from May 2001 to May 2002. We also accompanied a Neighborhood Police officer on a full day of rounds in a Hutong neighborhood and witnessed his activities firsthand.

Contrary to our initial apprehensions, Hutong dispute-resolution mechanisms and the basic norms employed by residents proved strikingly uniform from neighborhood to neighborhood. Similarly, the more "expert" perspectives of the Residents' Committee mediators and the Neighborhood Police officers were highly consistent with the reports offered by individual residents. This overall consistency of results across disparate institutional and geographical contexts allows meaningful reference to a single Hutong dispute-resolution "regime" encompassing a more or less coherent body of norms and institutions. It is to this regime that we now turn.

THE THREE-TIERED HUTONG DISPUTE RESOLUTION REGIME

Institutional Scaling and the Basic Menu of Dispute-Resolution Options

The Hutong dispute-resolution system is organized into three fundamental tiers, or layers, each involving different institutional actors and implying distinct dispute-resolution methods—an arrangement that can be termed "institutional scaling." When a dispute arises, residents choose the tier that is best suited to their own needs and the contingencies of the specific dispute at hand, and they will change tactics and move between tiers of the system (or rescale) as circumstances demand, especially if the dispute escalates or proves intractable.

Simple informal neighbor-to-neighbor negotiations make up the first tier of the dispute-resolution system, and indeed this is the default first option for residents who have grievances with their neighbors. Neighbor-to-neighbor negotiations often involve just the two parties involved in the dispute, but other nearby residents may participate, especially if they share common courtyard space or close social ties with the disputants. This mode of dispute resolution typically involves no formal rules whatsoever, so solutions are customized and flexible, formulated by the mutual consent of the parties involved and tailored to their specific needs (often with input from concerned neighbors). Similarly, there is no role for coercive state power or public institutions in this first tier, nor is there any formalized procedure involved—an aggrieved resident will simply approach the offending neighbor and suggest they discuss the problem privately.

The second tier of the Hutong dispute-resolution system involves more formal mediation of disputes by the local Neighborhood Residents' Committee (*juwei hui*) or special Neighborhood Police (*pianer jing*)—unique institutional actors that we characterize as "nonlegalistic public authorities." The Residents' Committee is a small body directly elected each year by residents of the neighborhood to handle certain common tasks (such as garbage disposal and sanitation) and to oversee implementation of certain public policies (like the one-child policy). Committee members are typically elected from among the neighborhood's residents and tend to be respected members of the local community. They are paid salaries with public money, and at least one of them—typically one with a reputation for fairness and good judgment—will have a specialized mandate to mediate disputes between residents.

The third tier of the Hutong dispute-resolution regime is comprised of formal legal institutions such as municipal police, Public Security Bureau (*gongan ju*) personnel, and the court system. These institutions bring the full weight of formal law, legal procedure, and the coercive power of the state to bear on disputes within their ambit. As a result, this third tier involves higher economic costs (including transaction costs), more social disruption, and a greater threat of punitive sanctions than the two lower tiers. Additionally, since formal legal rules—or policy decisions by political elites—are involved, solutions are not particularly flexible or customized.

The residents of Beijing Hutongs thus employ a three-tiered scalable dispute-resolution regime, the different layers of which imply varying degrees of legalism, cost, flexibility, social disruption, and access to state power. This system is evocative of more general dispute-resolution typologies in the literature, but with a unique and subtle twist. Most of the leading law and society scholarship presents a basic distinction between the world of "law," on the one hand, and the world of informal "norms," on the other. Under the conventional view, "law" (or other formalized rules) and "norms" are seen as presenting disputants with two binary options for dispute resolution.

Laws and other written rules are commonly associated with official (usually legal) institutions, adherence to some form of legal procedure (with its associated costs), and the application of coercive public power to enforce resolutions. "Norms," on the other hand, are commonly associated not with formal institutions or procedures but with informal enforcement regimes relying on social sanctions. Within the China law literature, leading scholar Donald Clarke similarly distinguishes between "external" and "internal" dispute-resolution mechanisms in Chinese society: "external" systems involve third-party mediators who have "no distinct relationship with the parties other than a specialized function as [a] dispute resolver" (such as formal legal institutions), while "internal systems" employ mediators who have authority "not because of [their] specialized function as dispute resolver[s] but because of some other distinct relationship with the parties" (such as family members).

Yet, the dispute-resolution regime discussed here is not binary, but tripartite. The first tier—informal neighbor-to-neighbor negotiation—certainly fits the traditional view of norm-based dispute resolution, as well as the "internal" category of Clarke's typology. No formal procedures are used, no preformulated rules are applied, and no formal institutions are involved. Individuals participate in mediation or negotiation because of their social relationships with disputants or their physical proximity to the disputed events. The third tier of the Hutong regime similarly fits the traditional conception of rule-based dispute resolution and Clarke's related "external" category. Lawyers, courts, and the police are summoned as neutral dispute-resolution experts with no prior relationship with the disputants, official procedures are followed, formal laws are applied, and state power is enforced to produce an officially mandated resolution.

The Hutong regime's second tier—that of the Residents' Committee and the Neighborhood Police—lies somewhere in between these two extremes. Both the Residents' Committee and the Neighborhood Police are institutional actors that specialize in dispute resolution, yet they also act as members of the disputants' community, enmeshed in the same web of social relationships as the disputants themselves. Indeed, as will be discussed, much of their moral authority stems precisely from their generalized social connections to disputants as fellow neighbors and sharers of a common social context. These two institutions are formalized and "public" in the sense that they are paid with public funds, have a mandate to represent community interests, and are established as government organs by formal elections or other legal procedures. Yet they are not able to apply coercive power in sanctioning parties, and they generally do not employ formal rules in resolving disputes. Some minimal level of formal procedure may be applied, especially by the Residents' Committee when summoned to mediate standing disputes, but this is often applied unevenly and tailored to the exigencies of individual cases.

This middle layer of nonlegalistic public authority in Beijing Hutongs suggests that the traditional distinction between laws and norms should be reconsidered, or at least the standard assumption that the use of informal norms precludes intervention by public institutions should be softened. Our field research suggests that institutionalized nonlegalistic public authorities can play a vital role in developing and enforcing informal social norms, and indeed they can often use norms to broker negotiations more efficiently and productively than purely private negotiators.

Our field research revealed a strong universal preference for norm-based, informal methods of dispute resolution among Beijing Hutong residents. The residents we interviewed reported a distinct bias against using formal legal rules or involving formal legal authorities in their affairs, which they generally regarded as inefficient and potentially troublesome. Of the sixty-five Hutong residents we interviewed, many of whom had lived in the same neighborhood since the 1950s, not one had ever hired a lawyer or been involved in litigation, and none reported ever calling the police about a dispute with a neighbor. In fact, most were quick to insist that relations with their neighbors were harmonious, and that they were not the kind of contentious people who would involve public authorities in private disputes.

Residents similarly reported a disinclination to summon third-party mediators from the Residents' Committee or the Neighborhood Police unless it was absolutely necessary. Despite the informal, rule-free nature of such mediations, less than one-third of the residents in our interview sample reported seeking mediation through either of these institutions.

Nonlegalistic public authorities like the Residents' Committee did appear to play a prominent role in the life of the community generally, however, as almost all interviewees reported regular contact with Residents' Committee members and Neighborhood Police officers in some capacity. Many interviewees also reported participating in Residents' Committee mediation of disputes involving other residents. But the vast majority of the residents we interviewed insisted that they preferred never to initiate third-party mediation. A baseline preference for informal, ad hoc, neighbor-to-neighbor negotiations was thus a constant refrain in our interviews, with norm-based mediation by the Residents' Committee or Neighborhood Police being a viable second choice, while invocation of formal rules (of any kind) or resorting to formal legal institutions were highly disfavored and accordingly rare.

Over 90 percent of the residents we interviewed reported that there are no written rules governing the use of common courtyard areas in Hutong neighborhoods. In other words, there are no official nuisance rules as that term is understood in the West. Instead, informal social norms dictate that each household may use the area around its doorway (roughly two square meters in area) in any way it wishes. The remaining courtyard areas—which generally account for most of the space in any given courtyard—are recognized as common space, and any proposed use of these areas must be approved by the other households adjoining the courtyard (that is, any single neighbor is able to veto any proposed use). This creates a variant of what [Michael] Heller has termed an "anticommons" in common courtyard areas. Alternatively, to invoke [Guido] Calabresi and [A. Douglas] Melamed's oft-cited typology, this scheme effectively grants all residents two entirely norm-based property-rule entitlements: one allowing them absolute control of designated household areas near their doorways and another granting them veto-power over proposed uses of common areas.

Under this regime, direct neighbor-to-neighbor bargaining generally resolves uncertainty as to what uses of common space are acceptable and the preferences of nearby neighbors are generally respected in this process. Of course, obstinate neighbors or particularly noxious uses or encroachments on common space can lead to intractable disputes. The Residents' Committee will step in to mediate between parties when private negotiation fails. We interviewed members of one household who had summoned the Residents' Committee to mediate a dispute with a neighbor who insisted on raising pigeons—and hence allowing them to discharge certain bodily functions—directly above the complainants' doorway. Another case we encountered involved a resident whose pet dog repeatedly relieved itself in common courtyard areas. In both cases, the Residents' Committee successfully intervened to vindicate the norm-based entitlements of the complainants, persuading the offending party to avoid such messes. Disputes over the use or expansion of kitchen facilities in courtyard areas also appeared typical, with private negotiations or Residents' Committee intervention similarly serving to uphold norms protecting property entitlements in courtyard spaces.

Resolution of noise complaints are also the exclusive province of informal norm-based solutions. The prevailing norm dictates that residents refrain from making more noise than is "necessary" under the circumstances. Residents' Committee mediators whom we interviewed reported that they were often summoned to mediate sometimes colorful disputes between neighbors embroiled in escalating battles of intrusive noisemaking.

A LOOK AHEAD: THE IMPLICATIONS OF LEGAL REFORM, URBAN DEVELOPMENT, AND SOCIAL CHANGE

Hutong dispute-resolution methods are time-tested, rooted in hundreds of years of cultural tradition and accumulated social practice. More importantly, they seem to be effective in maintaining social order within Hutong neighborhoods, and by definition, they seem to embody the methods most normatively acceptable to members of these communities. As such, legal reformers ignore Hutong norms at their peril. At the least, laws ill-fitted to existing norms can preclude the functioning of efficient norm-based dispute-resolution regimes and destroy social capital in the process. At the worst, such laws could actually discredit the legal system more generally, galvanize popular support for countervailing norms, and deepen social tendencies toward extralegality.

Conversely, new laws that dovetail with existing social norms will likely benefit from increased normative legitimacy among the populace and fewer problems surrounding their practical application. Ideally, new laws and legal institutions could harness efficient norm-based systems and incorporate both their substantive content and their institutional apparatus into new legal institutions. Legal reformers seeking to establish a "rule of law" in China will confront this coincidence of opportunity and peril in all areas of Chinese law where preexisting norm-based regimes exist (that is, almost everywhere). The Hutong regime discussed here provides but one particularly colorful and informative example.

REFERENCES

Clarke, Donald C. 1991. Dispute resolution in China. *Journal of Chinese Law* 5: 245, 248.

V LAW AND DEVELOPMENT AND LEGAL REFORM

INTRODUCTION

No society is static; all societies undergo social change, at all times, sometimes slow, sometimes fast. The founding fathers of sociological thought tried to identify trends in social change and relate them to changes in the law. Sir Henry Maine (1875) perceived a general trend from status to contract; Emile Durkheim (1911), from repressive to restitutive law; and Max Weber (1954), a trend toward rationalization of law. Empirically oriented law and society scholars have tried to analyze both general and specific issues in an attempt to explain how social change relates to changes in law and legal systems.

At what point does a group, community, or society develop a formal or specialized legal system? Richard Schwartz (1954), in a classic article, studied two Israeli settlements, one of which had a specialized judicial committee, and one of which did not. He argued that law (in the sense of formal and specific means of social control) appears when informal controls fail. Informal controls can suffice, however, in small groups in constant face-to-face interaction. A later study questioned Schwartz's findings (Shapiro 1975, 1996), arguing that even as face-to-face interactions in Israeli settlements decreased over time, specific legal organs failed to develop.

Other studies have asked how businesses and others cope in situations where there is no functioning legal system, or where the legal system functions badly or corruptly. McMillan and Woodruff (1999) studied contracting and dispute prevention in Vietnam. Businesspeople spent significant amounts of time trying to determine the reputation of those they might want to deal with; the weaknesses of the legal system meant they had to rely on business ethics rather than legal process. In Venezuela, Pérez-Perdomo (1996) found a similar situation, with the added feature that a businessperson who used the courts ran the risk of a bad reputation—a reputation as someone who seeks to profit from a slow and corrupt system of justice. Landa (1994), studying Chinese business communities in South Asia, found that ethnically homogeneous groups prefer to contract among themselves as a way of reducing costs of the uncertainty generated by imperfections in the legal order.

In some of these cases, the lack of a fully functional legal system does not seem to prevent a measure of economic growth and social change. Some studies have tried to identify substitutes for formal law, and such substitutes do develop, although whether they are adequate substitutes is an interesting question. Perhaps, if the rule of law prevailed in these societies, economic development would have taken a different, and presumably better, path. Even in societies with functioning legal systems, businesses and individuals might avoid the path of formal law. Winn (1994) makes explicit the thesis of marginality of law: studying contractual practices and contractual enforcement in Taiwan, she found very little use of the formal legal system law at a time when the country was experiencing phenomenal economic growth. During the 1990s, Vietnam experienced an impressive economic growth in the absence of a practically functioning legal system (McMillan and Woodruff 1999). In fact, social norms are powerful influences on behavior, even where there is a functioning and significant legal system, and the impact of legal rules, at least in some aspects of social life, is less decisive than commonly assumed (Macaulay 1963; Ellickson 1991).

Skepticism about the importance of formal law is widespread in the literature. But other law and society scholars have argued that law can be enormously relevant in some circumstances and in some areas of life. Forbath (1992) compared and contrasted the labor movement in the United States and England. In England, the labor movement was ultimately able to organize politically and also ultimately able to persuade Parliament to enact prolabor legislation on working conditions and economic issues. The trade unions moved into politics, and the Labor Party became one of the major political parties. The existence of a professional civil service also facilitated action through legislation. In the United States, the judges had the power of judicial review, and they used it to strike down labor legislation. The labor movement was not able to counter these decisions—and neither was the legislature. Hence the labor movement felt obliged to turn to collective bargaining, and it never was able to make use of the path followed by the labor movement in England. The different legal structure in these two countries had a huge impact, according to Forbath, in shaping politics and policy.

Law clearly does matter in many instances, but many factors interact in determining exactly what the impact of law is likely to be. Aubert (1989, 79), analyzing nineteenth-century Norway, points out that it is difficult to find concrete traces of influence, but "we are led to assume that the very existence of a fairly well developed legal system, a corps of relatively uncorrupt civil servants, and a growing legal profession contributed to the kind of trust that is conducive to economic growth."

Hurst (1964), Friedman (2005), and other historians have found many examples of the influence of law on American society in the nineteenth and twentieth centuries, but the impact of particular legal rules on specific social changes is elusive. Calavita (1986) shows that both proponents and skeptics were probably wrong regarding the effect of legal reform on labor safety in Italy. Work accidents decreased after the Italian Workers' Rights Act of 1970, but other factors besides the law itself could have had an impact on the frequency of work accidents. For example, Calavita (1986) pointed to recession as a powerful concomitant factor, and automation and technology might have also played a role. In a study of labor relations in Rotterdam and U.S. ports, Kagan (1990) found that law played an important role, but this role was hard to disentangle from organizational, economic, technological, and political elements.

Furthermore, given the complexity of social life, it is difficult to know if changes in law impact society or whether, on the contrary, it is social change that is molding the law. For example, a common perception is that easy divorce rules stimulate divorce rates and have a destructive effect on the family. In fact, it is the reverse that is more plausible, that is, that changes in society led to pressure to adopt easy divorce rules. Changes in gender relations, the appearance of women in the workforce and in higher education, along with the influence of films and the media, and changes in personality structure and general culture—all these suggest why the demand for divorce rose inexorably—and it was this demand, ultimately, that led to a liberalization of divorce rules and procedures (Jacob 1988; Friedman 2004; Théry 1993).

How social change impacts litigation rates over extended periods of time has been the subject of important studies for Spain (Toharia 1974), Belgium (Van Loon and Langerwerf 1990), Germany (Wollschläger 1990), California (Friedman and Percival 1976), Italy (Pellegrini 1997), and several Latin American and Mediterranean countries (Clark 1990). But it is hard to draw firm conclusions and make sound generalizations from these various studies. Except in cases of catastrophic events like war, it is difficult to predict what factors will affect litigation rates and to what degree.

Markovits (2002) has described the distinctive features of socialist legal systems, specifically focusing on the former Democratic Republic of Germany (East Germany). Under this regime, law and rules meant something different from what they meant in, say, West Germany, and the role of judges, lawyers, and prosecutors was quite different from their role in capitalist societies. Similarly, criminality and punishment were differently conceived (Łos 1991; Sanders and Hamilton 1992). Markovits (1992) has also, in an insightful study, documented the last days of the East German legal system—a rare study of a legal order that was in the process of disappearing.

Many societies have been attracted to the idea of producing or accelerating social and economic change, through modernizing or reforming the legal system. In the nineteenth century, Japan and various Latin American countries adopted modern codes and legislation with this in mind. China, Turkey, Ethiopia, and several other African countries did the same in the twentieth century. What was the impact of these attempts at massive legal change? In the law and society literature, the work by Starr (1980) is frequently cited. She studied the impact of the adoption of a civil code, inspired by the Swiss code, in rural Turkey. In a general way, the transplantation of law tends to encounter significant resistance in the receiving countries, and its precise impact is hard to predict; impact seems to depend both on the nature of the receiving society and on the field of law. Li (2003) studied how the intellectual property law enacted by Beijing found resistance in the provinces because of the economic and political situation in those provinces. Local governments are in charge of enforcement and their interest can differ from the central government. Piracy can provide economic activity to provinces that would tend to protect the intellectual property transgressors. (This work is excerpted here as Chapter 22.) A change in the rules of custody, in Taiwan, found greater acceptance in Taipei than in rural areas; the new rules displaced older rules that gave fathers preference, and these older rules, which conformed more to traditional patriarchal Chinese values, persisted outside of the metropolis (Liu 2002). (This work is excerpted here as Chapter 21.)

In the 1970s, the United States began a program to influence the law and legal culture of developing countries, mostly in Latin America. This effort, the law and development movement, placed particular emphasis on legal education, law schools, and, in general, the legal culture. Many scholars have concluded that the movement was a failure and was in fact misconceived from the outset (Trubek and Galanter 1974; Gardner 1980) even though its impact was sizeable (Garth and Sterling 1998; Tamanaha 1995). Efforts in Latin America itself to reform the legal system had begun before the law and development movement and continued after the American "missionaries" had departed (Pérez-Perdomo 2004).

In the 1990s, a new law and development movement appeared. Its basic assumptions were that law matters, and that economic growth and social development were associated with the strengthening of markets and legal institutions. In addition to efforts to change certain substantive legal rules, those who sponsored the movement emphasized strengthening the judiciary, the legislative process, and the administration of justice (Dezalay and Garth 2002b). There has been an effort to introduce, as well, alternative dispute-resolution mechanisms (Gómez 2008). (This work is excerpted here as Chapter 16.) The "new orthodoxy" has not lacked skeptics, in large part because the precise role of law and law reform in fostering economic growth is by no means as obvious as one might imagine (Ginsburg 2000). As was true in the 1970s, there were failures to use good research techniques and realistic studies of legal culture and legal institutions, before, during, and after the reform efforts. Many of the projects have been failures; this was true, for example, of criminal justice reform in Venezuela, which foundered in the face of strong cultural resistance and an adverse political environment (Alguíndigue and Pérez-Perdomo 2008, excerpted here as Chapter 18).

In Russia, law reform efforts have also found stiff cultural resistance (Hendley 2006, 1996). New rules are not necessarily understood, given previous experiences, and in general, old habits and attitudes die hard. But this does not mean that law and courts are completely useless. In another article Hendley (2004, also excerpted here as Chapter 20) analyzes those who go to court in Russia, finding surprising similarities with similar situations in the United States.

In several Latin American countries law and justice reforms have been successful in making the law more relevant to the protection of individual and collective rights, and for taking the protests of political minorities into account (McAllister 2008; Taylor 2008; Fix-Fierro 2003; Fix-Fierro and López Ayllón 2003; Bergoglio 2003; Smulovitz 2005; Uprimny Yepes 2007; Rodríguez, García-Villegas, and Uprimny 2003). The role of supreme courts or constitutional courts, too, has had an impact on legal and political systems in several Latin American countries (Cepeda Espinosa 2005; Wilson 2005; Arantes 2005) and, probably to a lesser extent, in East Asian countries (Ginsburg 2002). Law reform is not always a failure, but the enactment of legislation is usually just the beginning of a new social process.

The relationships between law and legal change are complex and elusive, and much more research needs to be done. Law reform efforts go on, in country after country, and the lack of evidence of success does not seem to stop these efforts. Certainly, in modern societies, which rely intensively on law, economic growth must depend to a certain extent on a functioning legal system. Protection of rights and freedoms also requires such a system. But the precise details—the how and the why—remain obscure.

REFERENCES AND SUGGESTIONS FOR FURTHER READING

Alguíndigue, Carmen, and R. Pérez-Perdomo. 2008. The inquisitor strikes back: Obstacles to the re-form of criminal procedure in revolutionary Venezuela. *Southwestern Journal of Law and Trade in the Americas* 15: 101.

Arantes, Rogério. 2005. Constitutionalism: The expansion of justice and the judicializatiion of poli-tics in Brazil. In *The judicialization of politics in Latin America*, ed. R. Sieder, L. Schjolden, and A. Angel, 231–62. London: Palgrave Macmillan.

Aubert, Vilhelm. 1989. Law and social change in nineteenth-century Norway. In *History and power in the study of law*, ed. J. Starr and J. Coller, 55–80. Ithaca, NY: Cornell University Press.

Bergoglio, María Inés. 2003. Argentina: The effects of democratic institutionalization. In *Legal cul-ture in the age of globalization: Latin America and Latin Europe*, ed. L. Friedman and R. Pérez-Perdomo, 20–63. Stanford: Stanford University Press.

Calavita, Kitty. 1998. Immigration law and marginalization in a global economy: Notes from Spain. *Law and Society Review* 32: 529.

———. 1986. Worker safety, law and social change: The Italian case. *Law and Society Review* 20: 187.

Cepeda Espinosa, Manuel José. 2005. The judicialization of politics in Colombia: The old and the new. In *The judicialization of politics in Latin America*, ed. R Seider, L. Schjolden, and A. Angel, 67–104. London: Palgrave Macmillan.

Clark, David. 1990. Civil litigation trends in Europe and Latin America since 1945: The advantage of intracountry comparisons. *Law and Society Review* 24: 549.

Dezalay, Yves, and B. Garth. 2002a. *Global prescriptions. The production, exportation, and importation of a new legal orthodoxy.* Ann Arbor: University of Michigan Press.

———. 2002b. *The internationalization of palace wars: Lawyers, economists, and the contest to trans-form Latin American states.* Chicago: University of Chicago Press.

Durkheim, Émile. 1911. *De la division du travail social.* 3d ed. Paris: Alcan.

Ellickson, Robert C. 1991. *Order without law: How neighbors settle disputes.* Cambridge, MA: Harvard University Press.

Fix-Fierro, Héctor. 2003. Judicial reform in Mexico: What next? *Beyond common knowledge: Empiri-cal approaches to the rule of law*, ed. Thomas Heller and Erik Jensen, 240–89. Stanford: Stanford University Press.

Fix-Fierro, Héctor, and Sergio López-Ayllón. 2003. "Faraway, So Close!" The rule of law and legal change in Mexico. In *Legal culture in the age of globalization: Latin America and Latin Europe*, ed. L. Friedman and R. Pérez-Perdomo, 285–351. Stanford: Stanford University Press.

Forbath, William E. 1992. Law and the shaping of labor politics in the United States and England. In *Labor law in America: Historical and critical essays*, ed. C. L. Tomlins and A. J. King, 201–30. Balti-more, MD: John Hopkins University Press.

Friedman, Lawrence M. 2005. *A history of American law*, 3d ed. New York: Simon & Schuster.

———. 2004. *Private lives: Family, individuals, and the law.* Cambridge, MA: Harvard University Press.

———. 2002. *American law in the 20th century.* New Haven, CT: Yale University Press.

Friedman, Lawrence M., and Robert Percival. 1976. A tale of two courts: Litigation in Alameda and San Benito counties. *Law and Society Review* 10: 267–301.

Gardner, James A. 1980. *Legal imperialism: American lawyers and foreign aid in Latin America.* Madi-son: University of Wisconsin Press.

Garth, Bryant, and J. Sterling. 1998. From legal realism to law and society: Reshaping law for the last stages of the social activist state. *Law and Society Review* 32: 409.

Ginsburg, Tom. 2002. Confucian constitutionalism? The emergence of constitutional review in Korea and Taiwan. *Law & Social Inquiry* 27: 763.

———. 2000. Does law matter for economic development? Evidence from East Asia. *Law and Society Review* 34: 829.

Gómez, Manuel. 2008. All in the family: The influence of social networks on dispute processing (A case study of a developing economy). *Georgia Journal of International and Comparative Law* 36: 291.

He, Xin. 2005. Why do they not comply with the law. *Law and Society Review* 39: 527.

Hendley, Kathryn. 2006. Assessing the rule of law in Russia. *Cardozo Journal of International & Comparative Law* 14: 347–91.

———. 2004. Business litigation in the transition: A portrait of debt collection in Russia. *Law and Society Review* 38: 305.

———. 1996. The role of law in the Russian economic transition: Coping with the unexpected in contractual relations. *Wisconsin International Law Journal* 14: 624–50.

Hurst, James Willard. 1964. *Law and economic growth: The legal history of the lumber industry in Wisconsin 1836–1915.* Cambridge, MA: Harvard University Press.

Jacob, Herbert. 1988. *Silent revolution: The transformation of divorce law in the United States.* Chicago: University of Chicago Press.

Kagan, Robert. 1990. How much does law matter? Labor law, competition and waterfront labor relations in Rotterdam and U.S. ports. *Law and Society Review* 24: 35.

Landa, Janet Tai. 1994. *Trust, ethnicity, and identity: The new institutional economics of ethnic trading networks, contract law, and gift-exchange.* Ann Arbor: University of Michigan Press.

———. 1981. A theory of the ethnically homogenous middleman group: An institutional alternative to contract law. *Journal of Legal Studies* 10: 349.

Li, Ling. 2003. The sky is high and the emperor is far away: The enforcement of intellectual property law in China. *Boletín Mexicano de Derecho Comparado* 108: 951.

Liu, Hung-En. 2001. Mother or father: Who received custody? The best interest of the child standard and judges' custody decisions in Taiwan. *International Journal of Law, Policy and the Family* 15: 185.

Łos, Maria. 1991. Los delitos de cuello rojo: Delitos de la elite en la URSS y Polonia. In *Corrupción y control, una perspectiva comparada,* ed. R. Pérez-Perdomo and R. Capriles. Caracas, Venezuela: Ediciones IESA.

Macaulay, Stewart. 1963. Non contractual relations in business: A preliminary study. *American Sociological Review* 28: 55.

Maine, Henry Summer. 1875. *Ancient law.* 5th ed. London: J. Murray.

Markovits, Inga. 2002. Justice in Lüritz. *American Journal of Comparative Law* 50: 853.

———. 1992. Last days. *California Law Review* 80: 55.

McAllister, Lesley K. 2008. *Making law matter: Environmental protection and legal institutions in Brazil.* Stanford: Stanford University Press.

McMillan, John, and Christopher Woodruff. 1999. Dispute prevention without courts in Vietnam. *Journal of Law, Economics & Organization* 15: 637.

Pellegrini, Stefania. 1997. *La litigiosità in Italia: Un analisi sociologico-giuridica.* Milan, Italy: Giuffrè.

Pérez-Perdomo, Rogelio. 2006. *Latin American lawyers: A historical introduction.* Stanford: Stanford University Press.

———. 2004. El movimiento de derecho y desarrollo y los intentos de cambio en los estudios jurídicos. In *Homenaje a Jorge Avendaño*, ed. J. de Belaunde and others. Lima, Peru: Pontificia Universidad Católica del Perú.

———. 1996. Seguridad jurídica, abogados y actividad judicial. *Seguridad jurídica y competitividad*, ed. M. E. Boza and R. Pérez-Perdomo. Caracas, Venezuela: Ediciones IESA.

Rodríguez, César M., García-Villegas, and R. Uprimny. 2003. Justice and society in Colombia: A sociological analysis of the Colombian courts. In *Legal culture in the age of globalization: Latin America and Latin Europe*, ed. L. Friedman and R. Pérez-Perdomo. Stanford: Stanford University Press.

Sanders, Joseph, and V. L. Hamilton. 1992. Legal cultures and punishment repertoires in Japan, Russia and the United States. *Law and Society Review* 26: 117.

Schwartz, Richard. 1954. Social factors in the development of legal control: A case study of two Israeli settlements. *Yale Law Journal* 63: 471.

Shapiro, Allan E. 1996. Law in the kibbutz. In *Social control and justice: Inside or outside the law*, ed. L. Sebba, 343–56. Jerusalem: Magnus Press; Hebrew University.

———. 1975. Law in the kibbutz: A reappraisal. *Law & Society Review* 10: 417.

Smulovitz, Catalina. 2005. Petitioning and creating rights: Judicialization in Argentina. In *The judicialization of politics in Latin America*, ed. Rachel Sieder, Line Schjolden, and Alan Angell, 161–86. New York: Palgrave Macmillan.

Starr, June. 1980. Dispute settlement in rural Turkey: An ethnography of law. *American Anthropologist* 82(3): 673–75.

Tamanaha, Brian Z. 1995. The lessons of law and development studies. *American Journal of International Law* 89: 470–86.

Taylor, Matthew M. 2008. *Judging policy: Courts and policy reform in democratic Brazil*. Stanford: Stanford University Press.

Théry, Irène. 1993. *Le démariage: Justice et vie privé*. Paris: Odile Jacob.

Toharia, José Juan. 1974. *Cambio social y vida jurídica en España*. Madrid, Spain: Edicusa.

Trubek, David, and M. Galanter. 1974. Scholars in self-estrangement: Some reflections on the crisis in law and development studies in the United States. *Wisconsin Law Review* 1062–95.

Uprimny Yepes, Rodrigo. 2007. La justice au cœur du politique: Potentialités et risques d'une judicialisation en Colombie. In *La fonction politique de la justice*, ed. J. Commaille and M. Kaluszynski. Paris: La Découverte.

Van Loon, F., and E. Langerwerf. 1990. Socioeconomic development and the evolution of litigation rates of civil courts in Belgium, 1835–1980. *Law and Society Review* 24: 283.

Weber, Max. 1954. *On law in economy and society*. Cambridge, MA: Harvard University Press.

Wilson, Bruce M. 2005. Changing dynamics: The political impact of Costa Rica's constitutional court. In *The judicialization of politics in Latin America*, ed. R. Sieder, L. Schjolden, and A. Angel, 47–66. London: Palgrave Macmillan.

Winn, Jane Kaufman. 1994. Relational practices and the marginalization of law: Informal financial practices of small business in Taiwan. *Law and Society Review* 28: 193.

Wollschläger, Christian. 1990. Civil litigation and modernization: The work of municipal courts of Bremen, Germany, in five centuries, 1549–1984. *Law and Society Review* 24: 583.

THE INQUISITOR STRIKES BACK

OBSTACLES TO THE REFORM OF CRIMINAL PROCEDURE IN REVOLUTIONARY VENEZUELA

Carmen Alguíndigue and Rogelio Pérez-Perdomo

Venezuela radically renovated criminal procedure in July 1998, approving a modern Código Orgánico Procesal Penal. The old criminal procedure, regulated in the Código de Enjuiciamiento Criminal of 1926, followed the most traditional rules of inquisitorial procedure (Chiossone 1981). Since confessions were a powerful form of evidence, police often applied their forceful tactics to extract desirable confessions. The lack of effective defense in cases involving poor defendants led to the frequent conviction of innocent people. In fact, the system did not have the means to distinguish guilty from innocent people. The Venezuelan criminal system crushed poor and uneducated suspects in its Kafaesque gears.

As criminal procedure was slow, particularly with poor and uneducated defendants, prisons were overpopulated. About 70 percent of the prison population was awaiting a judge's decision. Without conviction these prisoners were legally innocent. The prisons were violent. There were no reliable figures on duration of cases, but there were many horror stories of forgotten prisoners or cases with more than ten years waiting for a decision. The probability of being violated or killed in a prison was high (Pérez-Perdomo and Rosales 1999). In the 1990s, criminal justice was such a national shame that a number of higher judges, legal scholars, and distinguished lawyers promoted its radical restructuring.

At the same time that Venezuelans perceived the criminal procedure as flawed, the country was experiencing a sizeable increase in violent crime. Until the 1970s, criminality rates in Venezuela were relatively low. In the 1980s crimes against property increased. In response to this trend, the government relaxed the rules on gun control, and the citizens were invited to bear arms and defend their properties themselves. Few years later, homicides and other types of violent crime also rose. During the 1990s the annual homicide rate, which historically was below ten homicides per one hundred thousand inhabitants, rose to more than twenty per one hundred thousand. Venezuela's homicide rate was traditionally low for Latin American standards, but in the 1990s the rate attained the average for the region.

Reprinted from Carmen Alguíndigue and Rogelio Pérez-Perdomo, "The Inquisitor Strikes Back: Obstacles to the Reform of Criminal Procedure in Revolutionary Venezuela," *Southwestern Journal of Law and Trade in the Americas* 15: 101 (2008). Permission courtesy of the Southwestern Journal of Law and Trade in the Americas.

Armed robberies, kidnappings, and other violent crimes also increased. The perception was that something had to be done about the criminal justice system.

With this backdrop of such social expectations of change, Venezuela radically renovated its criminal procedure in July 1998. Some aspects of the code (suppression of secrecy in the *sumario*) entered in force immediately, but most important rules were to be applied starting in July 1999. Drafters of the code expected that the new rules would create a more efficient and equitable criminal justice system, which would provide legal certainty and would contribute to the fight against crime (*Código Orgánico Procesal Penal 1998*, exposición de motivos).

In the new code, the criminal procedure was entirely reorganized to be transparent, adversarial, neutral, and efficient. The model was the German criminal procedure. The secret phase of the old criminal procedure was abolished. Suspects had the right to a lawyer as soon as they were taken into custody or indicted. Prosecutors (and not judges) were given control over the indictment and supervision of police investigations. Judicial procedures became adversarial, oral, and speedy. Freedom became the rule. Preventive detention became the exception and had to be short. The trial should proceed immediately in a concentrated procedure. For more important crimes, citizens would be called to participate as jurors or lay assessors (*escabinos*). For the gravest crimes a nine-person jury would be called; for crimes of moderate gravity the court would be composed of one professional judge and two *escabinos*. For less important crimes the professional judge alone would resolve the matter. The code established a substantial reduction of penalties for defendants who confessed their guilt. This was the acceptance and regulation of plea bargaining. Criminal punishment could be avoided if there was an agreement with the victim to make reparations. Criminal courts were reorganized in order to guarantee fully neutral judges and more efficient operation. Judges themselves had different roles: the control judge supervised the criminal investigation; the decision judge attended the trial and issued the decision; and the judge *de ejecución* supervised the correct execution of punishment. Prisoners' human rights were fully guaranteed, at least on paper.

When Hugo Chávez became president in January 1999 he immediately called a Constituant Assembly. By December 1999 Venezuela had a new constitution, which recognized the principles of the new criminal procedure (Articles 44–50). The liberal principles were reinforced. But not everything was going well for the reform. Violent criminality rose. Many attributed this rise to the new criminal procedure and a controversy arose (Monteferrante and Pérez-Perdomo 2001). At the same time, the political changes following Chávez's election shook the judiciary, prosecutors, and investigative police.

Reforming criminal procedure entails complex social and political processes; it is not a mere change of the rules. This paper will analyze the state of the criminal justice system and the impact of the new procedure during the strife-filled years in Venezuela from 1999 to the present. In the first section, we will describe what changes have occurred both from the legislature and from the judiciary. In the second section, we will explore the return of the repressive criminal system in the context of Venezuelan legal culture and authoritarian political regime.

THE LEGISLATOR AS SORCERER'S APPRENTICE

Even before the new code was one year old, there were commissions studying its modification. In six years it has had been subjected to three legislative reforms that have emptied it of most of its liberal rules.

The first reform (March 2000) was presented as an "adaptation to the Venezuelan society" and a "necessary defense of society from criminality" implying that the code was considered ill adapted to the Venezuelan society and too lenient toward criminals. Although only five articles were changed, they were at the core of the liberal principles. The reform redefined *in flagrante delicto* to facilitate imprisonment without judicial intervention, increased the time for the judicial decision on imprisonment from twenty-four to seventy-two hours (the old rule was back), restricted the opportunities for defendants to compensate victims rather than serve time, and limited the reduction of punishment in violent crimes that carried a punishment of more than eight years of prison and in corruption crimes.

Opinion studies reflected the population's high sensitivity to violent crime. For example, *Percepción 21* of January 1999 stated that 22 percent of the population considered crime the main problem the country faced. A study by the Ministry of Justice found that 85 percent of the population perceived that violent crime was on the rise. Another opinion study by *Percepción 21* of April 2000 found that 35 percent considered crime the main problem of the country.

The National Assembly appointed a new commission to study the matter. After hearings, the president of the commission, Rep. Jordán Hernández, concluded that the criminal justice system was facing important difficulties. According to his report, there were not enough prosecutors; police laboratories were ill equipped; the system was staffed with people with insufficient training; there was not an integrated system of information and crime registry; there was not enough effort to inform the citizens in general of their new and important roles; and a system to protect jury members, lay judges, and victims was lacking. In addition, the penetration and enforcement of legislation on establishing justices of the peace, which could provide fora for conflict resolution in neighborhoods and decrease the level of violence, was insufficient (Asamblea Nacional 2001). The chief justice, the *fiscal general*, and several other high-level officials concurred regarding the need for better coordination and more resources for the system, but no effort at coordination was undertaken. The magical solution for this huge managerial problem was once more to reform the Código Orgánico Procesal Penal.

This time (2001) the reform was substantial: 178 articles were modified, 27 articles disappeared, and 48 new articles were introduced. The main features of this vast reform were (1) the further restriction of the principle of freedom, (2) the suppression of the jury trial, and (3) the curtailment of defendants' rights. The prosecutors were given six to eight months to present the accusation (*acto conclusivo*).[1] The possibility of decreeing the secrecy of incriminating evidence was expanded, affecting substantially the rights of defense. A kind of limbo was created for cases in which the prosecutors did not act. These cases could be

---

1. The *acto conclusivo* (concluding act) could be the accusation, the dismissal (*sobreseimiento*), or a nolle prosequi (*archivo fiscal*). *Código Orgánico Procesal Penal,* 2001, Art. 321.

sent to an archive but could be revived at any time, creating the category of quasi defendant. The police received new power including the possibility of directly asking the judge for permission to carry on new searches and investigation. These were major blows by the inquisitor on the liberal principles of 1998–99.

These revisions left very little of the original spirit of the 1998 code. Amazingly, data to support such legislative changes in 1998, 2000, and 2001 were largely absent. Only scattered figures were tossed about without explaining their basis. For example, the *fiscal general* asserted in a press release that procedural delays proceeded from the absence of juries. However, the *fiscal general* never explained how he arrived at this conclusion.

During the 1999–2001 period, a total of 334 jury trials were planned in the Caracas area, with 258 of them postponed. This represents a 77 percent postponement rate. The formation of juries was clearly a problem and was mainly attributable to (1) the lack of reliable lists to locate people, (2) lack of an organizational apparatus within the court administration to call in jurors, and (3) the population's lack of education and awareness for this new duty. However, the absence of parties to the trial was a more significant cause for the high postponement rate. It was responsible for 183 of the 258 delayed cases. Unfortunately, the remedy for postponement and delays was the suppression of juries, without any data being discussed. The information for 2002 (after the suppression of jury trials) shows a similar trend with increased numbers: 867 planned trials with only 144 (17 percent) actually taking place (Riego 2005, 128).

The reforms of the Código Orgánico Procesal Penal did not finish in 2001. In October 2006, in response to an increase in the incarcerated population, strikes and protests by prisoners, and a high level of violence in the prisons (www.observatoriovenezolanodeprisiones. org), the code underwent a new reform. This time the reform quietly liberalized the rules on requirements for alternative punishment and put some restrictions on preventive incarceration. In this reform only two articles were modified and one disappeared (*Ley de Reforma Parcial del Código Orgánico Procesal Penal* 2006). At the same time, the minister of interior and justice started the practice of giving instructions to the judges in order to decongest the prisons. These reforms of the reform and the executive branch's unconstitutional practices reflect the swing of the pendulum and a pragmatic response to a problem caused by the pro-incarceration policies in the reform of 2001. Of course, the minister of interior and justice will not be liberal with political prisoners.

All these changes were not capricious. The drafters of the 1998 code were aware of the population concerns about to the high level of violent crime. They probably thought that public, speedy, and fair trials would produce a visible association between crime and punishment, which would in turn have a dissuasive power on criminals. They admired Germany's liberal code, low crime rate, and very small incarcerated population. According to the principles of magical legalism, adopting similar rules would produce similar social results, even if the social context is different. Unfortunately wishful thinking frequently fails in legislative endeavours.

When the crime rate rose in 1999 and 2000, those who were unhappy with the new code quickly blamed this trend on its allegedly soft stance on crime. They did not look to the 1990s when the level of violent crime rose under the repressive code of 1925. As could be expected, the level of violent crime did not decrease as a consequence of the 2001 reform. The authoritarian branch of magical legalism was as wrong as the libertarian one. Violent crime is a complex social phenomenon and is difficult to control with reforms of the criminal procedure . . .

The other figures relevant for explaining the constant reform of criminal procedure are the ones focused on prison population. Traditionally, Venezuela has not had a high population in prison. During the 1990s, a time of increasing violent crime, the Venezuelan indicator of incarcerated population was similar to Spain and Costa Rica (approximately one hundred per one hundred thousand inhabitants, which is about one-sixth of the U.S. prison population rate), countries with much lower crime rates. This relatively low incarceration rate was not a product of the old Código de Enjuiciamiento Criminal. Rather, it was the combined result of the inefficiency of Venezuelan police and the criminal justice system and the special legislation that facilitated probation and alternatives to incarceration. The feature Venezuela shared with other Latin American countries was the high percentage of incarcerated people waiting for a judicial decision in their cases, the *presos sin condena* (Carranza 1983).

The data show that the prison population decreased as a consequence of the new rules in the Code of 1998. The decrease was particularly important among the defendants waiting for a decision. Since then the number of prisoners rose, and the percentage of condemned prisoners has tended to decrease. [Cristian] Riego observed that 90 percent of indicted people were in preventive prison. Based on this staggering statistic, it appears that the conditions of the past are returning. The inquisitor has struck back.

After all these reforms, the prisons are once again congested, and violence in the prisons remains a critical problem. Now the only difference is that prisoners seem more vocal. The Inter American Court of Human Rights took measures in favor of Venezuelan prisoners and required the Venezuelan government to inform the Court what it was doing to solve the problem.

The legislators and high officials in Venezuela have acted as the sorcerer's apprentices. They have unchained social forces without understanding their effects or the complex relationship between law and society. Facing the consequence of their improvisations, they try reversing direction, improvising once again. Chávez's *revolution* is the word used to justify radical changes in legislation without foreseeing social consequences. Let us consider the revolutionary goals and policies and their general impact on criminal justice.

LEGAL CULTURE, JUSTICE, AND REVOLUTION

The forward and backward movement of criminal procedural rules has an explanation in the Venezuelan legal culture and conception of legislation. Under the democratic regime controlled by political parties (1958–98), legislation was the business of elites. Select individuals would meet with party leaders, convince them of the need for and general convenience of a piece of legislation and then the leaders would mostly pass the legislation in Congress without much consultation. This was the case of the Código Orgánico de Procedimiento Penal. The group of lawyers and judges that promoted the new penal procedure found support in the international community. The Iberian American Institute of Procedural Law, the ILANUD, and people at the Inter American Development Bank and the

World Bank lent their support. Most law professors at Universidad Central de Venezuela and Universidad Católica Andrés Bello supported the radical change in the rules of criminal procedure. It was a change widely supported by the intellectual elite.

The reformers relied on the elite consensus and did not perceive the need for any study on how the reform could be perceived by the general population. The "consultations" they held were in fact information to describe the project. They did not pay any attention to Venezuelan external or popular legal culture. Our hypothesis is that in the popular culture the only conceivable form of punishment is prison or physical pain. If this hypothesis is well based, legislation that tried to restrict imprisonment could quickly be perceived as pro-criminal. No study of this culture was done, and no effort to educate the Venezuelan public was even attempted.

The Congress planned to implement the code throughout the country simultaneously, without the benefit of making adjustments for the difficulties of implementation. The very comprehensive character of the code, which included radical changes in the rules of preventive detention, restrictions on the police powers, orality, concentration, juries, and so on, made predictable that the reform of criminal justice would face severe difficulties.

The code was one of the last legislative acts that the former Congress passed, in 1998. In December of that year Hugo Chávez won the presidential election and the following Constituant Assembly swept out the old political elite. Those newly placed in power had no commitment to the reforming of criminal procedure. Among the new political elite, parties were not important and negotiations would have been considered a sign of weakness. These factors may help to explain the swift and radical change, which seemed to turn back the clock, particularly in sensitive areas like the limitation on preventive imprisonment.

In fact, the new authorities did not have a clear view of the implications of the 1998 code. In the years following the reform the country invested heavily in judicial reform but practically did nothing to improve the prosecution that was the new axis of criminal procedure.

Criminal courts were modernized. A new management system, called Juris 2000, was put in place. It required intensive use of computers, blind distribution of cases among judges, and measures intended to improve the management and conditions of work of judiciary personnel. The system facilitated following up cases to avoid the phenomenon of "forgotten prisoners" or forgotten cases. There was also a substantial increase in the number of criminal judges.

A report suggests that during this time criminal procedures quickened their pace. Unfortunately the report does not indicate the actual year of the study, size of the samples, and other technical information that could be used to determine its reliability.

While Juris 2000 effectively reduced the duration of criminal procedures, the report also shows a high degree of variability between the cities. For example, the average trial duration was nine months in Acarigua, while it was less than three in Merida. The research does not account for these differences, but they suggest an irregular application of the new management system. Other studies show a longer average duration: for 2002, Riego reported three hundred fifty days between accusation and trial in ordinary procedure, and forty-four days for abridged procedure. The sample was small and taken in Caracas. Reliable data is not abundant in Venezuela.

No similar attention was given to the prosecutorial office. The annual report that the *fiscal general* presented to the National Assembly in 2005 expressed that from the time the new code entered into full force in July 1999 to December 2004 more than two million cases were open. However, the number of prosecutors to deal with these cases was not substantially increased during this time. Venezuela had one of the lowest rates of prosecutors per inhabitants in Latin America and naturally the prosecutors' offices became the new bottlenecks of criminal justice. The *fiscal general* himself estimated that each prosecutor had a load of 2.9 cases in 2004. By 2006 this number has increased to 4.0. Very clearly, those who distributed resources among the various official actors of the criminal procedure did not understand the new centrality of the prosecutor's role.

Even if resources had been apportioned more evenly, this probably would have had little impact because ideologically the system was committed to repression, including the repression of political dissidence. In order to understand the new political system it is important to recognize that opposition is not tolerated. Any attempt to oppose the regime makes the opponent an enemy of the regime. A sanction will ensue. In most cases, the person is included in a list known as "Lista Tascón" that makes him or her ineligible for employment with the state or with a state organization or business. Even getting a passport could become more difficult. In more important cases a criminal indictment could follow.

Venezuela has experience with authoritarian governments. Previous dictators (Gómez, 1909–35; and Pérez Jiménez, 1952–58) established parallel repressive bodies that were not controlled by the judiciary. Those judges did not have to participate in the political repression (Pérez-Perdomo 2007; 2008). The Chávez's regime has not been able or willing to follow this course. The alternative has been to use the official penal system and accuse the person of a crime. In order to do so, the government needs legislation allowing preventive imprisonment and prosecutors and judges ready to act according to government wishes.

. . .

The examples of use of the justice system for political repression are very numerous. Political needs explain the changing rules and practices of hiring and dismissal, as well as the successive purges of judges and prosecutors. In the judiciary this included the suspension of all competitive public examinations (*concursos de oposición*) as the regular way of entering the judiciary. As the examination procedure gave tenure to judges, the lack of support for it among of new authorities is understandable. The new policy made almost all judges "provisional" and has destroyed the notion of a judicial career. About nine hundred judges, half of the entire judicial body, have been dismissed (Pérez-Perdomo 2007). Even the dismissal of provisional judges would require a process and grounds for the dismissal. However, the Comisión Judicial, a nonconstitutional entity, dismissed the judges in an executive way by voiding the appointment, a linguistic acrobatic feat. In 2006, the Supreme Tribunal decided to "regularize" the appointment of the provisional judges and organized a regularization course. Those judges approved in the course became *titular*. Because the course is not the open competitive public examination required by the constitution and legislation, the new "titular" judges do not have tenure and obviously can be dismissed any time through the mechanism of voiding their appointment. Thus, judges in Venezuela are completely dependent of the will of the Comisión Judicial. The judicial career has no meaning in these revolutionary times.

The Ley Orgánica del Ministerio Público of 1999 established competitive public examinations as a requirement for hiring new career-track prosecutors (Ley Orgánica del Ministerio Público 1999). These public examinations never took place, and only the prosecutors with more than ten years in their job got tenure. The reform of March 2007 suppressed this rule; nowadays all prosecutors can be freely hired and fired.

As consequence of these policies, judges and prosecutors in Venezuela are political appointees, and any decision that displeases the political powers generates the immediate dismissal of these disloyal functionaries.

The consequence of the repressive environment inside the judiciary and the Fiscalía General is mistrust, gossip, and low blows among the functionaries themselves or within power circles. In a June 8, 2005, the *fiscal general* wrote a letter complaining about the utter inefficiency of the prosecutors. He states that his office is full of cliques (*roscas*), irrational delays, and functionaries' inaction. "The excess of meetings (*reunionismo*) kills us and the indifference continues killing us after we are dead" (Oficio #DFGR-46.096, June 8, 2005).

Prosecutors may have reasons to be afraid. Any faux pas could produce their dismissal. By July 2005 more than two hundred prosecutors had been dismissed. In one case the consequence was much worse: Danilo Anderson was a prosecutor with important political cases. President Chávez and Fiscal General Rodriguez trusted him. One night, his car was blown up while he was driving. He was hailed as a revolutionary hero, but the crime was never solved. The rumors have offered many explanations, but it is likely that he was a victim of intense rivalries within the circles close to President Chávez.

The changes in criminal procedure in Venezuela have comprehensively altered rules of the organization and functioning of the judiciary and the Ministerio Público. In addition to these rule and organizational changes, there have been important investments as well. The justice system's budget has substantially increased. All these efforts have had an impact. In general terms, judicial and prosecutorial offices today look far more modern than twelve years ago. The offices have computers and servers; the spaces and furniture have a modern look. The average observer will notice that efficiency has improved. The decisions of the Supreme Tribunal are available on-line the same day of their publication; the archives of all courts are better organized, and so on.

But behind this façade, the observer would perceive the old bureaucratic and repressive mentality and a completely disorganized system. This is largely due to the lack of work on changing the legal culture. Very little has been done to reeducate judges, prosecutors, police officials, and other functionaries. Nothing has been done in relation to the broader citizens' legal and civil culture. This paper argues that this state of affairs is not an accident. The new regime requires repressive judges, prosecutors, and policemen, and very explicitly, it requires that they act in the political role of defenders of the Chávez regime. "Fatherland, socialism or death" is the constant message they receive and the orientation for their decisions.

President Chávez is the driving force behind the Venezuelan alleged socialist revolution. No part of the state (or society) can be indifferent. No part of the state can be independent. Judges should not be impartial. The enemies of the revolution, which includes anybody who disagrees with President Chávez about anything, should be punished under any pretext. In practical terms, authoritarianism has been accentuated, but Venezuela is still far from being a totalitarian society. Within the state, many people react with inaction, with morosity. This is not necessarily an ideological position but a question of survival. Inaction may be a safer way to survive.

The practical outcome of revolution has not been a new society. It is, rather, a disorganized society where crime has gone up and private businesses have stopped investing. Even the statistics are not published regularly. It is an authoritarian society in which the government needs a free hand to persecute dissidents. We are far from the spirit of the Código Orgánico Procesal Penal of 1998. The inquisitor has struck back with full force.

REFERENCES

Asamblea Nacional. 2001. *Informe de la Comisión Especial que estudia la reforma del Código Orgánico Procesal Penal.* Caracas: Asamblea Nacional.

Carranza, Elias. 1983. *El preso sin condena en América Latina y el Caribe: Estudio comparativo estadistico y legal de treinta paises y propuestas para reducir el fenomeno.* San José, Costa Rica: ILANUD.

Chiossone, Tulio. 1981. *Manual de derecho procesal penal venezolano.* 3d ed. Caracas: Universidad Central de Venezuela.

Monteferrante, Patricia, and Rogelio Pérez-Perdomo. 2001. Inseguridad y COPP: Qué se discute? Qué está en juego? *Debates IESA.* Caracas: Ediciones IESA.

Pérez-Perdomo, Rogelio. 2008. Estado, represión y justicia en tiempos de Gómez. Paper delivered at the VI Congreso de Investigación y Creación Intelectual. Caracas: Universidad Metropolitana.

———. 2007. Medio siglo de historia judicial en Venezuela (1952–2005). *Derecho y Democracia* 1: 22.

Pérez-Perdomo, Rogelio, and Elsie Rosales. 1999. La violencia en el espacio carcelario venezolano. *Revista de Derecho Penal y Criminología* 3: 293–316.

Republic of Venezuela. 1999. Ley Orgánica del Ministerio Público.

Republic (Bolivarian) of Venezuela. 2006. Ley de Reforma Parcial del Código Orgánico Procesal Penal.

———. 2005. Fiscalia General de la Republica. Oficio # DFGR-46.096, June 8.

Riego, Cristian. 2005. *Reformas procesales penales en América Latina: Resultados del proyecto de seguimiento.* Santiago, Chile: CEJA-JSCA 129.

19 JUDICIAL REFORM IN MEXICO

WHAT NEXT?

Héctor Fix-Fierro

THE DEMISE OF AUTHORITARIAN RULE
AND THE PARADOX OF JUDICIAL REFORM

Between 1929 and 2000, Mexico was ruled by a powerful and centralized authoritarian regime built around the presidency as the ultimate source of political authority and the so-called official party—the PRI—as its main instrument for social and political control. Liberal democracy was not abolished formally, and elections were held regularly, but vote fraud and manipulation prevented other parties from effectively challenging the system in the electoral area (Molinar 1991). Despite the PRI's quasi monopoly on power, the regime required as a source of legitimacy a certain degree of opposition. That led to cyclical attempts to open up spaces for minority parties in the Congress of the Union. This was controlled opposition: the PRI made sure not to endanger its majority and its control of political and electoral processes.

The electoral fraud that by all accounts took place in the presidential election of 1988 forced the new government—its legitimacy under fire—to negotiate, for the first time, electoral reform with the opposition. That reform (1990) and subsequent reforms in 1993 and 1994 revolved around the independence of the body charged with the organization of the elections, the reliability of the voters' register, and the mechanisms for settling electoral disputes.

Although the PRI was beginning to lose electoral support—it recognized the first loss of a governorship in 1989—it was still far from willing to surrender power. Postelectoral conflicts multiplied in several states, and then President Carlos Salinas de Gortari had to intervene, as an arbitrator of last resort, forcing the resignation of supposedly victorious PRI candidates and the designation of interim governors who were acceptable to the opposition.

In 1994 came tragedy. On January 1, the same day NAFTA entered into force, an indigenous guerilla movement in the southern state of Chiapas declared war on the Mexican

Reprinted from Héctor Fix-Fierro, "Judicial Reform in Mexico: What Next?," in *Beyond Common Knowledge: Empirical Approaches to the Rule of Law*, ed. Erik G. Jensen and Thomas C. Heller (Stanford: Stanford University Press, 2003). Permission courtesy of Stanford University Press.

government. On March 23, the PRI's presidential candidate was assassinated in Tijuana, a city close to the U.S. border. Later a prominent banker was kidnapped, and more violence followed. No wonder, then, that public security and the efficiency of the justice system became significant issues in the parties' electoral platforms.

A SILENT REVOLUTION

One last element of the 1994 judicial reform requires examination: its roots and significance in terms of the evolution of the legal system. Remember that the Mexican legal system was experiencing dramatic change during the first half of the 1990s, the result of economic liberalization and political reform (López-Ayllón 1997). That process of legal change was not restricted to substantive and procedural modifications. In fact, it can be argued that the Mexican legal system was undergoing a deep transition, a transition that would increase the impact of legal rules and institutions on people's lives. In the process, the legal system would take on a new role: the law would no longer be merely a symbolic resource, but an effective means for regulating social interaction (Fix-Fierro and López-Ayllón 2001; López-Ayllón and Fix-Fierro 2003). In other words, the law should not only institute but also regulate (López-Ayllón 1995). A careful analysis of recent events in Mexican public life—postelection conflicts in the early 1990s, the Chiapas rebellion in 1994, the bank creditors' movement in the later 1990s, the student strike at the National University (UNAM) in 1999–2000—shows the existence of powerful social forces. Where conflicts at one time would have been channeled to the political process, now they were being resolved through a more intensive use of legal means and institutions. The increasing orientation of social expectations toward the law can be interpreted as a sign of the growing autonomy of the legal system vis-à-vis the political system (Fix-Fierro and López-Ayllón 2001).

With respect to the judiciary, most reforms between 1917 and 1987 had the purpose either of changing the appointment procedures and the terms of office of the justices and federal judges, or of adjusting the composition and jurisdiction of the Supreme Court to help it cope with its crushing workload (Fix-Fierro 1999; see also Cossio Diaz 2001). By contrast, the 1987 reform can be said to have started a "judicial transition," in the sense that it introduced at least three very important changes that signaled a new direction in the evolution of the courts. First, it transferred to the collegiate circuit courts the final say in so-called legality *amparos*—that is, the review of judicial decisions where the incorrect interpretation of an ordinary statute is concerned, not a direct constitutional violation. The reform relieved the Supreme Court from this type of case—the reduction between 1987 and 1988 was about two thousand cases—clearing the way for the Court to specialize in constitutional matters. Second, the 1987 reform defined minimum guidelines for the organization of local courts and the appointment of local judges. Third, the reform established the first Electoral Tribunal. Although the tribunal had rather weak powers that proved completely inadequate to handle the electoral controversies of the 1988 election (Eisenstadt 1999), it was a significant step toward the full judicialization of the electoral process that was achieved less than a decade later, in 1996. Together, these three changes point to the professionalization, technicalization, and specialization of the judicial system, a trend that has been carried further by the 1994 and 1996 reforms.

Both the 1987 and, especially, the 1994 judicial reforms employ legal technology that reveals an awareness of contemporary trends in other legal systems. It is not by chance that several distinguished members of the Institute for Legal Research of the National University were closely involved with both reforms. As Yves Dezalay and Bryant Garth describe it, the institute is an academic center known for "investing in pure law" (1995, 25ff.) and for the importance it places on international legal developments. Thus, we can easily understand how the legal ideas cultivated at the institute were influential when the time came to modernize Mexico's legal system and to establish a national ombudsman for human rights and other institutions. It is also apparent why several members of the institute went into the government to help launch those institutions. By contrast, the 1999 reform, proposed by the Supreme Court itself, had shorter-term objectives and lacked an understanding of the Court's evolution toward a European-style constitutional court.

Judicial Reform in Mexico: Challenges and Perspectives

It should be fairly evident from the previous sections that judicial reform in Mexico is not primarily the result of foreign pressures or of the intervention of international development agencies: neither has played a significant role so far. Its roots run much deeper, and that is a source of both weakness and strength in the reform process.

It is a source of weakness insofar as the reform process has never proceeded on the basis of empirical analysis nor benefited from a systematic approach. In a sense, it has been a random process resulting from other changes. Therefore, it has lacked the definition of reform strategists and stakeholders. But the central idea behind Zedillo's December 1994 bill was and is essentially correct: political and economic change required a second wave of reforms aimed at the system of justice (see CIDAC 1994, chap. 1). This is why the rule of law appeared so prominently in the National Plan for Development 1995–2000 (Secretaria de Hacienda y Credito Publico 1995, chap. 2).

The 1994 judicial reform was supposed to be a first step toward strengthening the rule of law, but the financial crisis of 1995 redirected the government's reform impulses in view of more-pressing goals. Still, the 1994 reform started things rolling in the states. And in the long term, its impact will be more profound than appeared at first. If it is true that judicial reform in Mexico has been a response to social demands and expectations—not only to the interests of academic, political, and legal elites—then we can be fairly confident that the reform process will continue, albeit at its own pace and following its own logic.

. . .

The relationship between the federal and state courts merits a brief comment because it may become a prominent issue in the near future. As already mentioned, through the *amparo* suit the federal courts can review all decisions of state courts, and a high but unknown number of those decisions are actually reviewed. However, the present situation is perceived as unsatisfactory by both federal and state judges. The former complain about ever-growing caseloads and say that by correcting errors made in local judicial decisions, they are forced to do the job of state judges. The latter also have a number of complaints, ranging from the small percentage of *amparos* that are granted to the declining quality and growing inconsistency of federal judicial decisions (Concha Cantú and Caballero Juarez 2001, 164ff.; Fix-Fierro 2001). Therefore, they argue that the time has come for reclaiming the autonomy they lost to the federal courts at the end of nineteenth century.

Unfortunately, discussion to date on this topic has not been based on solid empirical evidence and a systematic analysis of viable solutions. Clearly, both federal and state judges are speaking out from their narrow interests, but there are other relevant interests involved, among them those of attorneys, litigants, and society at large. So, for example, a recent survey conducted by the newspaper *Reforma* among attorneys, law firms, and bar associations in twenty-three states shows that an overwhelming majority of respondents (86 percent) favors the status quo, and that only a small minority would like to see the *amparo* as a means for challenging state judicial decisions restricted or completely suppressed (Serna de la Garza 2003, 275). If no radical solutions are possible or wanted, perhaps Mexico should aspire to a judicial organization like that of the United States, in which the bulk of cases are handled efficiently and fairly by the state judiciaries, while the federal courts, in addition to hearing federal cases, exert only selective control over state judicial decisions. For this to happen, of course, state judiciaries—and the legal profession—must be perceived as trustworthy and effective by society at large (Fix-Fierro 2001). Also, judicial reform of this sort requires much more communication and cooperation between federal and state judiciaries.

Legal education and the legal profession also merit discussion here because they are not usually a part of the discourse on judicial reform. But it can be easily argued that both have significant consequences for that reform. In Mexico, legal education is very traditional. It is stagnant, still focusing on legal-theoretical models of the nineteenth century. Many professors have not stayed current with knowledge in the field, and the older ones are barely familiar with modern teaching techniques. Yet by many accounts, legal education in Mexico was satisfactory until the late 1960s and early 1970s, when enrollment in public law schools began to grow dramatically, resulting in a marked decline in quality (López-Ayllón and Fix-Fierro 2003).

How much do the failings of legal education affect the performance of the judiciary? We do not know for sure, but we can safely assume that a weak education does not contribute to building a more open and responsive judiciary. Although the system can use internal training to replace the outdated legal models students absorb during their stay in law school that is at best a stopgap measure. Consequently, there are strong reasons to believe that judicial reform—and, more generally, the modern rule of law—has much to gain from reform of legal education. But this is easier said than done.

Consider, for example, that law is the most popular area of study among Mexican students: about 190,000 students in 2001, well above the numbers in accounting and business administration. The number of law schools, especially small private schools, exploded during the 1990s (López-Ayllón and Fix-Fierro 2003). Although they require some sort of official recognition to issue law degrees, in truth there is no real control over the content and the quality of the education they provide. There is nothing equivalent to a bar examination in Mexico, so a university degree (and in certain cases, not even that) is all it takes to become a practicing lawyer.

It is easier to make the case for reform of the legal profession because lawyers' behavior has a direct impact on the judiciary's performance. Mexican judges complain that attorneys can be the most significant external obstacle to the operations of the courts. They refer to attorneys' lack of professional knowledge and to questionable practices, like using the press to apply pressure on the courts. A majority of civil and criminal judges interviewed for the Concha Cantú and Caballero Juarez study thought that attorney training and performance were "poor" or "bad" (2001, 188, 215ff.).

Mandatory bar affiliation has been proposed as a means of controlling lawyers' behavior and performance. Since the 1930s, the Barra Mexicana Colegio de Abogados, the most prestigious of Mexican bar associations, has debated the issue on several occasions. No conclusion has been reached yet, and even the considerable number of lawyers who favor mandatory affiliation concede that it will not be a panacea for the profession's ills (Barra Mexicana, Colegio de Abogados 2002, 61ff., 78). If, for whatever reason, mandatory affiliation was to become a prominent topic on the public agenda, it probably would not provoke too much resistance: lawyers' professional organization is not strong, and good lawyers may be ready to see their profession regulated somewhat.

Why have legal education and the legal profession been left out of the sweeping changes introduced in the Mexican legal and judicial systems during the past two decades? Why are reforms in these two areas absent from the public agenda? One possible answer lies in the autonomy and privacy accorded both institutions. Again, public and private law schools have to satisfy certain requirements to obtain recognition from the government and the right to grant law degrees. But those requirements are not very demanding, and beyond them, the schools enjoy a large degree of autonomy to decide the type and quality of education they provide. And the legal profession—or at least practicing attorneys—is not highly regulated by the government or by professional associations. Furthermore, lawyers seem able to deflect attention from their professional performance. If a case is lost and the "criminal" set free, or if an "innocent" is sent to prison, the public blames the judges, not the attorney. Finally, the fragmentary and unsystematic character of many reforms has effectively placed legal education and the legal profession well beyond their immediate objectives.

We asked above about the likelihood of additional reform of the judicial system. Certainly the failings of legal education and the legal profession in Mexico, as well as the trajectory of past reform, have an impact on the possibility of further reform. The new political stage, on which no party holds a majority in Congress (and that may not change in the near future), and the important role the judiciary has claimed for itself on that stage make it unlikely that sweeping changes of the sort passed in 1994 will be carried out again. Therefore, we are more likely to see smaller, incremental changes.

In the end, what is at stake is less the success of judicial reform, narrowly defined, than a new definition of the role of the courts in Mexican society. It is society that ultimately will determine how far judicial reform should go and where investment in judicial reform yields the highest returns. We can hardly doubt that in the long run, society will get more or less what it expects. It is just the present situation that seems so ambiguous and contradictory.

Despite society's demands for more substantive justice, as opposed to formal justice, the incentives for judges and lawyers to provide that justice have not been fundamentally altered so far. The people also demand and expect the courts to distinguish right from wrong, to be the "guardians of (democratic) promises" (Garapon 1996); but at the same time, according to opinion polls, they deny the courts their trust and confidence. Is this a motive for pessimism? Certainly not. We recently have lived through other changes, like the peaceful end of the PRI regime, which seemed impossible just ten or twenty years ago, and in a short time we have come to take those changes for granted. Why should judicial reform be different?

REFERENCES

Barra Mexicana, Colegio de Abogados. 2002. *80 años en la defensa de los valores del derecho (1922–2002)*. Mexico.

CIDAC. 1994. A la puerta de la ley. In *El estado de derecho en Mexico*, ed. H. Fix-Fierro. Mexico: CIDAC-Cal y Arena.

Concha Cantú, Hugo Alejandro, and Antonio Caballero Juarez. 2001. *Diagnostico sobre la administracion de justicia en las entidades federativas. Un estudio institucional sobre la justicia local en Mexico*. Mexico: UNAM-National Center for State Courts.

Cossio Diaz, José Ramon. 2001. La Suprema Corte y la teoria constitucional. *Politica y Gobierno* 8(1): 61–115.

Dezalay, Yves, and Bryant Garth. 1995. Building the new law and putting the state into play: International strategies among Mexico's divided elite. ABF working paper 9509. Chicago: ABF.

Eisenstadt, Todd. 1999. La justicia electoral en Mexico: De contradiccion en si, a norma juridica en una decada. Un analisis de casos de la evolucion de los tribunales federales electorales en Mexico (1988-1997) In *Justicia electoral en el umbral del siglo XXI. Memoria del III Congreso Internacional de Derecho Electoral (983–1050)*, ed. J. de Jesus Orozco Henriquez. Mexico: UNAM-IFE-TEPJF-UQRoo-PNUD.

Fix-Fierro, Héctor. 2001. El futuro del amparo judicial. *Bien Comun y Gobierno* 7(81): 5–16.

———. 1999. Poder Judicial. In *Transiciones y diseños institucionales*, ed. Maria del Refugio Gonzalez and Sergio López-Ayllón, 167–221. Mexico: UNAM.

Fix-Fierro, Héctor, and Sergio López-Ayllón. 2001. Legitimidad contra legalidad: Los dilemas de la transicion juridical y el estado de derecho en Mexico. *Politica y Gobierno* 8(2): 347–93.

Garapon, Antoine. 1996. *Le gardien des promeses. Justice et démocratie*. Paris: Editions Odile Jacob.

López-Ayllón, Sergio. 1997. *Las transformaciones del sistema juridico y los significados sociales del derecho en Mexico. La encrucijada entre tradicion y modernidad*. Mexico: UNAM.

———. 1995. Notes on Mexican legal culture. *Social and Legal Studies* 4(4): 477–92.

López-Ayllón, Sergio, and Héctor Fix-Fierro. 2003. "Faraway, so close!" The rule of law and legal change in Mexico, 1970–2000. *In Legal culture in the age of globalization: Latin America and Latin Europe*, ed. L. Friedman and R. Pérez-Perdomo, 285–351. Stanford: Stanford University Press.

Molinar Horcasitas, Juan. 1991. *El tiempo de la legitimidad: Elecciones, autoritarismo y democracia en Mexico*. Mexico: Cal y Arena.

Secretaria de Hacienda y Credito Publico. 1995. *Plan Nacional del Desarrollo 1995–2000*. Mexico.

Serna de la Garza, José Maria. 2003. Apuntes sobre el debate relativo al amparo casacion en Mexico. *Reforma Judicial, Revista Mexicana de Justicia* (Jan.–June) 1: 263–78.

BUSINESS LITIGATION IN THE TRANSITION

A PORTRAIT OF DEBT COLLECTION IN RUSSIA

Kathryn Hendley

WHY DO RUSSIAN FIRMS SUE ONE ANOTHER?

In Russia, as elsewhere, litigation is rarely the first course of action. Previous survey-based research supplemented by enterprise case studies demonstrates the widespread use of relational methods (for example, Hendley, Murrell, and Ryterman 2000; Hendley 2001). In this chapter, I am purposefully focusing on enterprises that chose to litigate. These enterprises did not rush to file their lawsuits. On average, about eleven months passed from the time the debt arose until litigation ensued. During this time, most creditors made some effort at resolving the case, usually starting with phone calls and ratcheting up to telegrams, letters, and personal visits over time.

In a series of follow-up questions to the victorious plaintiffs posed to the person who had handled the lawsuit, I explored motivation. Not surprisingly, repayment of the debt served as inspiration for virtually everyone. More interesting are the less obvious catalysts. Some issues that would probably emerge as significant in an adversarial setting, such as the United States, fade in importance in Russia. Very few creditors reported using litigation as a signal to other customers of the parameters of acceptable behavior. This makes sense given that case decisions are mostly unpublished and apply only to the parties involved. Third parties (including customers) are unlikely to learn of the outcomes, and if they do, they would not take them as a warning because variations in fact patterns might yield different results. Only a few creditors regard litigation as a mechanism for punishing an undisciplined trading partner.

Factors that are specific to Russia turn out to be more relevant. The uncertainty of the economic transition left the rules about when debts could be written off in flux. The vagaries of the tax code in effect during the 1990s, which some managers believed resulted in a tax rate of over 100 percent of income, created a powerful incentive to hide income (Berkowitz and Li 2000). One popular method was to pad financial records with fictitious debts in order to create the impression of no income (and, therefore, no taxes due). In conversations predating the study, some enterprise managers had reported that they preferred to have a court judgment in hand before writing off debt because it lessened the chances of challenges from the tax inspectorate. Along similar lines, I was also told that they occasionally resorted to the courts—even when the chances of collecting on a judgment were slim—in order to prove to the state authorities the genuineness of a debt. According to managers, an *arbitrazh* court judgment was viewed as definitive proof that a debt was not illusory. In a macabre twist on this logic, it seems that some organized crime groups insist on an *arbitrazh* court judgment before involving themselves in debt collection (Volkov 2002, 46).

Concerns over tax and accounting implications motivated a significant group of plaintiffs. A closer analysis indicates that these worries may be concentrated in Saratov. While only about one-quarter of the Moscow and Ekaterinburg enterprises reported being influenced by accounting, two-thirds of the Saratov enterprises declared it to be a catalyst (chi square = 15.02, 2 d.f., $p < 0.001$). The situation is even more lopsided vis-à-vis tax issues. While only 13 percent of the sample in Moscow and Ekaterinburg reported being motivated by tax concerns, 67 percent of the Saratov creditors claimed to be spurred into action by such concerns (chi square = 27.08, 2 d.f., $p < 0.001$). Given the small sample size, reading too much into these results would be premature, though they certainly warrant further investigation. What is inescapable is that state policies that seem unconnected to debt collection have influenced firms' strategies when faced with delinquent customers.

What similarities emerge among litigants motivated by a desire to obtain certification of debts for tax or accounting purposes? An analysis of my sample provides some provocative leads as well as some dead ends. Having access to legal expertise turns out to have little effect, probably because neither tax issues nor accounting matters are within the purview of in-house lawyers (even when they would seem to have legal implications) (for example, Hendley, Murrell, and Ryterman 2001). More telling is the length of the relationship between the parties. Petitioners involved in first-time transactions tend not to report tax or accounting concerns, but as the length of the relationship grows, such concerns become more pressing. This makes sense. As the lifespan of business relationships increases, so too does the likelihood of having side arrangements that might not stand up to scrutiny. When cash dried up during the 1990s, barter arrangements proliferated, often involving questionable valuations of the goods exchanged. Organizational structure turns out to matter, though not equally everywhere. Its effect is strongest in Saratov, where large enterprises (open joint-stock companies) emerged as the most uneasy over tax and accounting consequences. I had thought that the amount of the case would matter, hypothesizing that management's desire to have debts recognized as legitimate would intensify with the size of the debt. The data reveal a murkier picture. Once again, there was regional variation. My hypothesis was borne out only in Moscow, where the odds of being motivated by tax or accounting issues spiked for cases in excess of 500,000 rubles (approximately US$16,667). In Saratov and Ekaterinburg, such concerns were most likely to be manifested for smaller cases, for examples, cases ranging from 50,000 to 500,000 rubles. Precisely why they were absent from the larger cases is a puzzle.

The oddest aspect of business litigation in Russia is its persistence and, indeed, growth in the face of the well-known difficulties in collecting on judgments. This is one area where the stereotype mirrors the reality. A 1997 enterprise survey confirmed that managers regard enforcement as the single largest impediment to using the *arbitrazh* courts (Hendley, Murrell, and Ryterman 2000). Though the institution responsible for assisting in the collection of judgments underwent a wholesale reform in 1998, little had changed by the time of my 2001 study. Among my sample of one hundred nonpayment cases, only six of the debtor-defendants paid court judgments voluntarily (Hendley 2004). Most (64 percent) of the petitioners ultimately ended up getting some of what the court awarded them, but only after expending considerable effort to get the bailiffs or judicial enforcers (*sudebnye pristavy*) to do their job. So why bother suing? This seemingly pointless act makes sense only in context. The Russian firms that regularly turn to the *arbitrazh* courts believe themselves to have few alternatives. They are sure that the customer-debtor is not going to pay on its own. Through a lawsuit, they can get a court order that attaches to the debtor's bank account. If and when funds appear, the creditor will be paid automatically. If the bank account has been drained (as is often the case), then they can seek help from the bailiffs who are empowered to liquidate the debtor's assets to satisfy the judgment. Though litigation may bring no guarantees, it provides some hope.

HOW MUCH DOES BUSINESS LITIGATION COST IN RUSSIA?

The cost of litigating can serve as a powerful deterrent to creditors (for example, Silver 2002; Heise 2000; Priest and Klein 1984). The reduction of tangible costs, such as the time and money expended in pursuing a judgment, can spur litigation (for example, Ruhlin 2000; Blankenburg 1994). A full accounting of costs, however, ought to take into account not only the tangible but also the intangible, such as damage to the relationship with the delinquent customer (for example, Galanter and Rogers 1991). In Russia, the institutional structure yields different reactions. To be sure, no firm relishes the prospect of going to *arbitrazh* court. It is always less disruptive to find a solution through negotiations, which helps explain why firms with long histories together rarely take their disputes to court. Those who have experienced the judicial process complain about the inconvenience and absurdity of procedural rules, like their counterparts elsewhere. But the extent to which the process is punishing is qualitatively different. *Arbitrazh* courts generally eschew testimonial evidence, preferring to rely on documentary evidence, which means that top executives need not worry about having their character impugned through vigorous cross-examination. Nor is there any shame attached to being judged delinquent in fulfilling business responsibilities. The industrial downturn during the 1990s gave rise to an almost-universal lack of liquidity. The trick was staying in business with little or no cash flow. Managers almost took pride in accumulating debts that took them to the very tipping point for bankruptcy without falling into the abyss.

CONTEXTUALIZING THE RUSSIAN EXPERIENCE

Russian industrial enterprises are turning to the courts for assistance in recovering overdue debt in ever-increasing numbers, but they are not suing indiscriminately. Several patterns are clearly discernible. For the most part, creditors are using the courts to go after relatively small amounts and are doing so routinely. Almost without exception, they prevail, often receiving the full amount demanded in the original complaint. These lawsuits tend to involve trading partners with minimal histories together. It follows that the big-ticket disputes between long-term partners are being handled with informal relational methods. Most of the creditors were represented in the *arbitrazh* proceedings, and the data indicate that being represented was beneficial.

Certain aspects of creditors' experience in the *arbitrazh* courts stand out as well. Perhaps the most striking are the low costs associated with commercial litigation in Russia. Few participants bother to hire outside lawyers, preferring to rely on in-house counsel or to forego the use of lawyers entirely. The up-front filing fees are less of an obstacle than they first appear to be. The need to master the procedural intricacies of the system is mitigated by the willingness of *arbitrazh* judges to help uninitiated and even incompetent litigants through the process. This coddling may hamper the growth of the *arbitrazh* courts institutionally, but it unquestionably acts to even the playing field between experienced and inexperienced players. As a result, size and financial where-withal do not play the decisive role that might be expected.

The patterns found in Russian business debt litigation are basically consistent with what is predicted by the literature, though the specifics of the Russian case illustrate some of their limitations. Priest and Klein (1984) argue that creditors will go to court when the anticipated judgment exceeds the costs of going to court. Given the low cost of litigating in Russia and the virtual certainty of victory, the mystery is not why creditors are using the courts, but why they are not flocking to the courts in even greater numbers. Part of the explanation is provided by Galanter and Rogers' (1991) critique of the failure of Priest and Klein's cost-benefit model to take strategic behavior into account. Not all costs can be monetized. Litigation brings with it a danger of rupturing an ongoing business relationship. Though the nonadversarial nature of *arbitrazh* proceedings mutes this risk, it does not eliminate it entirely. A dispute is inherently contentious, and especially when large sums and/or friendships are involved, the relationship is unlikely to emerge unscathed. Thus, the reluctance of suppliers to U.S. auto assembly plants to bring their disputes to court for fear of severing the relationship is mirrored in the singular absence of Russian creditors with long-term relations from my sample (Kenworthy, Macaulay, and Rogers 1996, 653).

Instead, my sample is dominated by enterprises without much shared history. Anonymity tends to lower inhibitions to litigation (Cheit and Gersen 2000). When dealing with new customers that are delinquent, Russian managers see litigation as a no-lose proposition. After all, if customers renege at the outset—when they should be trying to make a good impression—then there is little chance that their behavior will improve (especially if the creditor tolerates it). As Macaulay has noted, when a relationship is irrevocably shattered, resorting to the courts can be "used for scavenger purposes to salvage something from the wreckage" (1977, 513). Russian creditors have learned through painful experience that waiting around to be paid by these new customers yields nothing. While litigation offers no guarantees, it does open the possibility of recovering all or part of the debt.

The literature highlights economic instability and uncertainty as factors that tend to stimulate litigation. The argument is that "they reduce the likelihood of long-term stable relationships among familiar parties, and thereby foster opportunism and mistrust. The basis for reliance on informal dispute resolution is eroded" (Kenworthy, Macaulay, and Rogers 1996, 633). But the sort of instability experienced by the U.S. auto industry during the second half of the twentieth century, which was the reference point for Kenworthy, Macaulay, and Rogers, pales in comparison to the economic collapse experienced by Russia after the disintegration of the Soviet Union. Confounding Macaulay's (1963, 62) prediction (which drew on [Soia] Mentschikoff's work on the Uniform Commercial Code) that truly profound uncertainty would be a death knell to commercial litigation because of the general inability to satisfy judgments, the pace of business litigation in Russia actually accelerated during its depression. And it increased even though those involved knew that collecting on judgments was a dicey proposition. To be fair, the prosperity of the Western world in recent decades has offered few opportunities to test Macaulay's prediction. The Russian case suggests that deep economic depression does not necessarily extinguish the desire to litigate.

At a more basic level, the Russian case confirms that uncertainty can retard the development of long-term relationships, which, in turn, can facilitate litigation. Initially, Russian managers found freedom of contract exhilarating, but the thrill wore off as interenterprise arrears mounted. Not paying became the norm, and one's reputation seemed to be enhanced by an ability to pile on more and more debt without tipping over into bankruptcy. The ability to shirk debt became a source of pride rather than shame. Moreover, the efforts of creditors to prevent delinquency fell flat. In the absence of reliable credit-rating agencies and/or a workable system of collateral, creditors were limited to demanding prepayment. But the existence of competitors willing to underbid on the percentage of prepayment required limited the ability of creditors to mitigate risk by insisting on full prepayment. Absent prepayment, only the existence of long-term relationships provided some minimal insurance that payment would be forthcoming. They came with a safety net of interpersonal relations among midlevel managers that had been forged over decades in oppressive conditions of constant material shortages. Not surprisingly, enterprises valued these long-term relationships and were loathe to risk them through litigation. Instead, they took their newer customers to court, reasoning that they had little to lose if the relationship soured, though most indicated in the interviews that they did not expect that outcome. Much like their counterparts in the United States in the late nineteenth century who did not have access to reliable credit ratings (Kagan 1984, 339–40), contemporary Russian manufacturers have no choice but to sell their goods to new and untested customers and hope for the best. Like their predecessors, they use the courts aggressively to collect these debts. Whether the emergence of a more stable financial system will bring an end to the practice of bringing petty debts to the courts (as happened in the United States) remains to be seen.

Looking beyond bilateral relationships, the distaste for litigation among some is no doubt motivated by the lingering skepticism toward law and legal institutions that persists as a legacy from the Soviet era. Notwithstanding the efforts at reform since the late 1980s, many enterprise managers remain openly dismissive of the capacity of the legal system to resolve disputes. The common wisdom that the courts are unusable reflects their contempt. Those who pursue legal remedies seem to do so without any expectation that they will actually collect the full amount owed, but with a sense that a lawsuit may marginally improve their chances of collecting some fraction of it. The low levels of voluntary compliance with the judgments of *arbitrazh* courts speak vividly to the lack of respect of most litigants for these courts. In such an environment, going to court is inevitably just one of a multitude of strategies that enterprises employ to encourage their customers to pay their debts.

Although the willingness of creditors to bring their complaints to the *arbitrazh* courts can fairly be seen as a hopeful sign in the struggle for the "rule of law" in Russia, the use of the *arbitrazh* courts for small-scale debt collection is hardly the most efficient use of limited judicial resources. As my data indicate, most of the cases are disputes in name only, in that the debtor has either explicitly acknowledged the debt or has done so implicitly by not challenging the creditor's petition. Under the new procedural code, these cases will no longer receive full-fledged hearings, but will be diverted into a "summary" process (*uproshchennoe proizvodstvo*) (APK 2002, Arts. 226–29), akin to the mechanism already in place in much of Europe (for example, Ruhlin 2000; Blankenburg 1994). According to the chairman of the Higher *Arbitrazh* Court, the new procedure will be "shorter and simpler" (Proskuryakova 2002). Whether the expectations of Russian policymakers that judges will be liberated from processing these petty debt cases will be met remains to be seen. Blankenburg's (1994) study of how such a regime worked in West Germany and the Netherlands demonstrates the powerful influence of the institutional structure in which the regime is embedded. The existence of a dense network of litigation alternatives diverted most Dutch creditors before they got to court. By contrast, the low cost and expeditiousness of the German system had the effect of promoting litigation. Given the current institutional environment in Russia, the German outcome seems more likely. Russian economic actors have been slow to embrace alternative dispute resolution. Given the novelty of the legislative change (which became effective only in September 2002), precisely how creditors will respond is unclear.

CONCLUSION

Russia's experience shows how deeply intertwined the processes of legal and economic reform are for countries making the transition from state socialism toward market democracy. The uneven development of institutions that are integral to the smooth functioning of business has given rise to unexpected patterns of behavior. Yet when studied carefully, the logic behind this seemingly irrational behavior comes into focus. Russian managers operate in a dog-eat-dog world, and absent reliable credit-rating agencies and a workable system of collateral, they have limited tools at their disposal for guaranteeing payment. The *arbitrazh* courts offer a cheap, quick, and nonconfrontational way of collecting on ever-mounting debt. The basic functionality of these courts is certainly an achievement, but one that rings somewhat hollow due to the limited ability to collect on judgments. To be sure, a reliable system of law and adjudication may be a significant factor in abetting economic development, but it is far from the only one. An effective contract law regime may come to matter only in an economy in which creditors can effectively demand meaningful collateral and debtors have enough wealth to provide it.

REFERENCES

APK [Arbitrazhny protsesual'nyi kodeks Rossiiskoi Federatsii]. 2002. Vestnik Vysshego Arbitrazhnogo Suda Rossiiskoi Federatsii, special supplement to no. 8.

Berkowitz, Daniel, and Wei Li. 2000. Tax rights in transition economies: A tragedy of the commons? *Journal of Public Economics* 76: 369–97.

Blankenburg, Erhard. 1994. The infrastructure for avoiding civil litigation: Comparing cultures of legal behavior in the Netherlands and West Germany. *Law and Society Review* 28: 789–808.

Cheit, Ross, and Jacob E. Gersen. 2000. Why businesses sue each other: An empirical study of state court litigation. *Law and Social Inquiry* 25: 798–816.

Galanter, Marc, and Joel Rogers. 1991. A transformation of American business disputing? Some preliminary observations. Institute for Legal Studies Working paper DPRP 10-3. University of Wisconsin Law School.

Heise, Michael. 2000. Justice delayed?: An empirical analysis of civil case disposition time. *Case Western Reserve Law Review* 50: 813–49.

Hendley, Kathryn. 2004. Enforcing judgments in Russian economic courts. *Post-Soviet Affairs* 20: 1–37.

———. 2001. Beyond the tip of the iceberg: Business disputes in Russia. In *Assessing the value of law in transition economies*, ed. P. Murrell, 20–55. Ann Arbor: University of Michigan Press.

Hendley, Kathryn, Peter Murrell, and Randi Ryterman. 2001. Agents of change or unchanging agents? The role of lawyers within Russian industrial enterprises. *Law and Social Inquiry* 26: 685–715.

———. 2000. Law, relationships, and private enforcement: Transactional strategies of Russian enterprises. *Europe-Asia Studies* 52: 627–56.

Kagan, Robert A. 1984. The routinization of debt collection: An essay on social change and conflict in the courts. *Law and Society Review* 18: 323–71.

Kenworthy, Lane, Stewart Macaulay, and Joel Rogers. 1996. "The more things change . . . ": Business litigation and governance in the American automobile industry. *Law and Social Inquiry* 21: 631–78.

Macaulay, Stewart. 1977. Elegant models, empirical pictures, and the complexities of contract. *Law and Society Review* 11: 507–28.

———. 1963. Noncontractual relations in business: A preliminary study. *American Sociological Review* 28: 55–67.

Priest, George L., and Benjamin Klein. 1984. The selection of disputes for litigation. *Journal of Legal Studies* 13: 1–55.

Proskuryakova, Iuliia. 2002. Veniamin Iakovlev: Biznes poluchil novye pravila resheniia spornykh voprosov. *Rossiiskaia Business-Gazeta*, July 30.

Ruhlin, Charles. 2000. Credit card debt collection and the law: Germany and the United States. In *Regulatory encounters: Multinational corporations and American adversarial legalism*, ed. R. A. Kagan and L. Axelrad, 255. Berkeley: University of California Press.

Silver, Charles. 2002. Does civil justice cost too much? *Texas Law Review* 80: 2073–121.

Volkov, Vadim. 2002. *Violent entrepreneurs: The use of force in the making of Russian capitalism*. Ithaca, NY: Cornell University Press.

21 MOTHER OR FATHER:

WHO RECEIVED CUSTODY?

THE BEST INTERESTS OF THE CHILD STANDARD AND JUDGES' CUSTODY DECISIONS IN TAIWAN

Hung-En Liu

INTRODUCTION

The Emergence of the "Best Interests of the Child" Standard in Taiwan

In 1994, the Grand Justices (Constitutional Court) of Taiwan declared unconstitutional the rule of preference for fathers' parental rights because it violated the fundamental right of equal protection irrespective of gender. In response to this important decision and pressure from Taiwanese women's movement groups, the Legislative Yuan (Congress of Taiwan) began amending the Family Book of the Civil Code. Finally, the "best interests of the child" standard for child-custody cases was promulgated in 1996.

For several decades before 1996, there had been the presumption of paternal custody for custody disputes in Taiwan. During this period, in some 80–90 percent of all custody cases, custody was awarded to fathers, and the court even tended to enforce the gender-biased presumption of paternal custody. Both women's rights and children's well-being were ignored. The best interests of the child standard was therefore enacted to eliminate the gender inequality and the disregard of child welfare in Taiwan's child-custody cases.

Although Taiwanese law has contained the best interests of the child standard, "law in books" is not equated with "law in action." In Taiwan, it is not unusual to find that while the "law in books" is almost perfect and completely logical, it just does not work in reality, especially when the law was transplanted from other countries. Sometimes changes in written law do not necessarily change judicial attitudes.

The basic belief of this study is that the effective date of a new law makes possible the inauguration of a series of empirical investigations for evaluating legal policy. We could and should reexamine the assumptions of the law, research its application in judicial and enforcing processes, and detect its effects to find out the extent to which it has improved the situation or created new problems that need to be settled. Based on this point of view and the

Reprinted from Hung-En Liu, "Mother or Father: Who Received Custody? The Best Interests of the Child Standard and Judges' Custody Decisions in Taiwan," *International Journal of Law, Policy and the Family* 15: 185 (2001). Permission courtesy of Oxford University Press.

fact that there is a lack of this kind of research, this thesis is intended to be an empirical and descriptive study on "law in action" of the best interests of the child standard in Taiwan.

FURTHER DISCUSSION

Why Many More Judges Award Custody to Mothers than Before

One of the most striking findings of this research is that, after 1996, judges dramatically more often awarded custody to mothers than fathers. As we have seen, in 75 percent of all contentious cases judges awarded custody to mothers. Given that in some 80–90 percent of cases prior to 1996 custody was granted to fathers, this overwhelming preponderance of preference for mothers cannot be explained merely by the enactment of the new law. Indeed, the new law abrogates the presumption of *paternal* custody, but it never adopts a presumption of *maternal* custody to substitute for it. While the new law merely adopts a gender-*neutral* standard (that is, the best interests of the child), why is there an overwhelming preference for mothers?

The cause of the phenomenon many people would think of first as the influence of the Taiwanese women's movement. Admittedly, women's groups have had a significant impact on the legislation and judicial practice in custody arrangements. From the beginning, it was women's groups raising the issues regarding the necessity to amend the law. Many leaders and active participants of these groups were female lawyers. They banded together in 1990 to promote the abrogation of the paternal presumption and to offer a draft of amendments. Then they made a lecture circuit of Taiwan to disseminate their ideas in different communities. They also lobbied the Ministry of Justice and the Congress to amend the law; however, except for a few Congresswomen and very few Congressmen, they did not receive much positive response. Feeling disappointed, the women's groups launched a street movement to put pressure on the government.

At the same time, along with some Congresswomen, they decided to file a petition to request the Grand Justices (Constitutional Court) to review the constitutionality of the law. Shortly afterward, the Grand Justices declared the law unconstitutional because it violated the equal protection clause in the Constitution, and this declaration forced Congress to amend the law immediately. Again, during the legislative process, the women's groups and the Xin Qin draft written by the women's league played a key role. In brief, there is no doubt that without the efforts of women's groups, there would not have been the new law in 1996.

However, the key role of women's groups in the legislative process, as described above, still cannot completely explain why judges awarded custody to mothers much more often than fathers after 1996. Not only is the new law merely gender-neutral, but the women's groups have never promoted a maternal preference. The role of women's movement and women's higher status in society than before may explain the fact that custody is granted to mothers more often than previously, but it cannot explain why it becomes *so* disproportionately more often. While women have only asked for *equality*, and the new law has merely adopted a gender-*equal* standard, why have judges changed their decision pattern from a paternal preference to the exactly opposite maternal preference?

The results of this research suggest that judges' perception of the gender-stereotyped role of women, along with the developing emphasis of child welfare, may have had a significant influence on the phenomenon. Specifically, since the new law required judges to pursue the best interests of the child, judges gave custody to mothers based on the view that placing children in their mothers' care is the most "natural" and the best for children. In fact, in the sample of seventy cases, many judges explicitly mentioned the importance of a "loving mother" or "mother's love and care" in their decisions, but *no* decision mentioning "loving father" or "father's love and care" has been found.

Several findings of this research can support this explanation. For instance, we have seen that in *all* the decisions that had considered "age of the child," judges granted custody to mothers. In the meantime, in *all* the decisions that had considered "parent-child relationship and affection," the custody was awarded to mothers too. Apparently, these decision patterns are in accord with the traditional idea of women's role as a natural loving mother, most fit to care for the child, especially a child of tender years.

As we have discussed, in Chinese/Taiwanese culture and tradition, mothers are always assumed to adopt an expressive role and to be the caregivers of children; the assumption is that mothers are better suited to nurture and raise children because of women's innate qualities. Even in today's society, the gender stereotyping and women's assumed duty to care for children are still deep-seated. Some empirical studies find that many women themselves also agree with this tradition and assumed duty. For example, according to an official survey conducted by Taiwan Province Government in 1993, 45.2 percent of women agreed or strongly agreed the traditional idea of "Nan Zhu Wai, Nu Zhu Nei" (males dominate the sphere outside families, and females dominate the domestic sphere), while only 29.1 percent of women disagreed or strongly disagreed with it. Another official survey conducted by Ministry of Interior indicates that 64.1 percent of women agreed that "managing household affairs and caring for children are women's natural duty," while only 6.5 percent of women thought this statement is unfair to women.

It is noteworthy, however, that the younger the women are, the higher their education is, and the more industrialized the areas in which they live are, the *less* the women agreed with the traditional ideas of gender stereotyping and the assumed duty to care for children.

In reality, in 1998, among all Taiwan's nuclear families in which only husbands were breadwinners, in 94.51 percent of them wives were mainly in charge of household affairs (including caring for children). Among the nuclear families in which the couple were both employed, still, in 90.52 percent of them were wives mainly responsible for household affairs. Only 31.61 percent of fathers spent more than three hours each day with their children between six and twelve years old, while 66.19 percent of mothers did so. Just as many researchers stress, even though more and more Taiwanese women have had a job outside their homes, they are still assumed to perform their duties in household affairs and child care. In other words, because gender stereotyping is so ingrained, women's labor force participation and concomitant economic independence do not necessarily enable them to be liberated from the duty of caring for children; instead, many of today's Taiwanese women bear a double burden—they have to perform their duties both inside and outside their homes.

Moreover, Taiwan's legal system and governmental policy always intentionally reinforced the perception of women's inherent role of being a mother and nurturing children. Legislation and policy continually connected women with child welfare; this policy has even been directly stipulated in the Constitution. Article 156 of the Constitution explicitly states, "The State, in order to consolidate the foundation of national existence and development, shall protect motherhood and carry out the policy of promoting the welfare of women and children." This is the only article mentioning "child welfare" in the Constitution, and clearly the Constitution makers believed that child welfare directly relates to motherhood. Not surprisingly, no "fatherhood" is ever mentioned in the Constitution; in fact, no "fatherhood" is mentioned in any legislation.

Another intriguing example is regarding national holidays in Taiwan. Before 1991, Women's Day and Children's Day were separated (March 8 and April 4, respectively). However, while Taiwan's government wanted to merge some holidays together in order to reduce the number of national holidays, these two days were immediately linked to each other because the government believed that they were "similar in essence." The result was that since then there is now only one "Women and Children's Day" on April 4. Certainly, the government has never considered merging Father's Day with Children's Day. Again, it is evident that Taiwan's government believed that child welfare is closely related to motherhood—the inherent role of mothers.

It should be noted that, *before* 1996, even though custody was mostly granted to fathers, in many cases, de facto, it was still noncustodial mothers who cared for their children. In other words, while fathers received custody *legally*, they were not necessarily the parents, *in reality*, responsible for nurturing their children. One reason of this phenomenon was that, due to the "presumption" of paternal custody, many fathers received custody *automatically* following divorce, even if they had not petitioned for it. Hence, we could not say the prevailing paternal custody prior to 1996 did not reflect the stereotyped gender role of women as caretakers of children. On the contrary, it was reflected in reality—"law in action"—though not directly reflected in the "law in books."

After 1996, this traditional perception and stereotype of women's role as an inherent better caretaker, associated with the best interests of the child standard, led to the phenomenon that judges much more often awarded custody to mothers. Combined with the tradition of considering economic competence as a necessary factor in deciding custody and the fact that more women became economically competent, they caused judges to grant custody to mothers more often but at the same time worsened the problem of women's double burden. Namely, economically competent mothers, usually the ones who are employed, would be more likely to be awarded custody because of the stereotyped gender role of being a better caretaker; therefore, they may need to both work outside their homes and take care of their children. From many judges' point of view, this double burden may be the best arrangement because it accords with both their belief of women's inherent qualities of being a better caretaker and their stress on the importance of economic resources—both comprise a main part of their ideas of what the best interests of the child should be.

The fact that many more mothers receive custody than do fathers is not absolutely good news for women. On the contrary, it may represent a start of the nightmare of the double burden requirement to many women. The courts increasingly award children to mothers not merely because of mothers' *rights*, but also because of mothers' *inherent duty* to be care-takers of their children. The disproportionate preference for mothers may not really be a victory for women; instead, through the appearance of the emphasis on the best interests of the child, it may tie women more tightly to their stereotyped social role and thus limit their career possibilities. We will discuss this further in a later section.

The Explanation of the Discrepancies Between Pingtung and Taipei

Another intriguing finding of this research is the discrepancies between decisions in Ping-tung and Taipei. We have seen that Taipei's judges were more likely to grant custody to mothers, and they took into account more factors in deciding custody. Taipei's judges also seemed to respect the child more and see the child more as an individual; they considered experts' opinion more often, and it appeared that they decided child custody more carefully than did the court in Pingtung. As to the consideration of the factor "support from relatives to care for the child," Taipei's judges tended to stress it more often than did Pingtung's judges. Meanwhile, Pingtung's judges tended to ignore the possible danger of awarding custody to the perpetrator of spousal abuse, but Taipei's judges might not. Taipei's judges also determined visitation arrangements on their own discretion much more often than did Pingtung's judges. It appears that Pingtung's judges were more likely to cling to the tradi-tional idea of not intervening in family affairs.

Several reasons may explain these discrepancies. To begin with, to determine custody arrangements, it is certain that, in each case, judges would have to consider each litigant's life status and socioeconomic background relevant to the factors listed in the new law of the best interests of the child standard. Naturally, the life status and socioeconomic background of litigants in a rural area, such as Pingtung, are different from those of the litigants in a highly industrialized area, such as Taipei. Meanwhile, the types of cases going to courts in different districts may also be different in the first place. These reasons can explain, for ex-ample, the fact that Taipei's judges took account of the factor "support from relatives to care for the child" more often than did Pingtung's judges.

Secondly, judges in different districts may have different levels of resources. This fact may lead to a difference in judges' possibilities to consider some factors. For instance, the fact that Taipei's judges took account of social workers' opinions much more often than did Pingtung's judges may be partly due to the insufficiency of social workers in rural areas.

Thirdly, judges' gender, age, educational background, and other attributes may have in-fluences on their decisions. Unfortunately, due to the limitation of available data, we cannot clearly depict the differences of attributes between judges in Taipei and judges in Pingtung. The only available attribute is judges' possible gender; however, we can only make conjec-ture based on their names, and it may not be accurate. Nonetheless, it appears that *almost all* decisions of Pingtung District Court in the sample were made by *male* judges; at Taipei District Court, about half of the decisions were made by *female* judges. We may need to conduct further research to reveal the correlation between judges' gender and the discrep-ancies mentioned above.

Fourthly, the newly developing theory of "frame switching" and "multicultural minds" in cultural psychology and cognitive psychology may render a valuable possible explanation. According to this theory, traditional Chinese/Taiwanese values emphasized in judges' socialization processes and life experiences are still embedded in their minds, along with legal norms learned afterward. In response to and being triggered by different social environments, they may shift to different cultural frames to decide their cases, although not intentionally or consciously. While the social environment in Pingtung is obviously more traditional and conservative than is Taipei, it is predictable that Pingtung's judges may be influenced—or more precisely, their inner traditional and conservative minds may be triggered—by the outer environment in which they work. Therefore, they may have a tendency to make some more conservative decisions in accord with traditional ideas.

Adverse Effects of the Current Judicial Practices

As we have seen, judges usually emphasize the economic resources of the parents and adopt the "all-or-none custody" decision pattern. These judicial practices are problematic for many reasons. To begin with, using parents' economic resources and occupation as a necessary factor in determining custody is unfair to mothers not only because of the structural gap in society, but also because many women have sacrificed their career opportunities to raise their children and take care of family. The economic criterion improperly ignores married women's contributions to their families other than wage earning. According to official surveys, in 1998, while the labor-force participation rate of married men (spouse present) and cohabiting men was 80.9 percent, the rate of married women (spouse present) and cohabitating women was only 46.5 percent, more than 76.8 percent of unemployed women were not employed because they needed to "take care of family" or "look after household affairs" (46.9 percent and 29.95 percent, respectively). To be more specific, 38.7 percent of married women (spouse present) did not go to work because they needed to take care of their children.

In addition to the unfairness to women, using the economic criterion may harm the child's best interests too. This criterion disregards the importance of the psychological and emotional needs of the child. By using economic resources as a necessary factor, custody may be awarded to an unfit or even dangerous father only because the mother does not have enough income, even though she has better parenting capability. Moreover, because the "all-or none custody" decision may cause the child to totally lose contact with the noncustodial parent, it may harm the child's psychological development.

The deficient legislation and judicial practices also have very adverse effects outside courtrooms. In Taiwan, a large percentage of divorce and relevant custody disputes have never entered any courts because consensual divorce only has to be registered at administrative agencies; in this case, parents can decide their own custody arrangements by an agreement. However, just as Mnookin and Kornhauser (1979) suggest, "the legal rules . . . give each parent certain claims based on what each would get if the case went to trial" and "the outcome that the law will impose if no agreement is reached gives each parent certain bargaining chips." Many studies attest that the phenomenon of "bargaining in the shadow of the law" is also apparent in Taiwan. For example, several studies prior to 1996 indicate that the old law obviously put wives at a great disadvantage in seeking divorce and child custody outside courts, as well as inside courts.

The decision pattern of "all-or-none custody," a pattern that uses finances as a necessary factor, disproportionately reduces the mother's bargaining power. Because the mother usually has fewer economic resources than does the father, it is highly predictable that the mother would avoid entering a court and make concessions in property division and alimony to receive custody. The mothers who care about and love their children the most will be most willing to accept an inferior bargain; that is, they will be "punished" the most. While divorce typically leads to a decline of economic status, this decision pattern further reduces the mother's opportunity to receive fair property division and alimony. The welfare of both the mother and the child in a divorced single-mother family may be severely damaged because of the concomitant financial difficulties.

Moreover, because they are afraid of losing their children, many mothers who do not have enough economic resources may give up the idea to seek divorce in the first place, even if they are victims of spousal abuse or their marriage has been intolerable. The mothers for whom their children matter most might be punished by losing the opportunity to improve their well-being or to merely protect themselves. Many of Taiwan's researchers and lawyers have attested to this phenomenon.

Some may argue that this study's explanations are somewhat self-contradictory because while this study has proven that mothers usually have fewer economic resources and that judges tend to use finances as a determinative factor in deciding custody, this does not explain why judges award custody to mothers much more often than fathers. However, this specious critique misreads this study's findings and explanations. On the one hand, the findings do *not* indicate, and this study has never so argued, that judges tended to use finances as a *determinative* factor, but the findings do show that judges tended to use finances as a *necessary* factor. Namely, parents who had more economic resources than did their former spouses did *not* necessarily always receive custody, but it is clear that judges tended to not award custody to the parents who did not have *enough* finances. In many judges' consideration, having enough economic resources was not sufficient, but it was necessary.

On the other hand, the result of a "double burden" on women can rebut the seemingly plausible critique. As has been discussed, the "double burden" means that women need to work outside their home to ensure their financial ability and play the role of inherent caretakers of their children at the same time. From many judges' point of view, this double burden may be the best arrangement, because it accords with both their belief in women's inherent qualities of being a better caretaker and their stress on the importance of economic resources in deciding custody. Not only so, but the whole legal system and governmental policy tended to reinforce this double burden on women, due to traditional ideas and the resort to the private welfare system based on a family unit.

However, this double burden on mothers obviously limits women's choice and possibilities in their life and careers. Just as Margaret Mead comments, the emphasis on the concept of mother-child's relationship is a "subtle form of anti-feminism which men are tying women more tightly to their children than has been thought necessary since the invention of bottle feeding and baby carriages." This double burden also marginalizes women in the labor market and thus limits their abilities to improve economic status because they usually need to be involved in informal employment to take care of their children. Many empirical studies consistently attest that the consideration of caring for children significantly affects women's choice of job; women tend to work informally when they have young children. Women's double burden is worsened by the lack of public child-care centers and the expensiveness of private daycare programs. Usually, women need to rely on their relatives (in most cases it is the child's grandparents) to care for their children while they are at work. As we have seen, judges' decisions also considered and reflected this social reality.

REFERENCES

Mnookin, Robert, and L. Kornhauser. 1979. Bargaining in the shadow of the law: The case of divorce. *Yale Law Journal* 88: 950.

22

THE SKY IS HIGH AND THE EMPEROR IS FAR AWAY

THE ENFORCEMENT OF INTELLECTUAL PROPERTY LAW IN CHINA

Ling Li

THE GROWING INTERNAL INCENTIVE STRUCTURE

The counterfeiting market in China has included almost everything from sneakers to liquor, shampoo to software. Between 1990 and 1997, the piracy issue had pushed the United States and China to the verge of major trade wars three times, in 1992, 1995, and 1996 respectively. For example, the trade sanction by the United States in 1992 was instigated by the United States's disappointment with China's neglect in enforcing copyright protection of U.S. works, particularly computer-software programs. From the following analysis of the internal incentive structures, including policy concerns, interest groups, and institutional arrangements, we can see that the enforcement of copyright law will be even harder than trademark law. Since the infringement of patents is not so serious as that of copyright or trademark, this paper will focus on the analysis of copyright and trademark.

Policy Concerns for Enforcement

In general, the justification for copyright protections is actually weak and unstable. The public has the right to get access to more knowledge, while the creators have the right as well to get remuneration for their works. The policy underlying copyright law states that society should give the creators some economic benefits in order to encourage individuals to strive for more intellectual achievements. However, problems arise regarding how much the public should pay, how much money is necessary to encourage people to continue intellectual exploration, and, more subtly, who should pay. Copyright protection always has to strike a balance between public and private interests.

In China, the justification for copyright protection can be more problematic. Deputy Director of the National Copyright Administration (NCA), Shen, once argued that the establishment of copyright protection in China could kill two birds with one stone: preventing Western cultural "junk" that would harm the younger generation and promoting

Reprinted from Ling Li, "The Sky Is High and the Emperor Is Far Away: The Enforcement of Intellectual Property Law in China," *Boletín Mexicano de Derecho Comparado* 108: 951 (2003). Permission courtesy of *Boletín Mexicano de Derecho Compardo.*

Chinese cultural exports that "in the past main western countries regarded as communist propaganda and shut the door to us." It appears that the main justification for copyright protection in China is more an ideological consideration than for the purpose of protecting people's private property and rights. This view is embodied in the Constitution of China, where Article 22 provides that "the State should promote the development of literature and art, the press, broadcasting and television undertakings, publishing and distribution services, libraries, museums, culture centers, and other cultural undertakings, that serve the people and socialism." This is the basic principle underlying the copyright law in China.

In contrast, justification for trademark law is stronger in China. Trademark is an indication of the source and quality of goods. It is the symbol of an enterprise's prestige and standards, distinguishing one product from another in the market. Therefore, trademark infringement usually relates to unfair competition among enterprises and misleading customers. In other words, trademark law protects not only the I[ntellectual] P[roperty] R[ights] holders' right but also the public's interest. Article 1 of the Chinese Trademark Law provides that the law has broad, general purposes, including the improvement of trademark administration, protection of exclusive rights to use trademarks, and encouragement of producers to warrant the quality of their goods and maintain the reputation of their trademarks. There is not much serious conflict between public and private interests in the trademark field as in the copyright field. This difference can also explain why the Chinese Trademark Law was promulgated in 1982, while a copyright law did not come into effect until June 1, 1991. Chinese officials justifiably regard the trademark laws as playing a key role in promoting China's commodity economy, ensuring product quality, and protecting consumer interests. Moreover, trademark infringements often come along with the inferior quality of products that harm public health, resulting in angry consumers or even riots, which is the most sensitive issue for the current Chinese government. It was recognized, "in a sense, to protect a famous trademark means to protect the life of an enterprise as well as the legitimate rights and interests of millions of consumers" (Human Rights China 1996).

The harm resulting from poorly made counterfeits has become a major concern of the current Chinese government. Accordingly, in July 1992, China implemented a nationwide crackdown on these goods. By September 1993, the courts had heard 68,989 cases involving counterfeit or shoddy goods, sentenced fifty people to prison, one person to death, and five people to life imprisonment. In October 1993, the courts gave a factory manager a life sentence and an assistant manger a seventeen-year sentence for manufacturing fake medicines. Six officials who accepted bribes for covering up illegal activities were also jailed. The government's recent effort to enforce the 1993 Product Quality Law is also an indication of the same concern. In addition, the Law on Protection for Customers' Rights was promulgated in 1993 and took effect in January 1, 1994.

Interest Groups

Obedience and enforcement of law are related to the interests of people and participants in the legal process. "How can law be obeyed? . . . Generally speaking, the direct motivation of obeying or resorting to law is that the law can bring to people convenience or benefits, including the psychological or emotional benefits. . . . In this sense, law must have the nature of utility . . . while it is not the only nature" (Zhu 2001). "The Chinese obey laws and observe rights if they are persuaded that it will be in their best interest to do so, just as people everywhere do" (Riley 1997). Therefore it is crucial to analyze whether there are any people in China who can benefit from IP protection.

Copyright Regime

The Media and Entertainment Industries   It has been argued that if the Chinese government paid more attention to the economic interests of copyright holders than to controlling the publication and press, the issue of copyright piracy could be resolved more efficiently. Actually, such control also restricts the economic interests of copyright holders. For example, in the media and entertainment industries, most of the domestic copyright holders are state-owned, and the government strictly controls the number of participants in these industries because the government is always attempting to strengthen its control of these industries. Usually the directors of state-owned enterprises care more about their political promotion than the economic interests of the enterprises. Even if they do care about the IPRs, they are not always powerful enough to push the government to enforce these rights because the deeply entrenched censorship system has stifled the directors' ability and freedom to develop the enterprises. It was reported that government monopolies have essentially controlled all aspects of the Chinese film industry, from production to distribution and exhibition, by way of the Ministry of Culture and related agencies. As for the other individual interested parties, namely, the writers, performers, and directors, though they can usually choose between a fixed remuneration or a return based on sales, after having regard to the piracy, they often choose to get fixed remuneration. Therefore, there is yet not a powerful group of domestic copyright holders who are eager to protect their copyright.

In addition, there are serious barriers for foreign IPR owners to access the Chinese market. According to the Motion Picture Exhibitors Association of America (MPEAA), China has also had an unofficial, unwritten, "shadowy" system of quotas for foreign films, video, and television. This system has effectively excluded direct participation by foreign interests and has provided a fertile ground for piracy. If the Chinese government relaxes or lifts the barriers to market access by foreign IPR owners, the foreign owners could sell their own goods in China and thereby displace, at least to some extent, pirated products. Moreover, absent such barriers, some U.S. producers could both sell their "authentic" products in Chinese market and monitor, if not police, infringement themselves. The control of market access has thus also weakened the potential force of foreign right-holders as a group to enforce the copyright laws.

With the development of technology, the pirated items are of increasingly high quality. It is natural for the customers to prefer the cheaper counterfeit rather than the expensive authentic product. According to the K. Y. General Manager of Shanghai CAV Home Entertainment Ltd., a Chinese-Singapore joint venture and China's largest distributor of Hollywood films on video, "Chinese consumers don't want to pay 36 yuan for a VCD, see it once or twice and give it away. . . . They would rather pay 6, 8, 10 yuan to see a pirated copy and then throw it away" (Smith 2000).

Additionally, Chinese copyright protection in the media industry is currently encountering much pressure from other industries, that is, VCD/DVD players. "Some people say the government has been reluctant to crack down on the pirates because the steady stream of cheap American movies has helped keep alive the state-owned factories producing videodisc players by millions" (ibid.). Without the availability of widespread pirated VCD/DVDs, the market for VCD/DVD players could not have emerged and prospered. "According to government reports, by the end of 1998, about 50 million Chinese families owned CVD/DVD players and were regular buyers of movie discs. . . . China produces 20 million VCD/DVD players annually, but current market demand is only half that amount" (ibid.). If the government enforced the copyright law strictly, the VCD/DVD player industry would collapse.

The Software Industry   As for the software industry, it is very much in its infancy in China. This is also why there has not been much resistance from the domestic manufacturers concerning piracy. Nonetheless, it is a growing industry, and continued piracy will not only harm foreigners' interests but also the development of the domestic software industry. However, some foreign software manufacturers' strategies in China also impede the development of domestic industry. These manufacturers realized that even if piracy did not exist, they might not gain a significant amount of business. This is because people are unwilling to pay high prices for genuine software resulting in a decrease in sales. Therefore, for the time being they do not attempt to combat piracy, but instead deliberately allow such activities to take place, hoping that their software can occupy a monopoly position in the market and become a necessity in many organizations. They hope to stop piracy when such a time comes, and they can become the only legitimate suppliers of such software and any future revisions. However, these foreign manufacturers do not realize that without the development of a domestic interest group for copyright protection, it is hard to push the Chinese government to stop piracy completely. Therefore, their strategy is indirectly slowing down the improvement of IP protection.

Trademark Regime

With the development of a market economy, more and more domestic private sectors have become trademark owners, such as Jianlibao (a drink), Wahaha (a drink), Sanxiao (a tooth brush), Yuanda (an air conditioner), and Lining (sports attire). They are often important sources of local revenue and employment. Thus, these trademark owners are able to have good connections with both local and national administrations and have become an important force for the enforcement of trademark law. It was reported that the revenue from private enterprises in Beijing in 2000 was 110 times of that in 1994. The private sector accounts for 18 percent of gross value industrial output (GVIO) today, while it was zero in 1978. With the Chinese market becoming more open, more and more foreign trademark owners have come into China. A lot of foreign trademarks have gained considerable shares of the Chinese market successfully, such as Coca-Cola, McDonalds, IBM, Panasonic, Motorola, and P[rocter] & G[amble]. These foreign trademark owners have also adopted a strategy of setting up joint ventures or licensing their products in China. For example, in January 2000 Colgate and Sanxiao set up their joint venture, Colgate Sanxiao in China. The joint-venture model could create an immediate economic incentive for Chinese enforcement of IP because the Chinese partners will certainly defend their mutual IPRs. The Chinese partner is more likely to have a better understanding of the nuances of political life in China, be more aware of impending upheavals, and maintain proper government contacts to safeguard joint venture's investments. Also, a local government is more willing to take action when a foreign investor has a government-linked partner and the government's own interest is at stake.

From the perspective of the consumers, Chinese consumers are more and more "brand-name" conscious. Name brand shops have mushroomed in big cities such as Shanghai. The country's increasingly aggressive advertising industry has also boosted public awareness of brand. Trademark recognition, just as in the United States, often motivates a consumer's decision to buy a certain product in China. Although there are still large amounts of counterfeit products in the Chinese market, they have more or less lost the original meaning of trademark infringement. Usually both the seller and the buyer know clearly that the goods are counterfeit because the buyer who purchases the counterfeit does not belong to the group of people who prefer to buy the authentic goods.

The individual's awareness of the benefits from trademark protection is also very important from a collective action perspective. For copyright, we assume that the collective will enjoy benefits over the long term so long as its members adhere to the law. However, for any individual member like the consumer, the incentive to defect from the law will still be great, since the individual who does defect by indulging in piracy will very often be better off in the short term than if he does not. Therefore it is difficult to encourage consumer collective action to protect copyright. As for trademark infringement, since fake goods are passed off as authentic goods, they involve cheating the consumers, and it is relatively easy to organize them to protest against trademark infringement. Early in 1983 the China Association for Protecting Consumers' Rights was established to protect consumers against fake goods and goods of inferior quality.

Institutional Arrangements

The administrative agency in charge of trademark, SAIC, is very powerful, more powerful than that of copyright, NCA. Because the NCA's authority was derived from the State Administration for Publication and Press, the regional copyright bureaus at the provincial level are affiliated with the local press and publication administrations. They are a "functional department" of the local government, rather than an administrative subsidiary of the NCA, except that they regularly receive "professional guidance" from the NCA. In contrast, the SAIC that handles trademark issues is a much larger agency than the NCA. It has a powerful network of local industry, commerce bureaus, and departments at the grassroots level throughout the country (Feng 1997, 15). Although the local trademark bureaus officially report to the local governments rather than to the SAIC, the SAIC traditionally has maintained much greater control over their work than the NCA over the local copyright administration. Originally the power of SAIC also helped it grab a larger share of power from courts, as [Peter] Feng indicated:

> Legal reform (in China) is politically a game of reallocation of existing jurisdiction as well as the awarding of new jurisdiction, among the powers that rule. Therefore government agencies must settle who . . . takes charge of enforcement for each new IP system. Consider-

ing all of the fiscal and political implications, the People's Court in the early 1980s was in no position to grab a larger share of power from other players, hence the earlier laws awarded more administrative duties to more powerful agencies such as the SAIC, and the later laws reduced administrative duties allocated to patent and copyright administrations.

In the field of trademark infringement, many foreign companies have chosen the administrative channel and have filed actions through the local AICs. The AICs are even willing to proceed with raids within one day of presentation of the case. When infringement is found, effective measures are used, such as sealing up or confiscating the goods. Decisions usually follow within a few months and generally involve stop orders or imposition of fines.

In contrast, in the area of copyright law enforcement, it is a regime not supported by a network as extensive as that provided by the local AICs. Therefore, companies are concerned about the availability of effective enforcement. Moreover, foreign copyright owners are required to direct administrative actions to the NCA at the national level. The NCA's powers and resources are presently not sufficient to handle the bulk of infringements effectively and efficiently. It was reported that the NCA is severely underfunded and understaffed, and it only employed as few as five people to tackle the task.

Usually, the NCA has to unite with other agencies to reinforce its power, and it acts in the name of antipornography to get stronger justification for its enforcement efforts. For example, in February 2000, five agencies, namely, the Ministry of Finance, the Ministry of Public Security (police department), the State Information and Publication Bureau, the National Copyright Administration, and the State "Sao Huang" (Antipornography) Task Force, jointly issued a rule entitled "Awarding Measures for the Reporting of Manufacturing and Selling of Pornography, Piracy and Other Illegal Publishing Activities." The National Working Group in charge of "antipornography" and "antipiracy and other illegal publishing activities" consists of officials from fourteen national departments and the Beijing City Council and is led by the State Press and Publishing Administration. In practice, if an infringer copied pornography items, the penalty might be much more serious. For example, in December 1995, Shenzhen police cracked down on a large amount of pirated audiovisual products illegally replicated by Q Company, and fifteen suspects from the company, including its manager-general, were arrested on the spot. The local prosecutor filed a lawsuit with the local same-level court. The court found that Q Company had been engaging in replication activities of pornographic and pirated VCD copies without any license of owners since May 1994. Up to December of 1995, Q Company had made eight million pirated and pornographic laser discs and videodiscs, with huge illegal gains of more than ten million RMB yuan. The court made a verdict as following: it sentenced the manager-general to twelve years' imprisonment for two crimes, infringing copyright crime and replicating pornographic products crime, and it imposed a fine of 300,000 yuan. The other fourteen culprits were also sentenced to imprisonment ranging from two–seven years.

It is also highly possible that NCA may come into conflict with other agencies at its bureaucratic level regarding the administration of the copyright law. For example, the Press and Publication Administration officially shared administration and enforcement responsibilities for the copyright law. The Ministry of Film, Radio, and Television formerly had exclusive responsibility for copyright matters and even conducted raids on suspected violators.

The fact that several agencies are responsible for the same task usually means every agency can shift its responsibility to others, which leads to more inefficiency. The lack of coordination among these agencies also decreases the NCA's authority and willingness to enforce the copyright law.

Changes in the Incentive for IP Protection

The change of domestic incentive structure will be the key to the improvement of IP protection. Using Taiwan as an example, as Professor [William] Alford (1995) asked:

> Were foreign pressure as certain an answer as its proponents believe, why was the ROC (Taiwan) able to resist it for decades during which the island state was highly dependent on U.S. economic and military support, only to yield to it at a time when Taiwan has the world's largest per capita foreign currency reserves and has carved out its own position in the international community?

An answer to this question, according to Alford, lies in the extraordinary economic, political, technological, and diplomatic changes that have occurred in Taiwan in the past decade and their implications for Taiwan's society and culture. Taiwan's explosive economic expansion, increasing awareness of the need of indigenous technology, ever-more-pluralistic political and intellectual life, growing commitment to formal legal process, and international aspirations have made evident the need for intellectual property law and nurtured domestic constituencies with good reasons for supporting it. Correspondingly, we cannot ignore the emergence of the new forces in China. China is now changing rapidly. The cultural industry is also becoming commercialized, especially in those areas that have little to do with politics. For example, there are emerging interest groups in the copyright regime. The Chinese computer industry grew 56 percent in 1996, and it is expected to have grown another 50 percent in 1997 and 1998 according to China's Ministry of Information Industry. The domestic software industry is valued at US$1–1.5 billion and is growing at 32 percent per annum. As the violation of Chinese IPR and resulting losses to Chinese right-holders increase, so will domestic pressure for better IPR protection.

The entertainment industry is also becoming a little more open and commercial as well. A deal reached by the United States and China on China's W[orld] T[rade] O[rganization] accession on November 16, 1999, did increase U.S. access to the Chinese film market. The number of American films allowed will be increased from ten films to fifty films in three years. The United States also gained the right for the American entertainment industry to distribute videos and sound recordings in China.

Indigenous right-holders also suffer much from the weak copyright protection. For example, even the Communist Party's own anticorruption propaganda film, "Life and Death Choice," is widely available in pirated copies across the country. There were also complaints from domestic singers. Tian Zhen, a famous Chinese singer, said to reporters, "I was busy with the promotion for my new works, but it is so depressing because of the sweeping piracy market. . . . People used to think authentic tapes and CDs are available in Xinhua Bookstore, but now even Xinhua Bookstore sells pirated works" (*Daily News* 2000). According to research by the Business Software Alliance, in 1997 the software industry provided China with

60,000 jobs and paid US$219.8 million revenue. For every decrease of 10 percent in the piracy rate, the software industry will provide China with 13,170 more jobs and US$77.7 million revenue.

Domestic right-holders have begun to actively promote the intellectual property law and conduct antipiracy activities by themselves. After the interview Tian Zhen's agents and the officials from the Beijing Cultural Bureau inspected several audio-visual shops to investigate the piracy. In 2000 some of the country's hottest singers in China gathered in the Shanghai International Art Festival, whose thesis is antipiracy. In addition, on May 26, 2000, the director of Shanghai Phrase Book Press announced that the press would give awards of up to 150,000 yuan to people who provided evidence of pirating their book, *Phrase Sea*. Many intellectual elites expressed their anger at the pirating of this Chinese authoritative dictionary.

We cannot dismiss the influence of these emerging IP holders in Chinese society. In the legislation process of copyright law and the discourse of China's accession to the Berne Convention, many famous writers and musicians such as Jiang Zilong, Ye Peiying, and Wang Liping made great efforts to ensure more copyright protection. Since these individuals are influential in Chinese society, political leaders tend to pay more attention to them. For example, Mr. Wang Liping, a highly respected musician in China, once wrote a letter to the National People's Congress, calling for copyright protection in China, before the enactment of the copyright law. Copies of this letter were sent to all the members of the Standing Committee of the National People's Congress. Moreover, some of the IP holders have natural connections with the media, or they are the media themselves, for example, the press, writers, and singers. This characteristic has made them more capable of using the media to influence policymaking or to promote the IP protection. Such large-scale publicity has been the main force for improving the Chinese people's awareness of IP rights. Early in the 1990s, there were some magazines that focused on IP protection in China. For example, "Quality Guarantee in China" (Zhonguo Zhiliang Wali Xing), started in 1993, has claimed that the publicity of IP protection is its focus.

Regarding the future enforcement of intellectual property protection, we should also pay attention to the association of IP interest holders. According to the experience of Taiwan, the private sector can be more effective than the government in battling counterfeits. As it was reported in the *United Daily*, when the government was launching an intensified campaign to crack down on piracy and counterfeiting in February 2000 for the coming Special 301 review, the Anti-Counterfeiting Coalition of Information Products, a local business alliance devoted to antipiracy efforts, confiscated 83,640 illegal software CDs and 85,268 copies of illegal video games. China also has numerous associations established by professional and industrial interest groups, including writers' associations, film producers, film distributors, audio-visual publishers, book publishers, and software manufacturers. However, these associations have broad administrative functions rather than focusing on IP rights protection. In February 1993, the Music Copyright Society of China was established to protect the copyright of the industry. In 1999, antipiracy alliances were also established in Beijing, Shanghai, Guangdong, Sichuan, Chongqing, and Jiangsu. They are partly designed to fill the manpower shortage of the NCP. The association should be more successful because they are more powerful than individuals to influence the government and can push them to enforce IP protection in China.

A Brief Conclusion on the Incentive Structures for IP Enforcement

In conclusion, we can see that trademark law has paved a relatively smoother way for enforcement than copyright in China, but both are changing in a good direction. Generally speaking, to enforce IPRs in China, the following three factors are crucial. First, there should be a sufficient number of domestic right-holders who have a stake in protecting their rights, such as the private trademark owners or some joint-venture right-holders. Secondly, such owners should get involved with the local economy, establish good connections with the government, and have the power to push the agencies to enforce their rights. However such power is sometimes restricted by political policies such as censorship and localism. Thirdly, there should be an efficient and independent institution in charge of the enforcement that is regarded as legitimate and necessary and willing to enforce these laws. Simply speaking, incentives are needed for the people to observe a new law and for the government to enforce the law.

FINAL REMARKS AND CONCLUSION

Final Remarks About the WTO

Some remarks should be given to China's accession to the WTO after fifteen years of trying. Under the T[rade] R[elated aspects of] I[ntellectual] P[roperty Right]s Agreement, one agreement under the WTO, China's obligations are not limited to merely enacting and amending formal laws. TRIPs, also administered by the WTO, require all WTO members to comply with the provisions of the enforcement requirement although a certain period of transition is granted. As a result, China's intellectual property enforcement regime will come under greater scrutiny within the WTO dispute procedure and the international community. Given the serious problem of piracy and the lack of effective measures, China's enforcement mechanism still has a significant way to go to achieve full compliance with the TRIPs enforcement obligations.

The WTO enforcement will make it easier for domestic interests to get privileges from the central government. For example, Article X of the G[eneral] A[greement on] T[ariffs and] T[rade] requires that member nations must publish their laws on trade and administer them in a "uniform, impartial and reasonable manner." Local protectionism with respect to the enforcement of IP law is obviously against this rule. However, this standard is very general and is not maintained by other GATT members either. The incentive structure at the local level, which is more decisive to improve the IP protection in China, is much more complicated. Most likely, the central government must still give privileges to local interests after a balance of international and domestic pressure, and its commitment to enforcement obligations remains difficult.

Moreover, there are also enforcement problems with the WTO rules. We cannot, by any means, expect the WTO to resolve the IP protection problem in China immediately or completely. It might be able to help China to reform its systems, including the legal, economic, and political ones, and thus nurture the ingredients required to cure the piracy problem. However, compliance with intellectual property rights legislation does not happen overnight. The WTO cannot substitute the formation of domestic incentives, though it may help their formation.

Conclusion

Since the adoption of the "reform and opening" as national policy in the late 1970s, China has been trying to develop foreign-related business, join the international economic community, and modernize some of its laws. Legal transplant has been an important way to achieve modernization and globalization in China. However, law is not "out of context." It cannot operate by itself. It is widely accepted that a foreign legal rule will not be transplanted successfully if it does not fit into a nation's social, political, and economic context. As Montesquieu (1751) said, "The political and civil laws of each nation must be proper for the people for whom they are made, so much so that it is a very great accident if those of one nation can fit another." After the transplant in the sense of legislation, the effectiveness of the law depends mainly on the domestic context.

This paper uses the transplant of IP law in China as a case to study the real force of a successful legal transplant and of globalization. It shows that the introduction of IP law in China has brought with it changes in Chinese society, such as rights awareness and social value toward IP. However, there remains the problem of ineffectiveness in the enforcement of the law. This paper illustrates that the problems with the ineffectiveness are mainly (1) the defects of the current system, and (2) the "marginalization" of the current system, for example, local protectionism. The cause of the problem is the lack of domestic incentives for people to observe the law and for the government to enforce the law.

This paper concludes that a successful legal transplant cannot be a mere project of the enactment of law. The establishment of efficient institutions and the changes of the conditions for enforcement are more important. In contemporary China, there are hopes for the improvement of the enforcement of IP law. For example, domestic IP holders are becoming more and more powerful with the establishment of a market economy and the process of privatization. China's accession to the WTO can also be expected to hasten this process and promote the rule of law in China. It can also provide foreigners with more opportunities to get involved with the local economy and get more legal protection.

From the case of Chinese IP law, we can see that although there is a global force working in our time, the effectiveness of the modernization of law and the real strength of globalization come from the domestic constituents. Although multinational organizations might add legitimacy to the international standard and help domestic reform, international pressure cannot substitute for internal will to legal reform. Since it is very complicated to change the domestic circumstances, and such changes usually take a long time, the success of the legal transplant cannot be achieved quickly. This will require not a project, but a lengthy process.

REFERENCES

Alford, William P. 1995. To steal a book is an elegant offense in intellectual property law. In *Chinese Civilization*. Stanford: Stanford University Press.

Daily News. 2000. http://dailynews.musi.com/11/chinese/83269.shtml.

Feng, Peter. 1997. *Intellectual property in China.* Hong Kong: Sweet and Maxwell Asia.

Human Rights China. 1996. China protects intellectual property rights. http://www.humanrights
-china.org/xiezhen/china/chanquan/091501.htm.

Montesquieu, Baron de (Charles-Louis de Secondat). [1751] 1989. *The spirit of laws.* Trans. Anne M.
Cohler, Basia Carolyn Miller, and Harold Samuel Stone. Cambridge: Cambridge University Press.

Riley, Mary L. 1997. *Protecting intellectual property rights in China.* Hong Kong: Sweet & Maxwell
Asia.

Smith, Craig S. 2000. A tale of piracy: How the Chinese stole the Grinch. *The New York Times*, December 12. http://www.nytimes.com/2000/12/12/world/a-tale-of-piracy-how-the-chinese-stole
-the-grinch.html.

Zhu, Suli. 2001. How can laws be obeyed? A review of law and religious. http://www.chinalawinfo
.com /fxsk/YDSG/review-contentasp?fid=14337 (accessed February 23, 2001).

VI LAW AND GLOBALIZATION

INTRODUCTION

Globalization is a catchword that describes some salient aspects of the contemporary world—a world of rapid social and technological change. In the last decades, the flow of information, money, and people across borders has grown dramatically. It is enough to mention the Internet, tourism, and immigration pressures as symptoms of these trends (Giddens 2000). The world, in many ways, has become truly a global village. The countries in the world are interconnected in ways that would have seemed unimaginable before. The current economic crisis (2010) is sad proof of that fact. This section of the reader will discuss some aspects of the consequences of globalization for the world's legal systems.

Business lawyering, mediation and adjudication of claims, and the formulation of rules and regulations can be carried out domestically, or in ways that transcend national borders. This is not new: the *jus gentium* was an international body of rules in ancient Rome, and interactions across boundaries have existed for centuries. One trait of contemporary times is the intensification of these exchanges and the strengthening of international lawyering. Trubek et al. (1994) have analyzed how some specific actors, like multinational business, specialized law firms, and international organizations and courts have become agents of globalization. This volume reproduces a section of this article. But actors are not necessarily global or national; people or organizations select among jurisdictions—national and international—that they feel are the best for obtaining the results they want, as Sikkink (2005) has shown for human rights activists in Latin America.

In a way, globalization is only a heightened and deepened form of modernization. Friedman (1994) has tried to list some of the characteristics of modern legal culture. These include a profound individualism, a consciousness of right and rights, and the willingness to enforce rights by judicial or other means (Friedman 1985). Another trait is the growing importance of concepts of human rights. The global age is also the age of human rights. This is a broader and more vital area of law than it was even fifty years ago, at the time of the Universal Declaration of Human Rights. Now people speak not only of "negative" rights, like freedom of speech, freedom of religion or property, but also about the so-called social (positive) rights, the right to education, health, housing, a healthy environment, and so on.

Human rights can be enforced in many national courts, but transnational courts, like the European Court of Human Rights, play an increasingly important role. Madsen (2007), in an article that is included here as Chapter 26, has documented the transformation of this court from a cold-war instrument to a true European Supreme Court. Arold (2007) has pointed out the importance of this Court and has discussed how it has created a kind of international legal culture in the area of human rights. In Latin America, the Inter American Court of Human Rights is also gaining importance (Buergenthal 1982; Lutz and Sikkink 2000). International courts, as they grow in significance, seem to stand for a global understanding of human rights, an understanding that transcends boundaries and national sovereignty (Stacy 2009). International NGOs, such as Amnesty International, or Human Rights Watch, also concern themselves with human rights. They publish information on the status of human rights in various countries, list the countries whose actions offend international standards, and they try to influence national political regimes (Sikkink 1993).

The growth, strength, and proliferation of international organizations are other manifestations of the closer integration of the world. The United Nations, UNESCO, the International Labor Organization, the World Trade Organization, the International Monetary Fund, the World Bank, the Organization of American States, the European Union, among many other organizations, all of these are loci for norm creation and dispute resolution. International organizations have become stronger and more numerous because of the increased need to regulate cross-border activities and international relations.

Some of these international organizations call themselves courts, and they behave like courts—for example, the international court that sits in The Hague, and the new International Criminal Court. The proliferation of international courts has been so intense that international law scholars discuss whether it is already a systemic problem (Kingsbury 1999). In addition, there are many other institutions—panels for dispute resolution, arbitration and mediation centers, and the like—that do international "legal" work, but they do not bear the label of "courts." Some of these are sponsored by chambers of commerce and other "private" organizations. Furthermore, many law firms and law schools (Sokol 2007; Dezalay 1990; Dezalay and Garth 1997, 2002; Trubek et al. 1994) have become internationalized and, in many respects, act as agents of the globalization of law.

One big question is how much globalization has affected ordinary people and their everyday interactions. A number of famous brands such as McDonalds and Coca-Cola are relatively easy to find virtually anywhere around the world. The same can be said about types of food like sushi, pizza, coffee, and croissants. In addition to the European countries where it has been traditionally produced, the wine we drink may come from Chile, South Africa, or California. Yet, to what extent do we really live in "one world" as the slogan of an airline advertisement announces? Mobile phones, computers, and other devices are almost universal, and thanks to modern technology we can easily communicate with people on the opposite side of the world and send them pictures and video in a matter of seconds. Many books are now available in electronic versions, and classes are being taught online. But it is important not to overestimate how much life has been globalized. Most people use their telephones, not to make international calls, but to communicate with family members and friends in their city or nearby. National law is still very important and many cross-border disputes will be resolved in local courts, on the basis of local law that the judge understands and applies (Gessner 1996).

Merryman (1981), Dezalay and Garth (1997), Appelbaum et al. (2001), among others, have called attention to the positive and negative aspects of globalization. On the one hand, there is an enormous expansion in tourism, which has important cultural consequences. Tourists are welcome in most countries; on the other hand, refugees, asylum-seekers, and people looking for a job and a better life are in general not welcome in many countries. They face bureaucratic hurdles, discrimination, and outright hostility in the wealthy countries to which they gravitate (Calavita 1998).

Law and practice define those who are welcome and those who are not. In Europe, citizens of the European Union can freely circulate; it is a sign of our times that a Polish plumber can find work in London and a Spanish carpenter can move to Warsaw. This is globalization, though defined in regional terms. For "extracommunitarian" people (mostly African and Latin American citizens) the reaction is different. Europe becomes "fortress Europe." Calavita's article (1998; here included as Chapter 23) shows how the formal Spanish policy of assimilation for immigrants in fact produces exclusion and illegalization. The living law, and official practices, contradict the formal purposes of the law. Massive immigration, however, along with reaction against it, derives its force from the brute facts of globalization. There is both a cultural and a technological aspect to the push for immigration. Dissemination of knowledge of conditions of life in Europe and modern transportation facilities join to make it likely for an Ecuadorian or a Moroccan to decide to immigrate "illegally" into Europe.

Modernization and globalization, as affirmations of individual worth, are both causes and effects of individualism; they are, moreover, deeply secular. Television, the cinema, and the Internet spread the gospel of material life, crowding out religious and traditional values, customs, and habits. This trend has generated a counter trend, which produces different results in different countries. Engel (2005; here included as Chapter 25) analyzes how religious feelings and the consciousness of right impact legal behavior in a midsize Thai city. One might ask: To what extent is Engel describing a general trend? In what societies will there appear phenomena of the sort he describes, and in which ones will it not?

Globalization increases world trade; businesses become international or multinational; they enter into contracts and other relations with suppliers or clients in many countries. The contracts are necessarily more detailed and require specialized legal knowledge. International-minded lawyers are profoundly useful to the international business community. However, international business law, even when it is highly formal, shares with local business law the fact that personal contacts are of vital importance, that contracts tend to be relational, that social norms influence the terms of contracts and the way they are carried out, and, last but not least, that at the end of the day, *guanxi* [personal connections] may often be vital to success.

Globalization has also gone hand in hand with democratization and the rule of law. The fall of communist regimes and the end of the cold war have led to a further outburst of democratic and constitutional regimes in many parts of the world. We now have agencies that provide worldwide evaluation of countries—scorecards, as it were, noting how much progress there is (or lack of progress) in protecting human rights, fundamental freedoms, property rights, and anticorruption measures. There is also a powerful counter-trend of religious resurgence. There are many theocratic regimes, particularly in the Middle East, and fundamentalist religion has been growing in strength. Some fundamentalists have opted for terrorism as a strategy. These fundamentalists are deadly enemies of modernity and secularism, even when they use modern means of communication and are organized globally. At the same time, the reaction again terrorism threatens to shake the foundations of the rule of law in the United States and in some European countries. As always, the world is a complicated, and ambiguous, place.

REFERENCES AND SUGGESTIONS FOR FURTHER READING

Appelbaum, R. P., W. L. F. Felstiner, and V. Gessner. 2001. Introduction: The legal culture of global business transactions. In *Rules and networks: The legal culture of global business transactions*, ed. R. P. Appelbaum, W. L. F. Felstiner, and V. Gessner, 1–38. Oxford: Hart Publishing.

Arold, Nina-Louisa. 2007. *The legal culture of the European Court of Human Rights.* Leiden, Netherlands: Martinus Nijhoff Publishers.

Buergenthal, Thomas. 1982. The Inter-American Court of Human Rights. *American Journal of International Law* 76: 231–45.

Calavita, Kitty. 1998. Immigration, law and marginalization in a global economy: Notes from Spain. *Law and Society Review* 32: 529.

Dezalay, Yves. 1990. The big bang and the law: The internationalization and restructuration of the legal field. *Theory, Culture & Society* 7: 279.

Dezalay, Yves, and B. Garth. 2002. *The internationalization of palace wars: Lawyers, economists, and the contest to transform Latin American states.* Chicago: University of Chicago Press.

———. 1997. Law, lawyers, and social capital: Rule of law versus relational capitalism. *Social and Legal Studies* 6: 109–41.

Engel, David. 2005. Globalization and the decline of legal consciousness: Torts, ghosts, and karma in Thailand. *Law and Social Inquiry* 30: 469.

Friedman, Lawrence M. 1994. Is there a modern legal culture? *Ratio Juris* 7: 117.

———. 1985. *Total justice.* New York: Russell Sage Foundation.

Gessner, Volkmar. 1996. International cases in German first instance courts. In *Foreign courts: Civil litigation in foreign legal cultures*, ed. V. Gessner. Aldershot, England: Dartmouth.

Giddens, Anthony. 2000. *Runaway world: How globalization is reshaping our lives.* New York: Routledge.

Kingsbury, Benedict. 1999. Foreword: Is the proliferation of international courts and tribunals a systemic problem? *International Law and Politics* 31: 679.

Lutz, Ellen, and Kathryn Sikkink. 2000. International human rights law and practice in Latin America. *International Organization* 54: 633.

Madsen, Mikael R. 2007. From cold war instrument to Supreme European Court: The European Court of Human Rights at the crossroad of international and national law and politics. *Law and Social Inquiry* 32: 137.

Merryman, John H. 1981. On the convergence (and divergence) of the civil law and the common law. *Stanford Journal of International Law* 17.

Pérez-Perdomo, Rogelio, and Lawrence M. Friedman. 2003. Latin legal cultures in the age of globalization. In *Legal culture in the age of globalization: Latin America and Latin Europe*, ed. L. Friedman and R. Pérez-Perdomo, 1–19. Stanford: Stanford University Press.

Sikkink, Kathryn. 2005. The transnational dimension of the judicialization of politics in Latin America. In *The judicialization of politics in Latin America*, ed. R. Sieder, L. Schjolden, and A. Angell, 263–92. London: Palgrave Macmillan.

———. 1993. Human rights, principled issue-networks, and soverignity in Latin America. *International Organization* 47: 411.

Sokol, Daniel. 2007. Globalization of law firms: A survey of the literature and a research agenda for further study. *Indiana Journal of Global Legal Studies* 14: 5–28.

Stacy, Helen. 2009. *Human rights for the 21st century: Sovereignty, civil society, culture.* Stanford: Stanford University Press.

Trubek, David M., Y. Dezalay, R. Buchanan, and J. R. Davies. 1994. Global restructuring and the law: Studies of the internationalization of legal fields and the creation of transnational arenas. *Case Western Reserve Law Review* 44(2): 407–98.

23

IMMIGRATION, LAW, AND MARGINALIZATION IN A GLOBAL ECONOMY

NOTES FROM SPAIN

Kitty Calavita

Scholars of immigration and globalization often argue that a paradox exists between the contemporary forces of globalization and the dismantling of economic borders on the one hand, and the increasingly restrictionist stance of Western capitalist democracies regarding immigration on the other. One example of this presumed paradox is the increasing ease with which capital and goods move in and out of Western Europe, while at the same time the "European Fortress" steps up control of its external borders. Perhaps even more conspicuous is the contrast between the North American Free Trade Agreement (NAFTA), which allows for the free movement of investments and goods between Mexico and the United States, and U.S. immigration policies that appear to be increasingly restrictionist.

Another theme that runs through much of the academic literature on immigration is the recurring gap between the declared intent of immigration laws and their outcomes. It is noted, for example, that despite concerted efforts to control immigration from developing countries, in most advanced capitalist democracies these efforts have been glaringly unsuccessful in controlling either the size of the flow or its composition, and in some cases have had a series of apparently unintended and counterproductive consequences (see Cornelius, Martin, and Hollifield 1994).

The study of Spanish immigration law on which this article is based was undertaken as a way to explore such apparent contradictions. As a country that has undergone enormous political and economic transformation in the last two decades—almost overnight joining the roster of Western capitalist democracies—and that arguably experiences the contradictions of advanced capitalist development in an intensified fashion, Spain provides an interesting case study for such analysis. As we will see, this recent immigration to Spain and the laws that purportedly attempt to control it can shed light not only on the contradictions of Spanish society, as Izquierdo (1996) notes, but also on the broader contradictions of immigration and immigration control in the new global economy.

· · ·

As I began this study of immigration laws in Spain, I was soon struck by the marked contrast between the integrationist rhetoric accompanying these laws and their actual content, which systematically marginalizes immigrants and circumscribes their rights. I argue here that as Spain's economy took off in the 1980s and it joined the emerging European Community, the economic importance of third world immigrants increased at the same moment that Spain was pressured by its European neighbors to control its borders, which had become the southern gate to the new Fortress Europe. The consequence was a series of contradictory policies that say one thing and do another. While the dual rationale of the 1985 law and its successors has been to control the borders while ensuring immigrants' rights, they do neither. Indeed, rather than controlling the number of immigrants entering Spain, these laws focus primarily on defining levels of social and economic inclusion/exclusion. I further argue that these policies are crafted in such a way that the predictable consequence is to marginalize third world immigrants and consign them to the extensive underground economy.

A central component of this marginalization concerns legal status. Not only do illegal immigrants "work scared and hard," as the former secretary of labor (Marshall 1978, 169) once said of undocumented immigrants in the United States, but they are excluded from most of the benefits of Spain's welfare state such as universal health care and social security, thus compounding their vulnerability and the urgency of their dependence on whatever work they can find. I will show here that the significant number of illegal immigrants (or "irregulars," as they are called) in Spain—and thus the high degree of marginalization of much of the country's immigrant stock—is the direct consequence of Spanish immigration law.

It has often been noted that law, at some fundamental level, creates illegality, in that without the boundaries of law, there are no "outlaws." But my argument here goes beyond this labeling theory insight. For Spanish immigration law actively and regularly "irregularizes" people, by making it all but impossible to retain legal status over time. Indeed, it makes little sense to draw distinctions between legal and illegal immigrants, as if they were different populations, because the law ensures that legal status is temporary and subject to continuous disruptions. In other words, not only does the law actively create "outlaws," but the boundaries between legal and illegal populations are porous and in constant flux, as people routinely move in and out of legal status. With lapses into illegality built into the system, Spanish immigration policy not only continually reproduces an extensive illegal population but also ensures the precariousness of its (temporarily) legal immigrants as well.

In the case discussed here, the point instead will be that the immigrant "other" is constructed as an outlaw (not vice versa), and that it is precisely immigrants' particular status as *workers* (not economic castoffs) that prompts this marginalization.

I hope that this analysis can make contributions at a number of levels. First, this research may help make sense of the apparent paradoxes outlined above. Not only has Spain only recently established its first immigration laws, as it experiences in fast motion and with considerable force the "internal and international contradictions" of advanced capitalist development, but these laws also offer a striking example of the intent/outcome discrepancy. My analysis addresses that discrepancy and in so doing begins to unpack the presumed paradox of heightened immigration restrictionism just as the forces of globalization increase. Indeed, I argue not only that there is no real paradox here but also that the current globalization and these particular forms of restrictionism go hand in hand.

Second, I hope to contribute to our understanding of the concepts of marginalization and social exclusion. Much of the discussion of immigrant marginalization and racism in European mass media and policy circles presumes that the dynamics of exclusion take place primarily at the level of culture (highlighting, for example, cultural differences between Muslim immigrants and the Western, Christian traditions of the host society, and calling for increased mutual respect and the undoing of stereotypes).

But my analysis demonstrates that marginalization and social and economic exclusion are not only—or even primarily—cultural issues but are systematically produced by law and the structural and economic imperatives it secures.

Finally, this case study of the legal construction of marginality may contribute to the ongoing discussion of the constitution of the marginalized "other" in late capitalist societies and the role of law in that process.

CONSTRUCTING IMMIGRANT MARGINALIZATION

Mercedes Jabardo, an anthropologist studying African farm labor in Catalonia, observed of the 1985 immigration law, "The new legislation [LOE] . . . generates irregularity among the vast majority of the immigrant community. . . . In other words, the Law creates the legal category of immigrant and . . . generates the category of the 'illegal'" (1995, 86–87). This is true in the obvious sense that before the LOE [Organic Law on the Rights and Liberties of Foreigners in Spain] there was no comprehensive immigration policy in Spain and thus no illegal immigrants. Similarly, the 1991 visa requirement for Moroccans, Peruvians, and Dominican Republicans ipso facto produced large numbers of illegal immigrants.

But the law produces "irregularity" in a more subtle way as well, for lapses into illegality are *built into* Spanish immigration law. This construction of illegality through law is the product of a variety of overlapping factors, the most important of which are the temporary and contingent nature of legal status and a series of bureaucratic catch-22s.

The temporary nature of legal resident status is a central component of Spain's policies toward foreigners. Spain grants nationality primarily according to the principle of *jus sanguinis* and not *jus soli*. This means that unless one has Spanish "blood," it is very difficult to obtain the full rights of Spanish citizenship. Thus, for example, children born of noncitizen parents on Spanish soil are not automatically conferred citizenship and indeed may from time to time be illegal, depending on their parents' status. Foreigners who marry Spanish citizens fare no better; as of 1996, illegal aliens who marry Spanish citizens must wait three years before they acquire even legal resident status.

There are few other routes to permanent legal status besides citizenship. Prior to 1996, it generally took ten years of continuous legal status before one could apply for permanent residence. Since the regulatory reform of 1996 (Real Decreto 155/1996, reproduced in Ministerio del Interior 1996), the waiting period has been reduced to six years. Nonetheless, very few applications for this permanent residence category have been received, largely because of the near impossibility of piecing together six years of uninterrupted work and residence permits (interview with Miguel Pajares, director of Immigrant Services, CCOO [Communist Union Confederation], Barcelona).

The temporary nature of legal status is underscored by the instability inherent in the very program purportedly designed to facilitate integration—the much-touted "regularization" of illegal aliens. The first of these regularizations was launched by the LOE in 1985–86. This was followed by the larger program of 1991 and a smaller one in 1996. While not technically "regularization" programs, the quota worker system established in 1993 for agriculture, construction, and domestic service has also become an avenue of regularization for those already residing in Spain.

All these legalization programs are specifically and exclusively for foreign *workers* (and, under some limited conditions, their families) and are contingent on either having a legitimate work contract or having had one in the recent past. The difficulties of illegal immigrants meeting this standard, given their concentration in the underground economy, are legion. Not only are underground employers often unwilling to formalize work contracts, but some clearly *prefer* the undocumented status of their workers and the vulnerability that status ensures. According to qualitative studies based on in-depth interviews with Latin American and African immigrants in and around Barcelona and Madrid, a number of immigrants have been fired for pursuing the possibility of legalization with their bosses (Valls et al. 1995; Pumares 1996). An Equatorial Guinean who lost his job when he asked his boss to help him with legalization put it this way, "Here when they hire an immigrant, they prefer that he work in conditions that are not legitimate, and preferably illegal, that way they can pay what they want and under conditions convenient to them." A Gambian immigrant explained, "If you work in the fields, and you go to your boss and ask for a contract, that's the day you lose your job" (quoted in Valls et al. 1995, 125, 127).

Those who do manage to get regularized find it difficult to retain their legal status. In fact, Spain's legalization programs *build in* a loss of legal status unless one can demonstrate on an annual basis that the original conditions persist (most important and most daunting, a formal work contract). Some immigrants do not qualify for renewal because the work contracts on which their regularization had been based have ended; in other cases, the original contract commitments were never fulfilled by employers. For example, among Moroccans it was not uncommon for "precontracts" to evaporate when the employer refused to pay social security or satisfy other formalities, leaving the newly legalized immigrants to work without a contract and making it impossible for them to renew their regularization at the end of the year (Pumares 1996, 87–89; Izquierdo 1996, 73).

Izquierdo points out that a large percentage of the women who secured domestic service positions through the 1993 and 1994 quota systems "have been reclaimed by the underground economy" (1996, 125). As he explains, "[It is] difficult for the regularized to maintain legal status, for they tend to work in precarious and unstable jobs in sectors (such as construction, textiles, agriculture and personal services) where irregular contracts and the underground economy are the norm" (73).

Statistics on immigrants who have not successfully renewed their regularization attest to this reality. Of the original 128,000 applicants for regularization in 1991, only 64 percent of them were legal after two years (150–51). The regularization program of 1985, which had drawn only 44,000 applicants, saw an even higher drop-off rate, with only one-third still legal after three years (Pumares 1996, 59). Izquierdo surveys the outcome of Spain's regularization programs and concludes ruefully, "A regularization program that maintains immigrants in illegality or sends a significant portion of the immigrant community back to that status, isn't worth much" (1996, 149).

The work permit system operates in conjunction with, and parallel to, these regularization programs. Foreign residents who have been legalized must secure a preliminary work contract with an employer, with which they then apply for a work permit. Seven kinds of work permits were provided for in the LOE regulations: Type A was for work of no longer than nine months; Type B lasted a maximum of one year, was only valid for one particular occupational activity and geographic area, and was renewable for one year; Type C lasted for five years and was valid for any occupation or region (preference was given to Latin Americans, Portuguese, Andorrans, Filipinos, Sephardic Jews, and Equatorial Guineans for this highly coveted type); Type D was for the self-employed, lasted one year, and was geographically limited; Type E lasted five years, with no geographical or occupational limitations. Type F was for EC members who resided in their own country and came into Spain only to work. As Santos has put it, "The result [of these multiple types of permits] is a system that keeps the alien in a constant state of uncertainty about the immediate future and necessitates engaging in frequent and trying bureaucratic proceedings" (1993, 120). Further, all these work permits are temporary, with the vast majority (Types A and B) lasting one year or less. As with regularization, securing a work permit—and renewing it when it expires—is contingent on maintaining a legitimate work contract, an insurmountable barrier for most third world immigrants.

Hurdles built into the legal requirements and Byzantine bureaucratic procedures compound these difficulties. For example, while Type A permits last only nine months, in order to renew them the applicant must wait twelve months from the date it was issued, *structuring in three months of illegal status*. Even those who secure permits that last one year inevitably experience periods of illegality. It is well known, for example, that in renewing these permits immigrants confront delays of up to six or eight months (Mariel 1994, 134; interview with Miguel Pajares, director of Immigrant Services, CC.OO, Barcelona). In some cases, it takes so long that the permit has almost expired by the time the immigrant receives it; there are even cases in which the permit has passed its expiration date by the time it is issued (Casey 1997, 25, 41). As Casey describes it, "The attitude of the administration seems to be to erect as many obstacles as possible to getting permits. . . . The consequence is to maintain immigrants in a position of continual supplication and permanent precariousness" (25). Borrás and Gonzalez concur: "Delays in the granting and renewing of permits and the excessive presence of short-term permits, place a large part of the immigrant population in a position of uncertainty and absolute precariousness" (1995, 213).

A catch-22 in the permit process also contributes to what one Spanish immigration law scholar calls the "institutionalized irregularity" of the system (Santos 1993, 111). In order to secure legal status, foreigners must (1) secure a work contract commitment from an employer; (2) take this precontract to the provincial Labor Department to apply for a work permit; (3) take this provisional work permit and other documents to the Department of Interior and the police for a residence permit; and finally, (4) secure a work/residence permit that authorizes them to live and work in Spain (again, usually expiring after one year). The catch-22 in this already complex circuit is that the labor contract, the work permit, and the residence permit are in effect mutually dependent on each other, a fact that one observer has called "the vicious circle in which clandestine immigrants are trapped" (de Lucas 1994, 92).

One Mexican worker living in Catalonia for three years described his experience, "The work permit was very difficult to get because [first] you need to present a work contract . . . but to get a work contract you need a permit, no? So, which comes first the chicken or the egg?" (quoted in Valls et al. 1995, 39). On some occasions, "there have been situations so absurd as immigrants losing their residence permit or work permit because one of them expired while waiting for the other to be issued" (40). A Gambian worker tells this story:

> My boss signed a year's precontract with me, but my work permit kept being delayed. . . . I went every two months to Barcelona to get the official stamp . . . well, after a year, still no work permit. One day, my boss says to me, "Well, the year is up already!"
>
> I say, "Yes, I know, but tomorrow I'm going to Barcelona again to see if I can get my papers." So, I go to the provincial authorities in the Interior, and they say, "Your papers are at the Labor Department," and I go to the Labor Department and they say, "Your papers are with Interior." When I go back to Interior, I tell them my name, they finally give me my papers, but then they say, "Oh, but your residence permit has expired."

Metaphors abound in describing these bureaucratic tangles. As one indignant member of the House of Representatives told his colleagues, "It is the famous fish that ate his tail: you can't get residence if you don't have a work permit and you can't get a work permit if you don't have residence" (Cortes Generales 1991, 4889).

Political decentralization and administrative discretion exacerbate the difficulties. As a member of the Immigrant Collective of Catalonia put it:

> [One] fact that characterizes Spanish immigration law is the frequent ambiguity of the concepts employed in its text, which results in very different interpretations in differing provinces and regions. That is what happened with the regularization of 1991, which gave rise to a veritable Tower of Babel between civil servants and applicants. (Kingolo 1994, 157)

It is not just that discretion was maximized but that in the process, "a veritable bureaucratic labyrinth came into being, in which the government institutions contradict each other" (Valls et al. 1995, 37). So contradictory and ambiguous are government policies that even the experts are divided on what it all means, with some declaring, for example, that all immigrants have a right to public education and health care and others citing government Decrees, "Instructions," "Circulars," and Constitutional mandates that seem to affirm just the opposite (see Santos 1993; Sagarra and Aresté 1995; Borrás and Gonzalez 1995). More important here, the lack of clarity heightens immigrants' insecurity and "can translate into an instrument for maintaining foreign workers in a clandestine status" (Santos 1993, 117).

Given the difficulties of securing permits, it is not surprising that most third world immigrants work without them, illegally. In 1996, with an immigrant worker population of about 300,000, fewer than 90,000 work permits—including renewals—were issued (Ministerio de Trabajo y Asuntos Sociales 1997, 201). Independent census studies of third world immigrant communities find a preponderance of "irregulars." According to Izquierdo's calculations, "Among Moroccan and Algerian immigrants, irregularity is the norm, not the exception" (1996, 24). Among African farm workers in Catalonia, it is estimated that four out of five workers are illegal (Jabardo 1995).

THE SOCIAL REALITY OF EXCLUSION AND MARGINALIZATION

Public opinion polls show Spaniards to be among the least anti-immigrant populations in Europe. The two most prestigious public opinion surveys in Spain, conducted by the Centro de Investigaciónes sobre la Realidad Española (CIRES 1995) and the Centro de Investigaciónes Sociológicos (CIS 1996), consistently report relatively low scores of racism and xenophobia, with the number of Spaniards who believe immigration to be a major problem remaining fairly low, even as the number of immigrants increases. Acts of violence against immigrants are by no means unknown, and there is some evidence that they are increasing, as documented by SOS Racismo (1995, 1996); nonetheless, their rates are low compared with other European countries.

Some have linked these limited expressions of xenophobia and anti-immigrant violence to the fact that Spain receives fewer immigrants than other developed countries (CIRES 1995). Others have pointed out that stereotypes, prejudices, and cultural exclusion—particularly directed against the Arab population—are indeed rampant in Spain, but that surveys are unlikely to tap these politically incorrect sentiments (de Lucas 1994, 1996; Santamaría 1993; Buisef 1994). Whatever its causes and contested sincerity, this laissez-faire stance toward immigrants, relative to other EC countries, contrasts markedly with the high degree of socioeconomic exclusion and marginalization actually experienced by the immigrant population in Spain. Extensive documentary evidence confirms what de Lucas (1994) sums up as "the existence of pockets of work, frequently clandestine, such that Moroccans, Guineans, and others, live in conditions of housing . . . health and wages that approach those of slavery."

The Centro de Investigaciones Sociologicas (Ramirez Goicoechea 1996) voluminous qualitative study of the life experiences of immigrants in Spain attests to the limited access of third world immigrants to social services, such as health clinics, as well as other life necessities. The inadequate housing of much of the immigrant population was dramatized in October 1994, when a large shanty-town outside Madrid that housed a significant portion of the city's Moroccan population burned to the ground, leaving thousands homeless (Izquierdo 1996). Recent studies and government reports confirm the more mundane realities of crowding, lack of sanitation, and the ghettoization of third world immigrants (Ramirez Goicoechea 1996; Valls et al. 1995; Pumares 1996; Comissionat de l'Alcaldia per a la Defensa dels Drets Civils 1995).

More important here, third world immigrants experience substantial marginalization in the labor market. As we saw above, they are concentrated in the underground economy and receive wages significantly below those of native workers. In study after study, they speak for themselves: Gambian gardeners paid 20,000 pesetas (roughly US$150) for a six-day week; Senegalese garment shop workers paid 28,000 pesetas a week working from eight at night to ten in the morning; a waiter who works for three weeks is terminated and not paid (Valls

et al. 1995, 136; Pumares 1996, 86). Jamal, a Moroccan immigrant, sums it up, "It is marginalized work . . . cleaning who knows what. . . . I go in a factory and, well, I do the worst jobs:
clean, gather, load, unload, do this, do that, whatever no one else can [*sic*] do" (quoted in
Valls et al. 1995, 131).

Turnover is high in these jobs, both because the workers cannot subsist long under these
conditions and because employment is unsteady and haphazard. As the Gambian gardener
cited above said, "The problem is, one week they give you work and the next week they don't.
You can't live like this" (137). Pumares (1996) found it not uncommon for these workers to
have seven or eight different jobs in a year, some of which overlapped with each other, in an
effort to make ends meet.

Sociologist Cesar Manzanos, addressing the double marginality of incarcerated immigrants, writes, "The situations of marginalization which the current socioeconomic system
produces are not residual categories, but necessary for its reproduction" (1994, 169). The
marginalization described here is similarly not "residual" but is the predictable consequence
of immigration policies that ensure immigrant vulnerability. The immigrants themselves
explain their vulnerability this way: "I don't like being illegal. Because being illegally in a
country means being without words; you can't speak, because if you open your mouth, [they
say] 'Where are your papers?' So, when I want to speak, I tell myself, 'I am here illegally'"
(quoted in Valls et al. 1995, 35). A Peruvian says, "They don't pay me much because, well,
because I'm irregular; if I was legal maybe they would pay me more, no?" (137). An Equatorial Guinean speaks of the low wages he received in one job and says, "I kept my mouth shut,
because I wasn't going to complain. If I complained, they'd show me the door" (137).

Spanish law requires that to file a labor complaint, a worker must have a work permit, thus
freeing employers of illegal workers from abiding by prevailing labor standards. A grower who
employs African farm workers explains the advantages of this system from his perspective, "I
try them out and if I see they don't work hard, I fire them" (quoted in Jabardo 1995, 88).

The subjective side of this vulnerability and marginalization is intense fear. Deportation
is relatively rare in Spain, but the threat of detection is all too real for many immigrants. A
provision in the LOE allows for administrative authorities to detain those they suspect are
deportable for up to forty days in immigrant detention centers (LOE, Art. 26). While statistics on the number thus detained are not available, extensive anecdotal evidence gathered
annually by SOS Racismo attests to the relative routineness of this practice and to the disruptions it wreaks on immigrants' lives (SOS Racismo 1995, 1996). One woman described
her fear, "I swear, sometimes I wet myself, I'm so scared. I don't have legal residence and
when I see the police, I'm terrified" (quoted in Valls et al. 1995, 50). An Algerian said, "Our
life is a continual flight from the police because we don't have papers. We live with permanent anxiety. It seems like we have a sign on our foreheads 'I am illegal'" (quoted in Dahiri
and Acosta 1994, 119). This fear of the police and vulnerability to detection has very tangible consequences. A Moroccan woman working as a domestic servant described turning
down a better-paying job when her employer threatened to report her to the police if she
left (Pumares 1996, 76).

Clearly, the production and reproduction of illegality through law enhances the precariousness and marginalization of those who are thereby illegalized. This marginalization is not

limited to the illegal population, however, but affects those who are (temporarily) legal as well. Indeed, in this system, there are few real distinctions between the two, since legal status is always a fragile state and almost inevitably gives way to periods of illegality. As Miguel Pajares, director of one of the largest union immigrant advocate groups in Barcelona, told me, "Immigrants in Spain always have to pass through periods of illegality."

Valls, Estrada, and Ferrer follow this logic through: "If this [marginalization] is true for immigrants all over the world, it is especially true in Spain, where it is so easy to go from a situation of legality to illegality. . . . The notion that there is a dichotomy of legal and illegal immigrants as if they were two intrinsically distinct categories, is false" (1995, 35).

Just as there is not a dichotomy between the illegal and the temporarily legal populations, so there is often little change in an immigrant's life as s/he goes from one to the other. Pumares, who studied Moroccan families in Madrid, described their disillusionment over this discovery: "There was a period, just after the regularization [of 1991], when Moroccans, hopeful over their new permits, tried to use them to get legal work, which many times turned out to be impossible" (1996, 81).

There is widespread recognition of this marginalization of immigrants in Spain. Not only immigrant advocates and academics but also politicians and the mass media decry the creation of immigrant "ghettos," even "apartheid," within Spanish society (Cortes Generales 1990, 2,112). And as we have seen, public policy is almost without exception rhetorically framed in terms of the need for integration and cultural tolerance. In marked contrast with this rhetoric, Spanish law systematically reproduces illegality, marginality, and precariousness. The social and economic exclusion and marginalization of Spain's immigrants is neither unpredictable nor incidental; rather, it is the most significant achievement of Spanish immigration law.

IMMIGRANTS AND OTHERS IN A POST-FORDIST ECONOMY

Of course, there is no smoking gun of intent here. A comprehensive search of parliamentary proceedings turned up surprisingly little real discussion on immigration policy, in large part because in Spain the debates accompanying parliamentary hearings take place off the record. The bulk of the published record consists of eloquent, formal statements extolling the dual virtues of controlling illegal immigration and integrating legal immigrants (reinforcing the misperception that illegal and legal immigrants are two distinct populations).

There may be no smoking gun, but there is nonetheless a lot of smoke in the air. For the marginalization that is systematically constructed by Spain's immigrant policies is eminently compatible with the economic flexibility that policymakers and employers repeatedly cite as the sole contribution of immigrants to Spanish society. An employer summed up the advantages of immigrant labor:

> Moroccans and Moors are better workers than the people around here: they are tougher [*sufridores*, or tolerate suffering]; and to work here you have to have the capacity to suffer. [Other] workers won't put up with what they put up with. They [other workers] come one week, but they don't last longer than that. These [immigrants] stay. (Quoted in Jabardo 1995, 85)

One observer of the role of African immigrants in Catalan agriculture describes their economic contribution this way:

> The competitive success of coastal agriculture is based on . . . a workforce that includes segmentation and hierarchy of tasks. It is a matter of being able to attract new farmworkers who occupy the lowest levels of the labor market. . . . It is not a coincidence that the development of this intensive agriculture is linked to the phenomenon of illegal immigration. . . .
>
> It is precisely their urgency and dependence that make the immigrant workers more economical for employers, even than Andalusian day laborers who . . . are not inclined to agree to the conditions that have been gradually getting more precarious. (Jabardo 1995, 81, 84)

Surveying the contribution of third world immigrants to agriculture and construction, Izquierdo argues there is a "structural dependence" on this pliable labor source (1996, 22).

There is nothing new in immigrants occupying the lowest rungs of the occupational hierarchy and enduring the worst working conditions and wage scales. An extensive immigration literature has for years documented the historical role of cheap immigrant labor (Bustamante 1978; Calavita 1984, 1992; Cornelius 1989; Marshall 1978; Castles and Kozack 1973). There are indications, however, that the contemporary situation is distinctive, particularly as it is unfolding in Spain. First, while in the past immigration to industrializing countries ebbed and flowed with the business cycles, decreasing and sometimes reversing direction during periods of high unemployment, today in Spain as in the rest of Western Europe and the United States, immigration flows are relatively unaffected by unemployment rates. This suggests that it is no longer simply an expanding economy that requires additional labor power, but a particular kind of labor power that is called for.

More specifically, the new immigration to Spain and other Western capitalist economies is occurring at a time of substantial post-Fordist restructuring. In Spain, as we saw earlier, this entails an expansion of the underground economy, rapid increases in the number of contingent and fixed-term contracts, and an emphasis on labor market flexibility. Pugliese describes these new conditions:

> The crisis of the Fordist model of production has serious consequences for labour demand and consequently on the occupational structure. . . . Very important for the occupational location of immigrants is a decrease in the amount of regular, steady, year-round employment. . . . Precarious employment tends to characterise many of the new jobs in industry and, above all, the service sector. Casualisation of the labour force is one of the most powerful trends in the labour market. . . . This explains why immigrants are located [even] . . . in regions where unemployment rates are high. (1995, 61–62)

Spanish politicians regularly and unself-consciously proclaim the dependence of the Spanish economy on third world labor, not simply as a way to supplement the labor supply (with a 23 percent unemployment rate, this would be a difficult argument to make), but to offset rigidity and enhance competitiveness in a post-Fordist global economy. Third world immigrants whose desperation and vulnerability have been reinforced by law are ideal for these purposes. The former director-general of migration has pointed out that a high unemployment rate and the need for immigrant workers are not mutually contradictory, noting that the Spanish labor market "contains certain rigidities" which third world labor helps counteract (quoted in Mercado 1992, 27). The 1993 law that established a guestworker system was accompanied by a government document addressing "the rigidities in the labor market" and a large "informal" sector that required an infusion of third-world workers (quoted in Izquierdo 1996, 163). The same year, the director-general of domestic policy announced that the government would not close the door to immigration, since "there are sectors of the labor market that are not occupied by Spaniards" (quoted in Vanguardia 1993). The 1994 Consejo de Ministro Plan for the Social Integration of Immigrants concluded that "rigidities in the labor market, resistance [of native populations] to move with employment opportunities, and high levels of social protection" (1995, 29) necessitated importing foreign workers, despite high levels of unemployment among the native population.

Third world immigrants who are excluded by law from the civil, political, and social rights that make up membership in Western democratic societies (Marshall 1950) are the perfect antidote to the "high levels of social protection" accorded to members of the modern welfare state and corresponding labor "rigidities."

CONCLUSION

[Dietrich] Thränhardt and [Robert] Miles comment on the effects of the current globalization, "There will be one single organized club of rich countries," with citizens of poor countries consigned to the margins (1995, 5). Furthermore, they argue, "Underlying and shaping the practice of exclusion are . . . racist conceptions of 'otherness'" (3).

Immigrants are in some ways the quintessential "other," having crossed physical borders to relocate in a community other than their own. Sociologist Georg Simmel (1950) long ago discussed the notion of the immigrant as "stranger"—physically present in a community but not part of it. More recently, Bourdieu has described the immigrant as "'atopos,' without place, displaced," a "bastard" between citizen and real outsider (1991, 9). And Rogers Brubaker talks about "the modern figure of the foreigner-not only as a legal category but as a political epithet . . . condensing around itself pure outsiderhood" (1992, 47).

But in this new economic and social order, it is more complicated than the dichotomies of immigrant/citizen or stranger/member imply. Legally, politically, and ideologically, the community has extended beyond the nation-state to include—in the case of Spain—the rest of Western Europe, or the European Community. Thus, not all foreigners come from "outside the community" and not all foreigners are "strangers" or "other." Increasingly, the determinant of who is truly an outsider to be restricted and controlled is based on the person's location in the global economy, not on his or her technical status as an immigrant.

Race, of course, plays a part in this exclusion, but is not the definitive criterion, nor could it be since race itself is socially constructed. Just as Italian and Spanish workers in Germany, France, and Switzerland in the 1950s and 1960s were considered racially and culturally inferior, only to become "Caucasians" and members of the European Community thirty years later, so it is with the marginalized workers of the Maghreb and certain South American countries in Spain that race, exclusion, and economic function are of one piece. The law plays a central role in this alchemy. For migrants who have crossed geographic borders, the law sorts and ranks and, for some, symbolically reconstitutes those borders. No longer physically out*siders*, they are now out*laws*.

The visa requirements imposed in 1991 for nationals of Peru and the Dominican Republic serve as a powerful example of the mutually constitutive effects of race, exclusion, and economics. For while in the past the preferences for Latin American countries were justified on the grounds of shared cultural traditions and heritage, these criteria are now trumped by development status. Thus, despite their cultural, religious, and linguistic ties to Spain, those from Peru and the Dominican Republic have fallen from their "preferred" status and are now defined as racially distinct outsiders. In the Spanish context, the "racist conception of 'otherness'" to which Thränhardt and Miles (1995, 3) refer is itself a product of marginal economic status and corresponding legal categories. In other words, the perception of certain immigrants as racially "other" is the consequence of their social, economic, and legal marginalization, rather than its cause.

The presumed paradox with which we began has thus unraveled. For in this era of globalization, immigration restriction largely entails the marginalization of people according to their location in this new economic order. As we have seen in Spain, despite the rhetoric of control and integration, immigration laws and policies have one conspicuous effect: instead of controlling immigration, they control the immigrant. Indeed, Spain's immigration policies are more accurately policies that define the parameters of foreigners' inclusion or exclusion in the national community and the corresponding limitations on their rights and freedoms.

This emphasis on denying immigrants' rights and marginalizing them from the national community is by no means unique to Spain. There are strong parallels between this control of the immigrant in Spain in lieu of entry controls and recent "immigration reforms" in the United States that focus almost exclusively on barring immigrants from welfare and social services (see Calavita 1996). And as summarized by Cornelius et al. , most other Western European countries have increasingly "whittled away at . . . the rights and protections previously accorded immigrants" (1994, 10; see also den Boer 1995).

We can take this one step further. Not only are globalization and immigration restriction of this sort not inconsistent, they are natural companions. For, as Spain's politicians are fond of pointing out, post-Fordist economies with an emphasis on flexibility derive substantial benefits from marginalized third world immigrants. As we have seen, law is a pivotal factor in shoring up this marginalization and the economic flexibility that is its welcome byproduct. Not only does immigration law sort people according to their inclusion/exclusion in the global economy, but—for third world peoples who cross geographic borders into developed countries—it recreates and perpetuates from within their outsider status.

REFERENCES

Borrás, Alegria, and Cristina Gonzalez. 1995. Aspectos generales de la integracion. In *Diez años de la Ley de Extranjeria: Balance y perspectivas*, ed. A. Borrás. Barcelona: Fondacion Paulino Torras Domenech.

Bourdieu, Pierre. 1991. Preface. In *L'immigration: Ou les Paradoxes de L'Alterite*, by Sayad Abdelmalek. Brussels: De Boeck-Wesmael.

Brubaker, Rogers. 1992. *Citizenship and nationhood in France and Germany*. Cambridge, MA: Harvard University Press.

Buisef, Dris. 1994. Medios de comunicacion y visions del Magreb. *Voces y Culturas* 6: 11–21.

Bustamante, Jorge. 1978. Commodity-migrants: Structural analysis of Mexican immigration to the U.S. In *Views across the border*, ed. S. Ross, 183–203. Albuquerque: University of New Mexico Press.

Calavita, Kitty. 1996. The new politics of immigration: "Balanced-budget conservatism" and the symbolism of proposition 187. *Social Problems* 43: 284–305.

———. 1992. *Inside the state: The Bracero Program, immigration and the INS*. New York: Routledge.

———. 1984. *U.S. immigration law and the control of labor: 1820–1924*. London: Academic Press.

Casey, John. 1997. La admision e integracion de los inmigrantes extranjeros. In *Las politicas publicas en España*, ed. J. Subirats and R. Goma. Madrid: Ariel.

Castles, Steven, and Godula Kozack. 1973. *Immigrant workers and class structure in Western Europe*. New York: Oxford University Press.

CIRES. 1995. *Informe CIRES: Actitudes hacia los inmigrantes*. October 1995. Madrid: BBK.

CIS. 1996. *Actitudes ante la inmigracion*. June 1996. Madrid: CIS.

Comissionat de l'Alcaldia per a la Defensa dels Drets Civils. 1995. *Alguns textos sobre la integracion dels treballadors estrangers i llurs families*. Barcelona: Ajuntament de Barcelona.

Consejo de Ministros. 1995. *Plan for the social integration of immigrants*. Madrid: Ministerio de Asuntos Sociales.

Cornelius, Wayne A. 1989. The U.S. demand for Mexican labor. In *Mexican migration to the United States: Origins, consequences, and policy options*, ed. W. A. Cornelius and J. A. Bustamante. La Jolla: Center for U.S. Mexican Studies, University of California, San Diego.

Cornelius, Wayne A., Philip L. Martin, and James F. Hollifield, eds. 1994. *Controlling migration: A Global perspective*. Stanford: Stanford University Press.

Cortes Generales 1991. Diario de Sesiones del Congreso de los Diputados. April 9, no. 100.

———. 1990. Diario de Sesiones del Congreso de los Diputados. June 13, no. 44.

Dahiri, Mohamed, and Diamantino Garcia Acosta. 1994. La inmigracion en España. In *Extranjeros en el Paraiso*, ed. el Colectivo Virico. Barcelona: Edicions La Lletra SCCL.

De Lucas, Javier. 1996. *Puertas que se cierran: Europa como Fortaleza*. Barcelona: Icaria.

———. 1994. *Europa ¿Convivir con la diferencia? Racismo, nacionalismo y derechos de las minorias*. Madrid: Editorial Tecnos.

Den Boer, Monica. 1995. Moving between bogus and bona fide: The policing of inclusion and exclusion in Europe. In *Migration and European integration: The dynamics of inclusion*, ed. R. Miles and D. Thränhardt, 92–111. London: Pinter.

Interview with Miguel Pajares, director of Immigrant Services, CCOO [Communist Union Confederation], Barcelona.

Izquierdo, Antonio. 1996. *La inmigracion inesperada*. Madrid: Editorial Trotta.

Jabardo, Mercedes. 1995. Etnicidad y mercado de trabajo: Inmgracion Africana en la agricultura catalana. *Perspectiva Social* 36: 81–95.

Kingolo, Saoka. 1994. El antirracismo desde la perspectiva de los colectivos de inmigrantes. In *Extranjeros en el Paraiso*, ed. el Colectivo Virico. Barcelona: Edicions La Lletra SCCL.

Manzanos, Cesar. 1994. Contribucion de la politica carcelaria estatal a la marginacion racial. In *Extranjeros en el Paraiso*, ed. el Colectivo Virico. Barcelona: Edicions La Lletra SCCL.

Mariel. 1994. El reto legal ante la extranjeria. In *Extranjeros en el Paraiso*, ed. el Colectivo Virico. Barcelona: Edicions La Lletra SCCL.

Marshall, F. Ray. 1978. Economic factors influencing the international migration of workers. In *Views across the border*, ed. S. Ross., 163–82. Albuquerque: University of New Mexico Press.

Marshall, T. H. 1950. *Citizenship and social class and other essays.* New York: Cambridge University Press.

Mercado. 1992. Miedo a lo desconocido. February 24: 27.

Ministerio del Interior. 1996. *Normativa basica de extranjeria.* Madrid: Secretaria General Tecnica del Ministerio del Interior.

Ministerio de Trabajo y Asuntos Sociales. 1997. *Boletin de Estadisticas Laborales.* April, no. 143. Madrid: Secretaria General Tecnica, Ministerio del Trabajo y Asuntos Sociales.

Pugliese, Enrico. 1995. New international migrations and the European fortress. In *Europe at the margins: New mosaics of inequality*, ed. Hadjimichalis and D. Sadler. New York: John Wiley and Sons.

Pumares, Pablo. 1996. *La integracion de los inmigrantes Marroquies: Familias Marroquies en la comunidad de Madrid.* Barcelona: Fundacion La Caixa.

Ramirez Goicoechea, Eugenia. 1996. *Inmigrantes en España: Vidas y experiencias.* Madrid: Centro de Investigaciones Sociologicas.

Sagarra, Eduard, and Pedro Aresté. 1995. Evolucion en la administracion desde 1985 en el tratamiento de la extranjeria. In *Diez años de la Ley de Extranjeria: Balance y perspectivas*, ed. A. Borrás. Barcelona: Fundacion Paulino Torras Domenech.

Santamaría, Enrique. 1993. (Re)presentacion de una presencia: La "Inmigracion" en y a traves de la prensa diaria. *Archipielago: Cuadernos de Critica de la Cultura* 12: 65–72.

Santos, Lidia. 1993. Elementos juridicos de la integracion de los extranjeros. In *Inmigracion e integracion en Europa*, ed. G. Tapinos. Barcelona: Itinera Libros.

Simmel, Georg. 1950. *The sociology of Georg Simmel.* Trans. and ed. Kurt H. Wolff. New York: Free Press.

SOS Racismo. 1996. *Informe anual sobre el racismo en el estado Español.* Barcelona: SOS Racismo.

———. 1995. *Informe anual sobre el racismo en el estado Español.* Barcelona: SOS Racismo.

Thränhardt, Dietrich, and Robert Miles. 1995. Introduction. In *Migration and European integration: The dynamics of inclusion*, ed. R. Miles and D. Thränhardt. London: Pinter.

Valls, Andreu Domingo, Jaume Clapes Estrada, and Maria Prats Ferrer. 1995. *Condicions de vida de la poblacio d'origen Africa i Llatinoamerica a la Regio Metropolitana de Barcelona: Una aproximacio qualitativa.* Barcelona: Diputacio de Barcelona.

24

LAW, LAWYERS, AND SOCIAL CAPITAL

RULE OF LAW VERSUS RELATIONAL CAPITALISM

Yves Dezalay and Bryant Garth

FAMILY CAPITALISM AND "DOUBLE HELIXES"

The criticisms we have made with respect to prevailing sociolegal models of the role of law in capitalism are based primarily on secondhand sources. The problem with such sources is that it is difficult without detailed empirical research to uncover the double role of lawyers in politics and power. We turn, therefore, to our own research in Latin America, and in particular Mexico (Dezalay and Garth 1996a), to explore the connections that may be found between law and social capital. After this presentation, we return to Asia, concentrating again on a rereading of other scholarly examinations of the role of law, business, and the state in Japan. Many of the traits described for Asia can be found in countries that have a completely different—far from Confucian—cultural tradition. For example, according to Larissa Adler Lomnitz and Marisol Perez-Lizaur (1987), Mexican businesses in the private sector have relied essentially on family resources to sustain themselves. The entrepreneur in Mexico is first and foremost a "paterfamilias of the industry" (Lomnitz and Perez-Lizaur 1987, 111) who "rules his enterprise much like his own family" (110). Indeed, the two worlds tend to get mixed: "Both family and business find their *raison d'etre* in each other" (124). Furthermore, when in conflict, the logic of family reproduction takes precedence over economic rationality. The leadership positions in the business, for example, are reserved to the sons, or if no sons are then available, to other relatives. And no matter how competent the substitute relatives may be, they must eventually cede their places to the direct family inheritors of the business. When that happens, the interim leaders are placed in related or client enterprises, further extending the family business network. In each generation, therefore, the process of concentration of capital is interrupted. Each of the sons wants *his* enterprise, and other relatives operate their own related businesses. The result is accordingly not one huge enterprise, but "family conglomerates," networks of enterprises linked through

Reprinted from Yves Dezalay and Bryant Garth, "Law, Lawyers, and Social Capital: Rule of Law versus Relational Capitalism," *Social and Legal Studies* 6: 109 (1997). © 1997 by Sage Publications. Reprinted by permission of Sage Publications.

their leaders more than through formal financial or legal ties—which are often nothing more than facades.

The ties of personal relationship dictate not only the modes of access to capital but also access to information and to contacts which open new markets and shape strategic choices: since "public information is scarce and unreliable . . . networks of relatives and friends represent the main source of business intelligence" (120). The talent of the male entrepreneur is measured by his ability to create and organize around him a network of contacts and information which permits him to seize new opportunities (109) or to protect against crises—which occur even in economies dominated by the state. Certainly these contacts are not limited to family members, but the networks are created and sustained around the families: "All close relatives are public relations agents of the entrepreneur, but his most dedicated public agent is his wife" (118).

These observations echo those made with respect to the Chinese diaspora and the entrepreneurs in Taiwan. The similarities can hardly be attributed to cultural proximity, but rather to the similar socioeconomic constraints faced by private entrepreneurs. These peripheral economies were not only confronted with an unstable international market requiring what Piore and Sabel (1984) term a "strategy of flexible accumulation," but they were also confronted with a very rigid division in the field of power between the state and private enterprise. The private actors could only count on their own resources, both financial and symbolic, and the symbolic were not incidental. The state not only represented a source of capital and information but intervened to assure the security and validity of transactions. Kept aside—or distrustful—of the state and its official legal system, however, private entrepreneurs concentrated on the family and invested their resources there, taking advantage of one of the oldest mechanisms for producing security and legitimacy.

In the case of Mexico, this division of the field of power is evident also in the world of law. We see a phenomenon that can be described as a "double helix" (Karady 1991), involving two parallel professional careers and tracks. Law schools, for example, recruit from two distinct social groups and lead subsequently to at least two distinct legal careers—one career as lawyer for the state, and the other as lawyer for private interests. This break in the legal field weakens both legal components. Private lawyers have no access to the state institutions—courts and doctrine—which produce the legitimacy of law, and they must therefore support themselves on the basis of family-based resources. Dependence on family resources hardly permits them to acquire autonomy with respect to their clients, who are also their relatives, and this is especially true when the clients tend to be their more influential and affluent relatives. Legal careers did not permit these lawyers to cross over to the prestigious political posts that the political field traditionally has offered to "well-born" lawyers. The divide has reinforced the lack of interest in law of the great families. Their most talented and ambitious children were encouraged to pursue other careers. In short, the social value of legal capital was devalued in the private sphere.

This loss of the social credibility of law in the private sphere, which weakened also its relative autonomy (Dezalay and Garth 1996a), had rather similar repercussions in the field of state institutions. Here also, the capital of social relations took the place of specific legal competence. Personal relations ("who you know") rather than knowledge (or "what you know") became the essential bases for a career. Thus, the practice of law in the state was inscribed in clientele relationships. As with the business families, this pattern developed out of strategic choices made in a specific political context. Individuals gained power in the political field by revitalizing certain social structures belonging to Mexico's cultural patrimony.

Political *camarillas*—the personal networks that dominated the Mexican ruling elite—were constructed initially to protect the revolutionary leaders in a period of great insecurity, but they functioned on a quasi-familial model. The model was one of exchange of favors between several generations, linked together by paternalist ties. It was a system of patrons and clients, mentors and disciples. According to Camp (1990, 85), these *camarillas* were "commonly referred to as the 'Revolutionary Family.'" In fact, as the reconstitution of a new state elite progressed, ties of consanguinity began to play an increasingly important role in the recruitment of these *camarillas* (97), but they were never determinant. The essential link was the mentor-disciple relationship constructed in elite academic institutions—which for a long time meant the faculty of law of the National Autonomous University of Mexico (UNAM).

These legally educated *camarillas* have been extraordinarily successful. They practically monopolized the power of the state (and the single dominant party, the PRI) for almost half a century. We thus see another illustration of a legal practice that relies on a combination of some degree of learned competence and personal ties—and where it is difficult to separate one from the other. This again suggests that, if not inseparable, both learned competence and personal ties are indispensable to the social authority of lawyers.

The exceptional success of lawyers in the field of the state had a paradoxical counterpart: judicial institutions lost much of their credibility by losing what little autonomy they had in relations of power. They tended to become the refuge of professionals possessing the least social capital. "Provincial cousins" who did not make it into the *camarillas* of power (and were not part of family business elites) formed the core of the local judiciary. They were subject in practice to the whims of the local *caciques* for their internal promotions—or even to hold their positions. Positions in the higher courts primarily served as payment for "second cousins" of the political players, or as a reward at the end of a career for those who had not already succeeded in gaining economic security. The autonomy of courts, as we have noted, was not promoted by either the lawyers in family enterprises or the state lawyers.

This brief presentation is necessarily rather schematic. The space for law and lawyers is not fixed, but is recomposed continually as a function of struggles that are at the same time internal and external. The families' transformation of what can be seen as "external" social relations modifies the equilibrium of "internal" forces and promotes new strategic initiatives. Such strategies are accelerating with the process of internationalization.

The nationalist politics of the Mexican government in the early 1970s obligated potential foreign investors to establish joint ventures with local partners. The most dynamic family enterprises were in demand and took advantage of the opportunities. They became multinational enterprises and adopted a more formalized mode of management—conforming to international practice. They invested in the law as part of the process, and the result was the emergence of a generation of business lawyers formed "in the American mode." The American-style lawyers then extended their influence with the restructuring of foreign debt in the 1980s and, later, with the movement toward the privatization and the building of institutions of internationalization in the 1990s.

On the strength of this growing experience and the concomitant development of important connections, including with legal elites in the United States and with governmental technocrats in Mexico, these lawyers for business entrepreneurs began to invest—publicly—in the field of state power. Prior to that time, as noted earlier, business lawyers had no public presence in government, instead remaining in backstage positions. Now these lawyers—often the progeny of the most cosmopolitan fraction of the great bourgeoisie of Mexican business—could present themselves as specialists in structuring transactions and, by extension, social relations. They could offer their expertise—and their connections, especially with allies in the media—in the service of a civil society that calls for more transparency in the administration of the state and the conduct of elections. They have, in short, adopted the northern model of the "gentleman lawyer". And, especially in the aftermath of the NAFTA agreement, they do not hesitate to mobilize public opinion from North American business, government and activist circles—in support of democracy and transparency.

This effort to reform the state, which mobilizes the rhetoric of law and especially that of human rights, coincides with efforts to bring judicial institutions up-to-date. These efforts include the installation of "parallel jurisdictions," exemplified by the National Commission of Human Rights in Mexico City. The commission serves as an ombudsman receiving numerous complaints against the activities of various local chiefs, police, or *caciques*—activities that until now had been given effective immunity in exchange for local support for the clientelist and paternalist activities of the PRI. Recently, in addition, there have been some relatively timid efforts to restore the credibility of high-court justice, which not only had been subject to political influence but had become further weakened by its own clientelism. Finally, this increased interest in law is seen in the multiplication of law schools and, again relatively timidly, in moving toward the professionalization of legal instruction.

Paradoxically, this investment in the law—and especially in learned law—coincided with a collapse in the number and status of the positions that legally educated politicians occupied in the field of the state. It was as if the eviction of a small elite of political lawyers, who had dominated the field of law while subordinating it to their political ambitions, left a place open to new strategies to (re)conquer power through the support of the law—lacking the power to count on political resources. Their demise left them to try, later or by other routes, to reconquer the terrain lost in the field of state power.

In a ten–year period, the *camarillas* of lawyers who had maintained a quasi monopoly on the leading positions of the PRI—and therefore of the state—had lost their place to *camarillas* of economists applying the same clientelist strategy of their elders (Centeno 1994), but aided by a learning that appeared more "modern" and above all cosmopolitan. The triumph of economists was represented by the presidencies of Salinas and Zedillo, both with U.S. PhDs in economics. To secure their autonomy from the faculties of law, the economists were very early adherents of the academic move to North America. These new generations of state technocrats were often the progeny of the lawyer politicians. They were able to exploit the old recipes of the paternalist state while speaking the same language as the new generations of managers, made in the U[nited] S[tates of] A[merica], who now control the business field. Even if the "double helix" of the Mexican elite remains inscribed in the institutions of the field of power, the boundary between the two worlds is eroding. The Americanization of learning is now providing common ground among different fractions of the elite.

RULE OF LAW VERSUS RULE BY LAW

The history of these transformations in the structure of the field of power—and accordingly in the legal field—underlines the contingent aspect of these social constructions, which, despite their pretensions, are neither universal nor necessary. The histories (or similar ones, such as Brazil, see Dezalay and Garth 1996c) can also, perhaps paradoxically, contribute to clarify certain questions about the possible evolution of the place of law in Asian capitalisms. Taiwan is not the only place in Asia where one can find examples of this double helix. It also can be found in Japan, Korea, and Singapore, even though these places are also characterized by strict ties between the bureaucracy of the state and the field of business.

These additional Asian examples reveal the same marked segmentation of the legal field—which strongly limits the autonomy of law in the field of power. This structural weakness reinforces the value of the social capital of personal relations to the detriment of a specific legal knowledge—in the field of economic power and also in the field of legal practice. The social history of Mexican law leads us to examine social and professional strategies that produce—or may seek to eliminate—this type of institutional split, which has also facilitated the growth of state paternalism and clientelism in and out of the legal field. We propose a structural reading of the triangular relationship involving the practitioners connected to legal institutions, the economic technocracy and the business bourgeoisie. Such a reading requires an analysis of the social capital of relations and clientele that each of these groups can mobilize in the service of its strategies to gain power. The *hypothesis* is that differentials in social capital explain the position of lawyers in the social field. Accordingly, a relatively restrictive definition of legitimate legal learning may reveal a handicap in the enterprise of accumulating the social capital in relation to other competitors in the field of power. After all, the *camarillas* were not only characteristic of Mexico. The same phenomenon of territorial strategies built on personal ties is found everywhere, even if under different names: *guanxi*, *batsu*, old-boy network, or *esprit de corps*.

In his classic study of the Japanese Ministry of Finance (MITI), Chalmers Johnson underlined the importance of generational peer groups (*keibatsu*) not only in career strategies but in the organization of the fight for power: "Even if not organized as a club, a class will sometimes meet and caucus as a body during periods of stress" (1982, 65–66). And while departmental heads no longer follow the pre-Second World War practice of arranging marriages of their subordinates in the interests of the department (56), the term *family* (78) continues to describe the close ties between high functionaries of the same administration.

The same phenomenon is found in the private sector—in very large enterprises and in the *keireitsu* (postwar business groups) where corporate and generational solidarities have progressively substituted themselves for the family ties that prevailed in the *zaibatsu* (powerful holding companies under the control of families) of the prewar period (Hamilton and

Biggart 1992). Finally, the forced retirement of the high functionaries of the public sphere and their "descent from heaven" (*amakudari*) into private business assures the continuing reactivation of ties between these two types of networks of personal relations. At the same time, the effective functioning of this "parachuting" comes from the fact that it is seen more as a family reunion than an imposition. Indeed, the two groups of individuals will no doubt have had continuous relations throughout their respective careers within the framework of administrative guidance—relations between the state addressed to business. Also, and perhaps above all, these two networks—public and private—have a common base, that of the Faculty of Law of the University of Tokyo, which Johnson described as the "batsu of all batsu" (1982, 59).

Here we have a surprising paradox—legal education is at the heart of a system of administrative guidance that all observers agree functions outside of the law:

> As a result of the lack of formal legal powers and the weakness of the few penal fines that did exist for noncompliance with administrative orders, Japanese government officials have been forced by necessity to rely on informal, extralegal sanctions when coercion is required. (Haley 1991, 160)

Similarly, the role of the courts has been carefully circumscribed. Miyazawa (1994a, 264ff.) thus describes in illuminating detail all the hierarchical norms put in place around the General Secretariat of the Supreme Court in order to preclude any judicial control over administrative discretion. In short, the boundary that separates the world of law and that of the technocracy is perfectly secure. And this "Chinese wall" is protected even more strongly by the efforts on each side by the hierarchical networks strictly controlled by a small elite of graduates of Todai.

In the face of this paradox of a boundary that is both strong and artificial, we may ask whether it is most appropriately characterized as a division of tasks or a division of symbolic labor. That is to say, there may be an historical compromise between different factions of power. The compromise—in a somewhat arbitrary manner—limits and fixes the respective territories of law and politics and of the social problems susceptible of treatment in the courts and those handled by paternalistic and bureaucratic means. Far from being the product of an old-age history, however, this border appears to have been consciously constructed in the aftermath of the crises of the 1930s. As scholars of Japan have shown, the work of construction was affected by nationalist elites anxious to stem a proliferation of court cases that seemed to threaten their paternalistic administration and social order. As Haley wrote, "Japan responded to the economic and political crises of the 1930s by redefining themselves and their culture. Drawing on certain elements of their tradition but ignoring others, they reinterpreted both their past and their present" (1991, 104).

As we have noted, it is easy to understand the reticence of a civil and military bureaucracy with respect to an imported technique capable of challenging their power and their networks of influence. They feared the development of a central role by the courts in the handling of social conflicts, or, worse still, transforming them into tribunals for the expression of political claims. It may appear surprising that the legal elites accepted this containment of legal controls that inevitably limited their sphere of influence. In fact, however, as shown by Haley, the legal elites collaborated in this revival of paternalist politics under the guise of "conciliation." Of course, the relative strength of forces was hardly favorable to this relatively recent and cosmopolitan fraction of the elite; they understandably chose to fight fire with fire—ceding some terrain—and participated in the counterreform effort. Even if the number of practitioners and cases was growing considerably in the 1920s, the social base of the recently imported institutions remained quite fragile. In exchange for their concessions, however, the Japanese *bengoshi* received an extension of their monopoly at the expense of foreign lawyers and nonlaw graduates. The acceptance of this politics of "containment" may also have benefited from the climate of concern within the profession created by the arrival of new recruits, proliferating in number in the absence of barriers to entry. Traditionally, the professional elites have tended to prefer a politics of scarcity, which they see as conducive to raising their social status and valorizing their knowledge. The promotion of conciliation was completely consistent with this Malthusian strategy. Indeed, combined with the economic crisis, the effects were to reduce the size of the bar by nearly one-third.

This tacit compromise involving a territorial limitation on the law and a more Draconian limitation in the number of new entrants was concretized after the Second World War under the aegis of the occupying government. From one perspective, this could be seen as reinforcing the power of the economic bureaucracy that had facilitated the Japanese war effort. Law was not to stand in the way of the bureaucracy. From another perspective, however, the elite of the bar got what it wanted. Its monopoly and its autonomy from the government were reinforced, and, most importantly, they were able to establish a competitive process for entry into the Legal Research and Training Institute—de facto creating a *numerus clausus.*

The effects of the Malthusian strategy multiplied with the passage of time. Neither the revenues nor the social prestige of the *bengoshi* suffered. The number of candidates competing for entry continued to multiply, despite the reduction in the percentage of successful applicants from 10 percent to 2 percent. But at the same time, the state technocracy had a power and sphere of influence that the courts did not touch. Lacking the power to mobilize the resources of law, the bureaucratic elite supported itself on networks of personal relationships that expanded with economic development. In a parallel manner, rather than spending energy exploring new domains for legal practice or new legal knowledges, the legal hierarchy devoted itself first to policing any initiatives that might call into question the division of tasks that, in fact, assigned a subordinate position to representatives of the legal order. This policing activity, for example, was directed against the efforts of the Young Lawyers Association, which sought to question the legal hierarchy and the compromise with the system of state paternalism.

As shown very well by Miyazawa, there are very close connections between the maintenance of the legal hierarchy and a disciplinary role fulfilled by the Supreme Court and a bureaucracy. "Powerful bureaucratic control of lower court judges by the Supreme Court General Secretariat insures this aversion to judicial activism" (Miyazawa 1994b, 153; Miyazawa 1994a, 264, 274–75). In short, to make a judicial career, they found it necessary to demonstrate a belief in an ideology of legal containment. Since the rigorous selection process resulted in very high material compensation and social prestige for those who succeeded, however, it was relatively easy to induce new recruits to conform to the prevailing ideology.

The subordination of legal practitioners and the justice system to a technocratic and paternalist ideology was therefore made more effective since it was imposed from the inside—even internalized. The Malthusian compromise was strengthened by the fact that the different categories of legal practitioners adhered to it completely. The inactivism of the judges was met by the inactivism of the *bengoshi*, easily dissuaded by their comfortable economic situation from appearing too entrepreneurial in exploring new markets: "Moreover, lawyers themselves have been reluctant to expand their sphere of influence" (1994b, 154).

These efforts dedicated to suppressing any hints of contestation of the ideology of containment show that the Japanese elites could not count on a "mentality" hostile to law. There were young judges or *bengoshi* ready to speak for the dominated in the political field. Following a pattern seen in many places, they sought to advance their own cause while shaking up the control of the legal hierarchy. In the same way, it is a safe bet that, as was the case in France with the *conseillers juridiques*, some practitioners of business law, whether salaried or independent, questioned the rules of a game that condemned them to be second-class professionals—prevented from mobilizing the potential resources of law and courts. The business law practitioners would naturally also form alliances with the potential competitors represented by foreign lawyers.

The so-called timelessness of the existing Japanese model is therefore far from established. The recent history of Europe provides support for this observation. We cannot exclude the possibility in Japan of an "Americanization" of legal practice. It is therefore interesting to observe that we find one of the strongest concentrations of Harvard Law School alumni in Japan, mainly in the bureaucratic and financial fields. These "hybrids" might seek to gain value in Japan for an expertise that, after all, is elsewhere considered dominant. While it is too early to say what will develop in Japan, the point is that the relationship among law, business, and the state is not necessarily stable.

LEGAL CAPITAL, SOCIAL CAPITAL, AND THE STRENGTHS OF THE AMERICAN MODEL

It is too early to predict a general Americanization of legal practice in the economic field. There is an impact, however, that can already be observed in Europe, Asia, and, increasingly, Latin America. It is useful, therefore, to examine the resources of this new symbolic imperialism. As we have already suggested, the phenomena of Americanization requires an explanation beyond asserting the merits of legal rationality and the rule of law.

Following the same approach used thus far in this article, we suggest that a structural explanation is required. What is exported is less an ensemble of concepts and rules and more a mode of organization that gives legal work a privileged status in palace wars. The combination of law schools and large law firms represents a formidable machine to reproduce elites. It permits elites to exploit their social capital in conjunction with legal capital. It also favors the accumulation of relational capital by facilitating the circulation of the different factions of the elite between different places of power.

From this point of view, as we have seen, this social construction of "power lawyering for the powerful" is in fact the structural equivalent of other regulatory mechanisms, in particular the *pantouflage* and "descent from heaven" that are central to the economic power of technocratic elites. These regulatory mechanisms, however, are inseparable from the states around which they have been constructed, while the law firms are able to maintain a distance from the state machinery while keeping their privileged access to it. This combination is especially useful in the international field, since it is necessary simultaneously to draw on national support and capital and maintain a distance from the national milieu (Dezalay and Garth 1996b). This distancing is necessary to foster the image of neutrality necessary for international credibility.

In contrast, the *grands corps* of the French state, like *guanxi* or old-boy networks, offer little that is exportable as delocalized and universal. Their local strength is also their weakness in the international market for expertise, since they are seen too openly as *national* champions competing in the new space of power. It is therefore not surprising that in France and China, for example, we see a shift in the technocracy toward the strategy of a legal career. Technocrats, and especially their offspring, are reconverting to "lawyers." And in this case the U.S. term—lawyer—accurately provides the meaning.

When these dominant elites choose the model of "lawyer" instead of what has been offered by their own national legal terrain, they do so not only because of the new international relations of power. They also tend to reject the local professional models that give little value to their social capital. There is no point in having a capital of political relationships when the field of legal practice is preoccupied with marking its *distance* from state politics. A local base of a narrow legal field would also serve poorly as a point from which to invest in the international legal field—which is characterized precisely by the close interconnection of the legal and the political. The weakness of institutional barriers between law and politics and legal capital and social capital, therefore, is another essential advantage of the North American model of legal practice—an advantage also with respect to other competitors in the market of expertise. The political is fed by the legal, and vice versa. Lawyers make the politics and produce the law—openly, without hiding behind a cult of traditions or legal technique, as has been the case in Europe. For these reasons, they have accumulated a political know-how quite useful in international legal relations—a field of practice that still has not conquered very much autonomy with respect to the political.

In sum, the advance of the "American model" comes from a mode of organization of work that permits lawyers to mobilize their social capital to gain privileged positions in the field of power. To formulate this hypothesis more exactly, the "rule of law" represents less the antithesis of *guanxi* than its continuation in a different framework and under other colors—those of professional ideology. This structural proximity between the two social institutions explains both their opposition at times and their possible reconciliation under the colors of law. This antagonism should be seen therefore as more tactical than fundamental. It is one of the ingredients and effects of the colonial and neo-imperialist fights. And it serves similar tactical purposes when the new American imperialism is promoted and presented under the colors of the market economy and the "rule of law." This does not mean that the results are unimportant, since the rules of the game can be transformed fundamentally. Formal law, for example, may play a greater role. But these occasional confrontations, despite their intensity, ought not to hide the profound continuity between the two modes of construction of social power—which facilitates a recomposition under the banner of professional ideology. This dressing up of relational capital in professional knowledge comes at a price for ruling elites (see Bourdieu 1989)—and brings changes in the rules of the game. But that is the price of legitimacy. The "*guanxi of law*," unlike the traditional *guanxi*, must pretend to be open to all and at everyone's disposal. Despite the openness, however, those dominant in the field of economic power remain best able to afford the luxury of the service of these legitimate intermediaries between business power and the state.

REFERENCES

Bourdieu, Pierre. 1989. *La noblesse d'etat*. Paris: Editions de Minuit.

Camp, Roderico. 1990. Camarillas in Mexican politics: The case of the Salinas cabinet. *Mexican Studies* 6: 85–108.

Centeno, Miguel. 1994. *Democracy within reason: Technocratic revolt in Mexico*. University Park: Pennsylvania State University Press.

Dezalay, Yves, and Bryant Garth. 1996a. Building the law and putting the state into play: International strategies among Mexico's divided elite. ABF working paper.

———. 1996b. *Dealing in virtue: International commercial arbitration and the construction of a transnational legal order*. Chicago: University of Chicago Press.

———. 1996c. Palace wars and the construction of the division of labor of domination in Brazil: How law was and still is at the center of the game. Unpublished.

Haley, John O. 1991. *Authority without power: Law and the Japanese paradox*. New York: Oxford University Press.

Hamilton, Gary, and Nicole Woolsey Biggart. 1992. Market, culture and authority: A comparative analysis of management and organization in the Far East. In *The sociology of economic life*, ed. M. Granovetter and R. Swedborg, 444–78. Boulder, CO: Westview Press.

Johnson, Chalmers. 1982. *MITI and the Japanese miracle: The growth of industrial policy*. Stanford: Stanford University Press.

Karady, Victor. 1991. Une nation de jurists. *Actes de la Recherche en Sciences Sociales* 90: 106–15.

Lomnitz, Larissa Adler, and M. Perez-Lizaur. 1987. *A Mexican elite family 1820-1980: Kinship, class and culture*. Princeton, NJ: Princeton University Press.

Miyazawa, Setsuo. 1994a. Administrative control of Japanese judges. In *Law and technology in the Pacific community*, ed. Philip Lewis, 263–81. Boulder, CO: Westview Press.

———. 1994b. The role of government and lawyers in the semiconductor/computer. In *Law and technology in the Pacific community*, ed. Philip Lewis, 137–58. Boulder, CO: Westview Press.

Piore, M., and C. Sabel. 1984. *The second industrial divide: Possibilities of prosperity*. New York: Basic Books.

25

GLOBALIZATION AND THE

DECLINE OF LEGAL CONSCIOUSNESS

TORTS, GHOSTS, AND KARMA IN THAILAND

David Engel

This article analyzes "injury narratives"—extended reflections on traumatic events placed in the broader context of individual life histories—which were provided by people who had been hospitalized for treatment in Chiangmai, Thailand. Coming from a variety of rural and urban settings, all the interview participants live in an environment marked by profound social, economic, and political transformations. Such changes are central to this study, since they reveal how a combination of forces often referred to as globalization interact with the identities of ordinary people and the worldviews in which law may or may not play a part. This is, then, a study of law and globalization, but it differs from much of the sociolegal scholarship that has come to typify the genre. It expresses skepticism about claims often made in the name of globalization, a term that is not always distinguishable from processes of social change that have long been studied under other headings: urbanization, modernization, and "development."

The literature on law and globalization usually tells a story of transformation initiated from the west or north. It traces the diffusion of norms and institutional practices from America and Europe as they flow east and south through new technologies and through new political and economic structures, leading to transformations at the national or transnational level. The relevant actors in such studies are typically members of the social elite, often Western or Western-educated and steeped in the liberal legal tradition. Although this type of research may examine instances of localized resistance to global power, and may point to the emergence of new sociolegal spaces and fields within the global order, its primary interest is in the movement of ideas and actors from the "center" outward and from the "top" downward. From this perspective, analysts often highlight the pervasiveness of American and European influences but less often provide insight into the thoughts and experiences of ordinary people "at ground level." By contrast, this study associates itself with research that asks a different question about law and globalization: How have the "time-

Reprinted from David Engel, "Globalization and the Decline of Legal Consciousness: Torts, Ghosts, and Karma in Thailand," *Law and Social Inquiry* 30: 469 (2005). Copyright © 2005 *Law and Social Inquiry*. Reproduced with permission of Blackwell Publishing.

space compression" and the "global cultural flows" affected the legal consciousness and everyday practices of ordinary people and the role law plays in their social interactions?

When the question is posed this way, the answers may be surprising and counterintuitive. Although it is said that globalization "accentuates individualism, and increases resort to law for the affirmation of individual rights" (Pérez-Perdomo and Friedman 2003, 5), the findings in this study suggest a trend away from liberal legalism among ordinary people in Thailand and a diminished regard for and use of law and legal institutions. Instead of an increase in the role of law, the Thai injury narratives suggest a new and important role of religion—in this case, of Buddhism. The emergence of a heightened form of religious consciousness rather than liberal legalism in everyday life may have implications for the study of globalization in other societies and in other regions of the world that have experienced a religious resurgence.

It might seem odd to focus on personal injuries in order to address these questions. Usually the scholars of law and globalization choose to study international trade, the environment, human rights, the legal profession, or even constitutional or administrative law. Torts and tort law have not been the site of much scholarly activity among students of globalization. The typical Thai case of injury caused by careless driving or a sporting mishap may seem remote from and irrelevant to the world of multinational corporations, NGOs, and international lawyers. Yet it is precisely this remoteness that makes the injury narratives of ordinary people such a valuable subject for inquiry. Here we can see with remarkable clarity how new information flows, new economic arrangements and activities, new patterns of internal migration, and new ideologies and religious belief systems create new human identities and new perceptions about the self and the community, and about social practices and responsibilities. In these stories, with their immediacy, intimacy, pain, and beauty, we can understand quite clearly how law and justice recede from the grasp of ordinary people even as they seek a vocabulary to express their sense of loss.

GLOBALIZATION IN CHIANGMAI

In 1975, Chiangmai was one of the more cosmopolitan of Thailand's upcountry cities, exposed to a variety of national and international influences, but any observer of Chiangmai today would be struck by the deep and extensive changes that have occurred as a result of expanded global interactions and socioeconomic transformations over the past quarter century.

THE STUDY

Because of the profound economic, political, and cultural influences it has experienced over the past twenty-five years, Chiangmai is an ideal setting in which to explore the connections between global influences and legal consciousness. The subject of "legal consciousness" has attracted considerable attention from sociolegal scholars, who have used a variety of methodologies to explore it. This study builds on research that explores the ways in which individuals tell stories about their lives, their experiences, their social relationships and interactions, and their sense of self. Such narratives are used primarily to understand the subjectivity of the narrators—how they interpret events, how they explain their own behavior and that of others, and how they view themselves in relation to the world around them and in relation to legal norms, procedures, and institutions.

In this study, as in a previous coauthored study of Americans with disabilities (Engel and Munger 2003), I encouraged interviewees to provide an extended narrative covering a broad sweep of time, in which the narrators described their lives from childhood to present and the changes that had occurred in their social environment over a period of many years. Within the broader narrative of their personal history they located the specific incident that had caused them to seek treatment in a hospital for physical injury. The primary value of such research is that it can demonstrate how individuals perceive themselves and their experiences in relation to broader systems of belief or social control. Although the "facts" recounted in these narratives may be of great importance to the narrator, this type of research does not necessarily seek external confirmation that they occurred as described, nor does it compare rival interpretations of events. The subjectivity of the narrator—in this case the interpretation offered by the injured person—is the object of study.

In order to record the injury narratives of ordinary people in Chiangmai, I identified a large hospital that treated patients from the entire province of Chiangmai and thus drew cases from a "jurisdiction" comparable to that of the provincial court. With the help of hospital staff, I obtained the names of ninety-three current or very recently discharged patients who were willing to participate in interviews. All had suffered physical injuries involving the conduct of another party. I selected thirty-five of these individuals for extensive, in-depth interviews, which I conducted, in Thai, at the hospital or at the interviewee's home or place of work. Participants were selected to provide a range of perspectives, based primarily on rural versus urban background, gender, circumstances of the injury, and age.

JUSTICE, BUDDHISM, AND LAW AVOIDANCE

Twenty-five years ago, before the radical transformations associated with "globalization" in Thailand, litigation rates were relatively low, yet remedies were often available to injury victims through locally sanctioned practices backed by community pressures. The norm among ordinary people who suffered injuries was "remedies without rights," in the sense that they turned to a well-established remediation process in which the law played only a small part. Today, recourse to law is even less frequent than before, as measured by tort cases per injury. At the same time, access to locally sanctioned remedies has been diminished by the process of social change, leaving most of the injury victims in this study with little or no compensation. The injury narratives, including the story told by Buajan,[1] suggest that a remedial vacuum now exists that could be—but thus far has not been—filled by law. They also suggest that an explanation for the absence of law can be found in the emergence of a new form of religious consciousness.

1. After leaving her child in school, Buajan stopped by a stand to buy pork. At this moment, a car backed up and injured her leg badly. She was taken to the hospital, had an operation, and, as a result, lost several months of work. The accident happened near a mango tree where several people had died in accidents, which indicated to Buajan that a ghost was present. The driver gave her some money, but she did not consider it sufficient compensation. Yet, she has not thought about making a legal claim, because, in her mind, the accident was caused not only by the driver of the car, but also by the ghost.—Eds.

Buajan's injury narrative, as we have seen, presents numerous causal explanations for the harm that has befallen her, including the effects of spirits, malevolent ghosts, bad stars, and negligence. Buajan, like nearly all the injury victims, also offers karmic explanations rooted in Buddhist doctrine, and these explanations point to the injured person's own misdeeds in a previous life or in her current existence. Although the injurer may be a wrongdoer, the deeper explanation makes him or her essentially an agent of the injury victim's own destiny, which was set in motion by her own bad choices and actions. Often, the injury narratives portray the two parties—injurer and victim—as locked in a karmic embrace that spans many existences. In this lifetime, the old man injured Buajan, but in a previous lifetime Buajan injured the old man, and so on. The cycle will continue through future reincarnations unless it can be stopped by a virtuous response rather than an aggressive effort to retaliate or merely to seek compensation. The Buddhist virtues of forgiveness, mercy, nonaggression, and selflessness represent the ideal response to injury, since they acknowledge the deeper issues of causality and are therefore most likely to bring an end to the suffering that has probably extended over many lifetimes.

The interpretive frame associated with Buddhist doctrine is deeply rooted in Thai culture and has been familiar to Thais for centuries. Although the karmic explanation of injury may seem conceptually inconsistent with village-level remedy systems that stressed the importance of injury payments by the injurer, Thais have long viewed these multiple interpretive frames as integrated with one another and part of a coherent whole. In this article, I suggest that the injury narratives may reveal a fragmentation of what was once an interlocking and coherent set of practices. Although Buajan and other injury victims offer multiple causal explanations, few if any of these explanations are associated with a remedy system that still functions effectively, at least in this lifetime. This was clearly the case with Buajan, who found that none of the interpretive frames she described could lead her to an outcome in which the old man would pay her adequately for the harm he had inflicted on her.

Buddhist beliefs and practices, it appears, are less and less connected to village-level cosmologies simply because individuals no longer live exclusively, if at all, in integrated village communities. In the injury narratives, Buddhism appears to have separated from its connections to village life and is described in less localized and more universalized doctrinal terms. This was true, in any event, for the thirty-five interviewees in my study, and they were selected specifically to provide a range of rural and urban backgrounds, occupations, and viewpoints. Without the remediation practices that were formerly part of daily life in Chiangmai province, injury victims now find themselves stripped of a set of choices that were once available to them. Their attachment to Buddhist beliefs and practices remains strong, but Buddhism without its roots in village-level practices seems to draw them away from the pursuit of a remedy. Globalized "mediascapes" have accentuated this new, delocalized form of Buddhism. The popular Dhammakaya temple, for example, has launched its own pay-TV channel ("Do heaven and hell exist? Where will we go after death? Why were we born? Only [the] DMC [TV channel] will tell you.") (Kongrut 2004). Although globalization has also brought increased exposure to the discourse of law, it is not obvious to ordinary people how to reconcile liberal legalism with religion. Buddhism and law now appear to be opposed to one another and to promote different and contradictory responses to injury.

Thai Buddhism, separated from the efficacious local remedy systems to which it was formerly linked, appears to counsel injury victims to absorb the harm that has been done to them without any aggressive attempt to obtain compensation. Those who attempt to follow its teachings settle for smaller payments than they think they deserve and, in some cases, receive nothing at all from their injurers. They explain such outcomes by pointing to their own karmic responsibility for the harm and by emphasizing their pursuit of a virtuous course of conduct as defined by Buddhist doctrine. The opposition of religiosity and legality in Chiangmai today is evident in the following examples drawn from the injury narratives.

Sawat, an agricultural extension worker whose motorcycle was struck by a car, attributes his serious injuries to his own karma. The other driver visited Sawat in the hospital and accepted total responsibility, yet Sawat refused to accept any payment from the driver or to file the papers that would provide payment by the other driver's insurance company. Although Sawat considers the other driver negligent, he thinks it is ultimately a matter of karma. Sawat did not receive justice, he acknowledges, and it may be better for people to invoke the law, but Sawat characterizes himself as typical of the people of northern Thailand who prefer to accept the consequences of their own karma rather than seek a remedy to which they are legally entitled.

Janya, a middle-aged civil servant whose husband was killed in a traffic accident ten years ago, suffered multiple fractures and lacerations when her motorcycle was struck at an intersection by a teenager driving a large motorcycle without a license. Janya thought she deserved about 30,000 baht in compensation. When the boy and his relatives offered 5,000 baht, Janya rejected any payment at all and instead agreed to serve as a witness in the boy's criminal prosecution for reckless driving. She was pleased that the court imposed a suspended sentence and hoped that two years of court supervision would help the boy to straighten out his life and resume his education. Janya thinks her injury was caused primarily by her own karma, and she guesses that she injured the boy in a previous life just as he injured her in their present lives. By forgiving him and rejecting his inadequate offer of compensation, Janya hopes that her bad karma will come to an end, and the cycle of injury and retaliation will not continue into the next life.

Aran is a young, accident-prone restaurant worker who came to Chiangmai city from a village background. His fractured knee required surgery following a motorcycle accident in which a teenage girl cut in front of him. She and her father apologized and promised to pay all the costs for lost wages, medical treatment, and repairs to his motorcycle, but after his surgery Aran never saw them again and received no compensation from them at all. Through the restaurant where Aran works, he has access to a health insurance plan that covered his hospital bills. Aran refuses to pursue the possibility of additional compensation by filing a civil or criminal case against the other driver. He believes that he suffers frequent injuries because of the bad karma he accumulated when he killed animals while working in a slaughterhouse. His mother finally made him stop and find other employment, but Aran thinks he has not used up his bad karma yet. His wife was later unfaithful to him, and she took his motorcycle and deserted him after his injury, but he forgives her. Aran believes that if he were to pursue a legal remedy against the teenage girl who injured him in this case, karma might cause his own daughter to encounter some accident or misfortune when she becomes a teenager. He is un-

willing to subject her to this risk, and he chooses to protect his daughter by forgiving his injurer in accordance with Buddhist teachings. Aran believes that the other driver and her father
will someday suffer the karmic consequences of their misdeeds and their broken promise to
provide compensation. It is, therefore, better for everyone if Aran allows the law of karma to
produce justice in the long term rather than to seek a legal remedy in the short term.

The stories of Buajan and of Sawat, Janya, and Aran are but four examples of a pattern
that emerged in most of the injury narratives. The injured individuals believed themselves
to be the victims of injustice and thought they were entitled to compensation from the other
party. Formerly, local remediation systems and community pressure would have compelled
compensation and, when they failed, might occasionally have encouraged injured persons
to pursue traditional remedies in the Chiangmai Provincial Court. Nowadays, as Buajan,
Sawat, Janya, and Aran acknowledge, local remedies are unavailable, and only the law can
compel the payment of damages, but they express a strong disinclination to pursue that
option. Instead, they invoke Buddhist doctrine to explain why they chose to forgive the
other party, accept little or no compensation, and end the karmic cycle of injury and response. The injury narratives reveal a form of legal consciousness in which Buddhist religious precepts, disconnected now from village-level systems of belief and social control,
predominate over legalism and rights consciousness.

What is the appeal of Buddhism to injury victims as they attempt to understand their
experience and determine what to do next? Buddhism provides a powerful and comprehensive interpretive framework through which individuals can explain who they are, why they
have encountered misfortune, and what they can and should do about it. It suits the world
in which injury victims now live, a world in which community pressures no longer reinforce
the expectation and pursuit of a remedy. It provides a discourse in which individuals can
claim a measure of justice and virtue even as they abandon other kinds of claims that they
could have made in times past. To those who believe in the workings of karma, Buddhism
offers not a rationalization for inaction but a different and more efficacious form of action
that, unlike the law, can end the cycle of injury and retribution. The invocation of Buddhist
precepts in response to an injury gives the interviewees greater control over the incident by
enabling them to confront the root cause of their suffering. Buddhism offers rewards that
appear greater than the rewards the law could provide, since—from a Buddhist perspective—the assertion of rights may ultimately prolong conflict and may in the long run contribute to suffering, misfortune, and distress.

The injury narratives reveal a form of legal consciousness in which Buddhism floats free
of its anchor in locality-based remediation systems. An expectation of "remedies without
rights"—shared by injury victims and the communities in which they lived—has given way
to an expectation of neither remedies nor rights. Instead, injury victims claim that they seek
to end the karmic cycle of pain and retaliation in this lifetime and in future reincarnations
by adhering to Buddhist principles of forgiveness and selflessness. Yet the injury narratives
also suggest that the absence of a remedy throbs like the pain of a missing limb. In the multiple perspectives so characteristic of the legal consciousness of ordinary Thai injury victims, the aspiration to religious virtue is at times coupled with an expression of unfairness
and frustration, because the compensation that was formerly routine has now become more

difficult to obtain. Indeed, it sometimes seems that the religiosity of forbearance is enhanced by the degree of unfairness the injury victims must virtuously accept.

When injury victims express unhappiness about the unavailability of a remedy, they do not use the language of rights nor refer to the law. They are no longer impelled by community pressure to seek compensation, and they do not consider the law as an option when negotiations break down. Their concept of injustice, despite the sweeping effects of globalization in Thai society, does not appear to have been shaped by liberal legalism. To probe their understanding more fully, I asked each interviewee to describe in general terms an example of injustice (in Thai, *khwaam mai pen tham*) that they or someone they knew had encountered. Interviewees' examples of injustice were varied and sometimes unexpected. For Saengkam, injustice is illustrated by the inequality between the high cost of fertilizer and the low market price she receives for her rice and vegetables. For Banchaa, injustice is illustrated on the highway when big cars cut off motorcycles. Several interviewees said that injustice was exemplified by a dispute whose resolution left one party angry and dissatisfied, regardless of who was right or wrong. Justice, by contrast, is achieved only when both parties accept the outcome, regardless of the equities in the dispute.

Responses of this kind suggest that the interviewees did not conceptualize justice and injustice in legalistic terms, or at least not in terms that map readily onto concepts of rights drawn from Western liberal legalism. The Thai term for justice, *khwaam pen tham*, derives from the word *dhamma* or dharma, which is rooted in traditional Hindu-Buddhist thought. *Khwam pen tham*, or dharma, refers to a cosmic law of existence governing all substances and beings in the universe according to their intrinsic nature. It is very broad, comprising the law of gravity as well as the law of torts. Dharma implies that cosmic rules will eventually produce appropriate results for virtuous acts and for acts lacking in virtue (Lingat 1973, 3–4; Engel 1978, 65).

From the responses of interviewees such as Saengkam, Banchaa, and Buajan herself, it appears that "injustice" implies not just a violation of legal rights but, more broadly, a perturbation or imbalance in the cosmic order. For that reason, the examples of injustice that they offer go beyond legal violations and refer to life experiences in which Thailand's economic crisis causes rice farmers' costs and profits to fall out of alignment or in which rich people flaunt their wealth and power by driving arrogantly and forcing poor people off the road. "Justice," then, does not imply narrow legal victories, but more broadly, a restoration of balance and harmony (compare Nader 1990). This is not an outcome that most Thai people associate with litigation.

Justice in this broader sense cannot, according to these interviewees, be achieved through the limited and often unreliable institutions of the legal system. The courts and the criminal justice system are in the hands of government officials, who have great power but cannot always be trusted to provide justice to ordinary people. Daaw, for example, who was subjected unwillingly to the authority of police investigators, refers to government officials as *khon mii sii*, literally "people with colors," referring to their official uniforms. Daaw was injured by an ambulance whose driver wore a uniform, and she was later interviewed by police, prosecutors, and other government officials in uniforms. She feels they were rude to her and threatened to make her the wrongdoer rather than the victim. Daaw concludes that "people with colors" stick together, and consequently, the legal system is more likely to produce injustice than justice:

> People with colors have . . . more of an advantage than we do. They think they work at the same place. They know each other. Something like that. We go to them, and we want them to help, but they don't help us. We don't get anything from them. Instead, they turn around and ask us angry questions. They should give us justice. . . . But at that time, I didn't have anyone who would help me. I was there alone. I thought, what can I do? I wanted them to give me justice, but they didn't give me any justice at all.

Many other interviewees agreed that "people with colors," including the civil servants who run the court system, are part of the problem and not part of the solution. As Somsak, a laborer, put it, the law is not there for people like himself in the "outer circle" (*roop nook*) of society, but only for wealthy people or government officials. Somsak was not alone in asserting that people like himself have no way to obtain justice. Both law and justice are, Somsak states, strictly for others and completely irrelevant to his life. Several interviewees expressed the opinion that justice could be obtained through the media. Both Pongsak and Jaemjai gave examples of unfair or corrupt behavior that they addressed by notifying newspapers and television reporters. They assumed that the media, rather than the legal system, offer a few individuals the possibility of achieving justice.

In injury cases, the loss of locality-based remediation systems has left individuals with a perception that human institutions are now less capable of providing compensation than in years past but that Buddhism provides an effective response that will ultimately reduce future harm and suffering. In the postglobalization era, liberal legalism does not feature more prominently in the legal consciousness of ordinary citizens. Interviewees express disapproval of the behavior of injurers and even of the officials who could hold wrongdoers accountable, but they do not couch their disapproval in legal terms. They may be familiar with the concept of rights (in Thai, *sit* or *sitthi*), but it is not a term they offer spontaneously, nor do they view the narrow thrust of law as capable of correcting injustice as they understand it.

REFERENCES

Engel, David. 1978. *Code and custom in a Thai provincial court.* Tucson: University of Arizona Press (Association for Asian Studies Monograph Series).

Engel, David, and Frank W. Munger. 2003. *Rights of inclusion: Law and identity in the life stories of Americans with disabilities.* Chicago: University of Chicago Press.

Kongrut, Anchalee. 2004. Dishing up Dhamma. *Bangkok Post*, November 7. http://www.bangkokpost.com/News/07Now2004_news03.php.

Lingat, Robert. 1973. *The classical law of India.* Trans. and additions J. Duncan M. Derret. Berkeley and Los Angeles: University of California Press.

Nader, Laura. 1990. *Harmony ideology: Justice and control in a Zapotec mountain village.* Stanford: Stanford University Press.

Pérez-Perdomo, Rogelio, and Lawrence M. Friedman. 2003. Latin legal cultures in the age of globalization. In *Legal culture in the age of globalization: Latin America and Latin Europe*, ed. Lawrence M. Friedman and Rogelio Pérez-Perdomo, 1–19. Stanford: Stanford University Press.

26

FROM COLD WAR INSTRUMENT

TO SUPREME EUROPEAN COURT

THE EUROPEAN COURT OF HUMAN RIGHTS AT THE CROSSROAD OF INTERNATIONAL AND NATIONAL LAW AND POLITICS

Mikael Rask Madsen

INTRODUCTION

This article analyzes the genesis and institutionalization of the European Convention for the Protection of Human Rights and Fundamental Freedoms (ECHR) as an example of the rise and transformation of European law since the postwar period. It centers on the role of the legal actors and their interface with diplomacy, and more generally politics, in the breakthrough of the European human rights institutions. It particularly explores the blurred boundaries between law and politics during the early period (1950–75) and how this also influenced the subsequent institutionalization of the ECHR: how the initial lack of institutional autonomy of the European Court and Commission, as well as the absence of a yet developed legal science or general knowledge on European human rights, allowed *national* political interests and conceptions to influence this laboratory of European law and integration. This subtle legal-political interplay was further replicated in the practices of many of the advocates of the ECHR. A considerable number of the most ardent promoters of the Convention were indeed operating within both legal and political fields, as well as they zigzagged between—and strategically utilized—the more national and international levels of actions. Eventually, and as reaction to the initial dynamics, the ECHR system gradually gained a higher degree of legal autonomy, which was achieved through a set of interdependent processes of institutionalization, legalization, and even scientification of European human rights.

The argument is straightforward and follows what might be regarded as a Weberian rationalization process, which can be illustrated by two contrasting ideal-types. The initial launch of the ECHR system was in many ways a cold war endeavor with clear geopolitical connotations, and only later was it turned into the sophisticated legal system we know today. Its initial operation was dominated by a group of high-level legal experts who managed to both develop its legal functionality and appear unthreatening to central national political interests. These jurists deployed a tacit understanding of the relationship between law and diplomacy, using the latter when confronted with high-political questions related to decolonization or high national politics. This particular understanding of the role of the institution—a specific elite discretion—generally helped legitimate and empower the system vis-à-vis the national political and diplomatic interests. Over time, and building on this institutional platform, the institution embarked on developing a more legalistic and dynamic understanding of the European Convention. This new enterprise took many of the member states by surprise as it sought both to harmonize the European protection of human rights and to create an up-to-date catalog of rights, which was far more comprehensive than what could have been predicted from the wording of the original text.

To analyze the emergence of European human rights law in a manner that captures the various interplays of law and politics and the national and international levels of action, this article insists on viewing the national and international levels as interdependently connected, as well as interdependently producing the ECHR system. It thus examines the emerging ECHR system from both an intrainstitutional perspective and from the point of departure of national legal and political strategies (see Dezalay and Madsen 2006). Underlining the import-export mechanisms between national and international legal and political fields, this approach seeks basically to reconsider the question of European institutionalization in a way that integrates the internal and external production of this nascent institutional space (Madsen and Dezalay 2002). The approach further emphasizes the agents as the transmitters and advocates of specific European agendas, yet analyzes these in regard to their national origins and interests. Ultimately, the objective is a sociology of Europeanization that centers on the *circulation* of ideas and models—how competing ideas and models were being promoted by a host of actors using their specific national and international resources, expertise, and other capital, and how these exchanges helped produce European law and institutions (see Bourdieu 2002, 1986). As noted above, a particularly striking dynamic of the institutionalization process of European human rights in Strasbourg was the institution's balancing of the new European law with national political interests and strategies. Throughout the analysis, I therefore emphasize the interplay between law, politics, and diplomacy. In practice, these terms were blurred, yet, on the conceptual level, some working definitions can be provided. I consider *law* as a set of systematized practices informed by a differentiated legal methodology and tradition and *politics* as both an institutional and more informal process of promoting and negotiating specific interests. Finally, *diplomacy* is seen as a specific international variant of *politics*, which is equally both formal and informal, as well as it is influenced by a particular set of issues, for example questions of "national sovereignty," the "international common good," etc.

A EUROPEAN HUMAN RIGHTS LAW:
THE METAMORPHOSIS OF A COLD WAR INSTITUTION

Having survived both the heated cold war and the politics of decolonization, the ECHR system benefited from the geopolitical changes of the 1970s, taking the air out of the anticolonial struggles and creating a new East-West dialog. Also, the growing human rights movement was increasingly involved in the new cause of criticizing the more distant perpetrators of human rights in Latin America or South Africa (Sikkink 1996). As part of these transformations, the demand for human rights *law* was growing, reflecting, for example, the strategies of Amnesty International of putting the *law of human rights* before the *politics of human rights* in order to recreate human rights in a more *neutral* form (Buchanan 2002; Dezalay and Garth 2002). As a vitalization of the dormant but very considerable legal tools available in the Convention, the ECHR system began to step out of the cloudy smokescreen of postwar political strategies and jump on the bandwagon of this new legal practice of human rights. This provided a further revelation. The network of grand professors and diplomats had in fact spent the period of cold war inertia nourishing the institution and its mechanisms—an effect virtually intrinsic to the appointment of such a high-level group of jurists—and these "tools" were far sharper than what could be anticipated from the *Cyprus* cases and the *Lawless* case. Also, a new set of judges and commissioners were making their entrance in the 1970s and, with that, a new approach to the enterprise.

In the early 1970s, emblematic of the fundamental changes in the human rights field, it was ironically the Irish government that filed an interstate complaint against the United Kingdom concerning the draconian interrogation measures used in Northern Ireland. In its decision of 1978, the Court eventually found that the interrogation techniques used by the British security forces in Northern Ireland were in violation of the Convention. The recourse to emergency arguments did not hold in this case—Article 3 (prohibition of torture) did explicitly not allow derogation in time of emergency (Article 15)—and it became an occasion that further underlined the beginning of the ECHR system's transformation, as well as the increased fine-tuning of its inborn legal utensils. Such cases of very serious violations of human rights, however, inevitably continued to push the system to the limit and were to be followed by routine allegations of politicized law—this was, for example, the case of the Thatcher government's response to the Court continuously finding the United Kingdom in violation of the ECHR during the 1980s (Ewing and Gearty 1990). But, at the same time, the ECHR started diversifying its business in the sense that it expanded its reach and was decreasingly only associated with these highly sensitive human rights cases. Whereas the restoration of justice in cases involving very serious claims, for example, torture, were a part of the institution's basic legal repertoire—and ultimately its justification—it was by developing a larger and far more comprehensive protection of a *procedural justice*, as well as an expansion of the catalog of rights, that it defined a new legal terrain (see Mowbray 2005).

With the new corps of judges in place, the institution was increasingly venturing into imposing a sort of minimum standards of an effective legal procedure and an expanding catalog of rights on the legal systems of the member states. These were drawn from the general terms of the ECHR but spiced up with the new ideal of interpreting the Convention dynamically. In addition to a set of younger new judges, among the central persons of the "new court," we find, for example, Pierre-Henri Teitgen, who made a comeback in the late 1970s to complete the term of René Cassin. The Court was, however, not unanimously progressive. As the development of the jurisprudence accelerated in the 1970s, so did the frequency of dissent from the English judge, Sir Gerald Fitzmaurice, another key judge of the court in the 1970s. A former legal adviser of the Foreign Office, judge on the ICJ, and member of the International Law Commission, Fitzmaurice's opposition to the new dynamic doctrines was considerable, and he sought to maintain the successful approach of the original Court (see Merrils 1982). Yet despite Fitzmaurice's many dissenting opinions, the game of European human rights law was changing. Good illustrations of this change are the cases of *Tyrer v. the U.K.* of 1978, which laid out the doctrine of the Convention as a "living organism," and *Marckx v. Belgium*, establishing the doctrine of an "effective and practical" protection of European human rights.

Tyrer v. the U.K. concerned Anthony M. Tyrer, a British citizen aged fifteen, who had been sentenced by the juvenile court of the Isle of Man to "three strokes of the birch" for his assault of a senior pupil. The issue was whether this corporal punishment was "degrading punishment" contrary to Article 3 of the ECHR. The response of the Court—with a ten-page dissenting opinion by Fitzmaurice—was that although such punishments might be acceptable to the citizens of the Isle of Man, the ECHR "is a living instrument ... [and] must be interpreted in the light of present-day conditions ... commonly accepted standards in the ... members states" (para. 31). This allowed for a dynamic interpretation of the contents of the ECHR and, with that, a new ideal of an up-to-date human rights protection that was further developed in subsequent cases. In *Marckx v. Belgium*, another key doctrine was laid out, the one of a "practical and effective" protection. The judgment basically obliged the member states to provide effective and reasonable possibilities to its citizens to benefit from the protection of the ECHR. In basic terms, the protection of the rights of ECHR was not an *abstract* but a *concrete* obligation of the member states and a failure to provide effective, practical access was to be a violation of the Convention.

This new progressive human rights doctrine took many of the member states by surprise. While most member states had assumed that their legal systems were generally operating on the basis of, if not up-to-date then fair procedures, the enforcement of this novel doctrine of European human rights made the caseload grow significantly. Seemingly far from the original postwar and cold war inspired objectives of the Convention, the build-up of this avant-garde law reflected how these institutions were increasingly managing to *neutralize* and even *naturalize* this originally politicized area of practice in the sense of transforming the Convention into a deeply specialized legal practice and discipline (see Bourdieu 1986). This veritable metamorphosis of the ECHR system was obviously helped by the Court's initial balancing between a more diplomatic role and the development of its own jurisprudence. If the system for the first fifteen to twenty years had focused on the build-up of reliable and respectable legal machinery, it was now using this legitimacy for taking a far more dynamic and expansive direction. The project was successful in the sense that the Court increasingly represented an important legal forum for contesting the claims of a broader group of applications, including the media, trade unions, and many others. This ultimately helped consolidate the Court's position in the larger, more fluid European legal field, as well as it allowed it to increasingly assume its role as supreme European Court vis-à-vis national legal fields.

This process of gaining access to the national production of human rights law was further facilitated by the set up of institutions in the various member states with the objective of researching and thereby systematizing this new area of law. Pioneering human rights research centers—such as the Essex and Nottingham Centers in the United Kingdom, the Danish Center for Human Rights, the Wallenberg Center in Sweden, the French centers in Nanterre and Strasbourg, and countless others—strongly contributed to this development. This emerging "scientificization" and systematization of human rights was however hardly a fait accompli. In the area of human rights, the distinction between law and politics remained hazy, as the area tended to attract jurists with clear political agendas and interests well into the 1980s. Nevertheless, the subject was becoming increasingly legalized and, thereby, *also* the turf for less politically industrious lawyers. These "pure jurists," driven by an almost entirely professional engagement, increasingly sought to bring the new subject into more traditional disciplines (for example, penal law), as well as impose an additional degree of "legality" on the subject. Above all, these intensified investments in European human rights were adding a new credibility to human rights *law*. It was a development where the law faculties played a key part but was soon followed by a significant number of private practitioners and national judges who also welcomed European human rights as a *legal* tool for reshaping and adjusting national ways of protecting human rights. Thereby, the Europeanized concept of human rights effectively entered the mainstream of the legal field, as well as it eventually became an issue related to the very politics of transforming the state (see Delmas-Marty 1989; see also Klug 2000).

This last paragraph should, however, not be read as an "end of history" account, a final step in what might be easily misread as a pure rationalization and institutionalization process. As argued elsewhere, Europe is always in the process of reconstruction (Dezalay and Madsen 2006). This was truer than ever in the 1990s when the European map had to be redrawn. While the ECHR system had greatly challenged the member states throughout the 1980s and early 1990s, the democratization of Eastern Europe became a very considerable challenge to the ECHR system itself. The institution had to integrate a very substantial number of new member states into its institutional framework, as well as it had to monitor human rights in respect to legal systems that had only recently been refurnished. To respond to this new and larger role, the ECHR system underwent a very considerable transformation to secure the regime's functionality in the new post-cold war era. In this regard, Protocol 11 provided the most significant reform. Coming into force in 1998, a new and permanent Court was set up and charged with an ever-increasing caseload derived from the approximately eight hundred million individuals from more than forty member states. While this new European "megasystem" of human rights protection became the appeal court for the citizens of the new democracies of Eastern Europe—numerically a growing group of applicants—this did not, however, mean that the old member states had finally solved their human rights issues, only adding to an increasingly heavy caseload. The question of delay, which had been imposed on national legal systems in hundreds of decisions, was illustratively swinging back to the ECHR system. Indeed, it seemed that the Strasbourg institutions were beginning to allow increasingly more *national* margin of appreciation as a way of limiting its own caseload. A new institutional balance was basically in the making.

CONCLUSION

This brief and obviously incomplete history of the ECHR is illustrative of the innovation of a new legal subject and practice that went along with, but also beyond, the political and legal genesis of the idea of *Europe*. Moreover, this story underlines the position of law as being both a unique social practice with clear links to the politics of the state and, at the same time, different from ordinary politics due to its differentiated ways of operating. Further, this sociological review of the constraints and issues that were at the center of the genesis and institutionalization of the ECHR provides an account of some of the original politics of European law and the role played by legal and quasi-legal actors in these processes. In great contrast to the current more or less naturalized category and practice of European human rights, this analysis underlines instead the constant interplay between law and diplomacy as a basic condition to the rise of postwar European law. As suggested, it was mainly due to the ability of the legal experts appointed to these nascent European institutions to navigate both cold war tensions and the simultaneous process of decolonization that it managed to gain a position not only in the emerging European legal field but also eventually in the national ones. Thus, "coming in from the cold" and indeed to the heart of the definition of European legal justice by imposing a novel doctrine of human rights law, these institutions came back with a curious boomerang effect, instigating not only a mere repatriation of Europeanized human rights law but also a more autonomous *European* human rights law as such (Madsen 2004).

These basic conclusions drawn from the specific history of the emergence of European human rights are also more generally evocative of the processes of Europeanization when analyzed from the point of departure of law and lawyers. When examined empirically in-depth, it appears that the processes of Europeanization have always been marked by the exchanges of national and international models and strategies. This was particularly obvious in the case of the pioneers of Europe, such as Pierre-Henri Teitgen, who explicitly pursued double careers in law and politics on both the national and European levels. Using their unique positions and multiple specializations, they became not only the couriers of the European idea, but also the middlemen involved in the import-export between the multiple levels concerned (see Dezalay 2004). They thereby helped to circulate both national foreign models and interests. Also, from the onset, the very definition of the boundaries of Europe was essentially a part of the strategies of institutionalizing this uncharted legal and political terrain. This observation should not be seen as only applicable for understanding the history of a different epoch—of literally the genesis of Europe—but also of the more contemporary issues of Europeanization (Dezalay and Madsen 2006). While a number of European fields have clearly achieved a certain degree of autonomy and thereby differentiated professional careers and knowledge than what was the case at the genesis of Europe, current emergent European fields are equally formed by professional-ideological, as well national-international, double-games related to European integration. This is not only due to the immediate political and legal interests in the definition of the European space but also because the European venues have become increasingly strategic for challenging national practices and vice versa. In the area of European human rights, for example, British lawyers involved in the battle with Thatcherism over civil rights and trade unionism during the 1980s started using European forums for relaunching and revalorizing their national policies, which ultimately helped accelerate certain European processes of human rights integration and institutionalization.

This last example from more recent European human rights politics highlights an essential feature of the European terrain, namely the continuous and striking interplay between its internal and external constructions. For the same reasons, the history of the European construction should not only be regarded as a story of the building of specific supranational institutions and the political interaction of states but also as the story of a particular set of political opportunities, which in turn contributed to the structuring of this social space. Among these, human rights offered a particular set of opportunities, which led to a European structuring process that both reproduced national knowledge and conventions. Yet, these were not only reinvented on the European level but were also reexported to the member states and, subsequently, to states in the periphery of the European construction seeking to comply with European law for entering the zone of Europe. In this sense, the European human rights system has become a very central institution continuously involved in translating the national-European exchanges into a European law, which reflects the changing political climates.

REFERENCES

Bourdieu, Pierre. 2002. Les conditions sociales de la circulation internationale des idees. *Actes de la Recherche en Sciences Sociales* 145: 3–8.

———. 1986. La force du droit. Elements pour une sociologie du champ juridique. *Actes de la Recherche en Sciences Sociales* 64: 3–19.

Buchanan, Tom. 2002. "The truth will set you free": The making of Amnesty International. *Journal of Contemporary History* 37(4): 575–97.

Delmas-Marty, Mireille, ed. 1989. *Raisonner la raison d'etat: Vers une Europe des droits de l'homme.* Paris: PUF.

Dezalay, Yves. 2004. Les courtier de l'international: Heritiers cosmopolites, mercenaries de l'imperialisme et missionnaires de l'universel. *Actes de la Recherche en Sciences Sociales* 151: 5–34.

Dezalay, Yves, and Bryant Garth. 2002. *The internationalization of palace wars: Lawyers, economists and the contest to transform Latin American states.* Chicago: University of Chicago Press.

Dezalay, Yves, and Mikael Rask Madsen. 2006. La construction europeenne au Carrefour du national et de l'international. In *Les formes de l'activité politique: Elements d'analyse sociologique XVIIIe-XXe siècle,* ed. Antonin Cohen, Bernard Lacroix, and Philippe Riutor. Paris: Presses Universitaires de France.

Ewing, K. D., and Connor A. Gearty. 1990. *Freedom under Thatcher: Civil liberties in modern Britain.* Oxford: Oxford University Press.

Klug, Francesca. 2000. *Values for a godless age: The story of the United Kingdom's new Bill of Rights.* London: Penguin.

Madsen, Mikael Rask. 2004. France, the UK and "Boomerang" of the internationalization of human rights (1945-2000). In *Human rights brought home: Socio-legal perspectives on human rights in the national context,* ed. Simon Halliday and Patrick Schmidt, 57–86. Oxford: Hart Publishing.

Madsen, Mikael Rask, and Yves Dezalay. 2002. The power of the legal field: Pierre Bourdieu and the law. In *An introduction to law and social theory*, ed. Reza Banakar and Max Travers, 189–204. Oxford: Hart Publishing.

Merrils, J. G. 1982. Sir Gerald Fitzmaurice's contribution to the jurisprudence of the European Court of Human Rights. *British Yearbook of International Law* 53: 119–27.

Mowbray, Alastair. 2005. The creativity of the European Court of Human Rights. *Human Rights Law Review* 5: 57–79.

Sikkink, Kathryn. 1996. The emergence, evolution and effectiveness of the Latin American human rights network. In *Constructing democracy, human rights, citizenship, and society in Latin America*, ed. Elizabeth Jelin and Eric Hershberg, 59-84. Boulder, CO: Westview Press.

27 EREWHON

THE COMING GLOBAL LEGAL ORDER

Lawrence M. Friedman

GLOBALIZATION OF LAW

If business and trade are globalized, and so too the culture of production and consumption, then there must also be a globalized sector of law. In the modern world, law is dense, ubiquitous, and pervasive. Some kind of legal order or legal culture must operate on the global level. But what does this legal order and culture consist of?

In answering that question we have to be careful not to exaggerate the importance of a global legal order. Most lawyers remain firmly rooted in their own legal habits and traditions, even if they work for transnational corporations. They deal mostly with local management problems, and they live in the world of domestic legal culture. Thousands of lawyers spend their days working on small real estate deals, drawing up wills, helping couples get a divorce, defending criminals, coping with contract disputes between small and medium companies, settling arguments over driveways and boundaries, and handling other issues that are confined to one particular locale. The legal world may be, in some ways, among the more primitive and less globalized sectors of modern life.

But the international legal sector does exist, and it is of growing importance. This follows from the facts of international trade and business. There are more and more huge multinational corporations—companies that are everywhere and nowhere, which operate in dozens of countries and have factories, offices, plants, and distribution centers all over the world. One can even speak of the "global assembly line in manufacturing." In the early 1990s, U.S. firms had more than eighteen thousand "affiliates overseas"; German firms had "even more." An official of Coca-Cola, speaking at Stanford Law School, announced (somewhat grandiosely) that Coca-Cola was not a U.S. company, but an international one; indeed, it operates in more than one hundred countries.

It seems quite clear that the international sector of the legal domain is growing rapidly.

Reprinted from Lawrence M. Friedman, "Erewhon: The Coming Global Legal Order," *Stanford Journal of International Law* 37: 347 (2001). Permission courtesy of *Stanford Journal of International Law*, Stanford University, School of Law.

One symptom is the rise of the transnational law firm. For example, in 1995, the old, famous Wall Street law firm of Sullivan and Cromwell, besides branches in other U.S. cities, had branches in London, Paris, Hong Kong, Melbourne, Tokyo, and Frankfurt. It is not only U.S. firms that have gone in for internationalization. A leading firm of solicitors in London has European branches from Brussels to Moscow as well as offices in Singapore, Bangkok, Hanoi, and Beijing. A Hamburg firm has offices in Bratislava, Budapest, New York, Hong Kong, and other places. An Italian firm adds Dubai and Tirana to the list.

In a way, then, the legal world has a form of diglossia—a technical word borrowed from linguistics. It refers to a "situation where two very different varieties of a language co-occur throughout a speech community," (Crystal 1992) usually divided into a "high" and a "low" version. The low version is used at home, on the street, and in popular literature and soap operas; the high version in speeches, newspapers, and formal literature. Diglossia is common in many parts of the world, and a mild form of it is almost universal. In the legal world, the language analogy may not be a bad one. There is a kind of internationalized law, or globalized law, which exists side by side with, or on top of, the national or local sector. It may well represent a minority, even a small minority, of lawyers' work, but its importance is clearly on the rise.

In today's world, people in, say, Estonia, are just as eager to dress internationally and eat international food as their government is to join NATO, the European Union, and other international organizations. But there is a certain tension between this desire to globalize and the desire to preserve local culture. Estonians amount to only about a million people. They speak Estonian, at least at home, and they treasure their linguistic heritage. But as they enter the world of international trade, or try to, they cannot expect to find deal makers from abroad who are comfortable speaking Estonian. Business cannot be conducted through grunts or sign language. It is possible to do business through interpreters, and this certainly happens often enough, but it is a clumsy arrangement at best. To smooth the process, a kind of lingua franca emerges. As it turns out, for historical reasons, the major candidate today is English. Regionally, there are rivals—Estonians probably still need to be fluent in Russian, for example, and they may find German or Swedish or Finnish exceedingly useful. But English seems likely to prevail internationally, and it is clearly going to dominate in transnational lawyering. In a prominent law firm in Warsaw, Poland, for example, of twenty-nine lawyers, twenty-six claimed fluency in English. This was the claim, too, of virtually all of the 150 lawyers in the largest law firm in Korea.

The dominance of English also means that U.S. ways of writing contracts and thinking about the law are likely to have more influence than they otherwise would in the coming global legal order. In some fields of law, U.S. institutions are said to be powerful models. It is obviously valuable, in brute money terms, for U.S. law firms to win the race for international business. One cannot rule out forms of subtle coercion from the world's only superpower and its citizens. But much of what looks like U.S. "influence" or power may simply reflect the fact that the United States, for various reasons, is ahead of the game in devising institutions that fit modern legal needs. The term imperialism, implied in the spread of U.S. law and U.S. lawyering abroad, may be a shade too strong. In part, what we have here is a matter of taste, like the spread of Coca-Cola. It is perhaps also sheer convenience and the fact that Americans were in the field fairly early, and because their style of lawyering suits the needs of the international order.

Substance and Style

There are, so far, serious gaps in the literature on the global sector of the legal order. A great deal has been published, but it runs heavily to doctrine. Dozens and dozens of articles deal with conflict of laws. There are also explanations of various treaties and the like, plus manifestoes and general essays like this one. Not much in the way of serious, rigorous, empirical research can be found.

What characterizes the globalized sector of the legal order? There is to begin with a body of hard law: that is, treaties, conventions, GATT and GATT-like arrangements, regional pacts like NAFTA and Mercosur, and the European Union. Some of these are truly international, others are regional, but they all, at any rate, aim at cross-national impact. Some of this "hard law" has also generated the beginnings of what we might call hard institutions— organizations which have the right or the duty to enforce norms and conventions. The World Trade Organization is an example.

Then there is what we might call a body of "soft law"—international customs, practices, and behaviors. There is a large literature on what some scholars describe as a new sort of *lex mercatoria*. The original *lex mercatoria* was a body of mercantile custom in the Middle Ages. It was closely associated with the Lombard merchants, who formed a kind of transnational business class. Quite a number of institutions of modern commercial law, relating to banking, negotiable instruments, and the like, grew out of customs and practices that were aspects of the *lex mercatoria*. The idea is that the transnational lawyers of today have their own customs, norms, and practices, and a sort of merchant law is emerging, without benefit of legislation, from their patterns of behavior.

Very likely there is less here than meets the eye. To be sure, some aspects of international business law have been formalized—standard contract forms provided by international trade groups, and such devices as the INCOTERMS, which the International Chamber of Commerce puts out. These "contractual provisions with legal or quasi-legal (customary) character" are supplemented by "codes of conduct with more or less sanctioning power," which form part of the international "normative order." All this is supposed to constitute, in Gessner's words, "autonomous norm creation within the international economy" (1994). But in the end all such customs and practices have to be validated somehow by national courts applying what they consider to be national law or rules that national law recognizes—or, as is often the case, the law that the parties to a contract may have stipulated.

The new *lex mercatoria* is associated, in particular, with the growing field of international arbitration, an area recently studied and described by Dezalay and Garth (1996). Commercial arbitration is "global" in the sense that it is not closely tied to any particular system of local law. It comes into play when the parties to contracts and deals agree to send problems and difficulties to arbitration. This way, they turn their problems over to a group of skilled and prestigious international practitioners and avoid, at least initially, the courts and the peculiarities of local legal systems. Most such arbitrators are lawyers, but they do not behave "legalistically." Their solutions are supposed to flow from social customs, norms, and understandings that are common to business people all over the world. Businesses tend to prefer to go to arbitration, which seems less drastic than going to litigation.

Lex mercatoria is a fairly fancy phrase and surely conveys something of a wrong impression. Wrong in two ways: first, in suggesting that these norms are precise, hard-edged, and precisely known; second, in suggesting that jet-set deal makers act in ways fundamentally different from national or local deal makers. After all, for example, commercial arbitration is also common in domestic systems of law. Business people everywhere choose to settle their affairs amicably, if they can, and especially if they have a continuing relationship. Like international business relationships, domestic business relationships are also often governed by customary practices and a sense of what is right and wrong—norms that are not necessarily recognized in the formal law.

Of course, without further research, there is not much that can be said about the norms, habits, and practices of the international deal makers, just as it is hard to say much about the local norms and customs of business people. The research is simply too thin. I suspect that deals and deal making have some general traits in common, at any level. This is because of the pervasive influence of unplanned convergence—the process that pulls systems of living law in the modern world closer together. There is nothing mysterious about this particular process. Moreover, all systems partake of the transnational commonality of products and desires. After all, in the modern world, there are problems and situations common to every developed country. Everybody has to deal with air traffic control, with international phone calls, with intellectual property, and with the tax problems of people and businesses that operate or live in more than one country. Common problems often lead to common solutions. But even when they do not, they generate a common vocabulary and a common conceptual framework.

It is, of course, an empirical question how far this convergence goes. It is widely believed that there remains an "American" way of drafting contracts, with every possible contingency spelled out, and a "Japanese" way, which simply sets out the general framework and leaves the rest, through a handshake or nod of the head, more or less to the good faith of the parties. Oddly though, it is the "Japanese" way which, on the surface at least, seems to presume more convergence. After all, the parties to a deal must share some kind of normative presupposition to make the handshake effective. The deal has to rest on an understanding, on a framework of custom. Between two Japanese business people, the handshake may mean one thing; in the international sphere it would be another matter entirely.

The literature about national styles of legal behavior is relevant to the question of how deeply economic and legal systems are converging. This literature tends to suggest deepseated and irreconcilable cultural differences between the "Confucian" countries of the Far East and the rest of the developed world. There is also an opposing literature which ridicules this idea. Some studies contrast family-style enterprise (supposed to be more prevalent in the same Confucian zone, with Latin America thrown in and perhaps Italy and France), and the more impersonal, market-oriented, managerial enterprises of the United States (with Britain perhaps also part of the bargain).

In her studies of the overseas Chinese, Janet Landa (1995) has tried to systematize the idea that there are efficiencies to be had in dealing only with kinsmen or members of one's own ethnic group. Obviously, the "American" style of business, which is more impersonal, makes more use of lawyers and presumably generates a different style of contractual legal behavior. Can family or clan-based businesses thrive in the shark-filled waters of international trade? There comes a point when you can no longer confine your deals to cousins and people from your hometown. As businesses move into the international arena, family businesses will have to take a deep breath and "Americanize"—they will also have to hire a batch of lawyers. Here, then, we see the primacy of culture again—a global economic and legal culture.

Risks, Misfortunes, and Opportunities

The globalization of risk and misfortune—the internationalization of problems—is also important for the legal order. Ulrich Beck has described what he calls the "risk society" (1986). His book, which attracted considerable attention, was stimulated by the Chernobyl disaster. A nuclear reactor in what was then the Soviet Union failed; radioactive winds swept over neighboring parts of Europe. Such winds, like global warming, have no respect for borders. Burning forests in Indonesia, acid rain, holes in the ozone layer: these are issues that transcend national interests.

Global problems are often caused by processes that may seem to be totally local. In a sense, the birth rate in Kenya is nobody's business but the Kenyans. But the soaring populations of African countries, in the first place, are in part due to modern medicine and technology—a transnational process which has cut back the rate at which little babies die. And a population explosion in Africa or Brazil does affect the rest of the world; it eats away at global resources and creates instabilities. Those cannot be contained in Africa; they inevitably spill over into other parts of the world. Genocide in Rwanda is also, in a sense, not a problem for, say, the Netherlands. But twentieth-century culture, with its emphasis on human rights, makes it difficult for the rest of the world to remain indifferent to wholesale slaughter, even if it confines itself to a single country. Cultural convergence includes not only consumption patterns but also the growing popularity of the notion of a single, overarching code of ethics, a code of human rights.

Again, the ravenous Chinese appetite for turtle meat or rhinoceros horns may seem of no concern to anybody else but the Chinese. The problem is, these tastes cannot be satisfied within the borders of China, since China has no rhinoceroses and too few turtles. The demand for these products could drive these poor creatures to the brink of extinction. In the world we live in, killing off pandas almost seems more unacceptable than killing off a lot of people inside "sovereign" countries. The culture of modernity includes the sense of global interconnection, and the environmental movement is both powerful and thoroughly modern. It of course transcends borders. The giant panda has become an international celebrity—the poster child for endangered species. It is not the only example of animal charisma. Condors, rhinoceroses, mountain gorillas, and leatherback turtles have their fan clubs as well. We live in a world in which some countries feel obliged to tell other countries not to kill whales, in which the United States bans the importation of ivory, and in which people are willing to spend millions to keep big, ugly raptors alive.

In a global age, it is almost impossible too, to keep maggots, beetles, weeds, and invasive pests from spreading all over the world: they come in cargo ships and fly along with passengers on the fastest jets. A plague of tree snakes on one island, mosquitoes in New York, fruit flies in California—the list is long and depressing. There is always the danger, too, that some exotic virus will leap from an animal host to human beings. Once it does so, it might conceivably spread all over of the world. This is, apparently, the history of the AIDS virus. Other viruses, just as deadly, may be lurking almost anywhere. All of this, of course, heightens the sense of interconnection.

Transnational risks are nothing new. Plagues never respected border lines, and the Black Death spread much further and killed vastly more people than the winds of Chernobyl. Still, it seems likely that there are more global risks today than ever. Never before were there risks, such as nuclear war or environmental devastation, which literally threatened to extinguish life on earth. Global risks are an obvious problem for the international order. These risks demand solutions on a scale as universal as possible. No one country can save the whales. No one country, not even a group of countries, can patch up the hole in the ozone layer. No one country can stop the proliferation of nuclear weapons or prevent genocidal wars. Yet the mechanisms for handling all these risks are severely underdeveloped. The international community has to rely on voluntary actions, treaties, conventions, and the like. It is hard to get everybody to sign on to these various instruments, and many countries, for political and economic reasons, will always be tempted to break the rules. Other countries are simply too weak, governmentally speaking, to enforce the treaties they sign. And there is no clear, or at least consistent, way to control, monitor, and discipline sovereign nations. All this suggests a need for hard and enforceable law that covers all nations. The whole world needs clean air and water, and it needs (in a less obvious sense) the rain forests and the steppes and the prairies and the coral reefs. Yet habitats and resources are located, legally speaking, within national borders, and a giant, invisible fence, called "national sovereignty," keeps foreigners, for the most part, out. More and more people recognize that laissez-faire here is intolerable. This suggests a need for hard law, and enforceable law: But where would this come from, and how?

There is another kind of risk which developed countries take very seriously. This is the global risk to standards of living. The vast increase in international trade has tied every major nation up in a single ball of string which cannot be untangled. Trade, after all, has consequences. Mostly, these are supposed to be good consequences. Everybody is better off with free trade; that, at any rate, is the gospel of orthodox economics. But "free trade," like the free market itself, is not just an absence, a negative, a form of liberty; it is an institution, and it presupposes customs, norms, and structures. And it is a process that ruthlessly hands out rewards and punishments. The invisible hand cares nothing about the standard of living in Belgium or Ghana. A rising tide is supposed to raise all the boats, but some of the boats, alas, are in poor condition and the rising tide sinks them to the bottom of the sea. Uncontrolled trade is, or can be, destructive. It has little or nothing to promise workers in sweatshops all over the third world, and it threatens to erode wages and protection for workers in the developed countries as well.

The conventional wisdom is that free trade and free markets are essential props of democracy and good government because they produce stability as well as wealth. But Amy Chua (1998) has argued that "free trade" under some conditions may actually undermine stability and democracy. This occurs when an ethnic minority, for example the whites in

South Africa and the overseas Chinese in Indonesia, are economically dominant. The minority gets to enjoy most of the benefits that global business brings to the country. Under such circumstances "development" can actually be destabilizing; it leads to "ethnonationalism" and conflict. Chua mentions Sri Lanka, Malaysia, and the former Soviet Republics as examples. There are no doubt counterexamples.

Development can threaten stability even without an ethnic minority. Development can increase the social and financial distance between rich and poor. An economist can argue—and perhaps correctly—that in the long run most people will benefit. But how far off is the long run? Poor people, and all people in fact, live in the short run—bread has to be put on the table today, not tomorrow. Developed countries, their banks, and the big world organizations seem far more concerned with getting rid of barriers to trade than in coping with the problems free trade may unleash. The erosion of borders may be as big a threat to social justice and social peace as the HIV virus.

Globalization is more than a matter of trade. It is also the movement of people. Thousands of men and women are migrating, legally or otherwise, from one country to another. This migration gives rich countries an ethnic and racial diversity which they may not particularly want. Some of these countries, Norway for example, were once fairly monotone demographically speaking, but no longer. When thousands and thousands bang on the doors of rich countries, pressure builds up to tighten laws of immigration and citizenship. Immigration, asylum, and citizenship rights were not high on the agenda of Germany and France in the nineteenth century; now they most definitely are.

Well into the twentieth century, most European countries were exporters of bodies, not importers; Swedes and Poles and Greeks and Italians left for the United States or Canada or Chile or Australia. The United States, like Argentina, Australia, and the other "immigration" countries, were at one time eager to recruit new citizens; they even advertised for souls in foreign countries. But they always did this on the assumption that the right sort of people would come. Nobody expected thousands of Chinese peasants or impoverished Tongans or Hindus to knock on the door. In the twentieth century, however, the cultural barriers to immigration have broken down. As I have argued, globalization is above all a cultural process. Television and the movies have spread the word to remote places; traditional societies are undergoing rapid change; in some countries, runaway growth in population puts strains on resources; land in the villages can no longer feed all the hungry mouths. There is a tremendous pool of surplus labor. As many as eighty million "expatriate laborers" are working all over the world, and tens of millions more would gladly join their ranks. Moreover, once there are colonies of fellow-countrymen in London or Rome or Sydney or New York—people who speak your language, serve your food, and practice your religion—it becomes easier and less alienating to leave your village or your country and move to the foreign city. The rich countries build fences around themselves, literally and legally, to protect themselves from a world in which cultural barriers against immigration have largely if not entirely broken down.

There is, however, an element of hypocrisy in this newly invigorated fence-building. Many of these societies have come to depend on legal or illegal migrants to do the dirty work, washing dishes and toilets, picking lettuce, and scrubbing floors. There is, in other words, a deliberate hole in the fence. The real policy, as opposed to the official policy, is to keep the hole the right size. For the better sort of jobs, however labor is in surplus in many of the wealthy countries. Factories are shutting down. They move to countries where labor works for pennies. High unemployment puts a strain on the welfare state, domestically, and internationally, increases the worry about erosion of labor standards. There are attempts to block the sale of goods made under conditions that would violate the law of rich countries. But the dogma of "free trade" sometimes stands in the way. Do the developed countries really need to buy sweaters and blouses made in sweatshops, or rugs woven by eight year olds?

The price of Western goods no doubt has to take into account costs of environmental controls and worker safety, not to mention the fact that the workers are used to a middle-class life. Third world countries pay (on the whole) little attention to safety and the environment, and the multinational corporations often seem to be beyond anybody's control. Shell Oil can pollute the Niger delta in Nigeria—and does—without much fear that the Nigerian government, or any government, will do something about it. The imperial countries are, in some ways, prisoners of multinational corporations just as much as the imperialized countries at the bottom of the heap.

The arguments for free trade are politically and economically powerful—almost beyond challenge. And "free trade" includes the free flow of capital. In fact, the argument seems to work politically for all of the factors of production except one: labor. Within the United States, or within the European Community, to be sure, people are free to move from place to place looking for jobs. But nobody dares extend the logic of free trade to immigration, although some purists insist that the world as a whole would be much better off if there were no barriers at all to migration. The rich countries, naturally, are totally convinced they would be much worse off if they opened their doors and let everybody in. There is absolutely no chance any country would adopt such a policy. Hence they all draw a sharp line between the movement of labor, and the movement of goods, money, capital of all sorts, and cultural commodities.

CONCLUSION

In sum, in the age of globalization, borders mean less and less, both culturally and economically. On the other hand, precisely because of their cultural and economic weakness, national borders in another sense matter more and more. After all, there was a time when people tended to stay where they were; a Spaniard or a Romanian, let alone a Sri Lankan, was born and died at home or near home; moving to Italy was unthinkable. This kind of demographic fixity is now a shambles. Control over borders prevents a politically intolerable movement of people—movement from places where they do not want to be, to places that seem more attractive, places that glitter with wealth and with jobs. The problem is not only economic; it seems to be cultural. Germans worry about the future of a Germany filled with "foreigners." France worries about the future of French culture in a multicultural world, a world that speaks English. The irony is that what threatens these cultures is, in fact, cultural convergence. It is the breakdown of barriers—especially cultural barriers. The same process that brings the croissant to Tokyo and the hamburger to Jakarta makes it easier to turn every country into a "melting pot."

It is not only the hamburger, pizza, and rock and roll that have internationalized; so too have concepts like the rule of law or basic human rights. In a way, a regime of human rights, enforceable against the state, is a kind of privatization. Just as the state sells off railroads, telephone companies, and nationalized industries, it is also privatizing some of its monopoly of violence and power. Constitutionalism and judicial review transfer some state power to the citizen. Of course, each country makes its own legal system, devises its own constitution, provides on its own for courts, the rule of law, and a bill of rights. But the global culture of rights, the recognition that some rights are inherent and universal—a characteristic of our period—has spread around the world with the same force and speed as modernity itself. To be sure, these rights are resisted by dozens of wicked and dictatorial regimes, by the world's kleptocracies, and by the strongholds of backlash and backwardness. Still, in the late twentieth century, more and more countries joined the club of democracy. Franco died, Hitler was defeated, the Greek colonels were overthrown. The Soviet Union let go of Poland, Hungary, and the rest of its satellites; then the Union itself dissolved. Pressure from below brought democracy to Korea and Taiwan. There is every hope that the regime of rights will win more converts.

The metaphor of the "global village" had its vogue. But the global order is nothing at all like a village. Villages were small, self-contained, and provincial. The world of pizza and the Internet is no village; it is not even a city, or a state, or anything easily described in conventional terms. It is erewhon—nowhere, and it is everywhere. Its future is obscure. Its legal future is equally obscure.

REFERENCES

Beck, Ulrich. 1986. *Risikogesellschaft* [Risk society]. Frankfurt am Main: Suhrkamp Verlag.
Chua, Amy. 1998. Markets, democracy, and ethnicity: Toward a new paradigm for law and development. *Yale Law Journal* 108: 1.
Crystal, David. 1992. *An encyclopedic dictionary of language and languages.* Oxford: Blackwell.
Dezalay, Yves, and Bryant Garth. 1996. *Dealing in virtue: International commercial arbitration and the construction of a transnational legal order.* Chicago: University of Chicago Press.
Gessner, Volkmar. 1994. Global legal interaction and legal cultures. *Ratio Juris* 7: 132, 137.
Landa, Janet Tai. 1995. A theory of the ethnically homogeneous middleman group: An institutional alternative to contract law. In *Trust, ethnicity, and identity: Beyond the new institutional economica of ethnic trading networks, contract law, and gift-exchange (economics, cognition, and society),* ed. Janet Tai Landa, 101. Ann Arbor: University of Michigan Press.

INDEX

The authorized representative in the EU for product safety and compliance is:
Mare Nostrum Group
B.V Doelen 72
4831 GR Breda
The Netherlands

www.ingramcontent.com/pod-product-compliance
Lightning Source LLC
Chambersburg PA
CBHW082138210326
41599CB00031B/6023